CHANGING LIVES THROUGH
LITERATURE

CHANGING LIVES
THROUGH
LITERATURE

Edited by

ROBERT P. WAXLER

and

JEAN R. TROUNSTINE

UNIVERSITY OF NOTRE DAME PRESS

Notre Dame, Indiana

Library of Congress Cataloging-in-Publication Data

Changing lives through literature / edited by Robert P. Waxler and
    Jean R. Trounstine.
        p.   cm.
    Includes bibliographical references.
    ISBN 0-268-00839-6 (alk. paper)
        1. American fiction—20th century.   2. United States—Social
life and customs—20th century—Fiction.   3. Prisoners—United
States—Books and reading.   I. Waxler, Robert P., 1944-   .
II. Trounstine, Jean R., 1946-   .
PS659.C48   1999
813′.5080355—dc21   98-54911

CONTENTS

ACKNOWLEDGMENTS

For the important work they have done to foster the Changing Lives through Literature program, we would like to thank a number of our colleagues: the professors who teach for the love of reaching those who need a voice; the judges and probation officers who tirelessly work with us to give offenders a better life; and in particular, Judges Robert Kane and Joseph Dever, as well as our first Executive Assistant, Linda Romano—all without whom the Changing Lives through Literature program would not have the impact it has today.

We would also like to thank the Gardiner Howland Shaw Foundation and the Massachusetts Foundation for the Humanities, whose financial support helped to get the program started; the University of Massachusetts, Dartmouth, and Middlesex Community College, who believed in the program from its inception; the Massachusetts State Legislature, for funding Changing Lives through Literature; the Office of Correctional Education in Washington, D.C., who gave us the opportunity to put together ideas for a book; our colleagues in other states and countries who have begun to put this program into practice; and the students themselves, whose insights have added to our understanding of great books.

A fine professional staff at the University of Notre Dame Press encouraged us from the onset and helped us enthusiastically in every step of our manuscript. Finally, we would like to thank our families for their inspiration, wisdom, and patience, and for sharing with us their love of literature.

CLTL AND THE POWER OF LITERATURE

Notes from the Editors

Robert P. Waxler—

I have always believed in literature, in its healing power, and in its ability to transform lives. I am not talking just about the words on a page or the book sitting peacefully on a shelf. No, that is not what I mean by literature. I mean something else, something that makes me part of the story that I am reading, or creating, or thinking about. Literature is always alive for me. It keeps me free.

When my son Jonathan was young, I would make up cowboy stories for him at bedtime. Cowboy Jonathan became a character of endless adventure riding off to meet his next challenge, returning home weary, yet always ready for another journey out. We were never certain what would happen to Cowboy Jonathan when he set out on his ride any particular night, but we cared about him, rooted for him, felt his danger, and celebrated his triumphs. He became part of our collective memory, and we carried with us traces of his story wherever we went.

Cowboy Jonathan lived in a mythical place between father and son. It is, as T. S. Eliot might say, a place of memory and desire, a place that remains as real and as significant as other locations of shared experience. That is, in part, what I mean by literature. Literature can give us a place in which to live and to dream.

In the early 1980s I received a National Endowment for the Humanities Summer Grant to participate in a seminar at Princeton on the topic of literature and society. The focus of much of our discussion that summer was on the role of literature in a society that was becoming increasingly fascinated by technology and the business of science. Was literature doomed to a place, at best, at the margins of this society? Was it possible that the power of numbers, of binary codes, and of quantitative analysis had become so seductive that a belief in literature was now as remote from the center of our consciousness as a faith in ancient religion?

I was not willing to give up that old-fashioned commitment to the magic of a good story. To me, Cowboy Jonathan was more central to human identity than a vast array of visual images speeding across a computer screen. Perhaps I was out of touch that summer, suffering from a bout of sentimental nostalgia. But I remained convinced that literature was the most important tool we had to humanize ourselves and society.

It was almost ten years later that I approached my good friend Bob Kane, a district court judge, with the idea to try the experiment which would eventually become the Changing Lives through Literature program. I wanted Bob to take eight to ten criminal offenders appearing before his bench, headed to jail, and sentence them instead to a series of literature discussions that I would design and facilitate at the University of Massachusetts, Dartmouth.

For the judge, it was a chance to break the dull round of a court system dizzy with turnstile justice. For me, it was an opportunity to talk about good books with a group that ordinarily would not come to the campus for such discussion. It was also a chance to demonstrate that literature did have the power to change lives.

We sat around a wooden table in the dean's office during that first series of discussions: eight criminal offenders who collectively had 148 convictions before coming into the program; a probation officer, Wayne St. Pierre, who proved to be very helpful in the development of the program; the judge, whose presence always made a difference; and myself. At times, others joined us: professors, lawyers, friends.

There was plenty of suspicion, of course, especially from those who thought this was a crackpot idea to begin with. Some administrators and professors worried that computers and other equipment would be stolen. Court officials agonized about what they saw as the coddling of criminals. Local citizens wondered why offenders should receive free education instead of punishment. To me, though, the issues were different: How did these men, often so bright and intelligent, get trapped in their present lives? To what extent would the reading and discussion of literature change them?

After the first twelve-week series of discussions, it was clear that the program was working. The men were reading to their children, talking about the stories to their girlfriends, thinking about continuing their education, and reconnecting with their families. As one of the men suggested, these discussions were as challenging to him as anything he had ever found peddling drugs on the streets. I too found myself thinking about the stories in new ways, seeing fresh perspectives, and understanding that the boundary between me and the criminal offenders was very thin indeed.

For me, these reading groups became an exploration into the meaning of democracy. People who had been pushed to the margins and refused a voice began to rediscover their identity and voice around that wooden table in the dean's office. The judge and I also began to deepen our sense of identity as we stripped away the privileges that came with our institutional titles and roles and learned that, like other men in the room, we too saw ourselves in the stories and characters we were reading about and discussing.

I believe that stories can save us from the chaos of our lives, perhaps from death itself. When we experience the unfolding of a good story, we experience the unfolding of our own selves. We journey through language and discover our identity reflected there as if in a mirror. I am convinced that through these discussions we have all learned to carry stories and characters around with us as we create that mythic place that brings us together. We have learned in the process that our lives are stories that we can create and shape.

I think of Mark M. in this context, a man who had spent one-third of his life in jail before entering the Changing Lives program. He was a heroin addict infected with HIV. Coming through the program, he decided to rewrite his story despite the death sentence looming over him. He started taking courses at the university, determined that he would get his college diploma. It is difficult to believe that anything will stop his heroic journey now. The story of his life has taken on a special meaning. It is a story of which we can all be proud.

Although this program was originally conceived as an alternative sentencing program, we have tried it inside prisons and jails with success. When I talk about the program, I like to point out how it enhances verbal skills through an engagement with language, how it opens experience to a multitude of perspectives, how it enriches our sense of human diversity, and how it makes us self-reflective and thoughtful. Good discussion of good literature connects us to each other no matter where we are.

Through this program, I have been fortunate to meet people like Mark M. and to create close friendships with people like my coeditor Jean Trounstine, who has done wonderful work developing the women's component of this program. A good story calls on us to exercise our minds, but it also reaches deep into the human heart. It evokes compassion. And, in the end, compassion makes Changing Lives through Literature worthy of participation. I can only hope that the readers of this book will find the selections that Jean and I have chosen as meaningful as we have. Let these moments of good literature become mythical places in your life, part of your collective memory and desire.

Jean R. Trounstine—

In 1986 I was teaching high school in an upper-middle-class town in Massachusetts where most students were white and Protestant and most families expected their children to go to college. When I was offered a part-time teaching job at Framingham Women's Prison, I jumped at the chance. It would supplement my salary; it was a college teaching position; I could teach writing in any way I wanted; and most of all, I knew I'd be working with women who had none of the privileges of my high school students. I wondered if they would have different understandings about the world.

Working behind bars, I found a community of women who had limited schooling. They came to class, some to find solace from the restrictions of prison life; others, out of boredom or for "Good Time"; but most of all, they came with a desire to learn. What I had to offer was my access to literature and ultimately to a world most had not experienced. To women who had street smarts and minds that needed challenge but who had never read books or written poetry, I first introduced writing, and later, theatre. By directing plays and listening to inmates' voices, I discovered that women prisoners had lives far richer than I had imagined, ideas that shocked and delighted me, and talent. Sometimes, I was sure that I was living with a secret that the rest of the world did not know. Women behind bars were a community with hopes, dreams, insights, and humor. They were teaching me to listen to their lives. As a result, they wrote poetry, short stories, and essays and appeared in eight plays that I directed at the women's prison.

In 1991, after I had started teaching at Middlesex Community College, I learned about Changing Lives through Literature (CLTL) from a teacher at Framingham Prison. She had attended a talk by Judge Kane, who mentioned the program in the southern part of our state begun by the judge and my future coeditor, Bob Waxler. CLTL was dramatically different than any program I had heard about since I'd started teaching behind bars. It offered probation and a reading seminar instead of jail to moderately literate offenders. It promised to work on the thinking skills of a person, getting them to look differently at their lives. Instead of concentrating on the text for its pure literary value, it encouraged readers to focus primarily on themes and characters. Thus a text became a way into a person's psyche rather than a purely fictional piece.

Since alternative sentencing ideas advocating literacy were not new, and since I had taught behind bars in college programs, it was not only the use of literature as an intervention that intrigued me. The fascination was that CLTL groups consisted of student-offenders, their probation officers, and the judge who sentenced them to the program. Literature discussion groups with offenders on the same playing field as judges and probation officers seemed unheard of in our criminal justice system. The notion that everyone's opinion about the story *mattered*, and no one had the final say, democratized the conversation. This brought me new ideas about choosing literature for a particular group, new ways of leading literature discussions, and a deeper understanding of how literature has the power to influence one's thinking.

At the time, the only CLTL program that existed was for men. The first group had a good success rate, and from conversations I had with the judge and Bob, I saw that we had similar views about the potential healing power of the humanities and arts. I was interested in expanding the current curriculum to include women's concerns. Most female offenders had read few books by female authors, and they had less confidence than their male counterparts about their reading abilities. They were used to identifying with the male hero since they didn't have a great deal of experience with readings about women. Women behind bars told me they had often been silent in class discussions and that they historically discounted their opinions. Some had never finished a book, and yet almost all wanted their children to learn to read. With Judge Joseph Dever, chief justice of the Lynn District Court, and probation officer Valrie Ashford-Harris, we brought Changing Lives through Literature to a group of women "sentenced to read" instead of sentenced to jail. Like the men's program, we met at an institution of higher learning. At the college where I taught, the president gave us her office for our classroom. Eventually, women from two towns in Massachusetts came together for our program and discussed great pieces of literature. Through the written word, we talked about women's work, men that left, families that failed, and dreams that bubbled up on the pages. Probationers argued with the judge about what was morally right, criticized characters' actions, spoke out forcefully about which characters they respected, and asked questions about plot turns. They began to let the books speak to them.

Seven years and many seminar programs later, Changing Lives has become an integral part of my life. It is certainly important that we have used the program with men and women outside of prison, and studies have been done showing that the women program-completers who return to crime commit very different crimes than those who do not complete CLTL. In our special graduation ceremony where the judge, probation officer, and I give diplomas, books, and flowers to the women in front of the first session of Lynn's District Court, we, like the men's program, seek to change the symbolism of the criminal justice system. Graduates become rewarded in a place where they were once shamed.

We now know that Changing Lives through Literature can be used with men and women in prison and with those whom we often call "alternative learners." In Texas as well as in Massachusetts, prisoners have graduated from CLTL groups and become better thinkers. Some practitioners are considering a CLTL program with juveniles. And recently, Bob and I presented the program in England, where practitioners who already use drama techniques in most prisons are considering its adoption. The program has received national and international attention because countries are desperate for solutions to the problems of crime.

Changing Lives is a way of looking at literature and a way of listening to others' insights. It is choosing literature with themes that resonate for a group, literature that speaks to readers' underlying issues. It is finding ways to engage the disengaged, giving voice to those who feel unheard, and it is a way to include those who have felt disenfranchised from our social system. CLTL is as much a way of approaching a literature discussion as it is a list of texts. And its methods can be used with groups that have members from diverse cultures, opinions, and backgrounds.

This book is an attempt to offer Changing Lives to the teacher and student. In this text we have included a number of pieces of literature chosen to resonate with the lives of those who often take part in our groups. We have organized the choices around great themes that have intrigued our readers, but the practitioner who picks up this book or the student who reads it may choose to go from section to section. All of the pieces of literature written by women that are included here have been used successfully with my groups and have provoked interesting discussions about issues as difficult as domestic violence, sexual abuse, or abandonment. Reading about survivors who struggle to keep a family together, make their way out of poverty, or become their own persons, can inspire us to succeed in our lives. Thus, by observing what characters do, how they solve problems, confront issues, and succeed or fail, we can learn to change our thinking and our behavior. By voicing our opinions and listening to those of others, we can change our way of being in the world.

In my CLTL groups, I use literature mostly written by women because the quests for identity seem to be different when presented from a female point of view. Women do not sail with Odysseus or look for the great white whale as much as they seek to understand their troubled father or find the strength to get out of a no-good relationship. When I include a work by a male author, I structure my discussion to get at ideas about the text with the understanding that the group is made up of women. So I come at it from a different angle. I have found that men and women often respond differently to the same texts. For example, "Greasy Lake," a short story which includes male violence against a woman, takes a different turn when we consider the potential for violence in the male characters rather than considering the text as a journey for male identity. The use of a story by a male author in an all-female group opens women up to the different ways we come at a text and perhaps helps us see some of the different ways we come at life. So too for the use of stories by female writers in an all-male group. The discerning teacher and student have a world of writing to choose from in this text.

The key to any piece of literature presented here is relevance. We have chosen these stories and novel excerpts because we have found that these stories are accessible to people. Although poetry, drama, and essays have much to offer, the story seems to creep inside us and we live in its grasp. We imagine ourselves somewhere in the story or see its characters in relationship to people we know. In discussion, instead of talking about ourselves and our downfalls, we are able to talk about the characters and their lives. Literature is also a protection. It enables us to process our own experiences without having to be confessional, but it is through the characters that we learn much about our lives.

Many of my students who first come into CLTL groups want

to know what reading books will do for them. "How," they ask cynically, "will reading have anything to offer me?" In the back of their minds, they are coming to please the courts or because they have tried everything else. That is exactly the kind of student, I tell them, that they should be. Desperate. Discriminating. Somewhere around the fourth book, they begin to see that reading is a lifelong way of learning about themselves and a way to begin changing some of the thought processes that have led them away from productive and meaningful lives. Those who have a tendency to see the world in black and white will begin to notice that literature offers a more complex approach and opens them up to a broader world view. No, I repeat to them, literature will not make a quick buck for you; it won't solve your problems. But it might give you insight on how you can change your life.

Both the editors—

As these personal accounts of our experience suggest, we believe that reading and discussing good literature can help transform lives. We have chosen the selections for this anthology with that purpose in mind. All the selections you find in this book have proven particularly successful in our CLTL program, and we are convinced that the reading and discussion of this literature can make a difference for all kinds of people struggling to discover meaning and direction in a world filled with complex problems.

CLTL was based on a vision that insisted that literature was the best tool we had in our culture to explore human identity and keep it alive. Guided by that vision, we have structured this anthology along lines that should make it valuable for any group at risk in these difficult times. In an important sense, we want this book to continue a conversation that CLTL helped to perpetuate, a conversation that demonstrates that literature can contribute to the building of moral character and to the development of good citizens.

Each of the four sections of the book begins with a short discussion about one of the many themes found in the selections of that particular section. Like the responses at the end of each selection, these brief remarks do not pretend to be inclusive. They are simply reflections. Yet they are often reflections deepened and sustained by conversations about the literature garnered from other readers. We are also grateful to the countless scholars who have added to our insight through their books and articles, as well as to the CLTL participants themselves.

In this sense, we think of our remarks as part of an ongoing discussion that we hope you will join, a conversation that repeats itself at times, but continually opens the literature to further inquiry and understanding. We call on you to keep that discussion alive. Your voice around the table makes such conversation worthwhile.

Designed to promote conversation, this book subtly insists upon more than one way of looking at literature. The reader will notice that after every story, both editors give their responses. The responses are often different, filled with contradictions, and aimed at showing you more than one way of seeing what you read. We hope that these responses will intrigue you, perhaps even cause you to have yet a different point of view.

All of us bring our own personal experiences to a text and thus come up with our own interpretations. This is one of the founding principles of Changing Lives through Literature. Diversity brings more than one approach. Because we differ in experiences, we see from different angles. Our gender differences may cause us to concentrate on one area of a story, whereas the differences in our ages may allow us other observations. Our religious, class, or racial backgrounds come into play as well. If you use this book by yourself, our responses will provide you with two different ways of looking at each story to provoke your thinking. If you use this book with a group, you will have the power of the other minds in the group as well.

This book hopes to reinforce the notion that responders can enlighten each other through conflict as well as through agreement. Many book groups today have caught on to this idea and use a "facilitator" to direct discussion so that every point of view is given its due. We feel that our book, both in its use of material by a range of male and female authors, and in its dual responses, underscores the strength in diversity.

We have also veered away from an approach which turns a response to a story into a list of fill-in-the-blank questions to be answered. By provoking your thinking, we hope to point out that literature is complex. It depends on themes that intersect, characters that conflict, plots that intertwine. It stimulates us to think, and even our individual thoughts may be multifaceted. Our book aims to show that good literature complicates the issues.

Finally, this book presents more than one point of view because doing so is a principle of our ever changing America. The people we see in our schools and our work places as well as in our courts are of all kinds, colors, and backgrounds. Changing Lives fosters a democratic way of running discussions based on the assumption that all ideas have weight and validity. We feel this makes our group participants more accepting of difference, thus turning our groups into better groups and our world into a better place.

Section One

VIOLENCE

INTRODUCTION

We believe that violence too often occurs because people have lost the ability to articulate their feelings and emotions. Instead they express their fear and rage through abusive behavior aimed either at themselves or at others. The causes of violent behavior are various: shame, low self-esteem, poverty, family breakdown, alcohol and drugs, and so on. The results are nearly always the same: chaos, confusion, fragmentation, and at times death.

We can neither deny violence nor avoid it. It seems part of our human condition. Unfortunately, we seem to give priority in our culture to immediate needs and primal desires rather than to the empathetic imagination and critical thinking. This anthology challenges that priority by using novels and short stories to explore and unfold the complexity and diversity of character and human consciousness. In this sense, through the selections, readers confront their own urge to violence, give it a shape, and come to understand it.

There is often something powerful about violence, giving it a ritualistic and ancient texture. It can renew us as well as destroy us. But too often it simply offers us a false sense of command and control, a phony assumption that we are superior to our victim. Men brutalize women, whites attack blacks, the wealthy marginalize the poor, nations struggle against nations: these are all forms of power creating a vicious circle of violence that threatens to tear apart the human fabric of society itself.

As Aristotle knew, literature can purge our violent emotions. A good story gives a form to violence and so leads us to the recognition that we can choose to do otherwise. It is not unusual to hear people tell us how the memory of a story has stopped them from committing another impulsive act of violence. In a moment of crisis, they have realized they have alternatives.

The selections we have chosen for this section offer up various perspectives on violence. Written by three men and two women, these five stories explore the meaning of violence in the human context and give us all a moment of self-reflection. Such stories can change us.

"Greasy Lake" by T. Coraghessan Boyle is a story that has the edge of adventure, and many readers, especially men, seem to identify with it. The three central characters journey into a world of unexpected violence, discovering their own dark side, a nightmare of primal energy. It is a world filled with mythic overtones of male violence, Oedipal desire, murder, and rape.

Emerging from the experience, the narrator in particular seems troubled. On the verge of tears, he has traveled through the seduction of violence to at least a partial recognition of the destructive forces of raw instinct. Like the reader, he is beginning to give shape to his experience as he works toward an understanding of the limits of his manhood and of his own mortality.

By contrast, Joyce Carol Oates explores the dilemma of young girls growing up in a sexually charged popular culture dominated by male aggression. In the story, Connie cannot escape the adolescent fantasies that make her an easy prey for male predators who gain a false sense of authority by sacrificing vulnerable teenage girls on the altar of sex and violence.

Connie must leave her family and home to achieve her womanhood, but her desire is shaped by the male gaze and the popular culture that surrounds her. She seems to have no alternative but to journey into that world of male control, a world that reminds all of us that men are capable of rape and murder.

Men, as well as women, need to be liberated from the cultural constructions that have given us this legacy of violence. *Affliction* by Russell Banks explores this legacy by reminding us how often lives are menaced and detroyed by the disease of alcoholism and family abuse.

In our selection from Banks's novel, Wade Whitehouse, a man afflicted with violence and humiliation, seems to be developing the destructive traits of his alcoholic father. The narrator, Wade's brother, knows that he too suffers from the wounds of an abusive upbringing, and that although the brothers have taken different roads, they are both products of the same family origins.

For Banks, there is no casy way to escape the legacy of male

violence passed from generation to generation. Like a mythic landscape, Banks's small New Hampshire town is filled with Oedipal
tension, the hunters and the hunted, the need for recognition, and
the desire to kill. Wade longs for relief from his affliction and from
the sins of the fathers, but in the end he can only release himself
from his condition by repeating the violence that he abhors. He is
locked into a cycle of violence that demands our attention and understanding if we are ever to break free from it.

The macho culture of Latin America can be interpreted as an
extreme version of male violence and narcissism, as "Solitude of
Blood" makes clear. The male landscape of such a culture is hard
and unforgiving. It allows neither daughters nor wives any space of
their own, except perhaps the space of a gentle and passionate
memory that runs deep within the blood.

The flip side of violence is humiliation and submission, a dual
construction that often defines male-female relationships and
binds those relationships into an intolerably narrow frame. Such
relations inevitably ignite blood lust, and blood is often spilled as
a public expression of the implications of such violence. In "Solitude of Blood," another story is also told. Women do not have to
sacrifice themselves in the external landscape of male domination.
In silence and solitude, they can remember the images of gentleness and passion that flow deep within the blood, the images that
men refuse to acknowledge at the cost of their own well-being.

We believe that the power of violence is part of life, but it needs
to be integrated into the expansive rhythm of our human development. In the selection from *Deliverance* by James Dickey, the narrator Ed lacks confidence in part because he does not trust the
impulses of his body. He lacks mastery and a sense of manhood because he has lost touch with the power that violence can unleash.
When he and Bobby face the brutality of the backwoodsmen, they
must count on Lewis to deliver them from death because they cannot count on themselves. By the end of the story, Ed will learn that
his responsibility includes the need to move beyond dependency to
a moment when he can confidently face that which he fears. For
Dickey, Ed is the new man at the end, the compassionate risk-
taker who has brought together his instincts and his human concern.

To read and discuss stories about violence can help us understand it and master it. These selections give all of us an opportunity

to feel the power of violence and to help give it a shape. Through that process, we believe, stories hold up a mirror for us to explore ourselves, and through that self-reflection we move to a position where we can make new choices and find alternatives to the destruction that violence often brings.

Greasy Lake

T. Coraghessan Boyle

It's about a mile down on the dark side of Route 88.

—BRUCE SPRINGSTEEN

There was a time when courtesy and winning ways went out of style, when it was good to be bad, when you cultivated decadence like a taste. We were all dangerous characters then. We wore torn-up leather jackets, slouched around with toothpicks in our mouths, sniffed glue and ether and what somebody claimed was cocaine. When we wheeled our parents' whining station wagons out into the street we left a patch of rubber half a block long. We drank gin and grape juice, Tango, Thunderbird, and Bali Hai. We were nineteen. We were bad. We read André Gide and struck elaborate poses to show that we didn't give a shit about anything. At night, we went up to Greasy Lake.

Through the center of town, up the strip, past the housing developments and shopping malls, street lights giving way to the thin streaming illumination of the headlights, trees crowding the asphalt in a black unbroken wall: that was the way out to Greasy Lake. The Indians had called it Wakan, a reference to the clarity of its waters. Now it was fetid and murky, the mud banks glittering with broken glass and strewn with beer cans and the charred remains of bonfires. There was a single ravaged island a hundred yards from shore, so stripped of vegetation it looked as if the air force had strafed it. We went up to the lake because everyone went there, because we wanted to snuff the rich scent of possibility on the breeze, watch a girl take off her clothes and plunge into the festering murk, drink beer, smoke pot, howl at the stars, savor the incongruous full-throated roar of rock and roll against the primeval susurrus of frogs and crickets. This was nature.

I was there one night, late, in the company of two dangerous characters. Digby wore a gold star in his right ear and allowed his father to pay his tuition at Cornell; Jeff was thinking of quitting school to become a painter/musician/head-shop proprietor. They were both expert in the social graces, quick with a sneer, able to manage a Ford with lousy shocks over a rutted and gutted blacktop road at eighty-five while rolling a joint as compact as a Toot-sie Roll Pop stick. They could lounge against a bank of booming speakers and trade "man"s with the best of them or roll out across the dance floor as if their joints worked on bearings. They were slick and quick and they wore their mirror shades at breakfast and dinner, in the shower, in closets and caves. In short, they were bad.

I drove. Digby pounded the dashboard and shouted along with Toots & the Maytals while Jeff hung his head out the window and streaked the side of my mother's Bel Air with vomit. It was early June, the air soft as a hand on your cheek, the third night of sum-mer vacation. The first two nights we'd been out till dawn, look-ing for something we never found. On this, the third night, we'd cruised the strip sixty-seven times, been in and out of every bar and club we could think of in a twenty-mile radius, stopped twice for bucket chicken and forty-cent hamburgers, debated going to a party at the house of a girl Jeff's sister knew, and chucked two dozen raw eggs at mailboxes and hitchhikers. It was 2:00 A.M.; the bars were closing. There was nothing to do but take a bottle of lemon-flavored gin up to Greasy Lake.

The taillights of a single car winked at us as we swung into the dirt lot with its tufts of weed and washboard corrugations; '57 Chevy, mint, metallic blue. On the far side of the lot, like the exo-skeleton of some gaunt chrome insect, a chopper leaned against its kickstand. And that was it for excitement: some junkie half-wit biker and a car freak pumping his girlfriend. Whatever it was we were looking for, we weren't about to find it at Greasy Lake. Not that night.

But then all of a sudden Digby was fighting for the wheel. "Hey, that's Tony Lovett's car! Hey!" he shouted, while I stabbed at the brake pedal and the Bel Air nosed up to the gleaming bumper of the parked Chevy. Digby leaned on the horn, laughing, and in-structed me to put my brights on. I flicked on the brights. This was hilarious. A joke. Tony would experience premature withdrawal and expect to be confronted by grim-looking state troopers with flashlights. We hit the horn, strobed the lights, and then jumped out of the car to press our witty faces to Tony's windows; for all we knew we might even catch a glimpse of some little fox's tit, and then we could slap backs with red-faced Tony, roughhouse a little, and go on to new heights of adventure and daring.

The first mistake, the one that opened the whole floodgate, was losing my grip on the keys. In the excitement, leaping from the car

with the gin in one hand and a roach clip in the other, I spilled
them in the grass—in the dark, rank, mysterious nighttime grass
of Greasy Lake. This was a tactical error, as damaging and irre-
versible in its way as Westmoreland's decision to dig in at Khe
Sanh. I felt it like a jab of intuition, and I stopped there by the open
door, peering vaguely into the night that puddled up round my feet.

The second mistake—and this was inextricably bound up with
the first—was identifying the car as Tony Lovett's. Even before the
very bad character in greasy jeans and engineer boots ripped out of
the driver's door, I began to realize that this chrome blue was much
lighter than the robin's-egg of Tony's car, and that Tony's car didn't
have rear-mounted speakers. Judging from their expressions, Digby
and Jeff were privately groping toward the same inevitable and unsettling conclusion as I was.

In any case, there was no reasoning with this bad greasy character—clearly he was a man of action. The first lusty Rockette kick
of his steel-toed boot caught me under the chin, chipped my favorite tooth, and left me sprawled in the dirt. Like a fool, I'd gone
down on one knee to comb the stiff hacked grass for the keys, my
mind making connections in the most dragged-out, testudineous
way, knowing that things had gone wrong, that I was in a lot of
trouble, and that the lost ignition key was my grail and my salva-
tion. The three or four succeeding blows were mainly absorbed by
my right buttock and the tough piece of bone at the base of my
spine.

Meanwhile, Digby vaulted the kissing bumpers and delivered
a savage kung-fu blow to the greasy character's collarbone. Digby
had just finished a course in martial arts for phys-ed credit and had
spent the better part of the past two nights telling us apocryphal
tales of Bruce Lee types and of the raw power invested in lightning
blows shot from coiled wrists, ankles, and elbows. The greasy character was unimpressed. He merely backed off a step, his face like
a Toltec mask, and laid Digby out with a single whistling round-
house blow . . . but by now Jeff had got into the act, and I was beginning to extricate myself from the dirt, a tinny compound of
shock, rage, and impotence wadded in my throat.

Jeff was on the guy's back, biting at his ear. Digby was on the
ground, cursing. I went for the tire iron I kept under the driver's
seat. I kept it there because bad characters always keep tire irons
under the driver's seat, for just such an occasion as this. Never
mind that I hadn't been involved in a fight since sixth grade, when

a kid with a sleepy eye and two streams of mucus depending from his nostrils hit me in the knee with a Louisville slugger; never mind that I'd touched the tire iron exactly twice before, to change tires: it was there. And I went for it.

I was terrified. Blood was beating in my ears, my hands were shaking, my heart turning over like a dirtbike in the wrong gear. My antagonist was shirtless, and a single cord of muscle flashed across his chest as he bent forward to peel Jeff from his back like a wet overcoat. "Motherfucker," he spat, over and over, and I was aware in that instant that all four of us—Digby, Jeff, and myself included—were chanting "motherfucker, motherfucker," as if it were a battle cry. (What happened next? the detective asks the murderer from beneath the turned-down brim of his porkpie hat. I don't know, the murderer says, something came over me. Exactly.)

Digby poked the flat of his hand in the bad character's face and I came at him like a kamikaze, mindless, raging, stung with humiliation—the whole thing, from the initial boot in the chin to this murderous primal instant involving no more than sixty hyperventilating, gland-flooding seconds—I came at him and brought the tire iron down across his ear. The effect was instantaneous, astonishing. He was a stunt man and this was Hollywood, he was a big grimacing toothy balloon and I was a man with a straight pin. He collapsed. Wet his pants. Went loose in his boots.

A single second, big as a zeppelin, floated by. We were standing over him in a circle, gritting our teeth, jerking our necks, our limbs and hands and feet twitching with glandular discharges. No one said anything. We just stared down at the guy, the car freak, the lover, the bad greasy character laid low. Digby looked at me; so did Jeff. I was still holding the tire iron, a tuft of hair clinging to the crook like dandelion fluff, like down. Rattled, I dropped it in the dirt, already envisioning the headlines, the pitted faces of the police inquisitors, the gleam of handcuffs, clank of bars, the big black shadows rising from the back of the cell . . . when suddenly a raw torn shriek cut through me like all the juice in all the electric chairs in the country.

It was the fox. She was short, barefoot, dressed in panties and a man's shirt. "Animals!" she screamed, running at us with her fists clenched and wisps of blow-dried hair in her face. There was a silver chain round her ankle, and her toenails flashed in the glare of the headlights. I think it was the toenails that did it. Sure, the gin

and the cannabis and even the Kentucky Fried may have had a hand
in it, but it was the sight of those flaming toes that set us off—the
toad emerging from the loaf in *Virgin Spring*, lipstick smeared on
a child: she was already tainted. We were on her like Bergman's
deranged brothers—see no evil, hear none, speak none—panting,
wheezing, tearing at her clothes, grabbing for flesh. We were bad
characters, and we were scared and hot and three steps over the
line—anything could have happened.

It didn't.

Before we could pin her to the hood of the car, our eyes masked
with lust and greed and the purest primal badness, a pair of headlights swung into the lot. There we were, dirty, bloody, guilty, dis-
sociated from humanity and civilization, the first of the Ur-crimes
behind us, the second in progress, shreds of nylon panty and span-
dex brassiere dangling from our fingers, our flies open, lips licked—
there we were, caught in the spotlight. Nailed.

We bolted. First for the car, and then, realizing we had no way
of starting it, for the woods. I thought nothing. I thought escape.
The headlights came at me like accusing fingers. I was gone.

Ram-bam-bam, across the parking lot, past the chopper and
into the feculent undergrowth at the lake's edge, insects flying up
in my face, weeds whipping, frogs and snakes and red-eyed turtles
splashing off into the night: I was already ankle-deep in muck and
tepid water and still going strong. Behind me, the girl's screams
rose in intensity, disconsolate, incriminating, the screams of the
Sabine women, the Christian martyrs, Anne Frank dragged from
the garret. I kept going, pursued by those cries, imagining cops and
bloodhounds. The water was up to my knees when I realized what
I was doing: I was going to swim for it. Swim the breadth of Greasy
Lake and hide myself in the thick clot of woods on the far side.
They'd never find me there.

I was breathing in sobs, in gasps. The water lapped at my waist
as I looked out over the moon-burnished ripples, the mats of algae
that clung to the surface like scabs. Digby and Jeff had vanished. I
paused. Listened. The girl was quieter now, screams tapering to
sobs, but there were male voices, angry, excited, and the high-
pitched ticking of the second car's engine. I waded deeper, stealthy,
hunted, the ooze sucking at my sneakers. As I was about to take the
plunge—at the very instant I dropped my shoulder for the first slash-
ing stroke—I blundered into something. Something unspeakable,

obscene, something soft, wet, moss-grown. A patch of weed? A
log? When I reached out to touch it, it gave like a rubber duck, it
gave like flesh.

In one of those nasty little epiphanies for which we are prepared by films and TV and childhood visits to the funeral home to
ponder the shrunken painted forms of dead grandparents, I understood what it was that bobbed there so inadmissibly in the dark.
Understood, and stumbled back in horror and revulsion, my mind
yanked in six different directions (I was nineteen, a mere child, an
infant, and here in the space of five minutes I'd struck down one
greasy character and blundered into the waterlogged carcass of a
second), thinking, The keys, the keys, why did I have to go and lose
the keys? I stumbled back, but the muck took hold of my feet—
a sneaker snagged, balance lost—and suddenly I was pitching face
forward into the buoyant black mass, throwing out my hands in
desperation while simultaneously conjuring the image of reek-
ing frogs and muskrats revolving in slicks of their own deliquesc-
ing juices. AAAAArrrgh! I shot from the water like a torpedo, the
dead man rotating to expose a mossy beard and eyes cold as the
moon. I must have shouted out, thrashing around in the weeds,
because the voices behind me suddenly became animated.

"What was that?"

"It's them, it's them: they tried to, tried to . . . *rape* me!" Sobs.

A man's voice, flat Midwestern accent. "You sons a bitches,
we'll kill you!"

Frogs, crickets.

Then another voice, harsh, *r*-less, Lower East Side: "Motherfucker!" I recognized the verbal virtuosity of the bad greasy character in the engineer boots. Tooth chipped, sneakers gone, coated
in mud and slime and worse, crouching breathless in the weeds
waiting to have my ass thoroughly and definitively kicked and
fresh from the hideous stinking embrace of a three-days-dead-
corpse, I suddenly felt a rush of joy and vindication: the son of a
bitch was alive! Just as quickly, my bowels turned to ice. "Come
on out of there, you pansy motherfuckers!" the bad greasy character was screaming. He shouted curses till he was out of breath.

The crickets started up again, then the frogs. I held my breath.
All at once there was a sound in the reeds, a swishing, a splash:
thunk-a-thunk. They were throwing rocks. The frogs fell silent. I
cradled my head. Swish, swish, thunk-a-thunk. A wedge of feldspar
the size of a cue ball glanced off my knee. I bit my finger.

It was then that they turned to the car. I heard a door slam, a curse, and then the sound of the headlights shattering—almost a good-natured sound, celebratory, like corks popping from the necks of bottles. This was succeeded by the dull booming of the fenders, metal on metal, and then the icy crash of the windshield. I inched forward, elbows and knees, my belly pressed to the muck, thinking of guerrillas and commandos and *The Naked and the Dead.* I parted the weeds and squinted the length of the parking lot.

The second car—it was a Trans-Am—was still running, its high beams washing the scene in a lurid stagy light. Tire iron flailing, the greasy bad character was laying into the side of my mother's Bel Air like an avenging demon, his shadow riding up the trunks of the trees. Whomp. Whomp. Whomp-whomp. The other two guys—blond types, in fraternity jackets—were helping out with tree branches and skull-sized boulders. One of them was gathering up bottles, rocks, muck, candy wrappers, used condoms, pop-tops, and other refuse and pitching it through the window on the driver's side. I could see the fox, a white bulb behind the windshield of the '57 Chevy. "Bobbie," she whined over the thumping, "come on." The greasy character paused a moment, took one good swipe at the left taillight, and then heaved the tire iron halfway across the lake. Then he fired up the '57 and was gone.

Blond head nodded at blond head. One said something to the other, too low for me to catch. They were no doubt thinking that in helping to annihilate my mother's car they'd committed a fairly rash act, and thinking too that there were three bad characters connected with that very car watching them from the woods. Perhaps other possibilities occurred to them as well—police, jail cells, justices of the peace, reparations, lawyers, irate parents, fraternal censure. Whatever they were thinking, they suddenly dropped branches, bottles, and rocks and sprang for their car in unison, as if they'd choreographed it. Five seconds. That's all it took. The engine shrieked, the tires squealed, a cloud of dust rose from the rutted lot and then settled back on darkness.

I don't know how long I lay there, the bad breath of decay all around me, my jacket heavy as a bear, the primordial ooze subtly reconstituting itself to accommodate my upper thighs and testicles. My jaws ached, my knee throbbed, my coccyx was on fire. I contemplated suicide, wondered if I'd need bridgework, scraped the recesses of my brain for some sort of excuse to give my parents—a tree had fallen on the car, I was blindsided by a bread truck, hit and run, vandals had got to it while we were playing chess at Digby's. Then I thought of the dead man. He was probably the only person on the planet worse off than I was. I thought about him, fog on the lake, insects chirring eerily, and felt the tug of fear, felt the darkness opening up inside me like a set of jaws. Who was he, I wondered, this victim of time and circumstance bobbing sorrowfully in the lake at my back. The owner of the chopper, no doubt, a bad older character come to this. Shot during a murky drug deal, drowned while drunkenly frolicking in the lake. Another headline. My car was wrecked; he was dead.

When the eastern half of the sky went from black to cobalt and the trees began to separate themselves from the shadows, I pushed myself up from the mud and stepped out into the open. By now the birds had begun to take over for the crickets, and dew lay slick on the leaves. There was a smell in the air, raw and sweet at the same time, the smell of the sun firing buds and opening blossoms. I contemplated the car. It lay there like a wreck along the highway, like a steel sculpture left over from a vanished civilization. Everything was still. This was nature.

I was circling the car, as dazed and bedraggled as the sole survivor of an air blitz, when Digby and Jeff emerged from the trees behind me. Digby's face was crosshatched with smears of dirt; Jeff's jacket was gone and his shirt was torn across the shoulder. They slouched across the lot, looking sheepish, and silently came up beside me to gape at the ravaged automobile. No one said a word. After a while Jeff swung open the driver's door and began to scoop the broken glass and garbage off the seat. I looked at Digby. He shrugged. "At least they didn't slash the tires," he said.

It was true: the tires were intact. There was no windshield, the headlights were staved in, and the body looked as if it had been sledge-hammered for a quarter a shot at the county fair, but the tires were inflated to regulation pressure. The car was drivable. In silence, all three of us bent to scrape the mud and shattered glass from the interior. I said nothing about the biker. When we were finished, I reached in my pocket for the keys, experienced a nasty stab of recollection, cursed myself, and turned to search the grass. I spotted them almost immediately, no more than five feet from the open door, glinting like jewels in the first tapering shaft of sunlight. There was no reason to get philosophical about it: I eased into the seat and turned the engine over.

It was at that precise moment that the silver Mustang with the flame decals rumbled into the lot. All three of us froze, then Digby and Jeff slid into the car and slammed the door. We watched as the Mustang rocked and bobbed across the ruts and finally jerked to a halt beside the forlorn chopper at the far end of the lot. "Let's go," Digby said. I hesitated, the Bel Air wheezing beneath me.

Two girls emerged from the Mustang. Tight jeans, stiletto heels, hair like frozen fur. They bent over the motorcycle, paced back and forth aimlessly, glanced once or twice at us, and then ambled over to where the reeds sprang up in a green fence round the perimeter of the lake. One of them cupped her hands to her mouth. "Al," she called. "Hey, Al!"

"Come on," Digby hissed. "Let's get out of here."

But it was too late. The second girl was picking her way across the lot, unsteady on her heels, looking up at us and then away. She was older—twenty-five or -six—and as she came closer we could see there was something wrong with her: she was stoned or drunk, lurching now and waving her arms for balance. I gripped the steering wheel as if it were the ejection lever of a flaming jet, and Digby spat out my name, twice, terse and impatient.

"Hi," the girl said.

We looked at her like zombies, like war veterans, like deaf-and-dumb pencil peddlers.

She smiled, her lips cracked and dry. "Listen," she said, bending from the waist to look in the window, "you guys seen Al?" Her pupils were pinpoints, her eyes glass. She jerked her neck. "That's his bike over there—Al's. You seen him?"

Al. I didn't know what to say. I wanted to get out of the car and retch, I wanted to go home to my parents' house and crawl into bed. Digby poked me in the ribs. "We haven't seen anybody," I said.

The girl seemed to consider this, reaching out a slim veiny arm to brace herself against the car. "No matter," she said, slurring the *t*'s, "he'll turn up." And then, as if she'd just taken stock of the whole scene—the ravaged car and our battered faces, the desolation of the place—she said: "Hey, you guys look like some pretty bad characters—been fightin', huh?" We stared straight ahead, rigid as catatonics. She was fumbling in her pocket and muttering something. Finally she held out a handful of tablets in glassine wrappers: "Hey, you want to party, you want to do some of these with me and Sarah?"

I just looked at her. I thought I was going to cry. Digby broke

the silence. "No, thanks," he said, leaning over me. "Some other
time."

I put the car in gear and it inched forward with a groan, shaking off pellets of glass like an old dog shedding water after a bath,
heaving over the ruts on its worn springs, creeping toward the highway. There was a sheen of sun on the lake. I looked back. The girl
was still standing there, watching us, her shoulders slumped, hand
outstretched.

——For Discussion——

RPW—

*Three nineteen-year-olds (the narrator, Digby, and Jeff), on the
third night of their summer vacation, cross way over the line, jour-
neying "a mile down on the dark side of Route 88," as the epigraph from Springsteen suggests. They are college kids, typical
middle-class suburban types, cruising in their parents' Bel Air,
trying to project an image of being "dangerous characters" in a
culture that plays with the idea that it is "good to be bad." They
want to find some last-minute excitement up at Greasy Lake, the
local hangout, before they head home. They discover much more
than they anticipate.*

*These young men enter a new territory of consciousness when
they get to Greasy Lake, lose the ignition key, and, metaphorically
at least, lose their footing in the darkness. For these three friends,
a practical joke turns into a living nightmare as they enter a world
they know little about, but one that is both frightening and ex-
hilarating because it taps into their own primal energy.*

*"What happened next? the detective asks. . . . I don't know, the
murderer says, something came over me. Exactly."*

*Yes, exactly. As a reader of this story, I am drawn up close
to the "gland-flooding" rush of male violence. I hear the Oedipal battle cry of men joined together in chorus—"motherfucker,
motherfucker"—and then witness the attack, the first Ur-crime,
a potential murder, quickly followed by the second Ur-crime, a
potential rape. Like the narrator inspired by lust and greed, gin
and cannabis, "flaming toes" and an image of female flesh (a fox)
pinned to the hood of a car, I am, for a moment, spellbound, jolted
only by the headlights of a Trans-Am pulling into the parking lot.*

And then with the narrator I retreat into the murky ooze of Greasy Lake itself.

And what does the narrator discover in this primordial ooze as he wrestles with his own darkness and mortality? Something he will never speak about for the rest of the story, something obscene, something soft and wet that gives like flesh itself, the flip side of rape and murder, a waterlogged carcass, death. With the background sounds of shattering headlights and the icy crush of his mother's windshield, the narrator must be considering not only the seduction and thrill of adventure and violence, but the destructive forces within that unleashing of raw instinct and energy. He doesn't want to party anymore on this night, just find his keys, go home, crawl into bed. He must be wondering what a trip on the dark side does to our human connectiveness and to ourselves. I am.

JRT—

Here is a short story that entices us to embrace three boys who learn that "being bad" is not as cool as it's made out to be. In fact, "being bad" can lead to murder and rape and a whole slew of evils that ultimately mean being untrue to one's essential "nature." Just as Greasy Lake has become a fetid wastepool where it once was pure, the three boys in the story set off on a course that, as seductive as it seems, can lead away from self.

Boyle does a good job at making us interested in and amused at the three wannabe bad guys, and yet the line between amusement and anger ends when the narrator and his cohorts almost rape "the fox." Here's where Boyle himself comes up short for me and for a lot of women in my classes. Why do we have to have a woman degraded for boys to grow up? The affection felt for the potheads dissipates as we are drawn into the seriousness of crime. It seems that the superficial level on which the boys live will always be unchangeable when it comes to their views on women. Yes, the narrator will go home after his night on the town, realizing that "being bad" can lead to a life of violence. He might stop partying every weekend and he might even get a real job. But there is nothing in the story that makes us believe he will respect women. To him, "the fox" remains the stereotypical drunk broad who might as well accompany big bikers. She remains a dark force, a "temptation," in the story. She symbolizes being swept up

*into the moment, and even if the boys refuse to be swept up again,
there is nothing to indicate that they come out of Greasy Lake and
their dark night of the soul respecting "the fox." She is dispensable
or usable, but certainly not two-dimensional.*

*It seems important to discuss how women and men play into
these views of women and how they can opt out of them. The boys
too are compelled by roles and the narrator can't stop playing
them. He goes from movie to movie, looking at his life dramatically and trying to be the star. The others are almost pawns in his
self-discovery, an evening of turnarounds. Questioning our roles,
our development of self, and the loss of innocence are all themes
that make this story important. Questions to ask might be: If you
were the narrator's parent, how would you talk to him after such
a night? What does it mean to go into one's darkest places? How
can we educate "the fox" to get her out of a Greasy Lake mental-
ity? Who or what is responsible for the potential violence in this
story?*

Where Are You Going,
Where Have You Been?

Joyce Carol Oates

FOR BOB DYLAN

Her name was Connie. She was fifteen and she had a quick nervous giggling habit of craning her neck to glance into mirrors, or checking other people's faces to make sure her own was all right. Her mother, who noticed everything and knew everything and who hadn't much reason any longer to look at her own face, always scolded Connie about it. "Stop gawking at yourself, who are you? You think you're so pretty?" she would say. Connie would raise her eyebrows at these familiar complaints and look right through her mother, into a shadowy vision of herself as she was right at that moment: she knew she was pretty and that was everything. Her mother had been pretty once too, if you could believe those old snapshots in the album, but now her looks were gone and that was why she was always after Connie.

"Why don't you keep your room clean like your sister? How've you got your hair fixed—what the hell stinks? Hair spray? You don't see your sister using that junk."

Her sister June was twenty-four and still lived at home. She was a secretary in the high school Connie attended, and if that wasn't bad enough—with her in the same building—she was so plain and chunky and steady that Connie had to hear her praised all the time by her mother and her mother's sisters. June did this, June did that, she saved money and helped clean the house and cooked and Connie couldn't do a thing, her mind was all filled with trashy daydreams. Their father was away at work most of the time and when he came home he wanted supper and he read the newspaper at supper and after supper he went to bed. He didn't bother talking much to them, but around his bent head Connie's mother kept picking at her until Connie wished her mother was dead and she herself was dead and it was all over. "She makes me want to throw up sometimes," she complained to her friends. She had a high, breathless, amused voice which made everything she said sound a little forced, whether it was sincere or not.

There was one good thing: June went places with girl friends of hers, girls who were just as plain and steady as she, and so when Connie wanted to do that her mother had no objections. The father of Connie's best girl friend drove the girls the three miles to town and left them off at a shopping plaza, so that they could walk through the stores or go to a movie, and when he came to pick them up again at eleven he never bothered to ask what they had done.

They must have been familiar sights, walking around that shopping plaza in their shorts and flat ballerina slippers that always scuffed the sidewalk, with charm bracelets jingling on their thin wrists; they would lean together to whisper and laugh secretly if someone passed by who amused or interested them. Connie had long dark blond hair that drew anyone's eye to it, and she wore part of it pulled up on her head and puffed out and the rest of it she let fall down her back. She wore a pull-over jersey blouse that looked one way when she was at home and another way when she was away from home. Everything about her had two sides to it, one for home and one for anywhere that was not home: her walk that could be childlike and bobbing, or languid enough to make anyone think she was hearing music in her head, her mouth which was pale and smirking most of the time, but bright and pink on these evenings out, her laugh which was cynical and drawling at home—"Ha, ha, very funny"—but high-pitched and nervous anywhere else, like the jingling of the charms on her bracelet.

Sometimes they did go shopping or to a movie, but sometimes they went across the highway, ducking fast across the busy road, to a drive-in restaurant where older kids hung out. The restaurant was shaped like a big bottle, though squatter than a real bottle, and on its cap was a revolving figure of a grinning boy who held a hamburger aloft. One night in mid-summer they ran across, breathless with daring, and right away someone leaned out a car window and invited them over, but it was just a boy from high school they didn't like. It made them feel good to be able to ignore him. They went up through the maze of parked and cruising cars to the bright-lit, fly-infested restaurant, their faces pleased and expectant as if they were entering a sacred building that loomed out of the night to give them what haven and what blessing they yearned for. They sat at the counter and crossed their legs at the ankles, their thin shoulders rigid with excitement, and listened to the music that made everything so good: the music was always in the background like music at a church service, it was something to depend upon.

A boy named Eddie came in to talk with them. He sat backwards on his stool, turning himself jerkily around in semi-circles and then stopping and turning again, and after a while he asked Connie if she would like something to eat. She said she did and so she tapped her friend's arm on her way out—her friend pulled her face up into a brave droll look—and Connie said she would meet her at eleven, across the way. "I just hate to leave her like that," Connie said earnestly, but the boy said that she wouldn't be alone for long. So they went out to his car and on the way Connie couldn't help but let her eyes wander over the windshields and faces all around her, her face gleaming with a joy that had nothing to do with Eddie or even this place; it might have been the music. She drew her shoulders up and sucked in her breath with the pure pleasure of being alive, and just at that moment she happened to glance at a face just a few feet from hers. It was a boy with shaggy black hair, in a convertible jalopy painted gold. He stared at her and then his lips widened into a grin. Connie slit her eyes at him and turned away, but she couldn't help glancing back and there he was still watching her. He wagged a finger and laughed and said, "Gonna get you, baby," and Connie turned away again without Eddie noticing anything.

She spent three hours with him, at the restaurant where they ate hamburgers and drank Cokes in wax cups that were always sweating, and then down an alley a mile or so away, and when he left her off at five to eleven only the movie house was still open at the plaza. Her girl friend was there, talking with a boy. When Connie came up the two girls smiled at each other and Connie said, "How was the movie?" and the girl said, "*You* should know." They rode off with the girl's father, sleepy and pleased, and Connie couldn't help but look at the darkened shopping plaza with its big empty parking lot and its signs that were faded and ghostly now, and over at the drive-in restaurant where cars were still circling tirelessly. She couldn't hear the music at this distance.

Next morning June asked her how the movie was and Connie said, "So-so."

She and that girl and occasionally another girl went out several times a week that way, and the rest of the time Connie spent around the house—it was summer vacation getting in her mother's way and thinking, dreaming, about the boys she met. But all the boys fell back and dissolved into a single face that was not even a face, but an idea, a feeling, mixed up with the urgent insistent pounding of the music and the humid night air of July. Connie's mother kept dragging her back to the daylight by finding things for her to do or saying, suddenly, "What's this about the Pettinger girl?"

And Connie would say nervously, "Oh, her. That dope." She always drew thick clear lines between herself and such girls, and her mother was simple and kindly enough to believe her. Her mother was so simple, Connie thought, that it was maybe cruel to fool her so much. Her mother went scuffling around the house in old bedroom slippers and complained over the telephone to one sister about the other, then the other called up and the two of them complained about the third one. If June's name was mentioned her mother's tone was approving, and if Connie's name was mentioned it was disapproving. This did not really mean she disliked Connie and actually Connie thought that her mother preferred her to June because she was prettier, but the two of them kept up a pretense of exasperation, a sense that they were tugging and struggling over something of little value to either of them. Sometimes, over coffee, they were almost friends, but something would come up—some vexation that was like a fly buzzing suddenly around their heads— and their faces went hard with contempt.

One Sunday Connie got up at eleven—none of them bothered with church—and washed her hair so that it could dry all day long, in the sun. Her parents and sister were going to a barbecue at an aunt's house and Connie said no, she wasn't interested, rolling her eyes to let her mother know just what she thought of it. "Stay home alone then," her mother said sharply. Connie sat out back in a lawn chair and watched them drive away, her father quiet and bald, hunched around so that he could back the car out, her mother with a look that was still angry and not at all softened through the windshield, and in the back seat poor old June all dressed up as if she didn't know what a barbecue was, with all the running yelling kids and the flies. Connie sat with her eyes closed in the sun, dreaming and dazed with the warmth about her as if this were a kind of love, the caresses of love, and her mind slipped over onto thoughts of the boy she had been with the night before and how nice he had been, how sweet it always was, not the way someone like June would suppose but sweet, gentle, the way it was in movies and promised in songs; and when she opened her eyes she hardly knew where she was, the back yard ran off into weeds and a fence-line of trees and behind it the sky was perfectly blue and still. The asbestos "ranch house" that was now three years old startled her it looked small. She shook her head as if to get awake.

It was too hot. She went inside the house and turned on the radio to drown out the quiet. She sat on the edge of her bed, bare-foot, and listened for an hour and a half to a program called XYZ Sunday Jamboree, record after record of hard, fast, shrieking songs she sang along with, interspersed by exclamations from "Bobby King": "An' look here you girls at Napoleon's—Son and Charley want you to pay real close attention to this song coming up!"

And Connie paid close attention herself, bathed in a glow of slow-pulsed joy that seemed to rise mysteriously out of the music itself and lay languidly about the airless little room, breathed in and breathed out with each gentle rise and fall of her chest.

After a while she heard a car coming up the drive. She sat up at once, startled, because it couldn't be her father so soon. The gravel kept crunching all the way in from the road—the driveway was long—and Connie ran to the window. It was a car she didn't know. It was an open jalopy, painted a bright gold that caught the sunlight opaquely. Her heart began to pound and her fingers snatched at her hair, checking it, and she whispered "Christ. Christ," wondering how bad she looked. The car came to a stop at the side door and the horn sounded four short taps as if this were a signal Connie knew.

She went into the kitchen and approached the door slowly, then hung out the screen door, her bare toes curling down off the step. There were two boys in the car and now she recognized the driver: he had shaggy, shabby black hair that looked crazy as a wig and he was grinning at her.

"I ain't late, am I?" he said.

"Who the hell do you think you are?" Connie said.

"Toldja I'd be out, didn't I?"

"I don't even know who you are."

She spoke sullenly, careful to show no interest or pleasure, and he spoke in a fast bright monotone. Connie looked past him to the other boy, taking her time. He had fair brown hair, with a lock that fell onto his forehead. His sideburns gave him a fierce, embarrassed look, but so far he hadn't even bothered to glance at her. Both boys wore sunglasses. The driver's glasses were metallic and mirrored everything in miniature.

"You wanta come for a ride?" he said.

Connie smirked and let her hair fall loose over one shoulder.

"Don'tcha like my car? New paint job," he said. "Hey."

"What?"

"You're cute."

She pretended to fidget, chasing flies away from the door.

"Don'tcha believe me, or what?" he said.

"Look, I don't even know who you are," Connie said in disgust.

"Hey, Ellie's got a radio, see. Mine's broke down." He lifted his friend's arm and showed her the little transistor the boy was holding, and now Connie began to hear the music. It was the same program that was playing inside the house.

"Bobby King?" she said.

"I listen to him all the time. I think he's great."

"He's kind of great," Connie said reluctantly.

"Listen, that guy's *great*. He knows where the action is."

Connie blushed a little, because the glasses made it impossible for her to see just what this boy was looking at. She couldn't decide if she liked him or if he was just a jerk, and so she dawdled in the doorway and wouldn't come down or go back inside. She said, "What's all that stuff painted on your car?"

"Can'tcha read it?" He opened the door very carefully, as if he was afraid it might fall off. He slid out just as carefully, planting his feet firmly on the ground, the tiny metallic world in his glasses slowing down like gelatine hardening and in the midst of it Connie's bright green blouse. "This here is my name, to begin with," he said. ARNOLD FRIEND was written in tarlike black letters on the side, with a drawing of a round grinning face that reminded Connie of a pumpkin, except it wore sunglasses. "I wanta introduce myself, I'm Arnold Friend and that's my real name and I'm gonna be your friend, honey, and inside the car's Ellie Oscar, he's kinda shy." Ellie brought his transistor radio up to his shoulder and balanced it there. "Now these numbers are a secret code, honey," Arnold Friend explained. He read off the numbers 33, 19, 17 and raised his eyebrows at her to see what she thought of that, but she didn't think much of it. The left rear fender had been smashed and around it was written, on the gleaming gold background: DONE BY CRAZY WOMAN DRIVER. Connie had to laugh at that. Arnold Friend was pleased at her laughter and looked up at her. "Around the other side's a lot more—you wanta come and see them?"

"No."

"Why not?"

"Why should I?"

"Don'tcha wanta see what's on the car? Don'tcha wanta go for a ride?"

"I don't know."

"Why not?"

"I got things to do."

"Like what?"

"Things."

He laughed as if she had said something funny. He slapped his thighs. He was standing in a strange way, leaning back against the car as if he were balancing himself. He wasn't tall, only an inch or so taller than she would be if she came down to him. Connie liked the way he was dressed, which was the way all of them dressed: tight faded jeans stuffed into black, scuffed boots, a belt that pulled his waist in and showed how lean he was, and a white pull-over shirt that was a little soiled and showed the hard small muscles of his arms and shoulders. He looked as if he probably did hard work, lifting and carrying things. Even his neck looked muscular. And his face was a familiar face, somehow: the jaw and chin and cheeks slightly darkened, because he hadn't shaved for a day or two, and the nose long and hawk-like, sniffing as if she were a treat he was going to gobble up and it was all a joke.

"Connie, you ain't telling the truth. This is your day set aside for a ride with me and you know it," he said, still laughing. The way he straightened and recovered from his fit of laughing showed that it had been all fake.

"How do you know what my name is?" she said suspiciously.

"It's Connie."

"Maybe and maybe not."

"I know my Connie," he said, wagging his finger. Now she remembered him even better, back at the restaurant, and her cheeks warmed at the thought of how she sucked in her breath just at the moment she passed him—how she must have looked to him. And he had remembered her. "Ellie and I come out here especially for you," he said. "Ellie can sit in back. How about it?"

"Where?"

"Where what?"

"Where're we going?"

He looked at her. He took off the sunglasses and she saw how pale the skin around his eyes was, like holes that were not in shadow but instead in light. His eyes were chips of broken glass that catch the light in an amiable way. He smiled. It was as if the idea of going for a ride somewhere, to some place, was a new idea to him.

"Just for a ride, Connie sweetheart."

"I never said my name was Connie," she said.

"But I know what it is. I know your name and all about you, lots of things," Arnold Friend said. He had not moved yet but stood still leaning back against the side of his jalopy. "I took a special interest in you, such a pretty girl, and found out all about you like I know your parents and sister are gone somewheres and I know where and how long they're going to be gone, and I know who you were with last night, and your best girl friend's name is Betty. Right?"

He spoke in a simple lilting voice, exactly as if he were reciting the words to a song. His smile assured her that everything was fine. In the car Ellie turned up the volume on his radio and did not bother to look around at them.

"Ellie can sit in the back seat," Arnold Friend said. He indicated his friend with a casual jerk of his chin, as if Ellie did not count and she should not bother with him.

"How'd you find out all that stuff?" Connie said.

"Listen: Betty Schultz and Tony Fitch and Jimmy Pettinger and Nancy Pettinger," he said, in a chant. "Raymond Stanley and Bob Hutter—"

"Do you know all those kids?"

"I know everybody."

"Look, you're kidding. You're not from around here."

"Sure."

"But—how come we never saw you before?"

"Sure you saw me before," he said. He looked down at his boots, as if he were a little offended. "You just don't remember."

"I guess I'd remember you," Connie said.

"Yeah?" He looked up at this, beaming. He was pleased. He began to mark time with the music from Ellie's radio, tapping his fists lightly together. Connie looked away from his smile to the car, which was painted so bright it almost hurt her eyes to look at it. She looked at that name, ARNOLD FRIEND. And up at the front fender was an expression that was familiar—MAN THE FLYING SAUCERS. It was an expression kids had used the year before, but didn't use this year. She looked at it for a while as if the words meant something to her that she did not yet know.

"What're you thinking about? Huh?" Arnold Friend demanded. "Not worried about your hair blowing around in the car, are you?"

"No."

"Think I maybe can't drive good?"

"How do I know?"

"You're a hard girl to handle. How come?" he said. "Don't you know I'm your friend? Didn't you see me put my sign in the air when you walked by?"

"What sign?"

"My sign." And he drew an X in the air, leaning out toward her. They were maybe ten feet apart. After his hand fell back to his side the X was still in the air, almost visible. Connie let the screen door close and stood perfectly still inside it, listening to the music from her radio and the boy's blend together. She stared at Arnold Friend. He stood there so stiffly relaxed, pretending to be relaxed, with one hand idly on the door handle as if he were keeping himself up that way and had no intention of ever moving again. She recognized most things about him, the tight jeans that showed his thighs and buttocks and the greasy leather boots and the tight shirt, and even that slippery friendly smile of his, that sleepy dreamy smile that all the boys used to get across ideas they didn't want to put into words. She recognized all this and also the singsong way he talked, slightly mocking, kidding, but serious and a little melancholy, and she recognized the way he tapped one fist against the other in homage to the perpetual music behind him. But all these things did not come together.

She said suddenly, "Hey, how old are you?"

His smile faded. She could see then that he wasn't a kid, he was much older—thirty, maybe more. At this knowledge her heart began to pound faster.

"That's a crazy thing to ask. Can'tcha see I'm your own age?"

"Like hell you are."

"Or maybe a coupla years older, I'm eighteen."

"Eighteen?" she said doubtfully.

He grinned to reassure her and lines appeared at the corners of his mouth. His teeth were big and white. He grinned so broadly his eyes became slits and she saw how thick the lashes were, thick and black as if painted with a black tarlike material. Then he seemed to become embarrassed, abruptly, and looked over his shoulder at Ellie. "*Him*, he's crazy," he said. "Ain't he a riot, he's a nut, a real character." Ellie was still listening to the music. His sunglasses told nothing about what he was thinking. He wore a bright orange shirt unbuttoned halfway to show his chest, which was a pale, bluish chest and not muscular like Arnold Friend's. His shirt collar was turned up all around and the very tips of the collar pointed out past his chin as if they were protecting him. He was pressing the transistor radio up against his ear and sat there in a kind of daze, right in the sun.

"He's kinda strange," Connie said.

"Hey, she says you're kinda strange! Kinda strange!" Arnold Friend cried. He pounded on the car to get Ellie's attention. Ellie turned for the first time and Connie saw with shock that he wasn't a kid either—he had a fair, hairless face, cheeks reddened slightly as if the veins grew too close to the surface of his skin, the face of a forty-year-old baby. Connie felt a wave of dizziness rise in her at this sight and she stared at him as if waiting for something to change the shock of the moment, make it all right again. Ellie's lips kept shaping words, mumbling along, with the words blasting in his ear.

"Maybe you two better go away," Connie said faintly.

"What? How come?" Arnold Friend cried. "We come out here to take you for a ride. It's Sunday." He had the voice of the man on the radio now. It was the same voice, Connie thought. "Don'tcha know it's Sunday all day and honey, no matter who you were with last night today you're with Arnold Friend and don't you forget it!—Maybe you better step out here," he said, and this last was in a different voice. It was a little flatter, as if the heat was finally getting to him.

"No. I got things to do."

"Hey."

"You two better leave."

"We ain't leaving until you come with us."

"Like hell I am—"

"Connie, don't foot around with me. I mean, I mean, don't fool *around*," he said, shaking his head. He laughed incredulously. He placed his sunglasses on top of his head, carefully, as if he were indeed wearing a wig, and brought the stems down behind his ears. Connie stared at him, another wave of dizziness and fear rising in her so that for a moment he wasn't even in focus but was just a blur, standing there against his gold car, and she had the idea that he had driven up the driveway all right but had come from nowhere before that and belonged nowhere and that everything about him and even about the music that was so familiar to her was only half real.

"If my father comes and sees you—"

"He ain't coming. He's at the barbecue."

"How do you know that?"

"Aunt Tillie's. Right now they're—uh—they're drinking. Sitting around," he said vaguely, squinting as if he were staring all the way to town and over to Aunt Tillie's backyard. Then the vision seemed to get clear and he nodded energetically. "Yeah. Sitting around. There's your sister in a blue dress, huh? And high heels, the poor sad bitch—nothing like you, sweetheart! And your mother's helping some fat woman with the corn, they're cleaning the corn—husking the corn—"

"What fat woman?" Connie cried.

"How do I know what fat woman. I don't know every goddam fat woman in the world!" Arnold Friend laughed.

"Oh, that's Mrs. Hornby. . . . Who invited her?" Connie said. She felt a little light-headed. Her breath was coming quickly.

"She's too fat. I don't like them fat. I like them the way you are, honey," he said, smiling sleepily at her. They stared at each other for a while, through the screen door. He said softly, "Now what you're going to do is this: you're going to come out that door. You're going to sit up front with me and Ellie's going to sit in the back, the hell with Ellie, right? This isn't Ellie's date. You're my date. I'm your lover, honey."

"What? You're crazy—"

"Yes, I'm your lover. You don't know what that is but you will," he said. "I know that too. I know all about you. But look: it's real nice and you couldn't ask for nobody better than me, or more polite. I always keep my word. I'll tell you how it is, I'm always nice at first, the first time. I'll hold you so tight you won't think you have to try to get away or pretend anything because you'll know you can't. And I'll come inside you where it's all secret and you'll give in to me and you'll love me—"

"Shut up! You're crazy!" Connie said. She backed away from the door. She put her hands against her ears as if she'd heard something terrible, something not meant for her. "People don't talk like that, you're crazy," she muttered. Her heart was almost too big now for her chest and its pumping made sweat break out all over her. She looked out to see Arnold Friend pause and then take a step toward the porch lurching. He almost fell. But, like a clever drunken man, he managed to catch his balance. He wobbled in his high boots and grabbed hold of one of the porch posts.

"Honey?" he said. "You still listening?"

"Get the hell out of here!"

"Be nice, honey. Listen."

"I'm going to call the police—"

He wobbled again and out of the side of his mouth came a fast spat curse, an aside not meant for her to hear. But even this "Christ!" sounded forced. Then he began to smile again. She watched this smile come, awkward as if he were smiling from inside a mask. His whole face was a mask, she thought wildly, tanned down onto his throat but then running out as if he had plastered make-up on his face but had forgotten about his throat.

"Honey—? Listen, here's how it is. I always tell the truth and I promise you this: I ain't coming in that house after you."

"You better not! I'm going to call the police if you—if you don't—"

"Honey," he said, talking right through her voice, "honey, I'm not coming in there but you are coming out here. You know why?"

She was panting. The kitchen looked like a place she had never seen before, some room she had run inside but which wasn't good enough, wasn't going to help her. The kitchen window had never had a curtain, after three years, and there were dishes in the sink for her to do—probably—and if you ran your hand across the table you'd probably feel something sticky there.

"You listening, honey? Hey?"

"—going to call the police—"

"Soon as you touch the phone I don't need to keep my promise and can come inside. You won't want that."

She rushed forward and tried to lock the door. Her fingers were shaking. "But why lock it," Arnold Friend said gently, talking right into her face. "It's just a screen door. It's just nothing." One of his boots was at a strange angle, as if his foot wasn't in it. It pointed out to the left, bent at the ankle. "I mean, anybody can break through a screen door and glass and wood and iron or anything else if he needs to, anybody at all and specially Arnold Friend. If the place got lit up with a fire honey you'd come running out into my arms, right into my arms and safe at home—like you knew I was your lover and'd stopped fooling around. I don't mind a nice shy girl but I don't like no fooling around." Part of those words were spoken with a slight rhythmic lilt, and Connie somehow recognized them—the echo of a song from last year, about a girl rushing into her boy friend's arms and coming home again—

Connie stood barefoot on the linoleum floor, staring at him. "What do you want?" she whispered.

"I want you," he said.

"What?"

"Seen you that night and thought, that's the one, yes sir. I never needed to look any more."

"But my father's coming back. He's coming to get me. I had to wash my hair first—" She spoke in a dry, rapid voice, hardly raising it for him to hear.

"No, your daddy is not coming and yes, you had to wash your hair and you washed it for me. It's nice and shining and all for me, I thank you, sweetheart," he said, with a mock bow, but again he almost lost his balance. He had to bend and adjust his boots. Evidently his feet did not go all the way down; the boots must have been stuffed with something so that he would seem taller. Connie stared out at him and behind him Ellie in the car, who seemed to be looking off toward Connie's right, into nothing. This Ellie said, pulling the words out of the air one after another as if he were just discovering them, "You want me to pull out the phone?"

"Shut your mouth and keep it shut," Arnold Friend said, his face red from bending over or maybe from embarrassment because Connie had seen his boots. "This ain't none of your business."

"What—what are you doing? What do you want?" Connie said. "If I call the police they'll get you, they'll arrest you—"

"Promise was not to come in unless you touch that phone, and I'll keep that promise," he said. He resumed his erect position and tried to force his shoulders back. He sounded like a hero in a movie, declaring something important. He spoke too loudly and it was as if he were speaking to someone behind Connie. "I ain't made plans for coming in that house where I don't belong but just for you to come out to me, the way you should. Don't you know who I am?"

"You're crazy," she whispered. She backed away from the door but did not want to go into another part of the house, as if this would give him permission to come through the door. "What do you . . . You're crazy, you . . . "

"Huh? What're you saying, honey?"

Her eyes darted everywhere in the kitchen. She could not remember what it was, this room.

"This is how it is, honey: you come out and we'll drive away,
have a nice ride. But if you don't come out we're gonna wait till
your people come home and then they're all going to get it."

"You want that telephone pulled out?" Ellie said. He held the
radio away from his ear and grimaced, as if without the radio the
air was too much for him.

"I toldja shut up, Ellie," Arnold Friend said, "you're deaf, get
a hearing aid, right? Fix yourself up. This little girl's no trouble
and's gonna be nice to me, so Ellie keep to yourself, this ain't your
date—right? Don't hem in on me. Don't hog. Don't crush. Don't
bird dog. Don't trail me," he said in a rapid meaningless voice, as
if he were running through all the expressions he'd learned but was
no longer sure which one of them was in style, then rushing on to
new ones, making them up with his eyes closed, "Don't crawl under my fence, don't squeeze in my chipmunk hole, don't sniff my
glue, suck my popsicle, keep your own greasy fingers on yourself!" He shaded his eyes and peered in at Connie, who was backed
against the kitchen table. "Don't mind him honey he's just a creep.
He's a dope. Right? I'm the boy for you and like I said you come out
here nice like a lady and give me your hand, and nobody else gets
hurt, I mean, your nice old bald-headed daddy and your mummy
and your sister in her high heels. Because listen: why bring them
in this?"

"Leave me alone," Connie whispered.

"Hey, you know that old woman down the road, the one with
the chickens and stuff—you know her?"

"She's dead!"

"Dead? What? You know her?" Arnold Friend said.

"She's dead—"

"Don't you like her?"

"She's dead—she's—she isn't here any more—"

"But don't you like her, I mean, you got something against her?
Some grudge or something?" Then his voice dipped as if he were
conscious of a rudeness. He touched the sunglasses perched on top
of his head as if to make sure they were still there. "Now you be
a good girl."

"What are you going to do?"

"Just two things, or maybe three," Arnold Friend said. "But I promise it won't last long and you'll like me that way you get to like people you're close to. You will. It's all over for you here, so come on out. You don't want your people in any trouble, do you?"

She turned and bumped against a chair or something, hurting her leg, but she ran into the back room and picked up the telephone. Something roared in her ear, a tiny roaring, and she was so sick with fear that she could do nothing but listen to it—the telephone was clammy and very heavy and her fingers groped down to the dial but were too weak to touch it. She began to scream into the phone, into the roaring. She cried out, she cried for her mother, she felt her breath start jerking back and forth in her lungs as if it were something Arnold Friend were stabbing her with again and again with no tenderness. A noisy sorrowful wailing rose all about her and she was locked inside it the way she was locked inside the house.

After a while she could hear again. She was sitting on the floor with her wet back against the wall.

Arnold Friend was saying from the door, "That's a good girl. Put the phone back."

She kicked the phone away from her.

"No, honey. Pick it up. Put it back right."

She picked it up and put it back. The dial tone stopped.

"That's a good girl. Now come outside."

She was hollow with what had been fear, but what was now just an emptiness. All that screaming had blasted it out of her. She sat, one leg cramped under her, and deep inside her brain was something like a pinpoint of light that kept going and would not let her relax. She thought, I'm not going to see my mother again. She thought, I'm not going to sleep in my bed again. Her bright green blouse was all wet.

Arnold Friend said, in a gentle-loud voice that was like a stage voice, "The place where you came from ain't there any more, and where you had in mind to go is cancelled out. This place you are now—inside your daddy's house—is nothing but a cardboard box I can knock down any time. You know that and always did know it. You hear me?"

She thought, I have got to think. I have to know what to do.

"We'll go out to a nice field, out in the country here where it smells so nice and it's sunny," Arnold Friend said. "I'll have my arms around you so you won't need to try to get away and I'll show you what love is like, what it does. The hell with this house! It looks solid all right," he said. He ran a fingernail down the screen and the noise did not make Connie shiver, as it would have the day before. "Now put your hand on your heart, honey. Feel that? That feels solid too but we know better, be nice to me, be sweet like you can because what else is there for a girl like you but to be sweet and pretty and give in?—and get away before her people come back?"

She felt her pounding heart. Her hand seemed to enclose it. She thought for the first time in her life that it was nothing that was hers, that belonged to her, but just a pounding, living thing inside this body that wasn't really hers either.

"You don't want them to get hurt," Arnold Friend went on. "Now get up, honey. Get up all by yourself."

She stood up.

"Now turn this way. That's right. Come over here to me—Ellie, put that away, didn't I tell you? You dope. You miserable creepy dope," Arnold Friend said. His words were not angry but only part of an incantation. The incantation was kindly. "Now come out through the kitchen to me honey and let's see a smile, try it, you're a brave sweet little girl and now they're eating corn and hotdogs cooked to bursting over an outdoor fire, and they don't know one thing about you and never did and honey you're better than them because not a one of them would have done this for you."

Connie felt the linoleum under her feet; it was cool. She brushed her hair back out of her eyes. Arnold Friend let go of the post tentatively and opened his arms for her, his elbows pointing in toward each other and his wrists limp, to show that this was an embarrassed embrace and a little mocking, he didn't want to make her self-conscious.

She put out her hand against the screen. She watched herself push the door slowly open as if she were safe back somewhere in the other doorway, watching this body and this head of long hair moving out into the sunlight where Arnold Friend waited.

"My sweet little blue-eyed girl," he said, in a half-sung sigh that had nothing to do with her brown eyes but was taken up just the same by the vast sunlit reaches of the land behind him and on all sides of him, so much land that Connie had never seen before and did not recognize except to know that she was going to it.

——For Discussion——

JRT—

Oates writes a suspenseful, horrifying rape story that forces us to see how easily the lives of young women, caught up in illusion and the promise of youth, can be destroyed at the drop of a dime. Connie is a typical teenager, obsessed with her looks, boys, and the music of her generation. It seems not to matter that Dylan sings to her and her alone; it could be Springsteen, or Smashing Pumpkins, Tupac Shakur, or any other male voice that could croon her into the daydream that befalls the young. Connie thinks she is infallible, in spite of what my students call her "normal dysfunctional family." Connie talks to the boys, makes out in their cars, "wears one thing at the [mall] and another at home." She even answers the door when Arnold drives up because she expects him to be slick and cool and safe. Connie hasn't known anything but safe, and that is the crux of this tale that Oates tells. We see how unsafe girls are when they are young, not because they are blind and deaf, but because they are rightfully innocent. Who then can protect them?

As mothers, the women in Changing Lives reading groups want to understand how to warn their daughters. Some are angry that Connie does not fight back more fiercely when Arnold, the rapist, lures her outside. Some bring up how much fear and disbelief she must have felt. Almost all believe Connie is a virgin and has no conception of the Arnolds of the world. The most interesting part of the discussion involves the comparison of their lives with Connie's.

For men, this story might be horrifying on other levels. Who is Arnold Friend and his sleazeball sidekick anyway? And who is responsible for the rape and ultimate murder of Connie? Does Connie's behavior justify the violence here? Can violence ever be justified?

RPW—

Fifteen-year-old Connie, with her long dark blond hair, is always checking herself out in mirrors or in the reflection of other people's faces. She needs to get out of her small asbestos ranch house, away from her jealous mother, her plain and chunky older sister, her bald and tired father. But where can an innocent adolescent American girl go—especially one filled with vanity and "trashy daydreams," one bathed and caressed by the shallowness of pop culture, one infatuated with the idea of boys and the sweet promise of sexual romance? Connie can go to the drive-in restaurant, to the sacred shopping plaza (and even down an alley with innocent Eddie). And she can wear her pullover jersey blouse in these places in an entirely different way from the way she wears it at home, the place she has already been.

The problem is that Connie's journey is doomed, doomed by her own vain desires and duplicity, doomed by the omnipresent music and voices and images of popular culture, and doomed by the menace of male violence masking itself as a familiar and exciting friend (perhaps even a savior).

Arnold Friend, with his black shaggy-haired wig, his metallic and mirrored sunglasses, his made-up face with its reassuring smile, and his overstuffed boots, is "only half real." He is our MTV rock star, tabloid celebrity, movie-of-the-week hero. He comes from nowhere and belongs nowhere. As a performer of popular culture, he arouses adolescent fantasies and heated desires. As a product of the trash daydreams he mimics, he is at first charming and alluring, then menacing, finally deadly. He becomes a male predator sacrificing teenage girls on the altar of sex and violence.

Connie cannot get away from Arnold Friend. "I'll hold you so tight you won't think you have to try to get away or pretend anything because you'll know you can't. And I'll come inside you where it's all secret and you'll give in to me and you'll love me—." Arnold always tells the truth. And the truth here is that as an adolescent girl Connie is doomed no matter which way she goes. As Arnold puts it: "The place where you came from ain't there any more, and where you had in mind to go is cancelled out."

Connie's father cannot protect her, nobody can, as Arnold Friend totally violates her, robbing her even of the pounding rhythm of her heart. But what else is there for a girl like Connie to do, "but be sweet and pretty and give in?"

Connie's sacrifice is not without its heroism. She protects her family from getting hurt, something they would not have had the courage to do for her. And in the end she knows where she is going: To the "vast sunlit reaches of the land" surrounding Arnold Friend, a land of death no doubt, but yet a land that appears to be her destiny.

from AFFLICTION

Russell Banks

CHAPTER 20

You will say that I should have known terrible things were about
to happen, and perhaps I should have. But even so, what could I
have done to stop them? By Friday, Wade was being driven by forces
that were as powerful as they were difficult to identify—for me
and for Margie, who were best situated to observe them, and certainly for people like Alma Pittman or Gordon LaRiviere or Asa
Brown. We had no choice, it seemed, but to react as we did to
Wade's actions that day and the next. In doing so, we were able
later to claim something like innocence, or at least blamelessness,
but by the same token, we were unable to affect his actions. To
have behaved differently would have required each of us to be pre-
scient if not omniscient and perhaps hard-hearted as well.

I cannot blame Gordon LaRiviere for his reaction to Wade that
morning, although, given what I know now, it may well have been
what drove Wade to his bizarre and violent actions later that day
and that evening. In fact, when Wade, after having left Alma
Pittman's, slammed his way into LaRiviere's shop, ignoring Jack
Hewitt and Jimmy Dame, and strode into LaRiviere's office, pushing right past Elaine Bernier's attempts to stop him, LaRiviere did
what I myself would have done under the same circumstances.

Wade came into the office already shouting. "You sneaky sonofabitch!" he bellowed. "I've got your number now, Gordon! All
these years," he said, panting, his eyes ablaze with a strange mixture of fury and sadness, "all these years I worked for you, since
I was a kid, goddammit, and I thought you were a decent man. I
thought you were a decent man, Gordon! I actually went around
feeling grateful to you! Can you fucking believe that! Grateful!"
He pounded both fists on LaRiviere's desk, bam, bam, bam, like an
enraged child.

Jimmy and Jack had appeared at the door behind Wade, while
Elaine Bernier, her face gray with fear, fluttered in the outer office
beyond them. LaRiviere calmly stood up, raising himself to his not
inconsiderable height and swelling his body like a tent, and said,

"Wade, you're done." He held out one hand, palm up. "Let me have the shop keys."

Wade looked around and saw Jack and Jimmy, both as grim as executioners, and he laughed. "You two, you don't get it, do you? You think you're free, but you're like slaves, that's all. You're this man's slaves," he said, and his voice changed again, became plaintive and soft. "Oh, Jack, don't you see what this man has done to you? Jesus Christ, Jack, you've turned into his slave. Don't you see that?"

Jack regarded Wade as if the man were made of wood.

"The key, Wade," LaRiviere said.

"Yeah, sure. You can have the key, all right. It's the key that's kept me chained and locked to you all these years," he said. "I give it back with pleasure!" He pulled his key ring from his pocket and worked one key free of it and dropped it into LaRiviere's extended hand. "Now I'm free." He stared into LaRiviere's unblinking eyes and said, "See how easy it is, Jack? All you got to do is give back what the man gave you, and you're free of him."

He turned, and Jack and Jimmy parted to let him pass. Elaine Bernier dodged to the side, and Wade walked through the outer office and was gone. Free.

From LaRiviere's, as far as we know, Wade drove straight home. It was midmorning by then, a sweetly bright day, warm enough to start the snow melting. Pop was out back, stacking firewood and splitting kindling for the stove, something he did almost every day at this hour, early enough for him to wield an ax with relative safety. He worked slowly, methodically, a brittle cautious man who seemed much older than he was, and he did not look up when Wade drove into the yard and parked Margie's car by the porch.

Margie was in the kitchen, drinking coffee and reading a week-old newspaper, and when Wade strode into the room, she folded the paper and looked up, ready now to talk with him about last night, about whatever it was that had happened in the back seat of the car: she did not know, really, what was going on between him and his father, but it was an ancient war, and she knew it was painful for Wade, and she was prepared to understand and sympathize. And as for the business of his being late, perhaps that could be explained: his car was obviously not here, so it must have broken down last night on the way home from work, too far from town to phone, and he had to walk all the way home in the snow, and somehow she had missed him on the road when she drove in to Wickham's, had driven right past him, poor guy, so that he had to turn around and walk back into town and was unable to get there until nine. Something like that, she was sure, had happened, and then at the restaurant and later in the car, when Pop had started in with his wild drunk-talk, Wade was probably so angry and feeling so guilty, too, that he just lost control, and that was why he slapped the old man.

But when she looked up from her newspaper and saw Wade, all these thoughts flew away, for she knew instantly that he was someone to be afraid of. His movements were abrupt and erratic, and his face was red and stiffly contorted, as if he were wearing a mask made from a badly photographed portrait of himself, and he was trembling: his hands shook; she could see the tremors from across the room as he pulled off his coat and draped it over a chair by the wall.

"I've got to talk to my brother," he announced. "Did you get my note? Yes, you did, I see it there. Listen, there's lots going on right now, and I've got to talk to Rolfe about some things," he said. "Everything okay? You got to go to work today, don't you?"

Margie nodded yes and watched him carefully, as Wade headed into the living room and grabbed up the telephone from the table next to the television set. "I'll only be a few minutes!" he called.

And that, of course, was when he telephoned me, at a time when I am not usually at home, but I happened on this occasion to have called in sick: it was a Friday, and I was suffering from some kind of mental exhaustion of my own, perhaps a delayed reaction to the funeral and my trip to Lawford, perhaps because of an obscure and complex and no doubt unconscious involvement with what Wade was going through—although at that time I was only marginally aware of what Wade was experiencing. At any rate, I had wakened that morning feeling unnaturally gloomy and peculiarly weak, unable to stand without my legs turning to water, so I had called the school and asked that a substitute take my classes for the day. Then, midmorning, the phone rang, and it was Wade.

It was an unusually long conversation. Wade was garrulous and intense at first, rapidly filling me in on the events of the previous evening. He left out, of course, certain details that would have put him in an unfavorable light, such as the slapping incident in the car, details that I obtained months later from various sources— Margie, Nick Wickham, Jimmy Dame, the deer hunters from Lynn,

Massachusetts. Then he told me the story, his version, of the bath-
tub incident, which I found somewhat disconcerting, since it was
so far from my own version of that story and because it happened
to be about me. And finally he got to the apparent point of his call,
to tell me what he had learned at Alma Pittman's this morning—
he did not mention his being fired by Gordon LaRiviere—and to
ask my advice on how to use this new information. "I know what
it *means*," he said. "I'm just running out of ways to use it."

"For what?" I asked.

"What do you mean, 'for what?' To help Jack, of course, and to
nail those sonsofbitches, the two Gordons, as old Alma calls them.
Jesus Christ, Rolfe, whose side are you on in this?"

"Yours, naturally," I assured him. But his intensity and the fe-
rocity of his feelings alarmed me. And his chaos and apparent
lack of focus, in spite of his obsession with this case, were causing me to react carefully. He switched from topic to topic, tone
to tone: one minute he would be railing against Mel Gordon, the
next he would be complaining about his toothache, which had per-
sisted for weeks now; he spoke with anxious sympathy about Jack
Hewitt, seeming almost to identify with the man, and then ram-
bled on at tedious length about his car's being in the garage and
having to borrow Margie's car and being unable to leave Pop alone
in the house for very long; he turned bitter for a few moments as he
spoke about Lillian and his custody suit, as he referred to it, and
then practically wept when he recounted how Lillian was keeping
him from being a good father to his own daughter.

It was an anxiety-producing conversation, to say the least, and I
felt one of my old migraines coming on, as if a penlight inside my
skull were being shined directly at my eyes from behind. I wanted
to get away from him, so I took over the conversation and spoke
with perhaps more authority than I normally would have. I do believe, however, that this was precisely what Wade wanted me to do
and why he had called me in the first place. While he was talking,
once it became evident to me that he had become hopelessly confused, I made notes on the yellow pad I keep by the phone, num-
bering his individual problems and putting them into relation to
one another: this is, after all, one of the ways I solve my own problems, by naming them and by placing them in order, so that solv-
ing the least of my problems leads finally to the solution of the
largest. Why not try to solve Wade's problems the same way? Thus,
when I decided to take over the conversation, I was able to speak

with clarity and force. He listened and, for all I know, may have been taking notes himself, because as it turned out, he followed my advice to the letter. Which is why I feel today less than innocent, less than blameless for what eventually happened. Of course, I had no way of knowing how Wade would botch things, no way of predicting how simple circumstances would thwart him and no way of anticipating the forms he would eventually discover to express his increasingly violent feelings.

Wade got off the phone with me and, as I had suggested, immediately called Merritt's garage to arrange to pick up his car. It was Chick Ward who answered, and when Wade said he was calling about his car, Chick laughed, a sneering knowing laugh, and said, "Wade, old buddy, there's good news and bad news. Which do you want first?"

"Just give me the facts, Chick. I'm in a hurry."

"Okay, the good news, old buddy, is we haven't got to your car yet. It only came in yesterday afternoon, you know. That's the good news, you understand." His voice was loud, as if he were talking for the benefit of an audience of listeners other than Wade.

"What the hell are you up to?"

"You want the bad news?" Wade could picture Chick grinning at the other end, standing in the garage and flashing a knowing wink at Chub Merritt and anyone else who happened to be there resuscitating LaRiviere's drowned pickup truck.

"Just tell me when you'll have it fixed. It's the starter motor, I'm pretty sure, it's been giving me trouble—"

"The bad news," Chick said, interrupting him, "is, the reason we ain't got to your car yet is we got a problem here with a truck somebody drove through the ice last night. Figured you'd know something about that, Wade."

Wade was silent for a second. "Yeah," he said. "I know about that."

"Yep. Figured. Chub also says to tell you that Gordon LaRiviere won't let you bill your job back to him. You'll have to pay for it yourself. Probably come to a couple hundred bucks, if it's a starter motor, like you say."

Wade said nothing. Money . . . he had none. No job, no money, no car, nothing.

"That okay with you, Wade?"

"Yeah. That's fine with me."

"Oh, I got some more of the bad news, Wade. You want to hear it?"

"Not particularly, you sonofabitch."

"Hey, I'm just the messenger, you know. I just work here."

"Tell me."

"Well, Chub, he says you're fired, Wade."

"Fired! He can't! He can't fire me! LaRiviere already did that this morning."

"Oh, yeah, Wade, he can. He's one of the selectmen, and he said to tell you to turn your badge in and clean out your office down to the town hall and leave your office key with his wife there. She'll be in the Board of Selectmen's office all day. He says he'll pull the CB and the police light off your car while he's got it down here. I guess they're town property, Wade."

"Let me talk to Chub," Wade said. "There's some things he ought to know. Put Chub on."

Chick muffled the phone for a few seconds, then came back on and said, "Chub says, he says to tell you he's too busy drying out your ex-boss's pickup truck to talk to you. Sorry."

"Look, you sonofabitch, put Chub on! I know a few things he ought to know, goddammit. Before he fires me, he should know what I know about a few people in this town. You put him on, you hear?"

Again, Chick muffled the phone. A moment passed, and then Wade heard the receiver click, and a dial tone buzzed in his ear.

Slowly, Wade laid the receiver back in its cradle. So Chub was in it too! Chub Merritt was working with them. He was probably taking a cut from Gordon LaRiviere and Mel Gordon, and as one of the selectmen, he had as much access to the tax records as LaRiviere did, so his job was to keep quiet about Northcountry Development Corporation and, among other things, help keep Wade out of the way.

The throb in his jaw seemed to continue the buzz of the dial tone, distracting him abruptly from his mania—for by now it was that, a mania—and made him remember my second piece of advice, to call a dentist, for heaven's sake, and get that tooth pulled. Take care of the little things first, the things that are distracting and handicapping you in your attempts to take care of the big things. Get your own car back, get your tooth pulled, let Pop take care of himself while you get your facts in order, and take your facts over the heads of the locals, whom you cannot trust, straight to the state police. Let the state police go to work on this. And then maybe try to get Jack Hewitt to turn himself in. But do it calmly, peacefully, rationally. Do not chase him around the countryside or go up against him in a bar or in LaRiviere's shop, where there will be other people around. Talk to his girlfriend or his father, talk to somebody he trusts, and explain what is at stake for him here. Jack no longer trusts you, Wade, so you might have to let someone else convince him that he must confess his crime and incriminate the others. Save that young man, and break the others. And while you are doing that, instruct J. Battle Hand to pursue your case against Lillian. Now that you have given him information that not only tarnishes Lillian's good-mother image but also implicates her own attorney, your Mr. Hand should be able to cut a deal that will force Lillian to give you back your rights as a father. In a few short weeks, before Christmas, maybe even before Thanksgiving, Wade, everything that now seems out of control and chaotic will be under control and orderly, and you and the fine woman who will soon be your wife and your lovely daughter Jill and your father will sit down to Thanksgiving dinner in the old family homestead together, and you will offer up a prayer to thank the Lord for all that He has given to you this year. And maybe I myself will join you at that table.

With the phone book in his lap, Wade flipped through the yellow pages and checked the Littleton listings for dentists: there were four, and he called one after the other in alphabetical order, asking, and then begging and finally shouting, for an appointment that afternoon. All four refused to see him. Two of them—I later learned, having called them myself—remembered hanging up in the middle of his rant, convinced that he was either crazy or dangerous or both.

Wade slammed down the phone, tossed the telephone book across the room, and when he stood up and turned around, he saw Margie standing by the door, watching him, mouth open, ashen-faced.

"What?" he said.

"What on earth is happening to you, Wade? Why are you acting this way?"

"What do you mean? It's my tooth! My fucking tooth! I can't even think anymore because of it!"

"Wade, I heard you talking. You got fired this morning, didn't you?"

"Look, that's just temporary, believe me. There's so much shit going to hit the fan in the next few days, my getting fired by LaRiviere and Chub Merritt won't matter a bit. Those sonsof-bitches are going to be out of business and doing time before I'm through." He paced around the room while he talked, and clamped his hand against his throbbing jaw, as if making sure that it was still attached to him. Behind Margie, Pop came into the kitchen from outside with a half-dozen chunks of wood in his arms and dumped them noisily into the woodbox. "There's a lot of stuff I haven't told you or told anyone yet, but by God, I'm going to blow this town wide open now," Wade said. "Don't worry, I'll get an-other job. I can find work doing lots of things around here. People are going to need me, anyhow. After this is over, and people see what's been going on behind their backs, they'll make me into a goddamned hero. You wait: when this blows, people will need me. Like the way Jill needs me, right? You'll see, I'll deliver. And I'll be the best goddamned father for her who ever lived. You need me. Even Pop, for Christ's sake, he needs me. So don't worry, I'll have a job, a good job, when this is over, and I'll take care of this house, fix it up, make it nice for all of us. And this town needs me too. They don't know it yet, but they do. The same as Jill and you and Pop. I'll be the town cop again, don't worry. Maybe now they think they can send me howling into a corner, like a kicked dog or some damned thing, some small irritating thing in the way, but by God, it'll be different soon."

Slowly, as if being shoved back by the force of his words, Margie retreated from the room toward the kitchen, where she lifted her coat from the hook by the door and picked up her pock-etbook, and while Wade paced and ranted on behind her, gesturing and explaining quite as if she were still standing at the living room door, she stepped outside.

She hurried down the steps and got into her car, started the mo-tor and backed out to the road, thinking, The man's crazy. One's a drunk, and the other's crazy. What on earth am I doing here? She could leave, she thought: her furniture was still in her old place in town, and she had not yet written to her ex-husband's parents in Florida to tell them that she had moved out. But all her clothes, her linens and personal belongings, photographs, papers, were in Wade's house, which was how she thought of the house now. Some-how the place smelled like Wade and looked like him: once a fine piece of country workmanship, symmetrical, handsomely proportioned, attractively located, the house was now broken down, disheveled, barely functional.

Wade was turning into his father, she suddenly realized. Wade, sober, sounded and acted the way his father did drunk. And his father was being eased out of existence altogether. She could see what was happening. She did not intend to turn into Wade's mother. She would stay in the house one more night, she decided, and tomorrow, when Wade went down to Concord to see that lawyer of his, she would move out.

*   *   *

The pain was worse than it had ever been: it had turned scarlet, had painted half of the inside of his face, was smeared from the point of his chin to his temple and was eating its way in toward the center. Wade's vision was affected now, and he saw things in discontinuous flutters and flashes—Pop was in the kitchen shucking his jacket; the television set was turned on, the horizontal control out of whack, the picture flipping again and again; Pop was seated on the couch in front of the television; was in the kitchen; was adjusting the horizontal control. Noises were unnaturally loud, followed by strange bits of silence: the sound of Pop opening the kitchen cabinet, unscrewing the top of his bottle, pouring whiskey into a glass and drinking it down—Wade heard it all clearly and at high volume, as if Pop had a microphone attached to him; and then the television came on, loud at first, suddenly silent, loud again; and the sound of Pop dropping an armload of wood into the woodbox, like a rock slide, punctuated by a hollow silence.

Pop was watching wrestling, his hands clapped onto his knees as if to hold them still, while Wade chased the pain in his face around the room, from window to window to door, as if his face were a dog in a pen looking for a way out. Pop said something about a dish antenna, he wished he had one of those dish antennas, they should buy one of those dish antennas, how much did a dish antenna cost, did Wade know how much people paid for those dish antennas you see all over town these days? *Shut up!* Wade shouted. *Just shut the fuck up!* The television audience was screaming, as a huge nearly naked man wearing a mask picked up another man and tossed him to the mat and leapt onto him, and the crowd shrieked with joy. Then the picture flipped again, and Pop got out of his seat and adjusted the knob and said he wished he had one of those dish antennas and sat back down, while the man with the mask flew through the air with his feet out and slammed the other man in the back, sending him staggering across the ring against the ropes, and the audience went crazy, booing, screaming, clapping hands, some even standing on their seats and shaking their fists. Then silence, as Wade stood by the window and looked out across the snow-covered backyard to the half-collapsed barn. A crow—in sharp black profile, like a silhouette, perched on a rafter—turned its head slowly, as if it knew it was being watched, until its beak was aimed at Wade like an accusing finger: *You!* Wade turned away, and the sound of the television bored into his head, the screams of the audience, the grunts and thuds of the wrestlers, the hearty voice of the announcer, strands of loud noise winding around one another and making a single shaft that drilled into his brain: Pop was out in the kitchen again; the television went silent; Wade heard the bottle being opened, the whiskey splashing into the glass, the sound of his father's mouth, lips, tongue, throat, as he swallowed. *Leave that fucking bottle out!* Wade shouted, and he strode into the kitchen, passed Pop coming the other way, grabbed the bottle from the counter and hurried outdoors.

The bright light of the sun against the snow blinded him, and he stood for a few seconds on the porch and struggled to see: he heard the wind sigh in the pines across the road, heard the crow call from the barn out back, heard gunfire from a distant clearing in the woods. Soon the blaze of light started to crack and crumble, and at last it fell apart in chunks of white that floated across Wade's field of vision. He stepped from the porch to the ground and walked around the porch to the woodshed attached to the end of the house, a three-sided lean-to open to the driveway, where Pop split, stacked and stored his firewood, and tools were kept on a rough workbench.

Wade entered the woodshed and once again could not see, blinded this time by darkness instead of light. He set the bottle on the bench and felt along the length of it, touching a hammer, tin cans filled with nails and screws, a rasp, a small monkey wrench, a gas can and parts of a chainsaw, a file, a splitting wedge, and finally, as the darkness softened to a gray haze, he reached the pair of channel-lock pliers that he knew were there—he had seen them the other night, Sunday, when he had come out here with a flashlight looking for tools to repair the furnace: Pop's tools, scattered and rusting, a drunk's tools, Wade had thought then.

He uncapped the bottle of whiskey and opened his mouth—it

hurt just to open it—and took a bite of whiskey the size of a tea bag and sloshed it around inside his mouth and swallowed: but he felt and tasted nothing, no grainy burn in his mouth or chest; nothing except the cold steel ripsaw of pain emanating from his jaw. He opened his mouth wider and touched the beak of the long-handled pliers to his front teeth, pulled his lip away with his fingers, forcing a cadaverous grin onto his mouth, and moved the pliers toward the dark star of pain back there. The jaws of the pliers angled away from the handles, like the head of a long-necked bird, and he managed for a second to lock them onto one of his molars, then released it and clamped them on the adjacent tooth. He withdrew the pliers and set them back down on the bench. The pain roared in his ears, like a train in a tunnel, and he felt tears on his cheeks.

He took another bite of whiskey, grabbed up the pliers and the bottle and walked quickly from the shed into the white wall of light outside, weeping and stumbling as he crossed the driveway and made his way to the porch without seeing, going on memory now—until he was back inside the house and could see his way through the gloom of the kitchen into the living room, where Pop sat in front of the television: the grunting huge men slammed their pink bodies against each other and the crowd shrieked with pleasure; Wade hurried past Pop, up the stairs and into the bathroom.

He set the bottle down on the toilet tank and looked into the mirror and saw a disheveled gray-faced stranger with tears streaming down his cheeks look back at him. He opened the stranger's mouth and with his left hand yanked back the lips on the right side, then took the pliers and reached in. He turned the face slightly to the side, so that he could see into it, pried the mouth open still further, and locked the pliers onto the largest molar in the back, squeezed and pulled. He heard the tooth grind against the cold steel of the pliers, as if the tooth were grabbing onto the bone, and he dug further into the gum with the mouth of the pliers and squeezed tightly again and pulled harder, steadily. It shifted in its bed, and he moved his left hand into place behind his right, and with both hands, one keeping the pressure on the tooth, the other lifting and guiding the pliers straight up against the jaw, he pulled, and the tooth came out, wet, bloody, rotted, clattering in the sink. He put the pliers down and reached for the whiskey.

When he passed Pop, he set the whiskey bottle down with pointed emphasis on the table beside him. Pop looked at the bottle for a second and up at Wade, and their eyes met and suddenly flared with hatred.

Neither man said a word. Abruptly, as if dismissing him, Pop looked back at the television. Wade grabbed his coat and hat from the hook in the kitchen, put them on and went outside, moving quickly through the sheets of bright light to the woodshed, where he picked up the gas can and headed on to the barn. His face felt aflame to him, burning from the inside out, as if the hole in his jaw were the chimney of a volcano about to erupt. Removing the tooth had opened a shaft, a dark tunnel, and sparks, cinders, hot gases flew up and scorched his mouth: he opened his mouth and spat a clot of hot blood into the snow and imagined it hissing behind him.

Inside the barn, it was dark and sepulchral. Wade emptied the gas from the can into Pop's truck and tossed the can aside. He stepped up on the running board and got into the driver's seat, took the key from his coat pocket, where it had remained since Wednesday, and after a few tries, got the motor running. The old truck shuddered and shook, and Wade backed it slowly out the huge barn door and along the narrow snowbanked lane that he and I had shoveled clear only two nights before, until he had it out on the road, where he aimed it toward town, worked the stickshift into first gear, and drove off.

——*For Discussion*——

RPW—

Rolfe Whitehouse, Wade's brother, is telling this story of male violence and humiliation. He knows that he escaped from his family and town to become a schoolteacher, but there is really no escape from the brutality both brothers experienced in their home as young boys. Rolfe could have been Wade. In a sense he is Wade, and so the story he tells is not only Wade's story, but his own.

In this chapter, it's clear that Wade has hit bottom. He is a man who "has no job, no money, no car, nothing." No wonder his girlfriend Margie Fogg wants to move out of the house and get away from Wade and his father. He is dangerous, and he is turning into his father. Who can blame Margie for wanting to get out! I wish she would stay to help him through this insanity, but Wade would probably just drag her down with him.

Wade is afflicted with the same disease that his father has, the affliction of male violence and impotent rage born out of shame and humiliation, nurtured by family abuse and alcoholism. Wade needs to be needed, but he cannot figure out how. He wants to be a good father and a good man, but he keeps tripping himself up.

Wade recently moved in with his father after the death of his mother, and now his life seems to be unraveling from every angle. He is in the midst of a custody battle to win back his daughter Jill from his ex-wife Lillian. He has just been fired by his boss, Gordon LaRiviere, the most powerful man in town. His car needs repairs, and he just drove a town truck through the ice last night. He also has an unbearable toothache which, like Wade himself, demands immediate attention.

In addition to all this, Wade seems obsessed with a conspiracy theory that he has developed, one of the many strange features of his bizarre and increasingly violent behavior. He is hell bent to expose this conspiracy and target the enemy. I imagine he wants to save the town. Then he can show the town who the real hero is: Wade Whitehouse, a man who is needed.

When Wade pulls out his own tooth with the rusty pliers from the woodshed, he seems to unleash the pent-up, volcanic rage that will prove to be his final undoing. I understand him, even admire his attempt to do battle with his demons, but I wish he hadn't let violence get the best of him. He's into dangerous territory, where demons often prevail.

As he drives his father's old truck from the barn, I am certain that Wade's destiny is being shaped by the affliction he is trying to escape. He has a disease that has been passed from one generation to the next, that male disease that has existed perhaps since the time before the first hunters.

JRT—

I agree with Margie, Wade's woman, that Wade has gone off the deep end and she should get out of his life. Here is a man bent on destruction of himself and whatever comes in his way. There are reasons, of course, and the narrator, Rolfe, Wade's teacher-brother, feels bound to show them to us. But still, I can't help but want to leave and drive far away from this scene with Margie.

The Wade we see in this chapter has blown it at his job. He wants to save himself, the town, his aging father, and his relationships with his daughter and Margie, but he is too angry to see *straight. We don't really get a sense here why he is so angry, but we can guess. No one appreciates Wade as a worker, a father, a lover, a son—basically as a man. He needs to be listened to, but more than that, he needs to blow off steam. And the chapter proceeds to show us that he will. "You will say that I should have known terrible things were about to happen," the narrator tells us in his opening lines. We witness a tragedy in the making: from Wade's dramatically throwing shop keys in his boss's face, to his need to phone his brother and tell him "some things"; from what his brother calls his obsession with a recent case, to losing his badge and police car; from railing on and on about injustice, to the gruesome scene where he pulls out his rotting tooth. We know that at the end of this chapter, Wade drives off into darkness, into a place where anything can happen. We imagine the worst.*

I can't say that I like Wade very much or feel much sympathy for him. It's not that I can't understand the frustration he must feel or the anger at being a man who lives on the edge of poverty. We do know he was not always so angry. He had a decent job; as a cop, he was once respected in the town. Now, as Margie says, he has become "broken down, disheveled, barely functional," an individual who seems to have chosen violence instead of responsibility. I say "chosen," because it seems to me he allows himself to be driven over the edge. He justifies his rage, and in a way, needs to act it out. I am drawn to know what he will do, but feel that it would be safer to get out of his way. Here is a man who can't be stopped by reason or love.

Solitude of Blood

Marta Brunet

The base was made of bronze, with a drawing of lacework flowers. The same flowers were painted on the reservoir glass, and a white spherical shade interrupted its extremities to allow the chimney to pass through. That lamp was the showpiece of the house. Placed in the center of the table, on top of a meticulously elaborate crocheted table cover, it was turned on only when there was a dinner guest, an unexpected, remote occurrence. But it was also lighted on Saturday night, every Saturday, because that eve of a worry-free morning could be celebrated in some way, and nothing could be better then, than to have the lamp spreading its brightness over the vivid tangle of paper that covered the walls, over the china cabinet so symmetrically decorated with fruit plates, soup tureens and formal stacks of dishes; over the doors of the cupboard, with decorative panels and the iron latch and its lock speaking of the same times as the grating that protected the window on the garden side of the house. Yes, every Saturday night, the lamplight traced out for the man and the woman a little hollow of intimacy, generally peaceful.

From living in contact with the earth, the man seemed made of telluric elements. In the south, in the mountains, looking at their reflection in the translucent eye of the lakes, the trees, polished by wind and by water, had strange shapes and startling qualities. In that wood worked by the pitiless harsh weather the man was carved. The years had made furrows in his face, and from that fallow field sprouted his beard, moustache, eyebrows, eyelashes. And his tangled mat of hair, coal black, crowned his head with a rebellious shock, which was always escaping over his forehead and which he would push back into place with a characteristic mechanical gesture.

Now, in the brightness of the lamplight, the large hands carefully shuffled a deck of cards. He spread the cards out over the table. Absorbed in the game of solitaire, slow and meticulous, because he was about to win, his features swelled with a kind of pleasantness. He hardly had any cards left in his hand. He drew one. He turned it over and suddenly the pleasantness turned into harshness. He gazed at the cards with rapt attention, the new card in his hand. He put down his remaining cards and tossed the big shock back, sinking and fixing his fingers in his hair. The pleasantness spread over his face again. He lifted his eyelids, and his eyes appeared like grapes, azure-blue. A cautious glance that became fixed on the woman, that found the woman's eyes, grey, so clear that in certain light or from a distance they gave the unsettling sensation of being blind.

"Just imagine that I'm not looking at you and go on with your trick . . . ," said the woman with a voice that sang.

"Will it turn out really badly?" asked the man.

"If it does, it does."

"It always fails to work for me! Come on, for God's sake! I'll do it again!" And he gathered the cards together to shuffle them.

Sometimes the game of solitaire "came out." Other times it "turned stubborn." But always at ten o'clock, the hours resonating in the corridor as they fell from the old clock, the man pulled himself up, looked at the woman, came toward her until he could put a hand on her head, and he caressed her hair, again and again, to conclude by saying, as he said that night:

"Until tomorrow, little one. Don't stay up for a long time, be sure the lamp is completely out and don't make a lot of noise with your phonograph. Let me drop off to sleep first . . . "

He left, closing the door. She heard his long strides through the corridor. Then she heard him go out onto the patio, saying something to the dog, turning around, going back and forth through the bedroom; she heard the bed creak, his heavy shoes falling one after the other, the bed creaking again, the man turning over, becoming quiet. The woman had abandoned the knitting in her lap. She was scarcely breathing, her mouth partially open, her whole self gathering in the sounds, separating them, classifying them, her auditory perception fine-tuned to such a point that all her senses seemed to have been transformed into one big ear. Tall, strong, her naturally brown skin tanned by the sun, she might have been any ordinary creole woman if her eyes had not set her apart, creating for her a face that memory, immediately, put in a place all by itself. Tension caused a little bead of perspiration to break out on her forehead. That was all. But she felt her chilled skin and, with an unconscious gesture, passed her hand slowly over it. Then, just as absent-mindedly, she looked at that hand. With every moment she seemed more tense, more like an antenna to receive signals.

And the signal came. From the bedroom, and in the form of a snoring sound, which was followed, arrhythmically, by others.

Her muscles went limp. Her senses opened up into an exact five-pointed star, each one doing its particular job. But the woman still remained motionless, with her expanding pupils fixed on the lamp.

When had she bought that lamp? One time when she went to the town, when she sold her habitual dozen children's outfits, knitted between one household chore and another, between chores that were always the same, methodically distributed over days that were indistinguishable one from another. She bought that lamp as she had bought the china cabinet, and the wicker furniture, and the wardrobe with the mirror, and the quilted eiderdown comforter. Yes, as she had bought so many things, so much . . . Of course, over so many years! How many years had it been? Eighteen. She was thirty-six now, and she was eighteen when she got married. Eighteen and eighteen. Yes . . . The lamp. The china cabinet. The wicker furniture . . . She never believed, of this she was sure, that by knitting she could earn money not only to dress herself, but to give herself household conveniences.

He said, no sooner had they gotten married:

"You have to be enterprising in order to establish your own little business and earn money for your necessities. Raise chickens or sell eggs."

She answered:

"You know I'm ignorant about these things."

"Look for something that you know how to do then. Something they taught you in school."

"I could sell candy."

"Give up on selling in this god-forsaken place. It ought to be something that can be carried all together once a month to the town."

"I could knit."

"That's not a bad idea. But it's necessary to buy wool," he added, suddenly uneasy. "How much would you need to get started?"

"I don't know. Let me check prices. And ask around in the store, to see if people are interested in knitted articles."

"If it doesn't come out being really expensive . . . "

And it did not turn out to be expensive, and it was definitely a good business enterprise. The wife of the store owner himself bought the first completed item for her son, which was merely a sample. A lovely little suit, such as no child had ever had in that "god-forsaken place," where the people handled money and acquired tasteless things in shops in which the barrel of fat was next to the bottles of perfume and the cheap woolens were next to the medicinal balm. Her business was a big success. People placed orders with her. She knitted for the whole region. She was able to raise her prices. She never had enough supplies for the orders that were pending. When he saw that she was prospering, he said one day:

"It's a good idea for you to give me back the ten pesos I lent you to begin your knitting. And don't spend all the money that you earn just on things for yourself. Of course I'm not going to tell you to give me this money, it's yours, yes, you've well earned it, and I'm not going to tell you to hand it over to me." He always repeated what he had just expressed, insisting, wanting to impress the idea on his own mind. "But now you see, now it's necessary to buy a big kettle and to fix the cellar door. You could easily assume responsibility for the household affairs, now that you have so much money at your disposal. Yes . . . , so much money."

She bought the big kettle, she had the cellar door repaired. And then, she bought, and she bought . . . Because it represented happiness to her to be converting that mess of a country house, eaten up by neglect, into what it was now, a house like hers there in the north, in the little town shaded by willows and acacias, with the river singing or rumbling down the valley, and the Andes right there, ever present, background for the little houses that seemed like toys: blue pink, yellow, with wide entrance halls and a jasmine bush perfuming the siestas, and facing the patio gate, a painted green bench, inviting casual conversation in the early evening, when the birds and the angelus were taking flight through the skies in the same air, and the peaks took on violent pinks and gentle violet colors, before falling asleep beneath the blanket of watchful gleaming stars.

She closed her eyelids, as if she too should fall asleep in the shelter of that vigilance. But she opened them again right away and listened again, certain of hearing the rhythm of the one who was sleeping. Then she picked herself up and with silent movements opened the cupboard, and from the highest shelf she went about taking down and placing on the table an old phonograph, improbably shaped, like a little cabinet whose open main doors revealed a set of zither strings, at an oblique angle over the mouth of the receiver, which was nothing but a small open circle in the sound chamber. Below, other doors, smaller, afforded a view of the green turntable. That phonograph was her own luxury item, not like the lamp, luxury of the house, but hers, hers. Purchased when the señora from "los Tapiales," passing through the town, had found her in the store and seen her knitted articles and asked her if she could make some overcoats for her little girls. What a beautiful woman, with a mouth so large and tender and a voice that dragged out her "rr's," as if she were a French lady; but she wasn't, and that really made her laugh. What a workload she had that summer! That was when she saw fulfilled her longing to have a phonograph with records and everything. He permitted her to buy it. That was what she earned all that money for!

"Just buy it, my dear. What's yours is yours, of course, but it would be good if you could also see about buying a poncho for me, for the wool flannel one is wearing through. Because the poncho is a real necessity, and since I have to get together money for another pair of oxen, it's not a matter of squandering funds, and since you are earning so much . . . But it's clear, yes, that you'll buy yourself the phonograph too, and before anything else . . . "

First she bought the poncho and immediately afterwards the phonograph. Never greater was her pleasure than being back at home, the phonograph set up on the table, listening insatiably to the cadence of the waltz or the march that was abruptly interrupted to let the sound of tolling bells be heard. They had sold it to her with the right to two records that she might choose carefully; yet he was impatient on seeing her indecisive after choosing the first one—which was the one with the waltz and the march on it—having to try out a whole album one record after another. Until he said, getting more and more impatient:

"It's getting late. Look how the sun is going down. We've got to go, yes. Night will catch us here if we don't. Take that one that you have set aside, and this one. One because you like it, and the other let's leave up to chance . . . ," and he pulled out at random a record from the box.

Which turned out to have Spanish songs filled with laments, which neither he nor she liked and which she tried in vain to exchange. And when, some time later, she hinted timidly at the idea of buying more records, he—with the claylike expression that he was accustomed to wearing when he was being negative—answered severely:

"No more fuss in the house. What you've got is enough and with that you can get along."

She never insisted. When she was alone, when he and his laborers were in the field working, she would take out the phonograph and in a standing position, with a vague uneasiness that she was "wasting time"—as he said—her hands together and a spiral of joy beginning to stir in her breast, she let herself sink sweetly into the music.

He did not like at all this "wasting time." She knew this well and did not allow herself to be carried away by the overwhelming desire to hear the waltz or to hear the march. But out of that habit of telling him, in minute detail, whatever she had done during the day, a habit to which he had made her accustomed since the beginning of their married life, she said, her eyelids open and her pupils dilated:

"I ground the flour for the workers, I mended your coat, I kneaded dough for the house . . . " She paused imperceptibly and added very gently: "I listened to the phonograph for a while and that's all . . . "

"Wanting to waste time . . . , time that's useful for so many things that bring in money, yes, to waste it . . . " He said it in different tones of voice, sometimes ascertaining a weakness in the woman, gently protective and condescending; sometimes absent-minded, mechanical, tossing back the rebellious shock of hair, troubled by another idea; sometimes stern, wooden and frightening her, she who had never been able to prevail over a dark, instinctive submissiveness of female animal to male, who in former years humiliated herself to her father and in the present, to her husband.

When she, without any hinting, bought that leather jacket for him, shiny as if it were waxed, black and long, which the storekeeper said was for a mechanic and which the rain could not seep into, like that which might fall in the stubborn downpours of the region; when she bought it and mysteriously brought it home and left the package in front of his place at the table—so that he might find it by surprise—the man, his mood softening on seeing it, passed his big hand over her soft hair, done up in braids and raised like a tiara on her head.

"You're a good old gal. Hard-working, like women ought to

be, yes. And listen, little one, tonight since its Saturday, light the lamp, and that way I can do my solitaire better. And when I go off to bed, you'll stay for a little while longer and play your phonograph. Yes, you'll play it, but when I'm sound asleep. You should have your pleasure too . . . "

Thus the custom was born.

She lowered the lamp's light a little. She went on tiptoes to the window and opened it, letting in the night and its silence. She went back to the table, carefully wound up the phonograph, put her hands together and waited.

Ta-ta . . . , ta-ta . . . , ta-ta-dum . . .

The march. And suddenly everything around her was blotted out; it disappeared submerged in the stridency of the trumpets and the roll of the drums, dragging her back through time, until leaving her in the plaza of the northern town, after eleven o'clock mass on a rainless Sunday, the drum major spinning the baton around and following after him, marching in step, the band taking the final turn along the parade route, with the children swarming in front, and a dog mixed in among their racing feet, while the ladies on their traditional bench commented on petty problems, the gentlemen talked about the wine harvest, and they—she and her sisters, she and her friends, arm in arm, with their braids uneasily sliding over breasts that were already swelling with sighs—passed and passed again in front of the grown-ups, crossing through groups of boys, who seemed not to see them, and on fixing their gaze on their surroundings only looked at one of them, absorbing them as if thirsty for fresh water, from a real spring, mouths avid, grown large with desire.

It was the occasion when new clothes were shown off. Sometimes they were pink or celestial blue. Sometimes they were red or sea colored, and this meant that throughout a sky of faded blue a few clouds shed their fleece and that the wind had carried away the last leaf of dark gold. She particularly remembered a red overcoat, with a round collar of white fur, curly and soft against her face and a muff like a little barrel, hanging from the collar by a cord, also white. And the warning from the mother:

"Put your hands in the muff and don't you take them out again. Of course, you can say hello to people . . . ," she added after a thoughtful pause.

They went back and forth, arm in arm. They whispered incomprehensible things, inaudible confidences that drew their heads together, murmurs scarcely articulated and that suddenly shook them in long bursts of laughter that left the trees perplexed, because it wasn't nesting season, or they stirred the trees to nod approvingly during that other time of year when the birds tried to add their own comments to those musical sounds. Sometimes, no, once, she raised her face to better catch the laughter that always seemed to fall on her from above, and from this foreshortened perspective, her pupils found the gaze of a pair of green eyes, as green as new grass and in the face of a boy darkened by the sun, strong and like a freshly sprouting field. Only an instant. But an instant to be carried home and treasured and placed in the depths of her heart, and to feel that a pang of anguish and a feeling of warmth and a vague desire to cry and pass soft fingertips over her lips suddenly tormented her, in the middle of reading, a chore, or a dream. To see him again. To have the feeling impressed on her again that life was stopping in her veins. For that second in which the green gaze of the boy fixed on her was the reason for her existence. Who was he? Was he from the town? No. Someone familiar? No. Perhaps a summer vacationer from a nearby area. She guarded her secret treasure. She talked less, she rarely laughed. But her pupils seemed to become enlarged, to flood her face in that search for the vigorous silhouette, dressed as the boys from the town did not dress. He arrived in a tiny car. It left him beside the club. He went to mass. She observed him from a distance, attentive and circumspect, in the presbytery, a little on the fringe of the group of men. When mass was over, he went to the candy store, filled the car up with packages, then took a walk around the plaza in order to go to the post office, retraced his steps, got into the car and left.

It was obvious that the other girls had noticed him. And dying of laughter over what he was wearing, in his golf or riding pants, they called him "Baggy Pants." To her hidden desperation.

The march continued filling the house with harmonious sounds. The bells burst in. As if pealing. Like on certain Sundays, when there was High Mass; but these were more sonorous bells, more harmonious, as if while they were pealing, pulsations of untapped joy were mixed with them.

The march ended. She shifted the needle, wound it again, turned the record over, and now the waltz began to spin around the table, music that seemed to be dancing, a beat that created soap bubbles, sometimes slowly, sometimes rapidly, radiating their colors.

She never found out what his name was, who he was, where he was from. One Sunday he didn't appear. Or the next. Or any other. A young girl raised the point:

"I wonder what's become of 'Baggy Pants'?"

"La Calchona, the Witch, has probably eaten him up," answered another, and they burst out laughing.

Her chest ached, and the sharp claw of sorrow dug at her throat. The corners of her mouth drew taut, and her eyes, like never before, filled her face. Once in the house, she sought out the most secluded corner, in the storage room, between the piano box and a pile of mattresses, and there she released her sorrow, she opened her heart, allowing her pain to escape and envelop her in its viscous mantle, adhering to her like new skin, moist and painful. The tears rained down her face. Never to see him again. The sobbing became stronger. What gaze was going to hold that magic for her? That burning that raged within her, she did not know where, as if waiting longingly for some unknown happiness. His name? . . . Enrique . . . Juan . . . José . . . Humberto . . . And if his name was Romauldo, like her grandfather's? It did not matter. She would always love him, whatever his name was . . . She would love him . . . Love him . . . Love him the way a woman loves, because she already was a woman and her fifteen years were ripening in her budding breasts, bringing a downy softness to her intimate zones and giving her voice a sudden dark tremolo. She would love him forever. She seemed to disintegrate into weeping. And suddenly she became still, sighing and still, without tears, her sorrow diluted, formless and distant. She signed again. She wiped her eyes. And she found herself thinking that probably they were looking for her all over the house, that she ought to go wash her tear-scorched face, that . . . Yes, it was shameful to confess it, but she was hungry. And she went out gently from among the stored items, watching carefully in order to leave without being seen and to go refresh her face in the courtyard water tank. Her mother stared at her occasionally, seeming confused, and would murmur repeatedly:

"What a woman my little girl's become . . . "

The father was more definitive in his conclusion and said at the top of his voice:

"Look, Maclovia, we have to marry this one off as soon as possible."

For years she wept her sorrow between the piano box and the stack of mattresses. Nobody ever found out anything. They lifted up her braids, which since then she wore like a tiara around her head. They lowered the hems of all her dresses. No one said that she was pretty. But there wasn't a man who did not become startled on seeing her, lost in the contemplation of her grey eyes, experiencing something akin to vertigo in the presence of her mouth, fleshy, intensely red. Her appearance was courteous and indifferent. She had to protect her memory, to keep her dream-fantasy safe, and only in a land of silence could she do this. Men looked at her, they stopped right next to her, but all of them, unanimously, went after other girls who were more accessible to their courtship.

The father introduced the future husband one day. He was from lands to the south, proprietor of a ranch, part of the estate of an old family in the region. Already an older man, of course not a "veteran"; this is what her mother said. As she also added: "A good catch."

Indifferent, she allowed them to interpret her acquiescence among themselves and they married her off. This man or another, it made no difference to her. For not a one of them was hers, the one she loved, that green gaze that filled her blood with tenderness. This one? The other one? What did it matter? And she had to get married, according to what her mother said, smiling and persuasive, and according to what her father ordered with his thundering voice that did not accept dissenting opinions.

She remembered the discomfort of her bridal gown, the crown that pressed against her temples and her terrible fear of ripping the veil. The groom whispered:

"It was so expensive . . . , be careful with it . . . "

The waltz ended. For a moment silence filled the house, a silence so complete that it was injurious. Because it was so complete that the woman began to sense the presence of her heart, and terror forced open her mouth, and then she heard the panting sound of her breathing. But she also perceived the snoring in the other room, broken off when the music was interrupted and which a soothed subconscious mind imposed again upon the sleeping man. Then she heard a cricket in the courtyard. She raised herself up slowly and looked, outside, at the black and spacious field that she knew was flat, without anything in the distance but the ring of the horizon. Flat. A plain. And in the midst of it herself and her vigil, intercepting memories, caressing the past. Lost on the plain. With no one for her tenderness, to look at her and kindle within her that passion that had moved through her blood before and made her mouth shudder under the trembling touch of her fingers. Alone.

She went back to the phonograph. She would have liked to repeat the magical experience. To spread out again the melodic canvas in order to project the images there once more. But no. The clock struck once. Ten thirty. If he were to wake up . . .

With the same caution as someone who handles living, fragile creatures, she put away the phonograph and the records, she closed the cupboard, and she put the key in her pocket. From the china cabinet she took out a small candle stick and lit the candle.

Then she turned off the lamp.

And she went out to the corridor, following after the light's mysterious glow, pursued by nightmarish shadows impinging on one another.

*　　*　　*

When she carried the rice pudding to the dining room, she believed she had made the last trip of the evening and that then she could sit down to wait for the guest to leave. But the two men, the lamp between them, dug in their spoons happily, like children, and once they had cleaned their plates, they both raised their heads and sat staring at her, eagerly, their mouths watering.

"Serve yourselves a little more," she said, bringing the platter up beside them.

"Of course, patrona; it's really a pleasure to eat this!" admitted the guest.

"It's that the old gal has a good hand for these things!" And the man added in a confidential manner, because the wine was spreading through his body: "Things that they taught her in school; it's worth the trouble to have an educated wife, friend; yes, I'm telling you, and believe me."

She waited, uncomfortable in her chair, her hands placed politely on the tablecloth. During the day they had eaten abundantly from a side of beef and the wine in the big jug was almost gone. It would be a matter of waiting around for awhile for the obligatory after dinner conversation and then the guest would leave. For his house was far away and the night was becoming windy, and over a background of pale stars enormous threatening clouds were creating shapes and then destroying them.

The man's voice caught her attention:

"And that coffee? Hurry, for the train won't wait . . . " And he laughed at his statement, hitting the table with his fist and making the lamp wobble back and forth.

Her trips to the kitchen weren't over . . . She went out to the corridor, thinking, disheartened, that the fire was probably already out and to revive it was a task that would take awhile. But under the ashes the red throbbing of the embers made her almost smile, and the water promptly boiled, and the coffee pot, important-looking with its two tiers, was on the tray, and she was once again walking through the darkened house, for the light of the reflector only seemed to thicken the blackness in the corners.

In the dining room the two men deliberated, sparing their words, their creole sullenness still in effect, because that meal was designated to close a deal for the purchase of some pigs that the guest had come from the town to see, and the afternoon had been spent in calculations, "I'll ask for this and offer you that," and they still were not arriving at anything concrete.

"On Monday I'll send you a messenger with the answer," said the guest.

"It's that tomorrow, Sunday, I have to give an answer to one of the parties that's also interested, and I can't put it off any longer, you understand, certainly; it's not good to just leave him waiting and to have him back out and you too and I lose a good buyer . . . "

"It's that you insist on such prices . . . "

"What the pigs are worth, friend; you won't find any better ones. There's not another litter like this anywhere around here, as you well know, yes . . . "

The woman had brought out the cups, the sugar; now she served them the coffee. Let them settle their business quickly and have the guest be on his way! And she sat down again, in the same position as before, so identical to, so like a cardboard cut-out and placed there, so erect, inexpressive and mysterious that, suddenly, the two men turned around to look at her, as if attracted by the ecstatic force that emanated from her.

The guest said:

"The patrona is so quiet!"

And the man, vaguely uncomfortable without knowing why:

"Serve some aguardiente, then."

She got up again, but this time not to go to the kitchen. She opened the cupboard and stood on her tiptoes to reach up above her the bottle that was stuck away in a corner behind the phono-graph. The guest, who was watching her do it, asked solicitously.

"Do you want me to help you, patrona? The bottle is pretty high up for you."

"Look at it, how troublesome the bottle is . . . , just like a woman. But that's what I'm here for, yes . . . ," exclaimed the man, and he reached up to take it down.

His hands bumped into the phonograph, and he added, de-lighted to find another token of respect to offer the guest:

"Let's tell the patrona to play the phonograph for us a little. I call it 'her noisemaker,' because you've got to see how it squawks; but she likes it and I let her get her pleasure out of it. That's the way I am, yes. Play something for my friend to hear. Put on what's prettiest. But first you'll serve us something, yes . . . "

He placed the bottle and the phonograph on the edge of the table. The woman had remained quiet, listening to what the man was saying. But when the big hands seized the little cabinet, a kind of resentment began to stir in her breast, slowly, hardly at all at first. The phonograph was her own property and nobody had any right to it. Never had anyone operated it, except for herself with her own hands, which were loving, as if for touching a child. She swallowed hard and then clenched her teeth, revealing the hard edge of her jaw, just like her father's and just like that of the distant grandfather who had come from the Basque Country. She thought that the aguardiente would make them forget the music and in-stead of the little glasses, green and deceiving, into which a thim-bleful of liquid hardly fit, she set out the other big wineglasses and filled them halfway. The men sniffed the aguardiente, then raised their eyes at the same time as they clinked the glasses, and in uni-son said:

"To your health!"

And they emptied their contents in one gulp.

"This is aguardiente!" the man said.

The guest answered with a whistle that seemed to get stuck in his puckered mouth, a gesture of stupor, because something was beginning to dance in his muscles without any intervention of his will, and this left him in this state, perplexed and so happy on the inside.

"Let's talk about the deal again," the man proposed. "It's a good idea now to get it decided, yes; my price is reasonable, as you

well know and you know you're getting pigs that'll bring double
the price, yes; fattened up in the feed pen and the boar almost a
purebred, outstanding pigs for ham . . . "

The other man smiled leisurely and nodded his assent.

"It's a deal, then?" asked the man. "It's a deal?"

"The aguardiente's good; one doesn't drink any better around
here, not even in the Piñeiros' hotel."

It was strange what he was feeling: still that sort of muscular
movement that now was polarizing in his knees and was hurling
his legs in every direction, irreducibly, just like a clown. And he
was so happy!

"Good aguardiente, of course, yes . . . ; it's a gift from my
father-in-law, who's from the vineyard region and he trades in
wines. Of the best quality. The deal is set?"

"What deal?" he asked stupidly, attentive to his desire to
laugh, to the impossibility of his laughing and to the disconsolate
feeling that was beginning to inundate him. And his legs under
the table dancing, dancing . . .

"The deal about the pigs, yes . . . "

"Oh! Really . . . But wasn't the patrona going to play the . . . ,
how did you call it . . . , the . . . , well . . . the phonograph?"

The woman hated him with a violence that might have destroyed him on becoming tangible. All the bad words that she had
heard in her existence, and that she never said, suddenly came to
her memory and they felt so alive to her that she was astonished
they did not turn around to look at her, terrified and speechless in
the face of this rude avalanche.

"It's a deal?"

"Music . . . , music . . . , life is short and one must enjoy it . . . "

But instead of reaching her hand out to the phonograph, the
woman had extended it toward the bottle and again she served
them, causing the wine glasses to overflow. And since each one,
absorbed in his own thoughts, had not seen that the glass had been
set in front of him, it was she who said, suddenly cordial:

"Serve yourselves!" And she made an inconclusive gesture of
invitation, a kind of greeting that stayed in the air, paralyzed,
while she watched them drink: "To your health!" And the hoarse
sound of her voice saying the toast surprised her.

"It's a deal?" insisted the man, his tongue tangled in his con-
sonants.

The other man did not hear a thing but only felt the tide of distress growing, at the same time as in his ears a cicada began its steady mid-afternoon sawing. And why were his legs dancing?

"Brother, I'm a good man . . . "I don't deserve this . . . " And the distress spilled over into a hiccough. "I don't want my legs to dance, my legs are mine, mine . . . Music . . . ," he shouted suddenly and he got up halfway, but he lost his momentum and fell down on top of the table.

The woman watched them, silent, with her eyes so open and inexpressive, so bright, so enormous in their greyness. They were not to come near her phonograph again, they were not to have it; it was hers; therein resided her inner life, her deliverance from colorless days. Outwardly she was similar to the plain, flat, with her husband's will cutting her level like the wind; but just as the current of water in all its forms passes under the layers of the earth, so she had within herself her singing water saying things from the past. The music belonged to her. To her, and pity anyone who came near it!

But the guest extended a heavy hand and placed it on the little doors of the phonograph, trying to open them. But he did not open them, because she, standing up violently and grabbing his hand harshly, said—also harshly:

"No. It's mine."

The guest looked at her, with his mouth curled up and trying to think some thought that he had just forgotten. Suddenly he remembered. And again he stretched out the hand that she had removed from the little door latch.

"I'm telling you, no!"

"Look how she's insulting me, brother . . . "

The man insisted greedily:

"It's a deal?"

"Music . . . ," answered the guest, stubbornly.

"Why don't you play something? Go ahead and raise a ruckus, little one, yes; something you like. Don't you see that we're going to close the deal?"

He would not put his hands on the phonograph. Not that, never. The guest had picked himself up and this time his muscles did obey him. But the woman prevented the attack and put herself inbetween, defensively. The other man reeled about the dining room, until bumping into the wall, and he turned around, inflamed with a criminal impulse, blinded to everything that was not his own idea.

"Music . . . , music . . . "

"Has she gone crazy? What's happening to her?" asked the man.

The guest was on top of her and she on top of the phonograph, defending it with her whole body. They struggled. The man looked at them for an instant, stunned, repeating:

"Has she gone crazy? Has she gone crazy?"

But when the guest gave a sharp cry because the woman's teeth were ripping into his hand, he rushed forward to separate them, to defend his friend, to defend his transaction, his deal already almost completed.

She kicked and bit them, behaving like an animal, furious, the way a puma in the wild might defend her cubs. The men did not know why they were getting punched, why they were rolling on the floor, why the table was reeling and the lamp was shifting its light back and forth in a swaying movement that was worse than the sensation in their stomachs. The phonograph fell with a crash and the strings reverberated, like the lament of a grove of trees whose leaves are ripped off by a strong wind. The guest was sitting on the floor, bewildered, and suddenly his cry broke into sobs that interrupted his hiccoughs. The man leaned against the window, astonished by everything and looking at the woman, her clothing in shreds, the magnificence of her hairdo undone, with a long slash on her face, cleaning herself off with the apron that was red with blood, her blouse stained, stubbornly intent on gathering from the floor the pieces of the broken records, looking at them and sobbing, cleaning the blood off herself, sobbing and looking for more pieces and cleaning off the blood and sobbing.

But the guest diverted his attention with his enormous hiccoughs.

"Brother . . . , I thought I was in the home of a brother . . . I've been insulted . . . I have . . . ," he lamented, stumbling as he spoke.

"Don't cry anymore, brother." And suddenly back to his idea and full of solicitude and tenderness: "It's a deal?"

"Swine, that's just what you are: swine . . . ," shouted the woman, and with her armload of pieces she left the dining room, closing the door with a resounding bang that startled the rats in the loft and caused the dog to gaze at her steadily, its sequin eyes sparkling in the gloom.

⋆　　⋆　　⋆

Outside the wind's mane was whipping about, unleashed in a frenetic gallop. The clouds had pressed themselves tightly together,

dense and black, imparting a dark tint to the environs and not allowing the outline of a single thing to be seen. As if the elements
had not yet been set apart. A cricket was giving witness, immuta-
bly, to its existence.

She fled, pressing the shattered records against her chest as she
went, feeling the flow of the blood through the wound, warm and
sticky on her neck, making its way inside to the fine skin of her
chest. She walked with her head down, breaking through the blackness and the wind. She walked. The house was far away, not just
erased by the darkness. The cricket, imperceptible, was left behind
tenaciously useless. She could be out on the plain and be the living center of her desolate surroundings; she could be in a valley
bounded by rivers and precipices; she could walk, walk, endlessly,
until she fell exhausted upon the hard earth, being grown over
evenly with identical weeds; she could suddenly slide down the
slope of the ravine and go crashing onto the smooth stones of a
river engorged with reddish sand; she could . . . Anything could
happen in this blackness of chaos, confusing and dreadful. For to
her nothing mattered.

To end it all. To die against the earth. To be destroyed in the ravine. Not to feel any more that corrosive ardor, bitter to her mouth
and clawing around inside her. To end it all. Not to make an effort any more to know what characteristic a certain day had, stubbornly persisting in extracting from the blurry sum a date to dif-
ferentiate it. Not to live like a machine amidst the daily shuffle
and the knitting, longing for Saturday to come in order to eat the
crumb of memories that was incapable of satiating her heart's craving for tenderness. To put an end to the sordidness surrounding
her, with its disguise of "do as you wish, but . . . ," of meticulous-
ness, of concealed vigilance. To be no more. Never again to return
to the house and find herself reporting what she had done and what
it had yielded, listening to the insinuation regarding what had to
be bought and what needed to be earned. To not get calluses on
her hands pounding wheat, neither with her eyes weepy from the
smoke of the oven, nor feeling her midsection aching in front of
the laundry tub. Never to take pains with painting a little board
and making a shelf, nor wallpapering the rooms, bedecking them
with flowers like an imitation garden. Never. Nor ever again to feel
him heaved over on top of her, panting and sweaty, heavy and without awakening any sensation in her other than a passive repugnance. Never.

The injury, which the air was turning cold, ached like a long stab wound. She touched it and found within the blood a hard point. A piece of glass. A spike-sized sliver from a broken glass that had buried itself there during the struggle, she did not know when. With a sort of insensitivity to the pain, she wiggled it to pull it out. She let out a groan. But furious with herself, in an abrupt tug that ripped her flesh more deeply, she pulled it out and tossed it away.

The blood was running through her fingers, around her neck, over her breasts. All stained and sticky, she kept going. To vanish. But first to sob, to shout, to howl. The wind, with its gusts, seemed to push its way inside her through her open flesh and make the pain intolerable. Greater still, sharper than the other pain which was destroying her feeling. Suddenly the hand that was gripping the apron, still holding the broken records, opened up and everything tumbled out over the ground. She took a few more steps and then fell face down sobbing, the sounds of which the wind seized with its strong hand and scattered throughout the surrounding area.

It was as if the water of those clear eyes could at last be water. She had the sensation that her mouth was opening for her, and she felt the strange noises being hurled from her throat and the scorched eyelids and wrinkled forehead and the salt from her weeping. And a hand clutching the wound, violently painful, and the blood running between her fingers and a braid of hair that must surely be soaked through and dampening her back. She raised herself up on one elbow; she turned her head. And she gave a sharp cry because a breath made her face feel warm and something inhuman terrified her to the point of losing consciousness.

The dog alternated periodically between sniffing her noisily, licking her hands, and sitting down—with his head raised on high, his snout stretched out toward mysterious omens—to deliver a long howl to the moon. He licked her face when the woman came to, and she knew instantaneously that it was the dog, although she did not know where she was. She sat up suddenly, and also suddenly she remembered her immediate situation.

It was as if she had not lived it. So strange, so alien to her. Almost like the sensation of the nightmare that had just become submerged in her subconscious. Was she fleeing from a dream; was she returning from some reality? A movement, on trying to stroke the dog, who was circling around her uneasily, gave her the exact shape of the facts. She groaned and the dog sought out her face again. But she pushed it aside, forcing it to lie down beside her. She pressed on the wound, which was oozing blood again, burning her as if she were being scalded.

She could bleed to death. To remain as she was, still in the night, in the cordial proximity of the dog until her blood went draining away and with it her life, that abhorrent life that she did not want to preserve for the benefit of another. Eliminating it, she avenged her constant state of humiliation, the animosities that had accumulated wordlessly, the resentment of a frustrated existence. To remove herself from the midst of things so that solitude might be the punishment for the man who would not have anyone to work, to produce and give an accounting of deeds and thoughts; the machine for his pleasure would have vanished and he would have to pay dearly to find another one so perfect as she. Not to see him again. Never to put in front of him the medium-done meat and see him chew with his surprisingly white teeth. Nor to see his gaze becoming clouded over, when desire made him reach out his hand to her futilely elusive body. Not to know that he was tangled up in subterranean calculations: "You'll buy this, because this little sum of money is to be stashed away and used to buy whenever possible the Urriolas' field, who are deep in debt and will finally have to sell, yes; or the field belonging to Valladares' widow, who with so many kids is not going to prosper, and they're going to put it up for auction, for the mortgage payments . . . " Waiting like a vulture, patiently, for the moment to take off with the prey. Land. Everything in him was reduced to that. To sell. To negotiate. To bring in money. And buy land, land.

To be no more. To think no more. To feel how the blood was slipping away through her fingers, running stickily over her chest, collecting in her lap, dampening her thighs.

The dog whined softly now, more and more restless. The woman, all of a sudden, opened her eyes, which no longer held any water other than that of their own clear irises, and she came face to face with a truth: to die was also never again to take out the memories of the past, that treasure chest with its images of tenderness. Never again to remember . . . To remember what? And in a rapid and incoherent superposition of images, snatches of scenes, fragments of sentences, she saw her mother sitting in front of the big gate, she saw herself with her sisters arm in arm, she saw the doves flying through the fragrant air of the garden. She perceived so exactly the smell of the jasmines that she inhaled longingly. But other images appeared: Herself crying between the piano box and the pile of mattresses; herself silent in the night under the moon's medallion in the bottom of the water tank; herself in front of the mirror, pinning a sprig of basil and some carnations into her braids, because Easter was an obstinately hopeful time; herself with her face turned around by the laughter and her eyes snaring the green gaze that stirred up a timid pigeon in her chest, so warm, so tender, so absolutely alive, that the surprise for her hand was not finding it sweetly nested there . . . All of that, never again. To die was also to renounce all of that.

Suddenly she stood up. Her legs felt unstable and little particles were dancing before her eyes. She closed them tight. She forced herself to hold herself erect. And also firmly she pressed the apron to her face, for she did not want the blood to flow through the wound, for she did not want the blood to abandon her, for death to leave her like an outspread rag in the middle of the field, on top of the mustard weeds, abandoned in the blackness with only the dog's protective custody. She wanted life, she wanted her blood, the branchwork of her blood, laden with memories.

She pressed the apron even harder against her cheek. She stared keenly into the night. Then she called the dog. She took it by its collar. And she said:

"Let's go home," and she followed it into the darkness.

Translated by Elaine Dorough Johnson

———*For Discussion*———

JRT—

Brunet paints a picture of a Latina woman who is bound to her controlling husband by duty rather than by love, a woman who lives "in the shadow of the lamp," catching late night moments and memories at her phonograph. The wife in this story has no name, and for most of the story she has only a sliver of existence where she is not "the wife."

In some ways, the story seems overdramatic for our modern American culture. An intense, brooding husband makes land deals and orders his wife to spend money on his necessities. The couple live in silences, in a house of somber darkness and shadows. The picture is almost melodramatic, but what speaks true is the portrait of an emotionally battered woman who lives in fear. Brunet hints at violence in her past, an arranged marriage, a sex life that is forced upon her, and a victim of a male-dominated culture. She seems to have no choice but to resort to memory and so claims her past as her only precious jewel. Her hour of freedom comes every night, after her husband has gone to bed, when she pulls out the phonograph that she bought with money from her knitting. Then she listens to waltzes and marches and remembers the boy whom she once loved, in the girlhood of her past. She is a depressing, hopeless woman. We wish she would get out of that house.

Brunet shows us that it is not so easy. Her heroine must fight fiercely for her soul. The phonograph records come under scrutiny one night when the husband is in the midst of a dinner deal with a guest. They drink too much, and the husband's desire to close the deal leads him to disregard his wife. The men demand music and the wife refuses, defending rights to the only thing she can claim as her own, the phonograph. Symbolically, she protects her past, her territory, her memories. The demands lead to a brawl and broken records. She calls the men "swine" and flees, broken records in her arms.

The most interesting discussion point in the story seems to be around what will happen to the heroine. In the woods, she wants to die, considers it at first, and then has a realization. If she were to die, she might lose her "self," the potential self it seems to me, her history and her future. Women actively engage in asking where she will go or if in fact she will return home. She has her dog. She says, "Let's go home." But the last lines might lead us to believe home may be a new place, an unknown place, perhaps a hopeful place. She follows her dog, after all, into the darkness. The question seems to be if she has the resources to live without her husband and find her own way or if she will return, shamefully, and lose even the small freedoms she had.

RPW—

At thirty-six, the woman (unnamed) in this story has been married half her life to a man blind "to everything that was not his idea." He is a man of schedules, calculations, and business deals, a ranch proprietor shaped by the land and by his sense of command over laborers and his wife alike. Her parents had arranged the marriage to this "older man," and she had been indifferent. She would always be instinctively submissive to men anyway; it was part of her nature, making her humiliate herself in front of her father and then in front of her husband. But when she married, she knew there was no man who could "kindle within her that passion that had moved through her blood" when she was fifteen. She had spotted "Baggy Pants" then gazing at her with his green eyes. I think that green-eyed gaze made all the difference. It filled her blood with tenderness forever. All that she could do after that was to protect that memory in silence and solitude. That was her reason for living. It made her powerfully attractive; it gave her a sensuous glow.

When her husband goes to sleep on Saturday night, the woman plays her phonograph, lowering the light from the lamp that she bought from her own hard work, and "letting in the night and its silence." The march music arouses memory and passion, transporting her back to the magical moment of the green gaze of the boy. For her, it is the moment of life in the midst of a black and flat plain stretching endlessly to the far horizon.

But such moments are difficult to hold onto, especially when a life is dominated by submission. When her husband entertains a guest to help facilitate a business deal, for example, she seems willing to play the servant, at least until the men insist that she take her phonograph out so they can listen to some music. For her that phonograph is like a tender child; for anyone else to touch it is a violation of her privacy, her memory of "Baggy Pants," and her warm desire. As the men grow drunk, they go on the attack. I picture a woman defending her phonograph; her husband defending his transaction, his heartless deal. Bleeding and clutching pieces of the broken records, the woman flees from the house.

Wandering outside, wounded and bleeding, she contemplates her death. She can end it all, eliminate her "abhorrent life . . . her constant state of humiliation." But then she realizes that "to die was also never again to take out the memories of the past, that treasure chest with its images of tenderness." In the end, she chooses life, her blood filled with desire for those "green eyes." It seems to me that she heads home into the darkness.

By contrast to so many stories in which women die at the end, often by their own hand, I suppose we should find some hope here. If so, it is a small light in the darkness.

from DELIVERANCE

James Dickey

I kept waking, and waking again, but when I was alive for good, the screen wire of the tent-front was gray and steady. Drew was deep in his sack, his head away from me. I lay with the flashlight still in one hand, and tried to shape the day. The river ran through it, but before we got back into the current other things were possible. What I thought about mainly was that I was in a place where none—or almost none—of my daily ways of living my life would work; there was no habit I could call on. Is this freedom? I wondered.

I zipped the sleeping bag down and rolled out, holding my breath, my own heat rising from me and fading away as I crawled free, with one quick look upward through the owl-hole. I pulled on my tennis shoes and bent toward the river sound, then stood up.

It was oddly warm and still and close, and the river was running with a heavy smoke of fog that moved just a little slower than the current must have been doing, rolling down the water in huge bodiless billows from upstream. It hovered at the bank while I watched, and overflowed, and in its silence I realized that I had been waiting for it to make a sound when it did this. I looked at my legs and they were gone, and my hands at my sides also; I stood with the fog eating me alive.

An idea came to me. I went back to my duffel bag, got out a two-piece suit of long underwear and put it on; it was almost exactly the color of the fog. My bow was backed and faced with white fiber glass, usually a disadvantage in green or brown woods but a very good thing now. I strung the bow, leaning on the live weight and resistance, took an arrow out of the bow quiver and went around behind the tents. The fog was seeping up over the canvas, swirling a little with the motion of deep water around Lewis and the others. It went back into the woods up what looked to be a long thin draw or little ravine, and I followed it, giving up my idea of waking Lewis and concentrating on being quiet. I couldn't see far ahead, but I knew that if I stayed in the draw, all I would have to do to get back down to camp, even if the fog got worse, would be to turn around and come back down until I practically—or actually—

stumbled over the tents. I concentrated on getting into some kind of relation to the woods under these conditions; I was as invisible as a tree.

At first I didn't have any idea of really hunting. I had no firm notion of what I was doing, except walking forward carefully, away from the river and into more and more silence and blindness—for the fog was now coming up past me and thickening straight back into my face—and carrying a bow and a nocked arrow and three other arrows in one hand and fingering the bowstring with the other. It tingled like a wire in my right-hand fingers, giving off an electric current that came from the woods and the fog and the fact that hunting and pretending to hunt had come together and I could not now tell them apart. Behind the tents, before I had got into the woods, I had figured that since I had the equipment to hunt and knew to some extent how to use it, I might as well make some show of doing what I said I had come for. All I had really wanted was to stay away a reasonable length of time, long enough for the others to wake and find me gone—I thought of just sitting down on the bank of the ravine and waiting for half an hour by my watch—and then walk back into camp with my bow strung and say I'd been out taking a look around. That would satisfy honor.

But now not; not quite. I was really looking and really listening, and a good many things came together in my legs and arms and fingers. I was a good shot, at least up to thirty-five yards, and the visibility I had was not going to be anything like that in the next half hour. I could do it, if I came on a deer; I felt certain I could, and would.

The fog was still heavy, but the draw-bottom began to climb, and as I went upward there was more light, first light through the fog and then things through the fog—leaves and twigs. The walls of the ditch—which I now saw was what I was in—were not as high now, barely to my shoulders, and I could see levelly along the ground into the woods a little way on both sides. Nothing moved, and there was also the quiet of nothing being there, though I did my best not to make a sound in case there was. The wet ground helped me; as far as I could tell I caused very little sound to come into the place, and thought perhaps that technically I didn't make such a bad hunter after all, at least for a little while.

Now I was walking up what was hardly more than a sunken track, caved in on both sides, with the last rags of mist around me. I knew I had better not go much farther or I might lose the ditch.

I stopped to turn around. There was nothing in any direction I hadn't already seen.

I started back, still looking as far off as I could into the woods rising slowly up to eye level right and left. The mist began to roll into my face in thin puffs. I was beginning to worry about walking right off past the tents into the river when to the left I saw something move. I stopped, and the fog rose exactly to my teeth. About fifteen yards from me, right at the limit of my vision, was a small deer, a spike buck as nearly as I could tell from the shape of his head. He was browsing, the ghost of a deer but a deer just the same. He lifted his head and looked directly at my face, which from his angle must have seemed like a curious stone on the ground, if he saw it. I stood there, buried to the neck in the ditch, in the floor of the forest.

He was broadside to me; I had shot a thousand targets one-quarter his size at the same distance, and when I recalled this— when my eyes and hands got together on it—I knew I could kill him just as easily as I could hit his outline on cardboard. I raised the bow.

He brought his head a little higher and lowered it again. I pulled the string back to the right side of my face and began to steady down. For a moment I braced there at the fullest tension of the bow, which brought out of me and into the bow about three fourths of my own strength, with the arrow pointing directly into his heart. It was a slight upshot, and I allowed for this, though at the range it wouldn't matter much.

I let go, but as I released I knew it was a wrong shot, not very wrong but wrong enough. I had done the same thing on key shots in archery tournaments: lifted my bow hand just as the shot went. At the sound of the bowstring the deer jumped and wheeled at about the time the arrow should have gone through him. I thought I might have hit him high, but actually I had seen the orange feathers flick and disappear over his shoulder. I may even have touched him, but I was fairly sure I had not drawn blood. He ran a few steps and turned, looking back around his side at me. I jerked loose another arrow and strung it, but my heart was gone. I was shaking, and I had trouble getting the arrow nocked. I had it only about halfway back when he took off for good. I turned loose anyway and saw the arrow whip badly and disappear somewhere above where he had been.

I was heaving and sweating as I drew in the fog and let it back out, a sick, steaming gas. Like that, I went downhill, part of the time with my hand at arm's length in front of my face. I saw the tents—one of them, then another thing like it—as low dark patches with something structured about them, clearly out of place here.

Lewis was up, trying to make a fire with wet twigs and branches. As I unstrung the bow, the others came out too.

"What about it, buddy?" Lewis said, looking at the two empty slots in the quiver.

"I got a shot."

"You did?" Lewis said, straightening.

"I did. A spectacular miss at fifteen yards."

"What happened? We could'a had meat."

"I boosted my bow hand, I think. I psyched out. I'll be damned if I know how. I had him. He was getting bigger all the time. It was like shooting at the wall of a room. But I missed, all right. It was just that little second, right when I turned loose. Something said raise your hand, and before I could do anything about it, I did it."

"Damn," Bobby said. "Psychology. The delicate art of the forest."

"You'll get another chance," Drew said. "We got a long ways to go yet."

"What the hell," I said. "If I'd hit him I'd be back in the woods now, tracking. He'd be hard to find in this fog. So would I."

"You could've marked the place you shot from and come back and got us," Lewis said. "We could've found him."

"You'd have a time finding him now," I said. "He's probably in the next county."

"I guess so," Lewis said. "But it's a shame. Where's my old steady buddy?"

"Your old steady buddy exploded," I said. "High and wide." Lewis looked at me.

"I know you wouldn't have, Lewis," I said. "You don't need to tell me. We'd have meat. We'd all live forever. And you know something? I wish you'd been up there and I'd been with you. I would'a just unstrung my bow and watched you put it right into the heart-lung area. Right into the boiler room. The pinwheel, at fifteen yards. What I was really thinking about up there was you."

"Well, next time don't think about me. Think about the deer."

I let that ride and went to drag the stuff out of the tents. Lewis finally got a kind of fire started. When the sun began to take on

height and force, the mist burned off in a few minutes. Through it
the river, which we could hardly make out at first, showed itself
more and more until we could see not only the flat of it and the
stitches of the current but down through it into the pebbles of the
stream-bed near the bank.

We had pancakes with butter and sorghum. After we finished,
Lewis went over to the stream to wash out the cooking stuff. I
pulled all the air mattresses out on the ground, unscrewed their
caps and lay on each in turn until the ground came up to me
through it and I was lying on the last sigh of air I had pumped into
it the night before. We rolled the tents, wet and covered with leaves
and pieces of bark, and lashed them into the canoes. I asked the
others if they thought we might team up differently this time, for
I was afraid that Lewis in his impatience might say something unpleasant to Bobby, and, since Bobby suddenly seemed to me on the
edge of exasperation with himself for coming, I thought it would
probably be best if I took him on. Drew would not have laughed,
or laughed in the right way, at the cracks that were Bobby's only
means of salvaging his civility, and I figured I would.

"How about it, tiger?" I said to Bobby.

"OK," he said. "How far can we get today, do you reckon?"

"Beats me," I said. "We'll get as far as we can. Depends on the
water, and how many places we have to walk through. Everybody
including the map says there's a gorge down below here, and that
sort of bothers me. But there's nothing we can do about it now."

Bobby and I got in and shoved off, and right away I could tell I
was in for a hard time. I was not in awfully good shape myself, but
Bobby was wheezing and panting after the first hundred yards. He
had no coordination at all, and changed the canoe from what it
had been with Drew's steady, serious weight in front to a nervous,
unstable craft that seemed bound and determined to do everything wrong, to get rid of us. I was sure that Lewis was disgusted
with Bobby, and just as sure that I would be, also, before much
longer.

"Easy," I said. "Easy. You're trying too hard. All we want to do
is hold this thing straight. We don't need to be pulling our guts out
to get there. Just let the river do it. Let George do it."

"George ain't doing it fast enough. I want to get the hell and
gone out of this goddamned place."

"Ah, now. It's not all that bad."

"It's *not*? Mosquitoes ate me up last night. My bites have got bites. I'm catching a fucking cold from sleeping on the fucking ground. I'm hungry as hell for something that tastes good. And I don't mean sorghum."

"Just steady down a little, and we'll get there . . . when we get there. It's not going to do your cold any good to dump in this river, you can bloody well bet."

"Fuck it," he said. "Let's get on with it. I'm tired of this woods scene; I'm tired of shitting in a hole in the ground. This is for the Indians."

After a while he settled down a little, and the back of his neck lightened its red. We dug a couple of strokes for every twenty-five yards, and the river moved us along. But I thought that the chances were pretty good, with my high center of gravity and his nerves, that we would spill before the day was out, especially if there were any fast stretches with lots of rocks. With the equipment and with Bobby and me, who were at least fifty pounds heavier than the other two, we were riding far too low in the water. We had too much stuff with us for the way we were teamed, and I signaled back to Lewis to pull over to the bank. He did, and we wallowed alongside the other canoe and tied up.

"Getting hot," Lewis said.

"Hot as the hinges," I said.

"Did you see that big snake back yonder?"

"No. Where?"

"He was lying up in the limbs of that old oak tree you went under about a mile and a half back. I didn't see him till you were right under him, and he lifted his head. I didn't want to make any fuss; thought it might make him nervous. I'm pretty sure it was a moccasin. I've heard of them dropping in boats."

"Shit fire," Bobby said. "That's all we need."

"Yeah," said Lewis. "I can imagine."

"Can you take on some of the stuff in our canoe, Lewis?" I asked. "We're awful low and logy."

"Sure. Go get the cooking equipment and the bedrolls. That ought to equalize us, just about. You can also let us have about half the beer that's left."

"Happy to. Everybody's going to need something to cool off with, today."

"Why do it just with beer?" Lewis said, unbuttoning his shirt. "It's shallow and slow here. I'm going to get wet."

I transferred the bedrolls and beer and the primus and other cooking equipment to the other canoe. Lewis was already in the water naked, booming overhand down the current with a lot of back showing, like Johnny Weismuller in the old Tarzan movies. He swam as well as he did everything else, and outran the current easily. Then he came back, his eyes glaring with effort at water level. I shucked off my coveralls and dived in, and so did Drew.

The river was very cold; it felt as though it had snow and ice in it, and had only just turned then to water. But it was marvelously clear and alive, and broke like glass around you and came together unhurt. I swam a little way into the current, and would gladly have given up all human effort—I was tired of human efforts of all kinds, especially my own—and gone on downstream either dead or alive, to wherever it would take me. But I swam back, a hard forty yards against the subtle tearing and downstream insistence, and stood up next to Lewis, who was waist deep with water crumpling and flopping at his belly. I looked at him, for I have never seen him with his clothes off.

Everything he had done for himself for years paid off as he stood there in his tracks, in the water. I could tell by the way he glanced at me; the payoff was in my eyes. I had never seen such a male body in my life, even in the pictures in the weight-lifting magazines, for most of those fellows are short, and Lewis was about an even six feet. I'd say he weighed about 190. The muscles were bound up in him smoothly, and when he moved, the veins in the moving part would surface. If you looked at him that way, he seemed made out of well-matched red-brown chunks wrapped in blue wire. You could even see the veins in his gut, and I knew I could not even begin to conceive how many sit-ups and leg-raises—and how much dieting—had gone into bringing them into view.

He dropped a hand on my shoulder and stirred the fur around. "What do you think, Bolgani the Gorilla?"

"I think Tarzan speak with forked tongue," I said. "I think Lord of Jungle speak with tongue of Histah the Snake. I think we never get out of woods. He bring us here to stay and found kingdom."

"Yeah," said Bobby from the bank. "Kingdom of Snakes is right."

Drew came out of the river near us. "Gosh that feels good," he said. "It really does. I never felt anything more wonderful in my life. Refreshing. You know, that's just what it is. I feel like I can go all day, now. You better come on in for a minute, Bobby."

"No thanks. Whenever you're ready, me and the other Fatso will just Fatso on down, the washed and the unwashed."

He sat with his knees drawn up, self-protective in the sun against the water-chill he could see on us. Our nipples were blue and drawn up, and my stomach muscles were beginning to heave against the moving underwater freeze. I climbed out and pulled on my sweaty coveralls. My head was fresh and cool while my body heated up, and I wanted to get back on the river before I began to melt again.

Bobby and I went over to our canoe and tried to figure out what else we might be able to transfer to the other one. We finally ended up taking only one tent, my bow, a six-pack of beer and Drew's guitar, for the wooden canoe was leaking a little and ours was more or less dry. We wrapped the guitar in the tent, got in and pushed off.

We rode a lot better now, and Bobby's paddling improved a good deal because of this, and maybe because he had convinced himself that the less trouble he was the quicker we'd get off the river.

The water was calm for a long time. We made turn after turn, sometime near one bank, and sometime near the other. I tried not to go under any more limbs, and this was easy enough to do. The river spread and slowed and quieted, and we had to paddle more than we had been doing. We could hardly feel any current at all; it was very faint, and when we rested it was as though we were drawn forward by something invisible underneath us, while the water around us stood still. We could hear sound far off in front, but it kept retreating downstream. Each turn opened out only on another stretch of river, gradually unfolding its woods along both banks. A heron of some kind flushed on the right. He swept downstream in front of us, going left, then right, then left-right, dipping quickly and indecisively. He would disappear around the next turn, then, as we came around it, would spring up again from leaves where we had not seen him and muscle himself into the air on long blue wings, giving a hoarse agonized inhuman cry and making a magnificent half-turn over the river ahead of us, then start downstream again with long wingbeats, the tips of his wings all but touching the water, so that wherever he was his shadow started up under him at each downstroke, vague and misshapen with the river. This continued through four or five turns, until we came around another one like the others and did not see him. He may have veered into the woods, but I thought that most probably he had learned to sit still, maybe nearing hysterical flight once again as we approached and went past, but managing to keep that long-necked, desperate cry in his throat until we had gone.

In the new silence the river seemed to go deeper and deeper under us; the colors changed toward denser greens as the sun got higher. The pace of the water began to pick up; we slid farther and farther with each stroke. I thought to myself that anyone fighting the brush along the bank could not keep up with us.

Every now and then I glanced down at the bow at my feet, big-handled and tense-looking, and at its two arrows slathered with house paint. The big orange feathers spiraled out of them, and the emery-wheeled edges of the broadheads shone in the sun like radium. Though I would have had to do a good deal of curious balancing to string the bow, I keep looking on both sides of the river for deer, hoping that we might float in on a big buck drinking. It was something to do.

We went through some deep, quickened water and floated out into a calm broad stretch of a long turn that slid us into a dim underpass of enormous trees, conifers of some kind, spruce or fir. It was dark and heavy in there; the packed greenness seemed to suck the breath out of your lungs. Bobby and I lifted our paddles clear of the river as by a signal, and we eased through the place the way the river wanted to go. Intense needles of light shook on the ripples, gold, hot enough to burn and almost solid enough to pick up from the surface like nails.

We came out among some fields grown up six or seven feet high in grass. A mottled part of the bank slipped into the water, and it took me a minute to realize it was a snake. He went across about twenty feet in front of us, swimming as if crawling, his head high, and came out on the opposite bank without changing his motion at all, a thing with a single spell, a single movement, and no barriers.

We went on, taking long slow swings at the water. I had fitted my stroke to Bobby's the best I could; I moved when he moved, and had got to the point where I could put my paddle in the water and lift it out at the same time he did. I thought he must surely be taking some satisfaction in the improvement, but I didn't say anything for fear of upsetting the rhythm.

After two hours from the time the heron left us we had drunk all the beer we had. The sun was eating my bald spot, and my nylon outfit was soaking with me. My tongue began to balloon in my mouth, and my backbone was splintering through the skin; I kept touching it between strokes to see if anything had given way. The edge of the seat was digging into my right thigh, for that was the only position in which I could get a good grip on the river. All the pains began to try to link up with each other and there was nothing I could do about it.

I looked back. The other canoe was just coming around. Lewis had lagged behind us because, I suppose, he wanted us in sight in case we got into trouble. Anyway, they were about half a mile back and disappeared as we rounded another curve, and I pointed with my paddle to the left bank. I didn't know whether they saw me or not, but I figured to flag them in when they came by. I wanted to lie up in the shade and rest for a while. I was hungry, and I sure would've liked to have had another beer. We dug in and swung over.

As we closed in on the left bank, a pouring sound came from under the trees; the leaves at a certain place moved as if in a little wind. The fresh green-white of a creek was frothing into the river. We sailed past it half-broadside and came to the bank about seventy-five yards downstream. I put the nose against it and paddled hard to hold it there while Bobby got out and moored us.

"This is too much like work," Bobby said, as he gave me a hand up.

"Lord, Lord," I said. "I'm getting too old for this kind of business. I suppose you could call it learning the hard way."

Bobby sat down on the ground and untied a handkerchief from around his neck. He leaned down to the river and sopped it, then swabbed his face and neck down, rubbing a long time in the nose area. I bent over and touched my toes a couple of times to get rid of the position that had been maiming my back, and then looked upstream. I still couldn't see the other canoe. I turned to say something to Bobby.

Two men stepped out of the woods, one of them trailing a shotgun by the barrel.

Bobby had no notion they were there until he looked at me. Then he turned his head until he could see over his shoulder and got up, brushing at himself.

"How goes it?" he said.

One of them, the taller one, narrowed in the eyes and face. They came forward, moving in a kind of half circle as though they were stepping around something. The shorter one was older, with big white eyes and a half-white stubble that grew in whorls on his checks. His face seemed to spin in many directions. He had on overalls, and his stomach looked like it was falling through them. The other was lean and tall, and peered as though out of a cave or some dim simple place far back in his yellow-tinged eyeballs. When he moved his jaws the lower bone came up too far for him to have teeth. "Escaped convicts" flashed up in my mind on one side, "Bootleggers" on the other. But they still could have been hunting.

They came on, and were ridiculously close for some reason. I tried not to give ground; some principle may have been involved.

The older one, looming and spinning his sick-looking face in front of me, said, "What the *hail* you think you're doin'?"

"Going downriver. Been going since yesterday."

I hoped that the fact that we were at least talking to each other would do some good of some kind.

He looked at the tall man; either something or nothing was passing between them. I could not feel Bobby anywhere near, and the other canoe was not in sight. I shrank to my own true size, a physical movement known only to me, and with the strain my solar plexus failed. I said, "We started from Oree yesterday afternoon, and we hope we can get to Aintry sometime late today or early tomorrow."

"*Aintry?*"

Bobby said, and I could have killed him, "Sure. This river just runs one way, cap'n. Haven't you heard?"

"You ain't never going to get down to Aintry," he said, without any emphasis on any word.

"Why not?" I asked, scared but also curious; in a strange way it was interesting to cause him to explain.

"Because this river don't go to Aintry," he said. "You done taken a wrong turn somewhere. This-here river don't go nowhere near Aintry."

"Where does it go?"

"It goes . . . it goes . . . "

"It goes to Circle Gap," the other man said, missing his teeth and not caring. "'Bout fifty miles."

"Boy," said the whorl-faced man, "you don't know *where* you are.

"Well," I said, "we're going where the river's going. We'll come out somewhere, I reckon."

The other man moved closer to Bobby.

"Hell," I said, "we don't have anything to do with you. We sure don't want any trouble. If you've got a still near here, that's fine with us. We could never tell anybody where it is, because you know something? You're right. We don't know where we are."

"A *stee*-ul?" the tall man said, and seemed honestly surprised.

"Sure," I said. "If you're making whiskey, we'll buy some from you. We could sure use it."

The drop-gutted man faced me squarely. "Do you know what the *hail* you're talkin' about?"

"I don't know what you're talking about," I said.

"You done said something about makin' whiskey. You think we're makin' whiskey. Now come on. Ain't that right?"

"Shit," I said. "I don't know whether you're making whiskey or hunting or rambling around in the woods for your whole fucking life. I don't know and I don't care what you're doing. It's not any of my business."

I looked at the river, but we were a little back from the bank, and I couldn't see the other canoe. I didn't think it could have gone past, but I was not really sure that it hadn't. I shook my head in a complete void, at the thought that it might have; we had got too far ahead, maybe.

With the greatest effort in the world, I came back into the man's face and tried to cope with it. He had noticed something about the way I had looked at the river.

"Anybody else with you?" he asked me.

I swallowed and thought, with possibilities shooting through each other. If I said yes, and they meant trouble, we would bring Lewis and Drew into it with no defenses. Or it might mean that we would be left alone, four being too many to handle. On the other hand, if I said no, then Lewis and Drew—especially Lewis— might be able to . . . well, to do something. Lewis' pectorals loomed up in my mind, and his leg, with the veins bulging out of the divided muscles of his thigh, his leg under water wavering small-ankled and massive as a centaur's. I would go with that.

"No," I said, and took a couple of steps inland to draw them away from the river.

The lean man reached over and touched Bobby's arm, feeling it with strange delicacy. Bobby jerked back, and when he did the gun barrel came up, almost casually but decisively.

"We'd better get on with it," I said. "We got a long ways to go." I took part of a step toward the canoe.

"You ain't goin' nowhere," the man in front of me said, and leveled the shotgun straight into my chest. My heart quailed away from the blast tamped into both barrels, and I wondered what the barrel openings would look like at the exact instant they went off: if fire would come out of them, or if they would just be a gray blur or if they would change at all between the time you lived and died, blown in half. He took a turn around his hand with the string he used for a trigger.

"You come on back in here 'less you want your guts all over this-here woods."

I half-raised my hands like a character in a movie. Bobby looked at me, but I was helpless, my bladder quavering. I stepped forward into the woods through some big bushes that I saw but didn't feel. They were all behind me.

The voice of one of them said, "Back up to that saplin'."

I picked out a tree. "This one?" I said.

There was no answer. I backed up to the tree I had selected. The lean man came up to me and took off my web belt with the knife and rope on it. Moving his hands very quickly, he unfastened the rope, let the belt out and put it around me and the tree so tight I could hardly breathe, with the buckle on the other side of the tree. He came back holding the knife. It occurred to me that they must have done this before; it was not a technique they would just have thought of for the occasion.

The lean man held up the knife, and I looked for the sun to strike it, but there was no sun where we were. Even so, in the intense shadow, I could see the edge I had put on it with a suburban grindstone: the minute crosshatching of high-speed abrasions, the wearing-away of metal into a murderous edge.

"Look at that," the tall man said to the other. "I bet that'll shave h'ar."

"Why'ont you try it? Looks like that'n's got plenty of it. 'Cept on his head."

The tall man took hold of the zipper of my coveralls, breathing lightly, and zipped it down to the belt as though tearing me open.

"Good God Amighty," said the older one. "He's like a god-damned monkey. You ever see anything like that?"

The lean man put the point of the knife under my chin and lifted it. "You ever had your balls cut off, you fuckin' ape?"

"Not lately," I said, clinging to the city. "What good would they do you?"

He put the flat of the knife against my chest and scraped it across. He held it up, covered with black hair and a little blood. "It's sharp," he said. "Could be sharper, but it's sharp."

The blood was running down from under my jaw where the point had been. I had never felt such brutality and carelessness of touch, or such disregard for another person's body. It was not the steel or the edge of the steel that was frightening; the man's fingernail, used in any gesture of his, would have been just as brutal; the knife only magnified his unconcern. I shook my head again, trying to get my breath in a gray void full of leaves. I looked straight up into the branches of the sapling I was tied to, and then down into the clearing at Bobby.

He was watching me with his mouth open as I gasped for enough breath to live on from second to second. There was nothing he could do, but as he looked at the blood on my chest and under my throat, I could see that his position terrified him more than mine did; the fact that he was not tied mattered in some way.

They both went toward Bobby, the lean man with the gun this time. The white-bearded one took him by the shoulders and turned him around toward downstream.

"Now let's you just drop them pants," he said.

Bobby lowered his hands hesitantly. "Drop . . . ?" he began.

My rectum and intestines contracted. Lord God.

The toothless man put the barrels of the shotgun under Bobby's right ear and shoved a little. "Just take 'em right on off," he said.

"I mean, what's this all . . . " Bobby started again weakly.

"Don't say nothin'," the older man said. "Just do it."

The man with the gun gave Bobby's head a vicious shove, so quick that I thought the gun had gone off. Bobby unbuckled his belt and unbuttoned his pants. He took them off, looking around ridiculously for a place to put them.

"Them panties too," the man with the belly said.

Bobby took off his shorts like a boy undressing for the first time in a gym, and stood there plump and pink, his hairless thighs shaking, his legs close together.

"See that log? Walk over yonder."

Wincing from the feet, Bobby went slowly over to a big fallen tree and stood near it with his head bowed.

"Now git on down crost it."

The tall man followed Bobby's head down with the gun as Bobby knelt over the log.

"Pull your shirt-tail up, fat-ass."

Bobby reached back with one hand and pulled his shirt up to his lower back. I could not imagine what he was thinking.

"I said *up*," the tall man said. He took the shotgun and shoved the back of the shirt up to Bobby's neck, scraping a long red mark along his spine.

The white-bearded man was suddenly also naked up to the waist. There was no need to justify or rationalize anything; they were going to do what they wanted to. I struggled for life in the air, and Bobby's body was still and pink in an obscene posture that no one could help. The tall man restored the gun to Bobby's head, and the other one knelt behind him.

A scream hit me, and I would have thought it was mine except for the lack of breath. It was a sound of pain and outrage, and was followed by one of simple and wordless pain. Again it came out of him, higher and more carrying. I let all the breath out of myself and brought my head down to look at the river. Where are they, every vein stood out to ask, and as I looked the bushes broke a little in a place I would not have thought of and made a kind of complicated alleyway out onto the stream—I was not sure for a moment whether it was water or leaves—and Lewis' canoe was in it. He and Drew both had their paddles out of water, and then they turned and disappeared.

——*For Discussion*——

RPW—

Ed, the narrator, wakes up early on this second day of a canoe trip down a white-water river winding like a snake through the backwoods of rural Georgia. He is camped with his three suburban buddies (Lewis, Drew, and Bobby), and as he rises in the morning fog, he senses that his ordinary habits will not help any longer in this wilderness. "Is this freedom?" he asks. Perhaps. It is certainly a journey into unknown territory, a journey that will test his manhood and deliver new knowledge of his own self.

Ed takes his bow and arrows into the woods, spots a deer, but then lifts his bow hand as he shoots, just as he has done "on key shots in archery tournaments." He misses the deer, and his second shot is even further from the mark. Ed is uncertain of himself, not sufficiently focused or confident, and too dependent on his buddy

Lewis. "I wish you'd been there and I'd been with you," he tells Lewis. "I would'a just unstrung my bow and watched you put it right into the heart-lung area." Ed admires Lewis's confidence, his perfectly-proportioned male body. It is as if he is counting on Lewis to deliver him.

By contrast to Lewis, Bobby is the typical victim, fat and out-of-shape. It is inevitable that Bobby will become the easy first target for the two men who step out of the woods to confront him and Ed as they make their way down the river. "You don't know where you are," the two backwoodsmen tell the surburbanites just before they unleash their primal rage. And how right these woodsmen are. Ed and Bobby have never been in a situation like this before. First terrorizing Ed with a knife that magnifies the hillbillies' brutality and carelessness, they then turn to the "plump and pink" Bobby, stripping him of his manhood, exposing how fragile our conception of human civilization and dignity can be.

Bobby's scream followed by his silent pain will remain with him, an everlasting wound and sense of shame. He will never recover. For the moment, only Lewis, coming up on the scene with Drew, offers any hope of deliverance from this violence. "He and Drew both had their paddles out of water, and then they turned and disappeared. . . . "

JRT—

This has to be one of the most terrifying scenes in literature. Two men, on a seemingly innocent journey into the wilderness, get separated from their two companions as they head down the river in a canoe. They meet up with brutal violation and the randomness of violence. Bobby is raped. Ed, the narrator, is tied to a tree and watches, horrified. We, the readers, understand that life is infinitely fragile, can change in a moment, and that human beings are capable of committing the worst kinds of horror against each other.

Dickey does not give us much hope here. There is the sense that there are some things in life you can never predict and will never recover from. That is for me what makes this passage so upsetting. There is no going back, no returning to the innocence of what once was. All you can do is go on and figure out how to understand what has occurred. I always wonder if there is only sur-

vival for these men and if forgiveness for such violence is ever pos-sible.

The perpetrators of the violence are as unlikable as can be. Two men (undoubtedly what writer Dorothy Allison and Dickey would both consider "white trash"), who might be drunk and surely are dirt poor, are worse even than the folks in Allison's Bastard Out of Carolina *(see section four). These aren't people we care to know. We don't want to consider if or why they are threatened by the men they violate. Who cares if the perpetrators were raped as children? Who cares if they have hard-luck lives? All that is important here is that they are nameless and hateful. When we discover in later chapters that Lewis, the outdoorsman of the bunch of four men, kills one of the rapists, we are vindicated and glad.*

Dickey forces us to consider that our journeys, seemingly filled with excitement or relaxation, are often journeys into the unknown and into a deeper part of ourselves. The men must find a way to confront what has happened, to understand it, and to decide how to deal with it in their lives when they return home. Although we can only imagine what this incident forebodes in terms of the rest of the trip, it seems clear that each man will be tested on this simple canoe trip into the wilderness.

IDENTITY/VOICE

INTRODUCTION

In an important sense, we use stories to explore identity. As we talk about literature, we know that, at a significant level, we are also talking about ourselves. Who are we? How do we connect with others? What are we all about? These are questions that prompt self-reflection, and it is the power of that self-reflection that we are pursuing when we talk about stories, the power of thinking which leads to an understanding of ourselves.

Know thyself, the philosopher insists. And for us it is that journey to locate ourselves in the world that makes life exciting and meaningful. That journey marks the human being as an educated person.

This approach suggests, no doubt, an old-fashioned sense of identity. Human beings have depth, imagination, passion, and an interior self often capable of battling the brutality and inhumanity always present in the world. The best literature helps us to discover this interior self.

As a good story unfolds, so too our identity unfolds, and we begin to glimpse, as if through a mirror, the shape of our self—our dreams, our expectations, our mortal limits. We are often not who we think we are. But as we experience a story through reading, we become that story and help to create it. And as we reflect on that story through discussion, we reflect ourselves and share our common humanity with others.

A good story gives voice to life and so stands in opposition to silence and death. In this sense, good literature always has a healing power. It gives us confidence and hope. Men and women often respond to different stories in different ways, however. We have provided in this section three selections written by women and two by men. As our comments following each selection suggest, the stories open themselves to various perspectives. They allow all of us to deepen our knowledge not only about how gender, race, and class contribute to our individual sense of identity, but also about how that pursuit of identity can lead to a recognition of our shared human condition.

The selection from *The Sea-Wolf* by Jack London is always popular, especially with men. The novel tells the story of a rugged sea captain, Wolf Larsen, and his first mate, Humphrey Van Weyden. Larsen is a man of great passion and rage. He believes that might makes right, and he has constructed a male identity on the foundation of power and control.

By contrast, Van Weyden is wimpish at first, a literary boy who lacks what Larsen clearly has. But as the story unfolds, Larsen's rough identity and commanding voice expose him as limited and self-destructive. The reader finally can judge his own sense of identity against Larsen's. "I used to be like Wolf Larsen," one of the men in our reading group once claimed. "I thought I could manipulate everyone. I was stupid then."

Van Weyden's identity and voice emerge and grow strong in *The Sea-Wolf*, while Larsen's fade and eventually die out. In "The Man Who Killed a Shadow" by Richard Wright, in contrast, the central character, Saul Saunders, finds himself always in the shadow of the dominant white society and has neither the resources nor the language to emerge free from that insidious power and control. He is a shadow among shadows, and the voices that he hears—the scream of a white woman, the official language of white justice— only function to make certain that his identity and voice remain invisible.

Only the third-person narrator at a distance can tell us the story of Saul Saunders. For Saul is a poor Southern black man whose self-expression is boxed in, limited to rage and violence, and finally to the peace of surrender. The structures of the white world keep Saul's identity invisible, even to himself.

By contrast, Tillie Olsen's story reminds us that at times it is the narrative voice itself that provides hope by bearing witness to a life lived, a life standing against silence and death. Olsen's "I Stand Here Ironing" gives us such hope, the voice of a mother standing at the ironing board, responding privately to all that has kept her and her daughter from fully flourishing. Like so many young mothers that we meet, the mother here is weighed down by the iron will of necessity and by guilt fostered by anxious love and fear. Yet she refuses to yield to that sense of fate and doom.

Tillie Olsen makes clear that the voice of the mother has its own power. It is capable of revealing and transforming the rhythm of necessity, like the relentless rhythm of the iron on its board. Through her own language, the mother becomes more than a mere victim. She gives expression to her struggle, and so reminds herself and her daughter, all of us in fact, that we need not be helpless victims before the brutal forces that bear down on us.

If Tillie Olsen offers us a mother's story, Ursula Le Guin gives us a wife's story, a story of caring and concern but also a story of mother anger. For Le Guin, our identity is tied to our sense of "the other," a sense of difference that often brings violence but also defines who we are.

As a good husband and father metamorphoses into the violent enemy, the good wife and mother also changes to protect her family. In Le Guin's story, the traditional violence of the white man is ironically driven to the margins by the blood lust of a sisterhood formed as a defense against the male demon. The hope is that such action will reaffirm gentleness and beauty, but the truth is otherwise. This is not a fairy tale but a wife's tale. We are limited by "the other," and for Le Guin, it is always against "the other" that we define ourselves. Without that painful limitation, we have only "the blessed darkness."

As the selection in this section from *The Bluest Eye* suggests, Toni Morrison also explores how a sense of difference contributes to the way we shape our identity and search for a voice. In a world that celebrates whiteness, the dark black skin of the Breedlove family only confirms their ugliness, filling them with self-hatred. Like Saul Saunders, the Breedlove's daughter, Pecola, exists in the shadows. She wishes she could disappear as she is, finally transformed into a different girl, beautiful with blue eyes.

If there is any hope in *The Bluest Eye*, it again comes from the narrative voice itself, from the young black woman who shapes memory and desire into a story that cannot save the Breedloves, but might save the reader and the narrator herself. As Morrison has suggested, it is this attempt "to transfigure the complexity and wealth of Black-American culture into a language worthy of the culture" that gives the story its purpose.

And it is something like this that we believe gives literature its power and success. Reading and discussing stories allow us to discover our identity and our meaning in the world. Through language, we recover our voice and our interior self.

from THE SEA-WOLF
Jack London

CHAPTER 6

By the following morning the storm had blown itself quite out and the *Ghost* was rolling slightly on a calm sea without a breath of wind. Occasional light airs were felt, however, and Wolf Larsen patrolled the poop constantly, his eyes ever searching the sea to the northeastward, from which direction the great trade wind must blow.

The men were all on deck and busy preparing their various boats for the season's hunting. There are seven boats aboard, the captain's dinghy and the six which the hunters will use. Three, a hunter, a boat puller, and a boat steerer, compose a boat's crew. On board the schooner the boat pullers and steerers are the crew. The hunters too are supposed to be in command of the watches, subject always to the orders of Wolf Larsen.

All this, and more, I have learned. The *Ghost* is considered the fastest schooner in both the San Francisco and Victoria fleets. In fact, she was once a private yacht, and was built for speed. Her lines and fittings—though I know nothing about such things—speak for themselves. Johnson was telling me about her in a short chat I had with him during yesterday's second dogwatch. He spoke enthusiastically, with the love for a fine craft such as some men feel for horses. He is greatly disgusted with the outlook, and I am given to understand that Wolf Larsen bears a very unsavory reputation among the sealing captains. It was the *Ghost* herself that lured Johnson into signing for the voyage, but he is already beginning to repent.

As he told me, the *Ghost* is an eighty-ton schooner of a remarkably fine model. Her beam, or width, is twenty-three feet, and her length a little over ninety feet. A lead keel of fabulous but unknown weight makes her very stable, while she carries an immense spread of canvas. From the deck to the truck of the maintopmast is something over a hundred feet, while the foremast with its topmast is eight or ten feet shorter. I am giving these details so that the size of this little floating world which holds twenty-two men may be appreciated. It is a very little world, a mote, a speck, and I marvel that men should dare to venture the sea on a contrivance so small and fragile.

Wolf Larsen has, also, a reputation for reckless carrying on of sail. I overheard Henderson and another of the hunters, Standish, a Californian, talking about it. Two years ago he dismasted the *Ghost* in a gale on Bering Sea, whereupon the present masts were put in, which are stronger and heavier in every way. He is said to have remarked when he put them in that he preferred turning her over to losing the sticks.

Every man aboard, with the exception of Johansen, who is rather overcome by his promotion, seems to have an excuse for having sailed on the *Ghost*. Half the men forward are deepwater sailors, and their excuse is that they did not know anything about her or her captain. And those who do know whisper that the hunters, while excellent shots, were so notorious for their quarrelsome and rascally proclivities that they could not sign on any decent schooner.

I have made the acquaintance of another one of the crew—Louis he is called, a rotund and jovial-faced Nova Scotia Irishman, and a very sociable fellow, prone to talk as long as he can find a listener. In the afternoon, while the cook was below asleep and I was peeling the everlasting potatoes, Louis dropped into the galley for a "yarn." His excuse for being aboard was that he was drunk when he signed. He assured me again and again that it was the last thing in the world he would dream of doing in a sober moment. It seems that he has been seal hunting regularly each season for a dozen years and is accounted one of the two or three very best boat steerers in both fleets.

"Ah, my boy"—he shook his head ominously at me—"'tis the worst schooner ye could iv selected, nor were ye drunk at the time as was I. 'Tis sealin' is the sailor's paradise—on other ships than this. The mate was the first, but mark me words, there'll be more dead men before the trip is done with. Hist, now, between you an' meself and the stanchion there, this Wolf Larsen is a regular devil, an' the *Ghost*'ll be a hell ship like she's always been since he had hold iv her. Don't I know? Don't I know? Don't I remember him in Hakodate two years gone, when he had a row an' shot four iv his men? Wasn't I a-layin' on the *Emma L.* not three hundred yards away? An' there was a man the same year he killed with a blow iv his fist. Yes, sir, killed 'im dead-oh. His head must iv smashed like an eggshell. An' wasn't there the governor of Kura Island, an' the chief iv police, Japanese gentlemen, sir, an' didn't they come aboard the *Ghost* as his guests a-bringin' their wives along—wee an' pretty little bits of things like you see 'em painted on fans. An' as he was a-gettin' under way, didn't the fond husbands get left asternlike in their sampan, as it might be by accident? An' wasn't it a week later that the poor little ladies was put ashore on the other side of the island, with nothin' before 'em but to walk home acrost the mountains on their weeny-teeny little straw sandals which wouldn't hang together a mile? Don't I know? 'Tis the beast he is, this Wolf Larsen—the great big beast mentioned iv in Revelation; an' no good end will he ever come to. But I've said nothin' to ye, mind ye. I've whispered never a word, for old fat Louis'll live the voyage out if the last mother's son of yez go to the fishes. Wolf Larsen!" he snorted a moment later. "Listen to the word, will ye! Wolf—'tis what he is. He's not blackhearted like some men. 'Tis no heart he has at all. Wolf, just wolf, 'tis what he is. D'ye wonder he's well named?"

"But if he is so well known for what he is," I queried, "how is it that he can get men to ship with him?"

"An' how is it ye can get men to do anything on God's earth an' sea?" Louis demanded with Celtic fire. "How d'ye find me aboard if 'twasn't that I was drunk as a pig when I put me name down? There's them that can't sail with better men, like the hunters, and them that don't know, like the poor devils of windjammers for'ard there. But they'll come to it, they'll come to it, an' be sorry the day they was born. I could weep for the poor creatures, did I but forget poor old fat Louis and the troubles before him. But 'tis not a whisper I've dropped, mind ye, not a whisper. Them hunters is the wicked boys," he broke forth again, for he suffered from a constitutional plethora of speech. "But wait till they get to cutting up iv jinks and rowin' 'round. He's the boy'll fix 'em. 'Tis him that'll put the fear of God in their rotten black hearts. Look at that hunter iv mine, Horner. 'Jock' Horner they call him, so quietlike an' easygoin', soft-spoken as a girl, till ye'd think butter wouldn't melt in the mouth iv him. Didn't he kill his boat steerer last year? 'Twas called a sad accident, but I met the boat puller in Yokohama an' the straight iv it was given me. An' there's Smoke, the black little devil—didn't the Roosians have him for three years in the salt mines of Siberia for poachin' on Copper Island, which is a Roosian preserve? Shackled he was, hand an' foot, with his mate. An' didn't they have words or a ruction of some kind? For 'twas the other fellow Smoke sent up in the buckets to the top of the mine; an' a piece at the time he went up, a leg today, an' tomorrow an arm, the next day the head, an' so on."

"But you can't mean it!" I cried out, overcome with the horror of it.

"Mean what?" he demanded quick as a flash. "'Tis nothin' I've said. Deef I am and dumb, as ye should be for the sake iv your mother; an' never once have I opened me lips but to say fine things iv them an' him, God curse his soul, an' may he rot in purgatory ten thousand years and then go down to the last an' deepest hell iv all!"

Johnson, the man who had chafed me raw when I first came aboard, seemed the least equivocal of the men forward or aft. In fact there was nothing equivocal about him. One was struck at once by his straightforwardness and manliness, which, in turn, were tempered by a modesty which might be mistaken for timidity. But timid he was not. He seemed, rather, to have the courage of his convictions, the certainty of his manhood. It was this that made him protest at the commencement of our acquaintance against being called Yonson. And upon this, and him, Louis passed judgment and prophecy.

"'Tis a fine chap, that squarehead Johnson we've for'ard with us," he said. "The best sailorman in the forecastle. He's my boat puller. But it's to trouble he'll come with Wolf Larsen, as the sparks fly upward. It's meself that knows. I can see it brewin' an' comin' up like a storm in the sky. I've talked to him like a brother, but it's little he sees in takin' in his lights or flyin' false signals. He grumbles out when things don't go to suit him, and there'll be always some telltale carryin' word iv it aft to the Wolf. The Wolf is strong, and it's the way of a wolf to hate strength, an' strength it is he'll see in Johnson—no knucklin' under and a 'Yes, sir, thank ye kindly, sir' for a curse or a blow. Oh, she's a-comin'! She's a-comin'! An' God knows where I'll get another boat puller! What does the fool up an' say when the old man calls him Yonson, but 'Me name is Johnson, sir,' an' then spells it out, letter for letter. Ye should iv seen the old man's face! I thought he'd let drive at him on the spot. He didn't, but he will, and he'll break that squarehead's heart, or it's little I know iv the ways iv men on the ships iv the sea."

Thomas Mugridge is becoming unendurable. I am compelled to mister him and to sir him with every speech. One reason for

this is that Wolf Larsen seems to have taken a fancy to him. It is
an unprecedented thing, I take it, for a captain to be chummy with
the cook, but this is certainly what Wolf Larsen is doing. Two or
three times he put his head into the galley and chaffed Mugridge
good-naturedly, and once this afternoon he stood by the break of
the poop and chatted with him for fully fifteen minutes. When it
was over and Mugridge was back in the galley, he became greasily
radiant and went about his work humming coster songs in a nerve-
racking and discordant falsetto.

"I always get along with the officers," he remarked to me in a
confidential tone. "I know the w'y, I do, to myke myself uppreci-
yted. There was my last skipper—w'y, I thought nothin' of drop-
pin' down in the cabin for a little chat and a friendly glass.
'Mugridge,' sez 'e to me, 'Mugridge,' sez 'e, 'you've missed yer
vokytion.' 'An' 'ow's that?' sez I. 'Yer should 'a been born a gentleman, an' never 'ad to work for yer livin'.' God strike me dead,
'Ump, if that ayn't wot 'e sez, an' me a-sittin' there in 'is cabin,
jollylike an' comfortable, a-smokin' 'is cigars an' drinkin' 'is rum."

This chitter-chatter drove me to distraction. I never heard a
voice I hated so. His oily, insinuating tones, his greasy smile, and
his monstrous self-conceit grated on my nerves till sometimes I
was all in a tremble. Positively, he was the most disgusting and
loathsome person I have ever met. The filth of his cooking was in-
describable, and as he cooked everything that was eaten aboard,
I was compelled to select what I ate with great circumspection,
choosing from the least dirty of his concoctions.

My hands bothered me a great deal, unused as they were to
work. The nails were discolored and black, while the skin was already grained with dirt which even a scrubbing brush could not
remove. Then blisters came in a painful and never-ending procession, and I had a great burn on my forearm, acquired by losing my
balance in a roll of the ship and pitching against the galley stove.
Nor was my knee any better. The swelling had not gone down, and
the cap was still up on edge. Hobbling about on it from morning
to night was not helping it any. What I needed was rest if it were
ever to get well.

Rest! I never before knew the meaning of the word. I had been
resting all my life and did not know it. But now, could I sit still
for one half hour and do nothing, not even think, it would be the
most pleasurable thing in the world. But it is a revelation, on the

other hand. I shall be able to appreciate the lives of the working people hereafter. I did not dream that work was so terrible a thing. From half past five in the morning till ten o'clock at night I am everybody's slave, with not one moment to myself, except such as I can steal near the end of the second dogwatch. Let me pause for a minute to look out over the sea sparkling in the sun, or to gaze at a sailor going aloft to the gaff-topsails or running out the bowsprit, and I am sure to hear the hateful voice. "'Ere, you, 'Ump, no sodgrin'. I've got my peepers on yer."

There are signs of rampant bad temper in the steerage, and the gossip is going around that Smoke and Henderson have had a fight. Henderson seems the best of the hunters, a slow-going fellow and hard to rouse, but roused he must have been, for Smoke had a bruised and discolored eye and looked particularly vicious when he came into the cabin for supper.

A cruel thing happened just before supper, indicative of the callousness and brutishness of these men. There is one green hand in the crew, Harrison by name, a clumsy-looking country boy, mastered, I imagine, by the spirit of adventure, and making his first voyage. In the light baffling airs the schooner had been tacking about a great deal, at which times the sails pass from one side to the other and a man is sent aloft to shift over the fore-gaff-topsail. In some way, when Harrison was aloft, the sheet jammed in the block through which it runs at the end of the gaff. As I understood it, there were two ways of getting it cleared, first by lowering the foresail, which was comparatively easy and without danger; and second by climbing out the peak-halyards to the end of the gaff itself, an exceedingly hazardous performance.

Johansen called out to Harrison to go out the halyards. It was patent to everybody that the boy was afraid. And well he might be, eighty feet above the deck, to thrust himself on those thin and jerking ropes. Had there been a steady breeze it would not have been so bad, but the *Ghost* was rolling emptily in a long sea, and with each roll the canvas flapped and boomed and the halyards slacked and jerked taut. They were capable of snapping a man off like a fly from a whiplash.

Harrison heard the order and understood what was demanded of him, but hesitated. It was probably the first time he had been aloft in his life. Johansen, who had caught the contagion of Wolf Larsen's masterfulness, burst out with a volley of abuse and curses.

"That'll do, Johansen," Wolf Larsen said brusquely. "I'll have you know that I do the swearing on this ship. If I need your assistance, I'll call you in."

"Yes, sir," the mate acknowledged submissively.

In the meantime Harrison had started out on the halyards. I was looking up from the galley door, and I could see him trembling, as with ague, in every limb. He proceeded very slowly and cautiously, an inch at a time. Outlined against the clear blue of the sky, he had the appearance of an enormous spider crawling along the tracery of its web.

It was a slight uphill climb, for the foresail peaked high; and the halyards, running through various blocks on the gaff and mast, gave him separate holds for hands and feet. But the trouble lay in that the wind was not strong enough nor steady enough to keep the sail full. When he was halfway out, the *Ghost* took a long roll to windward and back again into the hollow between two seas. Harrison ceased his progress and held on tightly. Eighty feet beneath, I could see the agonized strain of his muscles as he gripped for very life. The sail emptied and the gaff swung amidships. The halyards slackened, and though it all happened very quickly, I could see them sag beneath the weight of his body. Then the gaff swung to the side with an abrupt swiftness, the great sail boomed like a cannon, and the three rows of reef points slatted against the canvas like a volley of rifles. Harrison, clinging on, made the giddy rush through the air. This rush ceased abruptly. The halyards became instantly taut. It was the snap of the whip. His clutch was broken. One hand was torn loose from its hold. The other lingered desperately for a moment, and followed. His body pitched out and down, but in some way he managed to save himself with his legs. He was hanging by them, head downward. A quick effort brought his hands up to the halyards again, but he was a long time regaining his former position, where he hung, a pitiable object.

"I'll bet he has no appetite for supper." I heard Wolf Larsen's voice, which came to me from around the corner of the galley. "Stand from under, you, Johansen! Watch out! Here she comes!"

In truth, Harrison was very sick, as a person is seasick; and for a long time he clung to his precarious perch without attempting to move. Johansen, however, continued violently to urge him on to the completion of his task.

"It is a shame," I heard Johnson growling in painfully slow and correct English. He was standing by the main rigging, a few feet away from me. "The boy is willing enough. He will learn if he has a chance. But this is—" He paused awhile, for the word "murder" was his final judgment.

"Hist, will ye!" Louis whispered to him. "For the love iv your mother hold your mouth!"

But Johnson, looking on, still continued his grumbling.

"Look here," the hunter Standish spoke to Wolf Larsen, "that's my boat puller, and I don't want to lose him."

"That's all right, Standish," was the reply. "He's your boat puller when you've got him in the boat; but he's my sailor when I have him aboard, and I'll do what I damn well please with him."

"But that's no reason—" Standish began in a torrent of speech.

"That'll do, easy as she goes," Wolf Larsen counseled back. "I've told you what's what, and let it stop at that. The man's mine, and I'll make soup of him and eat it if I want to."

There was an angry gleam in the hunter's eye, but he turned on his heel and entered the steerage companionway, where he remained, looking upward. All hands were on deck now, and all eyes were aloft, where a human life was at grapples with death. The callousness of these men, to whom industrial organization gave control of the lives of other men, was appalling. I, who had lived out of the whirl of the world, had never dreamed that its work was carried on in such fashion. Life had always seemed a peculiarly sacred thing, but here it counted for nothing, was a cipher in the arithmetic of commerce. I must say, however, that the sailors themselves were sympathetic, as instance the case of Johnson; but the masters—the hunters and the captain—were heartlessly indifferent. Even the protest of Standish arose out of the fact that he did not wish to lose his boat puller. Had it been some other hunter's boat puller, he, like them, would have been no more than amused.

But to return to Harrison. It took Johansen, insulting and reviling the poor wretch, fully ten minutes to get him started again. A little later he made the end of the gaff, where, astride the spar itself, he had a better chance for holding on. He cleared the sheet and was free to return, slightly downhill now, along the halyards to the mast. But he had lost his nerve. Unsafe as was his present position, he was loath to forsake it for the more unsafe position on the halyards.

He looked along the airy path he must traverse, and then down to the deck. His eyes were wide and staring, and he was trembling violently. I had never seen fear so strongly stamped upon a human face. Johansen called vainly for him to come down. At any moment he was liable to be snapped off the gaff, but he was helpless with fright. Wolf Larsen, walking up and down with Smoke and in conversation, took no more notice of him, though he cried sharply once to the man at the wheel, "You're off your course, my man! Be careful, unless you're looking for trouble!"

"Aye, aye, sir," the helmsman responded, putting a couple of spokes down.

He had been guilty of running the *Ghost* several points off her course in order that what little wind there was should fill the foresail and hold it steady. He had striven to help the unfortunate Harrison at the risk of incurring Wolf Larsen's anger.

The time went by, and the suspense, to me, was terrible. Thomas Mugridge, on the other hand, considered it a laughable affair and was continually bobbing his head out the galley door to make jocose remarks. How I hated him! And how my hatred for him grew and grew, during that fearful time, to cyclopean dimensions. For the first time in my life I experienced the desire to murder, "saw red" as some of our picturesque writers phrase it. Life in general might still be sacred, but life in the particular case of Thomas Mugridge had become very profane indeed. I was frightened when I became conscious that I was seeing red, and the thought flashed through my mind: was I, too, becoming tainted by the brutality of my environment? I, who even in the most flagrant crimes denied the justice and righteousness of capital punishment?

Fully half an hour went by, and then I saw Johnson and Louis in some sort of altercation. It ended with Johnson flinging off Louis' detaining arm and starting forward. He crossed the deck, sprang into the fore-rigging, and began to climb. But the quick eye of Wolf Larsen caught him.

"Here, you, what are you up to?" he cried.

Johnson's ascent was arrested. He looked his captain in the eyes and replied slowly, "I am going to get that boy down."

"You'll get down out of that rigging, and damn lively about it! D'ye hear? Get down!"

Johnson hesitated, but the long years of obedience to the masters of ships overpowered him, and he dropped sullenly to the deck and went on forward.

At half after five I went below to set the cabin table, but I hardly knew what I did, for my eyes and brain were filled with the vision of a man, white-faced and trembling, comically like a bug, clinging to the thrashing gaff. At six o'clock, when I served supper, going on deck to get the food from the galley, I saw Harrison, still in the same position. The conversation at the table was of other things. Nobody seemed interested in the wantonly imperiled life. But making an extra trip to the galley a little later, I was gladdened by the sight of Harrison staggering weakly from the rigging to the forecastle scuttle. He had finally summoned the courage to descend.

Before closing this incident, I must give a scrap of conversation I had with Wolf Larsen in the cabin while I was washing the dishes.

"You were looking squeamish this afternoon," he began. "What was the matter?"

I could see that he knew what had made me possibly as sick as Harrison, that he was trying to draw me, and I answered, "It was because of the brutal treatment of that boy."

He gave a short laugh. "Like seasickness, I suppose. Some men are subject to it, and others are not."

"Not so," I objected.

"Just so," he went on. "The earth is as full of brutality as the sea is full of motion. And some men are made sick by the one, and some by the other. That's the only reason."

"But you, who make a mock of human life, don't you place any value upon it whatever?" I demanded.

"Value? What value?" He looked at me, and though his eyes were steady and motionless, there seemed a cynical smile in them. "What kind of value? How do you measure it? Who values it?"

"I do," I made answer.

"Then what is it worth to you? Another man's life, I mean. Come, now, what is it worth?"

The value of life? How could I put a tangible value upon it? Somehow I, who have always had expression, lacked expression when with Wolf Larsen. I have since determined that a part of it was due to the man's personality but that the greater part was due to his totally different outlook. Unlike other materialists I had met and with whom I had something in common to start on, I had nothing in common with him. Perhaps, also, it was the elemental simplicity of his mind that baffled me. He drove so directly to the core of the matter, divesting a question always of all superfluous details, and with such an air of finality, that I seemed to find myself struggling in deep water with no footing under me. Value of life? How could I answer the question on the spur of the moment?

The sacredness of life I had accepted as axiomatic. That it was in-
trinsically valuable was a truism I had never questioned. But when
he challenged the truism I was speechless.

"We were talking about this yesterday," he said. "I held that
life was a ferment, a yeasty something which devoured life that
it might live, and that living was merely successful piggishness.
Why, if there is anything in supply and demand, life is the cheapest
thing in the world. There is only so much water, so much earth,
so much air; but the life that is demanding to be born is limitless.
Nature is a spendthrift. Look at the fish and their millions of eggs.
For that matter, look at you and me. In our loins are the possibilities of millions of lives. Could we but find time and opportunity
and utilize the last bit and every bit of the unborn life that is in us,
we could become the fathers of nations and populate continents.
Life? Bah! It has no value. Of cheap things it is the cheapest. Everywhere it goes begging. Nature spills it out with a lavish hand.
Where there is room for one life, she sows a thousand lives, and
it's life eats life till the strongest and most piggish life is left."

"You have read Darwin," I said. "But you read him misunder-
standingly when you conclude that the struggle for existence sanc-
tions your wanton destruction of life."

He shrugged his shoulders. "You know you only mean that in
relation to human life, for of the flesh and the fowl and the fish
you destroy as much as I or any other man. And human life is in
nowise different, though you feel it is and think that you reason
why it is. Why should I be parsimonious with this life which is
cheap and without value? There are more sailors than there are
ships on the sea for them, more workers than there are factories or
machines for them. Why, you who live on the land know that you
house your poor people in the slums of cities and loose famine and
pestilence upon them and that there still remain more poor people,
dying for want of a crust of bread and a bit of meat—which is life
destroyed—than you know what to do with. Have you ever seen
the London dockers fighting like wild beasts for a chance to work?"

He started for the companion stairs but turned his head for a
final word. "Do you know the only value life has is what life puts
upon itself? And it is of course overestimated, since it is of necessity prejudiced in its own favor. Take that man I had aloft. He held
on as if he were a precious thing, a treasure beyond diamonds or
rubies. To you? No. To me? Not at all. To himself? Yes. But I do

not accept his estimate. He sadly overrates himself. There is plenty more life demanding to be born. Had he fallen and dripped his brains upon the deck like honey from the comb, there would have been no loss to the world. He was worth nothing to the world. The supply is too large. To himself only was he of value, and to show how fictitious even this value was, being dead he is unconscious that he has lost himself. He alone rated himself beyond diamonds and rubies. Diamonds and rubies are gone, spread out on the deck to be washed away by a bucket of seawater, and he does not even know that the diamonds and rubies are gone. He does not lose anything, for with the loss of himself he loses the knowledge of loss. Don't you see? And what have you to say?"

"That you are at least consistent," was all I could say, and I went on washing the dishes.

CHAPTER 7

At last, after three days of variable winds, we have caught the northeast trades. I came on deck after a good night's rest in spite of my poor knee to find the *Ghost* foaming along, wing-and-wing, and every sail drawing except the jibs, with a fresh breeze astern. Oh, the wonder of the great trade wind! All day we sailed, and all night, and the next day, and the next, day after day, the wind always astern and blowing steadily and strong. The schooner sailed herself. There was no pulling and hauling on sheets and tackles, no shifting of topsails, no work at all for the sailors to do except to steer. At night, when the sun went down, the sheets were slackened; in the morning, when they yielded up the damp of the dew and relaxed, they were pulled tight again—and that was all.

Ten knots, twelve knots, eleven knots, varying from time to time, is the speed we are making. And ever out of the northeast the brave wind blows, driving us on our course two hundred and fifty miles between the dawns. It saddens me and gladdens me, the gait with which we are leaving San Francisco behind and with which we are foaming down upon the tropics. Each day grows perceptibly warmer. In the second dogwatch the sailors come on deck stripped and heave buckets of water upon one another from overside. Flying fish are beginning to be seen, and during the night the watch above scrambles over the deck in pursuit of those that fall aboard. In the morning, Thomas Mugridge being duly bribed, the galley is pleasantly areek with the odor of their frying, while dolphin meat is served fore and aft on such occasions as Johnson catches the blazing beauties from the bowsprit end.

Johnson seems to spend all his spare time there or aloft at the crosstrees, watching the *Ghost* cleaving the water under press of sail. There is passion, adoration, in his eyes, and he goes about in a sort of trance, gazing in ecstasy at the swelling sails, the foaming wake, and the heave and the run of her over the liquid mountains that are moving with us in stately procession.

The days and nights are "all a wonder and a wild delight," and though I have little time from my dreary work, I steal odd moments to gaze and gaze at the unending glory of what I never dreamed the world possessed. Above, the sky is stainless blue— blue as the sea itself, which under the forefoot is of the color and sheen of azure satin. All around the horizon are pale, fleecy clouds, never changing, never moving, like a silver setting for the flawless turquoise sky.

I do not forget one night, when I should have been asleep, of lying on the forecastlehead and gazing down at the spectral ripple of foam thrust aside by the *Ghost*'s forefoot. It sounded like the gurgling of a brook over mossy stones in some quiet dell, and the crooning song of it lured me away and out of myself till I was no longer Hump, the cabin boy, nor Van Weyden, the man who had dreamed away thirty-five years among books. But a voice behind me, the unmistakable voice of Wolf Larsen, strong with the invincible certitude of the man and mellow with appreciation of the words he was quoting, aroused me.

> "Oh the blazing tropic night, when the wake's a welt of
>   light
>   That holds the hot sky tame,
> And the steady forefoot snores through the planet-
>   powdered floors
>   Where the scared whale flukes in flame.
>
> Her plates are scarred by the sun, dear lass,
> And her ropes are taut with the dew,
> For we're booming down on the old trail, our own
>   trail, the out trail,
> We're sagging south on the Long Trail—the trail that
>   is always new.

"Eh, Hump! How's it strike you?" he asked after the due pause which words and setting demanded.

I looked into his face. It was aglow with light, as the sea itself, and the eyes were flashing in the starshine.

"It strikes me as remarkable, to say the least, that you should show enthusiasm," I answered coldly.

"Why, man, it's living! It's life!" he cried.

"Which is a cheap thing and without value," I flung his words at him.

He laughed, and it was the first time I had heard honest mirth in his voice.

"Ah, I cannot get you to understand, cannot drive it into your head, what a thing this life is. Of course life is valueless, except to itself. And I can tell you that my life is pretty valuable just now—to myself. It is beyond price, which you will acknowledge is a terrific overrating, but which I cannot help, for it is the life that is in me that makes the rating."

He appeared waiting for the words with which to express the thought that was in him, and finally went on.

"Do you know, I am filled with a strange uplift; I feel as if all time were echoing through me, as though all powers were mine. I know truth, divine good from evil, right from wrong. My vision is clear and far. I could almost believe in God. But"—and his voice changed and the light went out of his face—"what is this condition in which I find myself? This joy of living? This exultation of life? This inspiration, I may well call it? It is what comes when there is nothing wrong with one's digestion, when his stomach is in trim and his appetite has an edge, and all goes well. It is the bribe for living, the champagne of the blood, the effervescence of the ferment, that makes some men think holy thoughts and other men to see God or to create him when they cannot see him. That is all, the drunkenness of life, the stirring and crawling of the yeast, the babbling of the life that is insane with consciousness that it is alive. And—bah! Tomorrow I shall pay for it as the drunkard pays. And I shall know that I must die, at sea most likely, cease crawling of myself to be all acrawl with the corruption of the sea; to be fed upon, to be carrion, to yield up all the strength and movement of my muscles that it may become strength and movement in fin and scale and the guts of fishes. Bah! And bah again! The champagne is already flat. The sparkle and bubble has gone out and it is a tasteless drink."

He left me as suddenly as he had come, springing to the deck with the weight and softness of a tiger. The *Ghost* plowed on her way. I noted the gurgling forefoot was very like a snore, and as I listened to it the effect of Wolf Larsen's swift rush from sublime exultation to despair slowly left me. Then some deepwater sailor from the waist of the ship lifted a rich tenor voice in the *Song of the Trade Wind:*

> *"Oh, I am the wind the seamen love—*
> *I am steady, and strong, and true;*
> *They follow my track by the clouds above,*
> *O'er the fathomless tropic blue.*
>
> *Through daylight and dark I follow the bark,*
> *I keep like a hound on her trail;*
> *I'm strongest at noon, yet under the moon,*
> *I stiffen the bunt of her sail."*

CHAPTER 8

Sometimes I think Wolf Larsen mad, or half mad at least, what of his strange moods and vagaries. At other times I take him for a great man, a genius who has never arrived. And finally, I am convinced that he is the perfect type of the primitive man born a thousand years or generations too late and an anachronism in this culminating century of civilization. He is certainly an individualist of the most pronounced type. Not only that, but he is very lonely. There is no congeniality between him and the rest of the men aboard ship. His tremendous virility and mental strength wall him apart. They are more like children to him, even the hunters, and as children he treats them, descending perforce to their level and playing with them as a man plays with puppies. Or else he probes them with the cruel hand of a vivisectionist, groping about in their mental processes and examining their souls as though to see of what soul-stuff is made.

I have seen him a score of times at table insulting this hunter or that with cool and level eyes and, withal, a certain air of interest, pondering their actions or replies or petty rages with a curiosity almost laughable to me who stood onlooker and who understood. Concerning his own rages, I am convinced that they are not real, that they are sometimes experiments, but that in the main they are the habits of a pose or attitude he has seen fit to take toward his fellowmen. I know, with the possible exception of the incident of the dead mate, that I have not seen him really angry, nor do I wish ever to see him in a genuine rage, when all the force of him is called into play.

While on the question of vagaries, I shall tell what befell Thomas Mugridge in the cabin, and at the same time complete an incident upon which I have already touched once or twice. The twelve-o'clock dinner was over one day and I had just finished putting the cabin in order when Wolf Larsen and Thomas Mugridge descended the companion stairs. Though the cook had a cubbyhole of a stateroom opening off from the cabin, in the cabin itself he had never dared to linger or to be seen, and he flitted to and fro once or twice a day like a timid specter.

"So you know how to play Nap," Wolf Larsen was saying in a pleased sort of voice. "I might have guessed an Englishman would know. I learned it myself in English ships."

Thomas Mugridge was beside himself, a blithering imbecile, so pleased was he at chumming thus with the captain. The little airs he put on and the painful striving to assume the easy carriage of a man born to a dignified place in life would have been sickening had they not been ludicrous. He quite ignored my presence, though I credited him with being simply unable to see me. His pale, wishy-washy eyes were swimming like lazy summer seas, though what blissful visions they beheld were beyond my imagination.

"Get the cards, Hump," Wolf Larsen ordered as they took seats at the table. "And bring out the cigars and the whiskey you'll find in my berth."

I returned with the articles in time to hear the cockney hinting broadly that there was a mystery about him, that he might be a gentleman's son gone wrong or something or other, also that he was a remittance man and was paid to keep away from England— "p'yed 'ansomely, sir," was the way he put it; "p'yed 'ansomely to sling my 'ook an' keep slingin' it."

I had brought the customary liquor glasses, but Wolf Larsen frowned, shook his head, and signaled with his hands for me to bring the tumblers. These he filled two thirds full with undiluted whiskey—"a gentleman's drink," quoth Thomas Mugridge—and they clinked their glasses to the glorious game of Nap, lighted cigars, and fell to shuffling and dealing the cards.

They played for money. They increased the amounts of the bets.

They drank whiskey, they drank it neat, and I fetched more. I do not know whether Wolf Larsen cheated or not—a thing he was thoroughly capable of doing—but he won steadily. The cook made repeated journeys to his bunk for money. Each time he performed the journey with greater swagger, but he never brought more than a few dollars at a time. He grew maudlin, familiar, could hardly see the cards or sit upright. As a preliminary to another journey to his bunk, he hooked Wolf Larsen's buttonhole with a greasy forefinger and vacuously proclaimed and reiterated, "I got money. I got money, I tell yer, an' I'm a gentleman's son."

Wolf Larsen was unaffected by the drink, yet he drank glass for glass, and if anything his glasses were fuller. There was no change to him. He did not appear even amused at the other's antics.

In the end, with loud protestations that he could lose like a gentleman, the cook's last money was staked on the game and lost. Whereupon he leaned his head on his hands and wept. Wolf Larsen looked curiously at him, as though about to probe and vivisect him, then changed his mind, as from the foregone conclusion that there was nothing there to probe.

"Hump," he said to me, elaborately polite, "kindly take Mr. Mugridge's arm and help him up on deck. He is not feeling very well.

"And tell Johnson to douse him with a few buckets of salt water," he added in a lower tone for my ear alone.

I left Mr. Mugridge on deck in the hands of a couple of grinning sailors who had been told off for the purpose. Mr. Mugridge was sleepily spluttering that he was a gentleman's son. But as I descended the companion stairs to clear the table, I heard him shriek as the first bucket of water struck him.

Wolf Larsen was counting his winnings.

"One hundred and eighty-five dollars even," he said aloud. "Just as I thought. The beggar came aboard without a cent."

"And what you have won is mine, sir," I said boldly.

He favored me with a quizzical smile. "Hump, I have studied some grammar in my time, and I think your tenses are tangled. 'Was mine,' you should have said, not 'is mine.'"

"It is a question, not of grammar, but of ethics," I answered.

It was possibly a minute before he spoke.

"D'ye know, Hump," he said with a slow seriousness which had in it an indefinable strain of sadness, "that this is the first time I have heard the word 'ethics' in the mouth of a man. You and I are the only men on this ship who know its meaning. At one time in my life," he continued after another pause, "I dreamed that I might someday talk with men who used such language, that I might lift myself out of the place in life in which I had been born and hold conversation and mingle with men who talked about just such things as ethics. And this is the first time I have ever heard the word pronounced. Which is all by the way, for you are wrong. It is a question, neither of grammar nor ethics, but of fact."

"I understand," I said. "The fact is that you have the money."

His face brightened. He seemed pleased at my perspicacity.

"But it is avoiding the real question," I continued, "which is one of right."

"Ah," he remarked with a wry pucker of his mouth, "I see you still believe in such things as right and wrong."

"But don't you—at all?" I demanded.

"Not the least bit. Might is right, and that is all there is to it. Weakness is wrong. Which is a very poor way of saying that it is good for oneself to be strong, and evil for oneself to be weak—or better yet, it is pleasurable to be strong because of the profits, painful to be weak because of the penalties. Just now the possession of this money is a pleasurable thing. It is good for one to possess it. Being able to possess it, I wrong myself and the life that is in me if I give it to you and forego the pleasure of possessing it."

"But you wrong me by withholding it," I objected.

"Not at all. One man cannot wrong another man. He can only wrong himself. As I see it, I do wrong always when I consider the interests of others. Don't you see? How can two particles of the yeast wrong each other by striving to devour each other? It is their inborn heritage to strive to devour and to strive not to be devoured. When they depart from this they sin."

"Then you don't believe in altruism?" I asked.

He received the word as if it had a familiar ring, though he pondered it thoughtfully. "Let me see, it means something about co-operation, doesn't it?"

"Well, in a way there has come to be a sort of connection," I answered, unsurprised by this time at such gaps in his vocabulary, which, like his knowledge, was the acquirement of a self-read, self-educated man whom no one had directed in his studies and who had thought much and talked little or not at all. "An altruistic act is an act performed for the welfare of others. It is unselfish, as opposed to an act performed for self, which is selfish."

He nodded his head. "Oh, yes, I remember it now. I ran across it in Spencer."

"Spencer!" I cried. "Have you read him?"

"Not very much," was his confession. "I understood quite a good deal of *First Principles,* but his *Biology* took the wind out of my sails, and his *Psychology* left me butting around in the doldrums for many a day. I honestly could not understand what he was driving at. I put it down to mental deficiency on my part, but since then I have decided that it was for want of preparation. I had no proper basis. Only Spencer and myself know how hard I hammered. But I did get something out of his *Data of Ethics.* There's where I ran across 'altruism,' and I remember now how it was used."

I wondered what this man could have got from such a work. Spencer I remembered enough to know that altruism was imperative to his ideal of highest conduct. Wolf Larsen evidently had sifted the great philosopher's teachings, rejecting and selecting according to his needs and desires.

"What else did you run across?" I asked.

His brows drew in slightly with the mental effort of suitably phrasing thoughts which he had never before put into speech. I felt an elation of spirit. I was groping into his soul-stuff as he made a practice of groping in the soul-stuff of others. I was exploring virgin territory. A strange, a terribly strange, region was unrolling itself before my eyes.

"In as few words as possible," he began, "Spencer puts it something like this: First, a man must act for his own benefit—to do this is to be moral and good. Next, he must act for the benefit of his children. And third, he must act for the benefit of his race."

"And the highest, finest, right conduct," I interjected, "is that act which benefits at the same time the man, his children, and his race."

"I wouldn't stand for that," he replied. "Couldn't see the necessity for it, nor the common sense. I cut out the race and the children. I would sacrifice nothing for them. It's just so much slush and sentiment, and you must see it yourself, at least for one who does not believe in eternal life. With immortality before me, altruism would be a paying business proposition. I might elevate my soul to all kinds of altitudes. But with nothing eternal before me but death, given for a brief spell this yeasty crawling and squirming which is called life, why, it would be immoral for me to perform any act that was a sacrifice. Any sacrifice that makes me lose one crawl or squirm is foolish, and not only foolish, for it is a wrong against myself and a wicked thing. I must not lose one crawl or squirm if I am to get the most out of the ferment. Nor will the eternal movelessness that is coming to me be made easier or harder by the sacrifices or selfishnesses of the time when I was yeasty and acrawl."

"Then you are an individualist, a materialist, and logically, a hedonist."

"Big words," he smiled. "But what is a hedonist?"

He nodded agreement when I had given the definition.

"And you are also," I continued, "a man one could not trust in the least thing where it was possible for a selfish interest to intervene?"

"Now you're beginning to understand," he said, brightening.

"You are a man utterly without what the world calls morals?"

"That's it."

"A man of whom to be always afraid—"

"That's the way to put it."

"As one is afraid of a snake, or a tiger, or a shark?"

"Now you know me," he said. "And you know me as I am generally known. Other men call me Wolf."

"You are a sort of monster," I added audaciously, "a Caliban who has pondered Setebos and who acts as you act, in idle moments, by whim and fancy."

His brow clouded at the allusion. He did not understand, and I quickly learned that he did not know the poem.

"I'm just reading Browning," he confessed, "and it's pretty tough. I haven't got very far along, and as it is I've about lost my bearings."

Not to be tiresome, I shall say that I fetched the book from his stateroom and read *Caliban* aloud. He was delighted. It was a primitive mode of reasoning and of looking at things that he understood thoroughly. He interrupted again and again with comment and criticism. When I finished, he had me read it over a second time, and a third. We fell into discussion—philosophy, science, evolution, religion. He betrayed the inaccuracies of the self-read man, and, it must be granted, the sureness and directness of the primitive mind. The very simplicity of his reasoning was its strength, and his materialism was far more compelling than the subtly complex materialism of Charley Furuseth. Not that I—a

confirmed and, as Furuseth phrased it, a temperamental idealist—
was to be compelled, but that Wolf Larsen stormed the last strong-
holds of my faith with a vigor that received respect, while not ac-
corded conviction.

Time passed. Supper was at hand and the table not laid. I became restless and anxious, and when Thomas Mugridge glared
down the companionway, sick and angry of countenance, I prepared to go about my duties. But Wolf Larsen cried out to him,
"Cooky, you've got to hustle tonight. I'm busy with Hump, and
you'll do the best you can without him."

And again the unprecedented was established. That night I sat
at table with the captain and the hunters, while Thomas Mugridge
waited on us and washed the dishes afterwards—a whim, a Caliban mood of Wolf Larsen's, and one I foresaw would bring me
trouble. In the meantime we talked and talked, much to the disgust
of the hunters, who could not understand a word.

———*For Discussion*———

RPW—

Wolf Larsen, captain of the Ghost, *is, as his name indicates, a
wolf, a primitive beast, a devil. He is a remarkable man, once met,
never forgotten. His Darwinian philosophy marks the boundaries
of his belief: Might makes right, survival of the fittest. But he is
more than his own philosophy implies.*

*Wolf keeps claiming that life is "a ferment, a yeasty some-
thing" with no chance for immortality, no soul. Based on the law
of supply and demand, life is cheap to Wolf; it is cannibalistic, a
business proposition, "a cipher in the arithmetic of commerce." I
think of Wolf when he is talking this way as if he were a radical
individualist committed to total self-sufficiency. But at the same
time I am reminded that no man is an island. Wolf is a materialist
dedicated to the power and strength of his own body, but he also
seems to be a lonely man in need of stimulating conversation in
the midst of the brutal environment of his small boat. He is a
reader and a self-educated thinker who craves the exercise of his
mind.*

*By contrast, Humphrey Van Weyden (Hump), taken uncon-
scious from the San Franciso Bay after the ferry-steamer he was*

on sank, is a well-educated literary critic, an idealist and dreamer who believes in morality and immortality. Van Weyden has lived a life of privilege and comfort. As Wolf well knows, when Van Weyden first came on board, he could not stand on his own two legs. Unlike Wolf, Van Weyden has never learned to take care of himself. Van Weyden may believe that life is sacred, but he has now been thrown into a world where life counts for nothing. He needs to acquire some of the strength of Wolf.

Of course like most rugged individualists, Wolf also needs to be number one, king of the hill. He knows that it is through his brutal power and strength that he can achieve and maintain that position. In this selection, for example, Wolf forces the country boy, Harrison, to stay out on the halyards even though it might cost Harrison his life. From Wolf's perspective, if Harrison falls it is a sign that he was not fit enough to live. Wolf also takes all of Thomas Mugridge's money in a card game. Why? Because he can. And because Mugridge is "a blithering imbecile" eager to get close to the captain. Wolf won't give the money back to Humphrey, although Mugridge had originally taken it from Humphrey. In a moral world, Wolf should give it back, but from Wolf's perspective Humphrey should never have allowed Mugridge to steal it from him in the first place. Humphrey needs to learn to take care of himself and not count on a moral code to protect him.

There will always be men on the boat with the certainty of their manhood and the courage of their convictions. In this selection, Johnson is such a man, straightforward and outspoken, willing to voice his feelings about Harrison's mistreatment and to insist that Wolf call him by his right name. As the mate Louis knows, Wolf hates such signs of strength, and it will only be a matter of time before Johnson is dead.

Wolf and Humphrey need each other because each lacks what the other has. Humphrey will continue to grow on his journey because he is willing to learn and expand. In the end, however, Wolf will not change. He remains remarkable, but he is defeated.

JRT—

Life had always been a "sacred thing," Hump, our narrator, tells us in these chapters of London's tale of men at sea. But here it "counted for nothing." The sailors might have been sympathetic to threats to the lives of their mates, but captains and masters mocked human life. Wolf Larsen doesn't blink when a man almost loses his life clinging to a sail. In fact, he says life is worthless, all, that is, except his own. What are we to make of this?

As difficult as it is may seem to understand this text without the whole tale, we know that Wolf Larsen represents threat. Threat to the status quo. Threat to what makes us comfortable. Threat to what we believe. What more perfect a place for London to raise questions about our existence than on the open seas where everything is up for grabs? On the one hand, Wolf represents virility and power—even his name signifies a hunger that preys on the helpless—and on the other hand, absolute self-centeredness. It would be easier to accept him as a character if he were uneducated, but he is well-read, knowledgeable, and worldly. He is a sort of monster, says Hump, capable of absolute lack of morality, but fascinating too for exactly that same reason. We know by the end of the eighth chapter that Wolf will challenge him, perhaps even destroy him, but we suspect he is gaining some strength through the life at sea.

London asks early on in these chapters if the struggle at sea creates its own kind of tension; if the environment creates the man. As we witness Hump begin to question what he is made of, his strengths and failings, his fortitude and fear, we too wonder what we would do aboard this ship if faced with Wolf.

The Man Who Killed a Shadow

Richard Wright

It all began long ago when he was a tiny boy who was already used, in a fearful sort of way, to living with shadows. But what were the shadows that made him afraid? Surely they were not those beautiful silhouettes of objects cast upon the earth by the sun. Shadows of that kind are innocent and he loved trying to catch them as he ran along sunlit paths in summer. But there were subtler shadows which he saw and which others could not see: the shadows of his fears. And this boy had such shadows and he lived to kill one of them.

Saul Saunders was born black in a little Southern town, not many miles from Washington, the nation's capital, which means that he came into a world that was split in two, a white world and a black one, the white one being separated from the black by a million psychological miles. So, from the very beginning, Saul looking timidly out from his black world, saw the shadowy outlines of a white world that was unreal to him and not his own.

It so happened that even Saul's mother was but a vague, shadowy thing to him, for she died long before his memory could form an image of her. And the same thing happened to Saul's father, who died before the boy could retain a clear picture of him in his mind.

People really never became personalities to Saul, for hardly had he ever got to know them before they vanished. So people became for Saul symbols of uneasiness, of a deprivation that evoked in him a sense of the transitory quality of life, which always made him feel that some invisible, unexplainable event was about to descend upon him.

He had five brothers and two sisters who remained strangers to him. There was, of course, no adult in his family with enough money to support them all, and the children were rationed out to various cousins, uncles, aunts, and grandparents.

It fell to Saul to live with his grandmother who moved constantly from one small Southern town to another, and even physical landscapes grew to have but little emotional meaning for the boy. Towns were places you lived in for a while, and then you moved on. When he had reached the age of twelve, all reality seemed to him to be akin to his mother and father, like the white world that surrounded the black island of his life, like the parade of dirty little towns that passed forever before his eyes, things that had names but not substance, things that happened and then retreated into an incomprehensible nothingness.

Saul was not dumb or lazy, but it took him seven years to reach the third grade in school. None of the people who came and went in Saul's life had ever prized learning and Saul did likewise. It was quite normal in his environment to reach the age of fourteen and still be in the third grade, and Saul liked being normal, liked being like other people.

Then the one person—his grandmother—who Saul had thought would endure forever, passed suddenly from his life, and from that moment on Saul did not ever quite know what to do. He went to work for the white people of the South and the shadowlike quality of his world became terribly manifest, continuously present. He understood nothing of this white world into which he had been thrown; it was just there, a faint and fearful shadow cast by some object that stood between him and a hidden and powerful sun.

He quickly learned that the strange white people for whom he worked considered him inferior; he did not feel inferior and he did not think that he was. But when he looked about him he saw other black people accepting this definition of themselves, and who was he to challenge it? Outwardly he grew to accept it as part of that vast shadow-world that came and went, pulled by forces which he nor nobody he knew understood.

Soon all of Saul's anxieties, fears, and irritations became focused upon this white shadow-world which gave him his daily bread in exchange for his labor. Feeling unhappy and not knowing why, he projected his misery out from himself and upon the one thing that made him most constantly anxious. If this had not happened, if Saul had not found a way of putting his burden upon others, he would have early thought of suicide. He finally did, in the end, think of killing himself, but then it was too late . . .

At the age of fifteen Saul knew that the life he was then living was to be his lot, that there was no way to rid himself of his plaguing sense of unreality, no way to relax and forget. He was most self-forgetful when he was with black people, and that made things a little easier for him. But as he grew older, he became more afraid, yet none of his friends noticed it. Indeed, many of Saul's friends liked him very much. Saul was always kind, attentive; but no one suspected that his kindness, his quiet, waiting loyalty came from his being afraid.

Then Saul changed. Maybe it was luck or misfortune; it is hard to tell. When he took a drink of whisky, he found that it helped to banish the shadows, lessened his tensions, made the world more reasonably three-dimensional, and he grew to like drinking. When he was paid off on a Saturday night, he would drink with his friends and he would feel better. He felt that whisky made life complete, that it stimulated him. But, of course, it did not. Whisky really depressed him, numbed him somewhat, reduced the force and number of the shadows that made him tight inside.

When Saul was sober, he almost never laughed in the presence of the white shadow-world, but when he had a drink or two he found that he could. Even when he was told about the hard lives that all Negroes lived, it did not worry him, for he would take a drink and not feel too badly. It did not even bother him when he heard that if you were alone with a white woman and she screamed, it was as good as hearing your death sentence, for, though you had done nothing, you would be killed. Saul got used to hearing the siren of the police car screaming in the Black Belt, got used to seeing white cops dragging Negroes off to jail. Once he grew wildly angry about it, felt that the shadows would some day claim him as he had seen them claim others, but his friends warned him that it was dangerous to feel that way, that always the black man lost, and the best thing to do was to take a drink. He did, and in a little while they were all laughing.

One night when he was mildly drunk—he was thirty years old and living in Washington at the time—he got married. The girl was good for Saul, for she too liked to drink and she was pretty and they got along together. Saul now felt that things were not so bad; as long as he could stifle the feeling of being hemmed in, as long as he could conquer the anxiety about the unexpected happening, life was bearable.

Saul's jobs had been many and simple. First he had worked on a farm. When he was fourteen he had gone to Washington, after his grandmother had died, where he did all kinds of odd jobs. Finally he was hired by an old white army colonel as chauffeur and butler and he averaged about twenty dollars every two weeks. He lived in and got his meals and uniform and he remained with the colonel for five years. The colonel too liked to drink, and sometimes they would both get drunk. But Saul never forgot that the colonel, though drunk and feeling fine, was still a shadow, unreal, and might suddenly change toward him.

One day, when whisky was making him feel good, Saul asked the colonel for a raise in salary, told him that he did not have enough to live on, and that prices were rising. But the colonel was sober and hard that day and said no. Saul was so stunned that he quit the job that instant. While under the spell of whisky he had for a quick moment felt that the world of shadows was over, but when he had asked for more money and had been refused, he knew that he had been wrong. He should not have asked for money; he should have known that the colonel was a no-good guy, a shadow.

Saul was next hired as an exterminator by a big chemical company and he found that there was something in his nature that made him like going from house to house and putting down poison for rats and mice and roaches. He liked seeing concrete evidence of his work and the dead bodies of rats were no shadows. They were real. He never felt better in his life than when he was killing with the sanction of society. And his boss even increased his salary when he asked for it. And he drank as much as he liked and no one cared.

But one morning, after a hard night of drinking which had made him irritable and high-strung, his boss said something that he did not like and he spoke up, defending himself against what he thought was a slighting remark. There was an argument and Saul left.

Two weeks of job hunting got him the position of janitor in the National Cathedral, a church and religious institution. It was the solitary kind of work he liked; he reported for duty each morning at seven o'clock and at eleven he was through. He first cleaned the Christmas card shop, next he cleaned the library; and his final chore was to clean the choir room.

But cleaning the library, with its rows and rows of books, was what caught Saul's attention, for there was a strange little shadow woman there who stared at him all the time in a most peculiar way. The library was housed in a separate building and, whenever he came to clean it, he and the white woman would be there alone. She was tiny, blonde, blue-eyed, weighing about 110 pounds, and standing about five feet three inches. Saul's boss had warned him never to quarrel with the lady in charge of the library. "She's a crackpot," he had told Saul. And naturally Saul never wanted any trouble; in fact, he did not even know the woman's name. Many times, however, he would pause in his work, feeling that his eyes were being drawn to her and he would turn around and find her staring at him. Then she would look away quickly, as though ashamed. "What in hell does she want from me?" he wondered uneasily. The woman never spoke to him except to say good morning and she even said that as though she did not want to say it. Saul thought that maybe she was afraid of him; but how could that be? He could not recall when anybody had ever been afraid of him, and he had never been in any trouble in his life.

One morning while sweeping the floor he felt his eyes being drawn toward her and he paused and turned and saw her staring at him. He did not move, neither did she. They stared at each other for about ten seconds, then she went out of the room, walking with quick steps, as though angry or afraid. He was frightened, but forgot it quickly. "What the hell's wrong with that woman?" he asked himself.

Next morning Saul's boss called him and told him, in a nice, quiet tone—but it made him scared and mad just the same—that the woman in the library had complained about him, had said that he never cleaned under her desk.

"Under her desk?" Saul asked, amazed.

"Yes," his boss said, amused at Saul's astonishment.

"But I clean under her desk every morning," Saul said.

"Well, Saul, remember, I told you she was a crackpot," his boss said soothingly. "Don't argue with her. Just do your work."

"Yes, sir," Saul said.

He wanted to tell his boss how the woman always stared at him, but he could not find courage enough to do so. If he had been talking with his black friends, he would have done so quite naturally. But why talk to one shadow about another queer shadow?

That day being payday, he got his weekly wages and that night he had a hell of a good time. He drank until he was drunk, until he blotted out almost everything from his consciousness. He was getting regularly drunk now whenever he had the money. He liked it and he bothered nobody and he was happy while doing it. But dawn found him broke, exhausted, and terribly depressed, full of shadows and uneasiness, a way he never liked it. The thought of going to his job made him angry. He longed for deep, heavy sleep. But, no, he had a good job and he had to keep it. Yes, he would go.

After cleaning the Christmas card shop—he was weak and he sweated a lot—he went to the library. No one was there. He swept the floor and was about to dust the books when he heard the footsteps of the woman coming into the room. He was tired, nervous, half asleep; his hands trembled and his reflexes were overquick. "So you're the bitch who snitched on me, hunh?" he said irritably to himself. He continued dusting and all at once he had the queer feeling that she was staring at him. He fought against the impulse to look at her, but he could not resist it. He turned slowly and saw that she was sitting in her chair at her desk, staring at him with unblinking eyes. He had the impression that she was about to speak. He could not help staring back at her, waiting.

"Why don't you clean under my desk?" she asked him in a tense but controlled voice.

"Why, ma'am," he said slowly, "I just did."

"Come here and look," she said, pointing downward.

He replaced the book on the shelf. She had never spoken so many words to him before. He went and stood before her and his mind protested against what his eyes saw, and then his senses leaped in wonder. She was sitting with her knees sprawled apart and her dress was drawn halfway up her legs. He looked from her round blue eyes to her white legs whose thighs thickened as they went to a V clothed in tight, sheer, pink panties; then he looked quickly again into her eyes. Her face was a beet red, but she sat very still, rigid, as though she was being impelled into an act which she did not want to perform but was being driven to perform. Saul was so startled that he could not move.

"I just cleaned under your desk this morning," he mumbled, sensing that he was not talking about what she meant.

"There's dust there now," she said sternly, her legs still so wide apart that he felt that she was naked.

He did not know what to do; he was so baffled, humiliated, and frightened that he grew angry. But he was afraid to express his anger openly.

"Look, ma'am," he said in a tone of suppressed rage and hate, "you're making trouble for me!"

"Why don't you do your work?" she blazed at him. "That's what you're being paid to do, you black nigger!" Her legs were still spread wide and she was sitting as though about to spring upon him and throw her naked thighs about his body.

For a moment he was still and silent. Never before in his life had he been called a "black nigger." He had heard that white people used that phrase as their supreme humiliation of black people, but he had never been treated so. As the insult sank in, as he stared at her gaping thighs, he felt overwhelmed by a sense of wild danger.

"I don't like that," he said and before he knew it he had slapped her flat across her face.

She sucked in her breath, sprang up, and stepped away from him. Then she screamed sharply, and her voice was like a lash cutting into his chest. She screamed again and he backed away from her. He felt helpless, strange; he knew what he had done, knew its meaning for him; but he knew that he could not have helped it. It seemed that some part of him was there in that room watching him do things that he should not do. He drew in his breath and for a moment he felt that he could not stand upon his legs. His world was now full of all the shadows he had ever feared. He was in the worse trouble that a black man could imagine.

The woman was screaming continuously now and he was running toward the stairs. Just as he put his foot on the bottom step, he paused and looked over his shoulder. She was backing away from him, toward an open window at the far end of the room, still screaming. Oh God! In her scream he heard the sirens of the police cars that hunted down black men in the Black Belts and he heard the shrill whistles of white cops running after black men and he felt again in one rush of emotion all the wild and bitter tales he had heard of how whites always got the black who did a crime and this woman was screaming as though he had raped her.

He ran on up the steps, but her screams were coming so loud that when he neared the top of the steps he slowed. Those screams would not let him run any more, they weakened him, tugged and pulled him. His chest felt as though it would burst. He reached the top landing and looked round aimlessly. He saw a fireplace and before it was a neat pile of wood and while he was looking at that pile of wood the screams tore at him, unnerved him. With a shaking hand he reached down and seized in his left hand—for he was left-handed—a heavy piece of oaken firewood that had jagged, sharp edges where it had been cut with an ax. He turned and ran back down the steps to where the woman stood screaming. He lifted the stick of wood as he confronted her, then paused. He wanted her to stop screaming. If she had stopped, he would have fled, but while she screamed all he could feel was a hotness bubbling in him and urging him to do something. She would fill her lungs quickly and deeply and her breath would come out at full blast. He swung down his left arm and hit her a swinging blow on the side of her head, not to hurt her, not to kill her, but to stop that awful noise, to stop that shadow from screaming a scream that meant death ... He felt her skull crack and give as she sank to the floor, but she still screamed. He trembled from head to feet. Goddamn that woman ... Why didn't she stop that yelling? He lifted his arm and gave her another blow, feeling the oaken stick driving its way into her skull. But still she screamed. He was about to hit her again when he became aware that the stick he held was light. He looked at it and found that half of it had broken off, was lying on the floor. But she screamed on, with blood running down her dress, her legs sprawled nakedly out from under her. He dropped the remainder of the stick and grabbed her throat and choked her to stop her screams. That seemed to quiet her; she looked as though she had fainted. He choked her for a long time, not trying to kill her, but just to make sure that she would not scream again and make him wild and hot inside. He was not reacting to the woman, but to the feelings that her screams evoked in him.

The woman was limp and silent now and slowly he took his hands from her throat. She was quiet. He waited. He was not certain. Yes, take her downstairs into the bathroom and if she screamed again no one would hear her ... He took her hands in his and started dragging her away from the window. His hands were wet with sweat and her hands were so tiny and soft that time and again her little fingers slipped out of his palms. He tried holding her hands tighter and only succeeded in scratching her. Her ring slid off into his hand while he was dragging her and he stood still for a moment, staring in a daze at the thin band of shimmering gold, then mechanically he put it into his pocket. Finally he dragged her down the steps to the bathroom door.

He was about to take her in when he saw that the floor was spotted with drippings of blood. That was bad ... He had been trained to keep floors clean, just as he had been trained to fear shadows. He propped her clumsily against a wall and went into the bathroom and took wads of toilet paper and mopped up the red splashes. He even went back upstairs where he had first struck her and found blood spots and wiped them up carefully. He stiffened; she was hollering again. He ran downstairs and this time he recalled that he had a knife in his pocket. He took it out, opened it, and plunged it deep into her throat; he was frantic to stop her from hollering . . . He pulled the knife from her throat and she was quiet.

He stood, his eyes roving. He noticed a door leading down to a recess in a wall through which steam pipes ran. Yes, it would be better to put her there; then if she started yelling no one would hear her. He was not trying to hide her; he merely wanted to make sure that she would not be heard. He dragged her again and her dress came up over her knees to her chest and again he saw her pink panties. It was too hard dragging her and he lifted her in his arms and while carrying her down the short flight of steps he thought that the pink panties, if he would wet them, would make a good mop to clean up the blood. Once more he sat her against the wall, stripped her of her pink panties—and not once did he so much as glance at her groin—wetted them and swabbed up the spots, then pushed her into the recess under the pipes. She was in full view, easily seen. He tossed the wet ball of panties in after her.

He sighed and looked around. The floor seemed clean. He went back upstairs. That stick of broken wood . . . He picked up the two shattered ends of wood and several splinters; he carefully joined the ends together and then fitted the splinters into place. He laid the mended stick back upon the pile before the fireplace. He stood listening, wondering if she would yell again, but there was no sound. It never occurred to him that he could help her, that she might be in pain; he never wondered even if she were dead. He got his coat and hat and went home.

He was nervously tired. It seemed that he had just finished doing an old and familiar job of dodging the shadows that were forever around him, shadows that he could not understand. He undressed, but paid no attention to the blood on his trousers and shirt; he was alone in the room; his wife was at work. When he pulled out his billfold, he saw the ring. He put it in the drawer of his night table, more to keep his wife from seeing it than to hide it. He climbed wearily into bed and at once fell into a deep, sound sleep from which he did not awaken until late afternoon. He lay blinking blood-shot eyes and he could not remember what he had done. Then the vague, shadowlike picture of it came before his eyes. He was puzzled, and for a moment he wondered if it had happened or had someone told him a story of it. He could not be sure. There was no fear or regret in him.

When at last the conviction of what he had done was real in

him, it came only in terms of flat memory, devoid of all emotion, as though he were looking when very tired and sleepy at a scene being flashed upon the screen of a movie house. Not knowing what to do, he remained in bed. He had drifted off to sleep again when his wife came home late that night from her cooking job.

Next morning he ate the breakfast his wife prepared, rose from the table and kissed her, and started off toward the Cathedral as though nothing had happened. It was not until he actually got to the Cathedral steps that he became shaky and nervous. He stood before the door for two or three minutes, and then he realized that he could not go back in there this morning. Yet it was not danger that made him feel this way, but a queer kind of repugnance. Whether the woman was alive or not did not enter his mind. He still did not know what to do. Then he remembered that his wife, before she had left for her job, had asked him to buy some groceries. Yes, he would do that. He wanted to do that because he did not know what else on earth to do.

He bought the groceries and took them home, then spent the rest of the day wandering from bar to bar. Not once did he think of fleeing. He would go home, sit, turn on the radio, then go out into the streets and walk. Finally he would end up at a bar, drinking. On one of his many trips into the house, he changed his clothes, rolled up his bloody shirt and trousers, put the blood-stained knife inside the bundle, and pushed it into a far corner of a closet. He got his gun and put it into his pocket, for he was nervously depressed.

But he still did not know what to do. Suddenly he recalled that some months ago he had bought a cheap car which was now in a garage for repairs. He went to the garage and persuaded the owner to take it back for twenty-five dollars; the thought that he could use the car for escape never came to his mind. During that afternoon and early evening he sat in bars and drank. What he felt now was no different from what he had felt all his life.

Toward eight o'clock that night he met two friends of his and invited them for a drink. He was quite drunk now. Before him on the table was a sandwich and a small glass of whisky. He leaned forward, listening sleepily to one of his friends tell a story about a girl, and then he heard:

"Aren't you Saul Saunders?"

He looked up into the faces of two white shadows.

"Yes," he admitted readily. "What do you want?"

"You'd better come along with us. We want to ask you some questions," one of the shadows said.

"What's this all about?" Saul asked.

They grabbed his shoulders and he stood up. Then he reached down and picked up the glass of whisky and drank it. He walked steadily out of the bar to a waiting auto, a policeman to each side of him, his mind a benign blank. It was not until they were about to put him into the car that something happened and whipped his numbed senses to an apprehension of danger. The policeman patted his waist for arms; they found nothing because his gun was strapped to his chest. Yes, he ought to kill himself . . . The thought leaped into his mind with such gladness that he shivered. It was the answer to everything. Why had he not thought of it before?

Slowly he took off his hat and held it over his chest to hide the movement of his left hand, then he reached inside of his shirt and pulled out the gun. One of the policemen pounced on him and snatched the gun.

"So, you're trying to kill us too, hunh?" one asked.

"Naw. I was trying to kill myself," he answered simply.

"Like hell you were!"

A fist came onto his jaw and he sank back limp.

Two hours later, at the police station, he told them everything, speaking in a low, listless voice without a trace of emotion, vividly describing every detail, yet feeling that it was utterly hopeless for him to try to make them understand how horrible it was for him to hear that woman screaming. His narrative sounded so brutal that the policemen's faces were chalky.

Weeks later a voice droned in a court room and he sat staring dully.

". . . The Grand Jurors of the United States of America, in and for the District of Columbia aforesaid, upon their oath, do present:

"That one Saul Saunders, on, to wit, the first day of March, 19—, and at and within the District of Columbia aforesaid, contriving and intending to kill one Maybelle Eva Houseman . . . "

"So *that's* her name," he said to himself in amazement.

". . . Feloniously, wilfully, purposely, and of his deliberate and premeditated malice did strike, beat, and wound the said Maybelle Eva Houseman, in and upon the front of the head and in and upon the right side of the head of her, the said Maybelle Eva Houseman, two certain mortal wounds and fractures; and did fix and fasten about the neck and throat of her, the said Maybelle Eva Houseman, his hand or hands—but whether it was one of his hands or both of his hands is to the Grand Jury aforesaid unknown—and that he, the said Saul Saunders, with his hand or hands as aforesaid fixed and fastened about the throat of her, did choke and strangle the said Maybelle Eva Houseman, of which said choking and strangling the said Maybelle Eva Houseman, on, to wit, the said first day of March, 19—, and at and within the said District of Columbia, did die."

He longed for a drink, but that was impossible now. Then he took a deep breath and surrendered to the world of shadows about him, the world he had feared so long; and at once the tension went from him and he felt better than he had felt in a long time. He was amazed at how relaxed and peaceful it was when he stopped fighting the world of shadows.

" . . . By force and violence and against resistance and by putting in fear, did steal, take, and carry away, from and off the person and from the immediate, actual possession of one Maybelle Eva Houseman, then and there being, a certain finger ring, of the value of, to wit, ten dollars."

He listened now with more attention but no anxiety:

"And in and while perpetrating robbery aforesaid did kill and murder the said Maybelle Eva Houseman; against the form of the statute in such case made and provided, and against the peace and government of the said United States of America."

P.S. Thereupon Dr. Herman Stein was called as a witness and being first duly sworn testified as follows:

" . . . On examination of the genital organs there was no evidence of contusion, abrasion, or trauma, and the decedent's hymen ring was intact. This decedent had not been criminally assaulted or attempted to be entered. It has been ascertained that the decedent's age was 40."

——*For Discussion*——

RPW—

Saul Saunders, a poor Southern black man, lives in the shadow of the white world of segregation. He cannot get an emotional grip on his life. His mother and father die when he is very young. Sepa-

rated from his five brothers and two sisters, he moves from place to place with his grandmother until she too passes suddenly from his life. As he grows to fear what he does not know, especially the white shadows that surround him, only whiskey seems to relieve his anxiety and tension, blunting his rage and making life bearable. For Saul, only "the dead bodies of rats" that he kills as an exterminator are real, substantive evidence of what he can do.

Eventually Saul goes to work as a janitor in the National Cathedral, where he encounters a "queer shadow," a middle-aged white woman, who insists that he clean under her desk. Saul and the woman are shadows to each other and in a sense shadows to themselves. I think they are both forced into acts that they do not want to perform. With her dress "drawn halfway up her legs," the white woman seems anxious to be caught in the black man's gaze, ready to spring with naked thighs onto his sexed body. And for Saul Saunders, such apparent desire overwhelms with its "sense of wild danger," as he is split in two, watching himself do what he knows he should not do.

When the white woman begins to scream, Saul can only hear that scream as a death sentence for him as a black man. He does not think of her as a human being, or even as a sexual object; she is simply a shadow to him, a scream that must be silenced. After he kills her, he does not think of fleeing. The experience is emotionally flat for him, a fleeting encounter with a shadow, an event that he will never be able to explain.

At his trial, the courtroom brims with the official language of white shadow justice, offering up one version of the events but certainly not Saul's story. We learn that Saul's victim did have a name, Maybelle Eva Houseman, that she was forty years old, and that she died a virgin. We do not hear Saul's voice at the trial, but we know that he is "relaxed and peaceful" at last. He has "surrendered to the world of shadows about him." He has given up the struggle of life.

JRT—

Eldridge Cleaver, who spent years in prison, first on a marijuana charge and later for rape, calls the white woman "the ogre" in Soul on Ice, letting her symbolize all that is not attainable for black men in a world where white men rule. After serving time for minor drug charges, Cleaver's anger, fueled by incarceration, led him to rape white women, after practicing on blacks. Cleaver shows how his rage at being denied access to the privileges of good education, safe streets, and secure jobs led him to this thinking and to thought patterns which he later reviles when he returns to prison. He says the price for hating others is hating oneself and, in a sense, putting one's soul on ice.

Wright too gives us a character who is denied access to the world of white men. Wright shows us how it is almost logical that Saul Sanders lives unobtrusively in a world of shadows, much like Cleaver. Here Saul lives in the "shadow of his fears." Wright says in the first paragraph that Saul "lived to kill one of them," implying that it was destiny that Saul would kill that which provoked his fear. Fears of what? Of never being accepted as a full member of society; of never being permitted the fruits of security; of always being the blackhearted soul. We, however, in the 1990s hope that Saul can learn other ways to deal with a broken childhood, mediocre bosses, no support, and even a world dominated still by racism and brutality. Unlike Cleaver, Wright's antihero does not regret his actions, shows no remorse, and is only relieved when at last he is convicted of murdering the white woman, the symbol of all his torments. He "had to kill" her to stop her from haunting him.

Symbolism aside, it's tedious for women to be used to represent what men can't get. We take a lot of abuse for desiring what we can't have, tempting innocent men, and over and over providing the apple in the garden of Eden. Saul falls and pays dearly. We're reduced to symbols and don't even get a chance.

But seriously, couldn't a real Saul find a way out? Is Wright's message that society is so hopelessly stacked against a black man that he is forced into crime? I don't believe that Wright aims us towards that conclusion. The shadow world is there for all of us, no matter what gender, race, or background. It seems that Saul needs a friend other than alcohol, something to do with his life, a family that means something to him, and the belief that he can carve out a place for himself in this world. Cleaver did, and once he left blaming the ogre behind, he found personal responsibility in spite of a crippled world. What are the options that Saul has today?

I Stand Here Ironing

Tillie Olsen

I stand here ironing, and what you asked me moves tormented back and forth with the iron.

"I wish you would manage the time to come in and talk with me about your daughter. I'm sure you can help me understand her. She's a youngster who needs help and whom I'm deeply interested in helping."

"Who needs help." . . . Even if I came, what good would it do? You think because I am her mother I have a key, or that in some way you could use me as a key? She has lived for nineteen years. There is all that life that has happened outside of me, beyond me.

And when is there time to remember, to sift, to weigh, to estimate, to total? I will start and there will be an interruption and I will have to gather it all together again. Or I will become engulfed with all I did or did not do, with what should have been and what cannot be helped.

She was a beautiful baby. The first and only one of our five that was beautiful at birth. You do not guess how new and uneasy her tenancy in her now-loveliness. You did not know her all those years she was thought homely, or see her poring over her baby pictures, making me tell her over and over how beautiful she had been—and would be, I would tell her—and was now, to the seeing eye. But the seeing eyes were few or nonexistent. Including mine.

I nursed her. They feel that's important nowadays. I nursed all the children, but with her, with all the fierce rigidity of first motherhood, I did like the books then said. Though her cries battered me to trembling and my breasts ached with swollenness, I waited till the clock decreed.

Why do I put that first? I do not even know if it matters, or if it explains anything.

She was a beautiful baby. She blew shining bubbles of sound. She loved motion, loved light, loved color and music and textures. She would lie on the floor in her blue overalls patting the surface so hard in ecstasy her hands and feet would blur. She was a miracle to me, but when she was eight months old I had to leave her daytimes with the woman downstairs to whom she was no miracle at

all, for I worked or looked for work and for Emily's father, who
"could no longer endure" (he wrote in his good-bye note) "sharing
want with us."

I was nineteen. It was the pre-relief, pre-WPA world of the depression. I would start running as soon as I got off the streetcar,
running up the stairs, the place smelling sour, and awake or asleep
to startle awake, when she saw me she would break into a clogged
weeping that could not be comforted, a weeping I can hear yet.

After a while I found a job hashing at night so I could be with
her days, and it was better. But it came to where I had to bring her
to his family and leave her.

It took a long time to raise the money for her fare back. Then
she got chicken pox and I had to wait longer. When she finally
came, I hardly knew her, walking quick and nervous like her father, looking like her father, thin, and dressed in a shoddy red that
yellowed her skin and glared at the pockmarks. All the baby love-
liness gone.

She was two. Old enough for nursery school they said, and I did
not know then what I know now—the fatigue of the long day, and
the lacerations of group life in the kinds of nurseries that are only
parking places for children.

Except that it would have made no difference if I had known.
It was the only place there was. It was the only way we could be
together, the only way I could hold a job.

And even without knowing, I knew. I knew the teacher that
was evil because all these years it has curdled into my memory,
the little boy hunched in the corner, her rasp, "why aren't you outside, because Alvin hits you? that's no reason, go out, scaredy." I
knew Emily hated it even if she did not clutch and implore "don't
go Mommy" like the other children, mornings.

She always had a reason why we should stay home. Momma,
you look sick. Momma, I feel sick. Momma, the teachers aren't
there today, they're sick. Momma, we can't go, there was a fire
there last night. Momma, it's a holiday today, no school, they
told me.

But never a direct protest, never rebellion. I think of our others
in their three-, four-year-oldness—the explosions, the tempers, the
denunciations, the demands—and I feel suddenly ill. I put the iron
down. What in me demanded that goodness in her? And what was
the cost, the cost to her of such goodness?

The old man living in the back once said in his gentle way: "You should smile at Emily more when you look at her." What *was* in my face when I looked at her? I loved her. There were all the acts of love.

It was only with the others I remembered what he said, and it was the face of joy, and not of care or tightness or worry I turned to them—too late for Emily. She does not smile easily, let alone almost always as her brothers and sisters do. Her face is closed and somber, but when she wants, how fluid. You must have seen it in her pantomimes, you spoke of her rare gift for comedy on the stage that rouses laughter out of the audience so dear they applaud and applaud and do not want to let her go.

Where does it come from, that comedy? There was none of it in her when she came back to me that second time, after I had had to send her away again. She had a new daddy now to learn to love, and I think perhaps it was a better time.

Except when we left her alone nights, telling ourselves she was old enough.

"Can't you go some other time, Mommy, like tomorrow?" she would ask. "Will it be just a little while you'll be gone? Do you promise?"

The time we came back, the front door open, the clock on the floor in the hall. She rigid awake. "It wasn't just a little while. I didn't cry. Three times I called you, just three times, and then I ran downstairs to open the door so you could come faster. The clock talked loud. I threw it away, it scared me what it talked."

She said the clock talked loud again that night I went to the hospital to have Susan. She was delirious with the fever that comes from red measles, but she was fully conscious all the week I was gone and the week after we were home when she could not come near the new baby or me.

She did not get well. She stayed skeleton thin, not wanting to eat, and night after night she had nightmares. She would call for me, and I would rouse from exhaustion to sleepily call back: "You're all right, darling, go to sleep, it's just a dream," and if she still called, in a sterner voice, "now go to sleep, Emily, there's nothing to hurt you." Twice, only twice, when I had to get up for Susan anyhow, I went in to sit with her.

Now when it is too late (as if she would let me hold and comfort her like I do the others) I get up and go to her at once at her moan or restless stirring. "Are you awake, Emily? Can I get you something?" And the answer is always the same: "No, I'm all right, go back to sleep, Mother."

They persuaded me at the clinic to send her away to a convalescent home in the country where "she can have the kind of food and care you can't manage for her, and you'll be free to concentrate on the new baby." They still send children to that place. I see pictures on the society page of sleek young women planning affairs to raise money for it, or dancing at the affairs, or decorating Easter eggs or filling Christmas stockings for the children.

They never have a picture of the children so I do not know if the girls still wear those gigantic red bows and the ravaged looks on the every other Sunday when parents can come to visit "unless otherwise notified"—as we were notified the first six weeks.

Oh it is a handsome place, green lawns and tall trees and fluted flower beds. High up on the balconies of each cottage the children stand, the girls in their red bows and white dresses, the boys in white suits and giant red ties. The parents stand below shrieking up to be heard and the children shriek down to be heard, and between them the invisible wall: "Not to Be Contaminated by Parental Germs or Physical Affection."

There was a tiny girl who always stood hand in hand with Emily. Her parents never came. One visit she was gone. "They moved her to Rose Cottage," Emily shouted in explanation. "They don't like you to love anybody here."

She wrote once a week, the labored writing of a seven-year-old. "I am fine. How is the baby. If I write my leter nicly I will have a star. Love." There never was a star. We wrote every other day, letters she could never hold or keep but only hear read—once. "We simply do not have room for children to keep any personal possessions," they patiently explained when we pieced one Sunday's shrieking together to plead how much it would mean to Emily, who loved so to keep things, to be allowed to keep her letters and cards.

Each visit she looked frailer. "She isn't eating," they told us.

(They had runny eggs for breakfast or mush with lumps, Emily said later, I'd hold it in my mouth and not swallow. Nothing ever tasted good, just when they had chicken.)

It took us eight months to get her released home, and only the fact that she gained back so little of her seven lost pounds convinced the social worker.

I used to try to hold and love her after she came back, but her body would stay stiff, and after a while she'd push away. She ate little. Food sickened her, and I think much of life too. Oh she had physical lightness and brightness, twinkling by on skates, bouncing like a ball up and down up and down over the jump rope, skimming over the hill: but these were momentary.

She fretted about her appearance, thin and dark and foreign-looking at a time when every little girl was supposed to look or thought she should look a chubby blonde replica of Shirley Temple. The doorbell sometimes rang for her, but no one seemed to come and play in the house or be a best friend. Maybe because we moved so much.

There was a boy she loved painfully through two school semesters. Months later she told me how she had taken pennies from my purse to buy him candy. "Licorice was his favorite and I brought him some every day, but he still liked Jennifer better'n me. Why, Mommy?" The kind of question for which there is no answer.

School was a worry to her. She was not glib or quick in a world where glibness and quickness were easily confused with ability to learn. To her overworked and exasperated teachers she was an over-conscientious "slow learner" who kept trying to catch up and was absent entirely too often.

I let her be absent, though sometimes the illness was imaginary. How different from my now-strictness about attendance with the others. I wasn't working. We had a new baby, I was home anyhow. Sometimes, after Susan grew old enough, I would keep her home from school, too, to have them all together.

Mostly Emily had asthma, and her breathing, harsh and labored, would fill the house with a curiously tranquil sound. I would bring the two old dresser mirrors and her boxes of collections to her bed. She would select beads and single earrings, bottle tops and shells, dried flowers and pebbles, old postcards and scraps, all sorts of oddments; then she and Susan would play Kingdom, setting up landscapes and furniture, peopling them with action.

Those were the only times of peaceful companionship between her and Susan. I have edged away from it, that poisonous feeling between them, that terrible balancing of hurts and needs I had to do between the two, and did so badly, those earlier years.

Oh there are conflicts between the others too, each one human, needing, demanding, hurting, taking—but only between Emily and Susan, no, Emily toward Susan that corroding resentment. It seems so obvious on the surface, yet it is not obvious. Susan, the second child, Susan, golden- and curly-haired and chubby, quick and articulate and assured, everything in appearance and manner Emily was not; Susan, not able to resist Emily's precious things, losing or sometimes clumsily breaking them; Susan telling jokes and riddles to company for applause while Emily sat silent (to say to me later: that was *my* riddle, Mother, I told it to Susan); Susan, who for all the five years' difference in age was just a year behind Emily in developing physically.

I am glad for that slow physical development that widened the difference between her and her contemporaries, though she suffered over it. She was too vulnerable for that terrible world of youthful competition, of preening and parading, of constant measuring of yourself against every other, of envy, "If I had the copper hair," "If I had that skin. . . . " She tormented herself enough about not looking like the others, there was enough of the unsureness, the having to be conscious of words before you speak, the constant caring—what are they thinking of me? without having it all magnified by the merciless physical drives.

Ronnie is calling. He is wet and I change him. It is rare there is such a cry now. That time of motherhood is almost behind me when the ear is not one's own but must always be racked and listening for the child cry, the child call. We sit for a while and I hold him, looking out over the city spread in charcoal with its soft aisles of light. "*Shoogily,*" he breathes and curls closer. I carry him back to bed, asleep. *Shoogily.* A funny word, a family word, inherited from Emily, invented by her to say: *comfort.*

In this and other ways she leaves her seal, I say aloud. And startle at my saying it. What do I mean? What did I start to gather together, to try and make coherent? I was at the terrible, growing years. War years. I do not remember them well. I was working, there were four smaller ones now, there was not time for her. She had to help be a mother, and housekeeper, and shopper. She had to set her seal. Mornings of crisis and near hysteria trying to get lunches packed, hair combed, coats and shoes found, everyone to school or Child Care on time, the baby ready for transportation. And always the paper scribbled on by a smaller one, the book looked at by Susan then mislaid, the homework not done. Running out to that huge school where she was one, she was lost, she was a drop; suffering over the unpreparedness, stammering and unsure in her classes.

There was so little time left at night after the kids were bedded down. She would struggle over books, always eating (it was in those years she developed her enormous appetite that is legendary in our family) and I would be ironing, or preparing food for the next day, or writing V-mail to Bill, or tending the baby. Sometimes, to make me laugh, or out of her despair, she would imitate happenings or types at school.

I think I said once: "Why don't you do something like this in the school amateur show?" One morning she phoned me at work, hardly understandable through the weeping: "Mother, I did it. I won, I won; they gave me first prize; they clapped and clapped and wouldn't let me go."

Now suddenly she was Somebody, and as imprisoned in her difference as she had been in anonymity.

She began to be asked to perform at other high schools, even in colleges, then at city and statewide affairs. The first one we went to, I only recognized her that first moment when thin, shy, she almost drowned herself into the curtains. Then: Was this Emily? The control, the command, the convulsing and deadly clowning, the spell, then the roaring, stamping audience, unwilling to let this rare and precious laughter out of their lives.

Afterwards: You ought to do something about her with a gift like that—but without money or knowing how, what does one do? We have left it all to her, and the gift has as often eddied inside, clogged and clotted, as been used and growing.

She is coming. She runs up the stairs two at a time with her light graceful step, and I know she is happy tonight. Whatever it was that occasioned your call did not happen today.

"Aren't you ever going to finish the ironing, Mother? Whistler painted his mother in a rocker. I'd have to paint mine standing over an ironing board." This is one of her communicative nights and she tells me everything and nothing as she fixes herself a plate of food out of the icebox.

She is so lovely. Why did you want me to come in at all? Why were you concerned? She will find her way.

She starts up the stairs to bed. "Don't get me up with the rest in the morning." "But I thought you were having midterms." "Oh, those," she comes back in, kisses me, and says quite lightly, "in a couple of years when we'll all be atom-dead they won't matter a bit."

She has said it before. She *believes* it. But because I have been dredging the past, and all that compounds a human being is so heavy and meaningful in me, I cannot endure it tonight.

I will never total it all. I will never come in to say: She was a child seldom smiled at. Her father left me before she was a year old. I had to work her first six years when there was work, or I sent her home and to his relatives. There were years she had care she hated. She was dark and thin and foreign-looking in a world where the prestige went to blondeness and curly hair and dimples, she was slow where glibness was prized. She was a child of anxious, not proud, love. We were poor and could not afford for her the soil of easy growth. I was a young mother, I was a distracted mother. There were other children pushing up, demanding. Her younger sister seemed all that she was not. There were years she did not want me to touch her. She kept too much in herself, her life was such she had to keep too much in herself. My wisdom came too late. She has much to her and probably little will come of it. She is a child of her age, of depression, of war, of fear.

Let her be. So all that is in her will not bloom—but in how many does it? There is still enough left to live by. Only help her to know—help make it so there is cause for her to know—that she is more than this dress on the ironing board, helpless before the iron.

——*For Discussion*——

JRT—

I often use this story at the first class of Changing Lives, when women are nervous about their ability to succeed and their fear goes back and forth like the iron in Olsen's story. I read it aloud to them while they follow along. There are mixed reactions. Surprise that this took place in the Depression, before Welfare and at a time when men without jobs left their wives out of shame. Anger that the mother had more children when Emily seemed so unprovided for. Sympathy for the narrator's attempt to make up love she can never make up, and concern for Emily, the daughter, who may have overcome her crippled past through performing on stage.

The story serves as a springboard for readers to see that there exists more than one point of view. The mother goes back and forth with her anxieties about her daughter (as only a mother can?), and Emily tugs at us with worry (what will become of her?). The story also shows concern about how we all live our lives, implying that reconsideration, reevaluation, and making tough choices are not the province of the few but of the many.

This story also asks us to think about Emily. She seems neglected, maybe even abandoned. Yet Emily is loved, as the mother shows us over and over, in spite of the fact that the mother couldn't always do her best. She is thought about, agonized over, and as we discover, raised without Welfare. She is the cause of the mother's prayer at the end of the story. What does it mean to not be the "dress on the ironing board, helpless before the iron"? What does it mean to have the child or be the child of a mother who raises you alone? What difference is there in birth order to the way we feel about our children?

RPW—

The narrator, a mother, moves, like the iron, back and forth over the past, giving voice to her own private response to a request from her daughter Emily's counselor to come in and talk with her. The mother knows she cannot "total it all" for the well-meaning bureaucrat, nor does she want to. Instead, standing over her ironing board, she attempts to understand a mother's "anxious love," a mother-daughter relationship shaped by a tightness of worry and fostered by an age of depression, war, and fear.

There is a sense of necessity and circumstance here: poverty shaming a father until he abandons the household; a single mother obligated to leave her daughter so she can work; and then "a new daddy" having little to do with Emily. Understandably, there is not much "motherly warmth" for this daughter either: few smiles for Emily to respond to, few moments of attention even after her sister Susan is born.

Yet Emily is more than the "dress on the ironing board, helpless before the iron." She is "thin and dark," "not glib or quick," slow in physical development, asthmatic. She has few friends, is disappointed in young love, and cannot compete with her younger sister. But she has left "her seal" on the family. Emily has a legendary appetite; she has given the word "shoogily" (comfort) to the family as part of its inherited discourse; and she can capture an audience with her comic pantomimes. Her gift will not fully flourish, but how many gifts do?

The mother in this story is driven by the relentless rhythm of the iron, yet she is the one ironing. In the same sense, she is driven by necessity, yet is able to reveal that necessity through her use *of language. Her hope is that Emily will be left free ("Let her be") to develop her life as best she can in the midst of all of life's limitations. It is a mark of her tenacity and courage that she can accept the belief that she is a mother who has done what she can for her daughter.*

This mother is free of sentimentality and constricted judgment. She is more than a mere victim of life, and she gives cause for her daughter to know that she need not be a victim either. To me, she is heroic.

The Wife's Story

Ursula K. Le Guin

He was a good husband, a good father. I don't understand it. I don't believe in it. I don't believe that it happened. I saw it happen but it isn't true. It can't be. He was always gentle. If you'd have seen him playing with the children, anybody who saw him with the children would have known that there wasn't any bad in him, not one mean bone. When I first met him he was still living with his mother, over near Spring Lake, and I used to see them together, the mother and the sons, and think that any young fellow that was that nice with his family must be one worth knowing. Then one time when I was walking in the woods I met him by himself coming back from a hunting trip. He hadn't got any game at all, not so much as a field mouse, but he wasn't cast down about it. He was just larking along enjoying the morning air. That's one of the things I first loved about him. He didn't take things hard, he didn't grouch and whine when things didn't go his way. So we got to talking that day. And I guess things moved right along after that, because pretty soon he was over here pretty near all the time. And my sister said—see, my parents had moved out the year before and gone south, leaving us the place—my sister said, kind of teasing but serious, "Well! If he's going to be here every day and half the night, I guess there isn't room for me!" And she moved out—just down the way. We've always been real close, her and me. That's the sort of thing doesn't ever change. I couldn't ever have got through this bad time without my sis.

Well, so he come to live here. And all I can say is, it was the happy year of my life. He was just purely good to me. A hard worker and never lazy, and so big and fine-looking. Everybody looked up to him, you know, young as he was. Lodge Meeting nights, more and more often they had him to lead the singing. He had such a beautiful voice, and he'd lead off strong, and the others following and joining in, high voices and low. It brings the shivers on me now to think of it, hearing it, nights when I'd stayed home from meeting when the children was babies—the singing coming up through the trees there, and the moonlight, summer nights, the full moon shining. I'll never hear anything so beautiful. I'll never know a joy like that again.

It was the moon, that's what they say. It's the moon's fault, and the blood. It was in his father's blood. I never knew his father, and now I wonder what become of him. He was from up Whitewater way, and had no kin around here. I always thought he went back there, but now I don't know. There was some talk about him, tales, that come out after what happened to my husband. It's something runs in the blood, they say, and it may never come out, but if it does, it's the change of the moon that does it. Always it happens in the dark of the moon. When everybody's home and asleep. Something comes over the one that's got the curse in his blood, they say, and he gets up because he can't sleep, and goes out into the glaring sun, and goes off all alone—drawn to find those like him.

And it may be so, because my husband would do that. I'd half rouse and say, "Where you going to?" and he'd say, "Oh, hunting, be back this evening," and it wasn't like him, even his voice was different. But I'd be so sleepy, and not wanting to wake the kids, and he was so good and responsible, it was no call of mine to go asking "Why?" and "Where?" and all like that.

So it happened that way maybe three times or four. He'd come back late, and worn out, and pretty near cross for one so sweet-tempered—not wanting to talk about it. I figured everybody got to bust out now and then, and nagging never helped anything. But it did begin to worry me. Not so much that he went, but that he come back so tired and strange. Even, he smelled strange. It made my hair stand up on end. I could not endure it and I said, "What is that—those smells on you? All over you!" And he said, "I don't know," real short, and made like he was sleeping. But he went down when he thought I wasn't noticing, and washed and washed himself. But those smells stayed in his hair, and in our bed, for days.

And then the awful thing. I don't find it easy to tell about this. I want to cry when I have to bring it to my mind. Our youngest, the little one, my baby, she turned from her father. Just overnight. He come in and she got scared-looking, stiff, with her eyes wide, and then she begun to cry and try to hide behind me. She didn't yet talk plain but she was saying over and over, "Make it go away! Make it go away!"

The look in his eyes, just for one moment, when he heard that.

That's what I don't want ever to remember. That's what I can't forget. The look in his eyes looking at his own child.

I said to the child, "Shame on you, what's got into you!"—scolding, but keeping her right up close to me at the same time, because I was frightened too. Frightened to shaking.

He looked away then and said something like, "Guess she just waked up dreaming," and passed it off that way. Or tried to. And so did I. And I got real mad with my baby when she kept on acting crazy scared of her own dad. But she couldn't help it and I couldn't change it.

He kept away that whole day. Because he knew, I guess. It was just beginning dark of the moon.

It was hot and close inside, and dark, and we'd all been asleep some while, when something woke me up. He wasn't there beside me. I heard a little stir in the passage, when I listened. So I got up, because I could bear it no longer. I went out into the passage, and it was light there, hard sunlight coming in from the door. And I saw him standing just outside, in the tall grass by the entrance. His head was hanging. Presently he sat down, like he felt weary, and looked down at his feet. I held still, inside, and watched—I didn't know what for.

And I saw what he saw. I saw the changing. In his feet, it was, first. They got long, each foot got longer, stretching out, the toes stretching out and the foot getting long, and fleshy, and white. And no hair on them.

The hair begun to come away all over his body. It was like his hair fried away in the sunlight and was gone. He was white all over, then, like a worm's skin. And he turned his face. It was changing while I looked. It got flatter and flatter, the mouth flat and wide, and the teeth grinning flat and dull, and the nose just a knob of flesh with nostril holes, and the ears gone, and the eyes gone blue—blue, with white rims around the blue—staring at me out of that flat, soft, white face.

He stood up then on two legs.

I saw him, I had to see him, my own dear love, turned into the hateful one.

I couldn't move, but as I crouched there in the passage staring out into the day I was trembling and shaking with a growl that burst out into a crazy, awful howling. A grief howl and a terror howl and a calling howl. And the others heard it, even sleeping, and woke up.

It stared and peered, that thing my husband had turned into, and shoved its face up to the entrance of our house. I was still bound by mortal fear, but behind me the children had waked up, and the baby was whimpering. The mother anger come into me then, and I snarled and crept forward.

The man thing looked around. It had no gun, like the ones from the man places do. But it picked up a heavy fallen tree branch in its long white foot, and shoved the end of that down into our house, at me. I snapped the end of it in my teeth and started to force my way out, because I knew the man would kill our children if it could. But my sister was already coming. I saw her running at the man with her head low and her mane high and her eyes yellow as the winter sun. It turned on her and raised up that branch to hit her. But I come out of the doorway, mad with the mother anger, and the others all were coming answering my call, the whole pack gathering, there in that blind glare and heat of the sun at noon.

The man looked round at us and yelled out loud, and brandished the branch it held. Then it broke and ran, heading for the cleared fields and plowlands, down the mountainside. It ran, on two legs, leaping and weaving, and we followed it.

I was last, because love still bound the anger and the fear in me. I was running when I saw them pull it down. My sister's teeth were in its throat. I got there and it was dead. The others were drawing back from the kill, because of the taste of the blood, and the smell. The younger ones were cowering and some crying, and my sister rubbed her mouth against her forelegs over and over to get rid of the taste. I went up close because I thought if the thing was dead the spell, the curse must be done, and my husband could come back—alive, or even dead, if I could only see him, my true love, in his true form, beautiful. But only the dead man lay there white and bloody. We drew back and back from it, and turned and ran, back up into the hills, back to the woods of the shadows and the twilight and the blessed dark.

——*For Discussion*——

JRT—

Ursula Le Guin is a science fiction writer who tricks us in this story. At first we imagine werewolves, but lo and behold, as we reread, we see that the man is not turning into a wolf. The wolf is turning into a man: his skin is like a "worm's"; his body becomes tall and long; "he stood up on two legs." After that passage where we have been stumped, then delighted, we're voracious. We go back over and over, noticing how cleverly Le Guin sets us up. The male goes hunting. He joins his friends and sings at the lodge. "It always happens in the dark of the moon." All of the references we thought were about females are about female wolves: "my own dear love. . . . my sister's teeth." So, the first level of this tale seems to be based on reversals.

The next level seems to be about men and women. Even the female wolf fears when her mate comes home and smells strange. Le Guin's implication is that men can change, are able to intimidate their spouses, even their children in this duality. On the one hand, he was gentle. Then he changes into "the hateful one," a man instead of a wolf, but also an abuser of sorts, a father who puts fear into the youngest with "the look in his eyes." We feel shades of sex-abuse, physical battering, and emotional scarring, partly because of the prevalence of violence in our world, and also because of the way Le Guin tells the story. The female wolves in the story must kill the hateful one, or else he will kill them, send his stick into their house and destroy the family's lair. By the end of the tale, we have domestic violence and women who kill to protect their young. Not the best answer, we say, but Le Guin draws us in partially because the narrator, the female wolf, seems so innocent.

The story is most enjoyable to me as a way to think how we might be perceived by animals. Humans are so self-centered, Le Guin seems to say, that we forget that other creatures exist. Her tricking us is exactly the point. We could never imagine this tale as one about wolves because we are so centered on our own civilization. We may be the ones with the curse in our blood if we do not take care of our environment, enact laws about senseless killing of animals, and nurture our pack.

RPW—

We are not accustomed to stories about animals turning into human beings (or at least, "a man thing"); nor do we usually anticipate a story about "mother anger" when the world seems so full of male violence. Betrayal, however, is something we know all too well.

As the wife tells us: "He was a good husband, a good father. I

don't understand it. I don't believe in it. I don't believe that it happened. I saw it happen but it isn't true." We don't want to believe
"it happened," but "it" did: a metamorphosis, a transformation,
a change from animal to "wereman," from good husband to "the
enemy."

He seemed like the perfect husband and father, gentle and caring, leading the singing at the Lodge Meeting, respected by the
community. So what happened? Like so many others, he was
drawn to find those like himself, those who have the curse in their
blood, those like his father before him. His own child begins to
find him strange, and then the wife herself witnesses firsthand the
metamorphosis. He becomes a white man, standing on two legs.
He becomes "the other," "the hateful one," a violent man filled
with blood lust.

What can a wife do at such a moment? Stalked by a man with
a weapon ready to kill, she is filled with fear and grief, terror and
rage. She calls her pack together, and led by her sister, they attack,
in turn, with their own blood lust. The wife hopes that this will
exorcise the demon, get rid of the curse, and bring her good husband back in his full beauty. But if that were to happen, we would
simply be listening to a fairy tale, and this is not that kind of
fantasy; it is a wife's story. He is a dead white man who would
never have returned to his youthful days of joy and family.

And the wife? She can go back with those she can count on,
back to the shadows, the twilight, the "blessed darkness."

from THE BLUEST EYE

Toni Morrison

HEREISTHEFAMILYMOTHERFATHER
DICKANDJANETHEYLIVEINTHEGREE
NANDWHITEHOUSETHEYAREVERYH

The Breedloves did not live in a storefront because they were having temporary difficulty adjusting to the cutbacks at the plant. They lived there because they were poor and black, and they stayed there because they believed they were ugly. Although their poverty was traditional and stultifying, it was not unique. But their ugliness was unique. No one could have convinced them that they were not relentlessly and aggressively ugly. Except for the father, Cholly, whose ugliness (the result of despair, dissipation, and violence directed toward petty things and weak people) was behavior, the rest of the family—Mrs. Breedlove, Sammy Breedlove, and Pecola Breedlove—wore their ugliness, put it on, so to speak, although it did not belong to them. The eyes, the small eyes set closely together under narrow foreheads. The low, irregular hairlines, which seemed even more irregular in contrast to the straight, heavy eyebrows which nearly met. Keen but crooked noses, with insolent nostrils. They had high cheekbones, and their ears turned forward. Shapely lips which called attention not to themselves but to the rest of the face. You looked at them and wondered why they were so ugly; you looked closely and could not find the source. Then you realized that it came from conviction, their conviction. It was as though some mysterious all-knowing master had given each one a cloak of ugliness to wear, and they had each accepted it without question. The master had said, "You are ugly people." They had looked about themselves and saw nothing to contradict the statement; saw, in fact, support for it leaning at them from every billboard, every movie, every glance. "Yes," they had said. "You are right." And they took the ugliness in their hands, threw it as a mantle over them, and went about the world with it. Dealing with it each according to his way. Mrs. Breedlove handled hers as an actor does a prop: for the articulation of character, for support of a role she frequently imagined was hers—martyrdom. Sammy used his as a weapon to cause others pain. He adjusted his behavior to it, chose his companions on the basis of it: people who could be fascinated, even intimidated by it. And Pecola. She hid behind hers. Concealed, veiled, eclipsed—peeping out from behind the shroud very seldom, and then only to yearn for the return of her mask.

This family, on a Saturday morning in October, began, one by one, to stir out of their dreams of affluence and vengeance into the anonymous misery of their storefront.

Mrs. Breedlove slipped noiselessly out of bed, put a sweater on over her nightgown (which was an old day dress), and walked toward the kitchen. Her one good foot made hard, bony sounds; the twisted one whispered on the linoleum. In the kitchen she made noises with doors, faucets, and pans. The noises were hollow, but the threats they implied were not. Pecola opened her eyes and lay staring at the dead coal stove. Cholly mumbled, thrashed about in the bed for a minute, and then was quiet.

Even from where Pecola lay, she could smell Cholly's whiskey. The noises in the kitchen became louder and less hollow. There was direction and purpose in Mrs. Breedlove's movements that had nothing to do with the preparation of breakfast. This awareness, supported by ample evidence from the past, made Pecola tighten her stomach muscles and ration her breath.

Cholly had come home drunk. Unfortunately he had been too drunk to quarrel, so the whole business would have to erupt this morning. Because it had not taken place immediately, the oncoming fight would lack spontaneity; it would be calculated, uninspired, and deadly.

Mrs. Breedlove came swiftly into the room and stood at the foot of the bed where Cholly lay.

"I need some coal in this house."

Cholly did not move.

"Hear me?" Mrs. Breedlove jabbed Cholly's foot.

Cholly opened his eyes slowly. They were red and menacing. With no exception, Cholly had the meanest eyes in town.

"Awwwwww, woman!"

"I said I need some coal. It's as cold as a witch's tit in this house. Your whiskey ass wouldn't feel hellfire, but I'm cold. I got to do a lot of things, but I ain't got to freeze."

"Leave me 'lone."

"Not until you get me some coal. If working like a mule don't give me the right to be warm, what am I doing it for? You sure ain't bringing in nothing. If it was left up to you, we'd all be dead. . . . " Her voice was like an earache in the brain. " . . . If you think I'm going to wade out in the cold and get it myself, you'd better think again."

"I don't give a shit how you get it." A bubble of violence burst in his throat.

"You going to get your drunk self out of that bed and get me some coal or not?"

Silence.

"Cholly!"

Silence.

"Don't try me this morning, man. You say one more word, and I'll split you open!"

Silence.

"All right. All right. But if I sneeze once, just once, God help your butt!"

Sammy was awake now too, but pretending to be asleep. Pecola still held her stomach muscles taut and conserved her breath. They all knew that Mrs. Breedlove could have, would have, and had, gotten coal from the shed, or that Sammy or Pecola could be directed to get it. But the unquarreled evening hung like the first note of a dirge in sullenly expectant air. An escapade of drunkenness, no matter how routine, had its own ceremonial close. The tiny, undistinguished days that Mrs. Breedlove lived were identified, grouped, and classed by these quarrels. They gave substance to the minutes and hours otherwise dim and unrecalled. They relieved the tiresomeness of poverty, gave grandeur to the dead rooms. In these violent breaks in routine that were themselves routine, she could display the style and imagination of what she believed to be her own true self. To deprive her of these fights was to deprive her of all the zest and reasonableness of life. Cholly, by his habitual drunkenness and orneriness, provided them both with the material they needed to make their lives tolerable. Mrs. Breedlove considered herself an upright and Christian woman, burdened with a no-count man, whom God wanted her to punish. (Cholly was beyond redemption, of course, and redemption was hardly the point—Mrs. Breedlove was not interested in Christ the Redeemer, but rather Christ the Judge.) Often she could be heard discoursing with Jesus about Cholly, pleading with Him to help her "strike the bastard down from his pea-knuckle of pride." And once when a drunken gesture catapulted Cholly into the red-hot stove, she screamed, "Get him, Jesus! Get him!" If Cholly had stopped drinking, she would never have forgiven Jesus. She needed Cholly's sins desperately. The lower he sank, the wilder and more irresponsible he became, the more splendid she and her task became. In the name of Jesus.

No less did Cholly need her. She was one of the few things abhorrent to him that he could touch and therefore hurt. He poured out on her the sum of all his inarticulate fury and aborted desires. Hating her, he could leave himself intact. When he was still very young, Cholly had been surprised in some bushes by two white men while he was newly but earnestly engaged in eliciting sexual pleasure from a little country girl. The men had shone a flashlight right on his behind. He had stopped, terrified. They chuckled. The beam of the flashlight did not move. "Go on," they said. "Go on and finish. And, nigger, make it good." The flashlight did not move. For some reason Cholly had not hated the white men; he hated, despised, the girl. Even a half-remembrance of this episode, along with myriad other humiliations, defeats, and emasculations, could stir him into flights of depravity that surprised himself—but only himself. Somehow he could not astound. He could only be astounded. So he gave that up, too.

Cholly and Mrs. Breedlove fought each other with a darkly brutal formalism that was paralleled only by their lovemaking. Tacitly they had agreed not to kill each other. He fought her the way a coward fights a man—with feet, the palms of his hands, and teeth. She, in turn, fought back in a purely feminine way—with frying pans and pokers, and occasionally a flatiron would sail toward his head. They did not talk, groan, or curse during these beatings. There was only the muted sound of falling things, and flesh on unsurprised flesh.

There was a difference in the reaction of the children to these battles. Sammy cursed for a while, or left the house, or threw himself into the fray. He was known, by the time he was fourteen, to have run away from home no less than twenty-seven times. Once he got to Buffalo and stayed three months. His returns, whether by force or circumstance, were sullen. Pecola, on the other hand, restricted by youth and sex, experimented with methods of endurance. Though the methods varied, the pain was as consistent as it was deep. She struggled between an overwhelming desire that one would kill the other, and a profound wish that she herself could

die. Now she was whispering, "Don't, Mrs. Breedlove. Don't."
Pecola, like Sammy and Cholly, always called her mother Mrs.
Breedlove.

"Don't, Mrs. Breedlove. Don't."

But Mrs. Breedlove did.

By the grace, no doubt, of God, Mrs. Breedlove sneezed. Just
once.

She ran into the bedroom with a dishpan full of cold water
and threw it in Cholly's face. He sat up, choking and spitting. Naked and ashen, he leaped from the bed, and with a flying tackle,
grabbed his wife around the waist, and they hit the floor. Cholly
picked her up and knocked her down with the back of his hand. She
fell in a sitting position, her back supported by Sammy's bed frame.
She had not let go of the dishpan, and began to hit at Cholly's
thighs and groin with it. He put his foot in her chest, and she
dropped the pan. Dropping to his knee, he struck her several times
in the face, and she might have succumbed early had he not hit
his hand against the metal bed frame when his wife ducked. Mrs.
Breedlove took advantage of this momentary suspension of blows
and slipped out of his reach. Sammy, who had watched in silence
their struggling at his bedside, suddenly began to hit his father
about the head with both fists, shouting "You naked fuck!" over
and over and over. Mrs. Breedlove, having snatched up the round,
flat stove lid, ran tippy-toe to Cholly as he was pulling himself up
from his knees, and struck him two blows, knocking him right
back into the senselessness out of which she had provoked him.
Panting, she threw a quilt over him and let him lie.

Sammy screamed, "Kill him! Kill him!"

Mrs. Breedlove looked at Sammy with surprise. "Cut out that
noise, boy." She put the stove lid back in place, and walked toward
the kitchen. At the doorway she paused long enough to say to her
son, "Get up from there anyhow. I need some coal."

Letting herself breathe easy now, Pecola covered her head with the
quilt. The sick feeling, which she had tried to prevent by holding
in her stomach, came quickly in spite of her precaution. There
surged in her the desire to heave, but as always, she knew she
would not.

"Please, God," she whispered into the palm of her hand.
"Please make me disappear." She squeezed her eyes shut. Little
parts of her body faded away. Now slowly, now with a rush. Slowly

again. Her fingers went, one by one; then her arms disappeared all
the way to the elbow. Her feet now. Yes, that was good. The legs
all at once. It was hardest above the thighs. She had to be real still
and pull. Her stomach would not go. But finally it, too, went away.
Then her chest, her neck. The face was hard, too. Almost done,
almost. Only her tight, tight eyes were left. They were always left.

Try as she might, she could never get her eyes to disappear. So
what was the point? They were everything. Everything was there,
in them. All of those pictures, all of those faces. She had long ago
given up the idea of running away to see new pictures, new faces,
as Sammy had so often done. He never took her, and he never
thought about his going ahead of time, so it was never planned.
It wouldn't have worked anyway. As long as she looked the way
she did, as long as she was ugly, she would have to stay with these
people. Somehow she belonged to them. Long hours she sat looking in the mirror, trying to discover the secret of the ugliness, the
ugliness that made her ignored or despised at school, by teachers
and classmates alike. She was the only member of her class who
sat alone at a double desk. The first letter of her last name forced
her to sit in the front of the room always. But what about Marie
Appolonaire? Marie was in front of her, but she shared a desk with
Luke Angelino. Her teachers had always treated her this way. They
tried never to glance at her, and called on her only when everyone
was required to respond. She also knew that when one of the girls
at school wanted to be particularly insulting to a boy, or wanted to
get an immediate response from him, she could say, "Bobby loves
Pecola Breedlove! Bobby loves Pecola Breedlove!" and never fail to
get peals of laughter from those in earshot, and mock anger from
the accused.

It had occurred to Pecola some time ago that if her eyes, those
eyes that held the pictures, and knew the sights—if those eyes of
hers were different, that is to say, beautiful, she herself would be
different. Her teeth were good, and at least her nose was not big
and flat like some of those who were thought so cute. If she looked
different, beautiful, maybe Cholly would be different, and Mrs.
Breedlove too. Maybe they'd say, "Why, look at pretty-eyed Pecola.
We mustn't do bad things in front of those pretty eyes."

> *Pretty eyes. Pretty blue eyes. Big blue pretty eyes.*
> *Run, Jip, run. Jip runs, Alice runs. Alice has blue eyes.*
> *Jerry has blue eyes. Jerry runs. Alice runs. They run*

with their blue eyes. Four blue eyes. Four pretty
blue eyes. Blue-sky eyes. Blue-like Mrs. Forrest's
blue blouse eyes. Morning-glory-blue-eyes.
Alice-and-Jerry-blue-storybook eyes.

Each night, without fail, she prayed for blue eyes. Fervently, for a year she had prayed. Although somewhat discouraged, she was not without hope. To have something as wonderful as that happen would take a long, long time.

Thrown, in this way, into the binding conviction that only a miracle could relieve her, she would never know her beauty. She would see only what there was to see: the eyes of other people.

She walks down Garden Avenue to a small grocery store which sells penny candy. Three pennies are in her shoe—slipping back and forth between the sock and the inner sole. With each step she feels the painful press of the coins against her foot. A sweet, endurable, even cherished irritation, full of promise and delicate security. There is plenty of time to consider what to buy. Now, however, she moves down an avenue gently buffeted by the familiar and therefore loved images. The dandelions at the base of the telephone pole. Why, she wonders, do people call them weeds? She thought they were pretty. But grown-ups say, "Miss Dunion keeps her yard so nice. Not a dandelion anywhere." Hunkie women in black babushkas go into the fields with baskets to pull them up. But they do not want the yellow heads—only the jagged leaves. They make dandelion soup. Dandelion wine. Nobody loves the head of a dandelion. Maybe because they are so many, strong, and soon.

There was the sidewalk crack shaped like a Y, and the other one that lifted the concrete up from the dirt floor. Frequently her sloughing step had made her trip over that one. Skates would go well over this sidewalk—old it was, and smooth; it made the wheels glide evenly, with a mild whirr. The newly paved walks were bumpy and uncomfortable, and the sound of skate wheels on new walks was grating.

These and other inanimate things she saw and experienced. They were real to her. She knew them. They were the codes and touchstones of the world, capable of translation and possession. She owned the crack that made her stumble; she owned the clumps of dandelions whose white heads, last fall, she had blown away; whose yellow heads, this fall, she peered into. And owning them made her part of the world, and the world a part of her.

She climbs four wooden steps to the door of Yacobowski's Fresh Veg. Meat and Sundries Store. A bell tinkles as she opens it. Standing before the counter, she looks at the array of candies. All Mary Janes, she decides. Three for a penny. The resistant sweetness that breaks open at last to deliver peanut butter—the oil and salt which complement the sweet pull of caramel. A peal of anticipation unsettles her stomach.

She pulls off her shoe and takes out the three pennies. The gray head of Mr. Yacobowski looms up over the counter. He urges his eyes out of his thoughts to encounter her. Blue eyes. Blear-dropped. Slowly, like Indian summer moving imperceptibly toward fall, he looks toward her. Somewhere between retina and object, between vision and view, his eyes draw back, hesitate, and hover. At some fixed point in time and space he senses that he need not waste the effort of a glance. He does not see her, because for him there is nothing to see. How can a fifty-two-year-old white immigrant storekeeper with the taste of potatoes and beer in his mouth, his mind honed on the doe-eyed Virgin Mary, his sensibilities blunted by a permanent awareness of loss, *see* a little black girl? Nothing in his life even suggested that the feat was possible, not to say desirable or necessary.

"Yeah?"

She looks up at him and sees the vacuum where curiosity ought to lodge. And something more. The total absence of human recognition—the glazed separateness. She does not know what keeps his glance suspended. Perhaps because he is grown, or a man, and she a little girl. But she has seen interest, disgust, even anger in grown male eyes. Yet this vacuum is not new to her. It has an edge; somewhere in the bottom lid is the distaste. She has seen it lurking in the eyes of all white people. So. The distaste must be for her, her blackness. All things in her are flux and anticipation. But her blackness is static and dread. And it is the blackness that accounts for, that creates, the vacuum edged with distaste in white eyes.

She points her finger at the Mary Janes—a little black shaft of finger, its tip pressed on the display window. The quietly inoffensive assertion of a black child's attempt to communicate with a white adult.

"Them." The word is more sigh than sense.

"What? These? These?" Phlegm and impatience mingle in his voice.

She shakes her head, her fingertip fixed on the spot which, in her view, at any rate, identifies the Mary Janes. He cannot see her view — the angle of his vision, the slant of her finger, makes it incomprehensible to him. His lumpy red hand plops around in the glass casing like the agitated head of a chicken outraged by the loss of its body.

"Christ. Kantcha talk?"

His fingers brush the Mary Janes.

She nods.

"Well, why'nt you say so? One? How many?"

Pecola unfolds her fist, showing the three pennies. He scoots three Mary Janes toward her—three yellow rectangles in each packet. She holds the money toward him. He hesitates, not wanting to touch her hand. She does not know how to move the finger of her right hand from the display counter or how to get the coins out of her left hand. Finally he reaches over and takes the pennies from her hand. His nails graze her damp palm.

Outside, Pecola feels the inexplicable shame ebb.

Dandelions. A dart of affection leaps out from her to them. But they do not look at her and do not send love back. She thinks, "They *are* ugly. They *are* weeds." Preoccupied with that revelation, she trips on the sidewalk crack. Anger stirs and wakes in her; it opens its mouth, and like a hot-mouthed puppy, laps up the dredges of her shame.

Anger is better. There is a sense of being in anger. A reality and presence. An awareness of worth. It is a lovely surging. Her thoughts fall back to Mr. Yacobowski's eyes, his phlegmy voice. The anger will not hold; the puppy is too easily surfeited. Its thirst too quickly quenched, it sleeps. The shame wells up again, its muddy rivulets seeping into her eyes. What to do before the tears come. She remembers the Mary Janes.

Each pale yellow wrapper has a picture on it. A picture of little Mary Jane, for whom the candy is named. Smiling white face. Blond hair in gentle disarray, blue eyes looking at her out of a world of clean comfort. The eyes are petulant, mischievous. To Pecola they are simply pretty. She eats the candy, and its sweetness is good. To eat the candy is somehow to eat the eyes, eat Mary Jane. Love Mary Jane. Be Mary Jane.

Three pennies had bought her nine lovely orgasms with Mary Jane. Lovely Mary Jane, for whom a candy is named.

——*For Discussion*——

JRT—

This chapter's epigraph is a section of a Dick and Jane reader from the 50s where mom and pop had two kids, a white picket fence, and lived in a big house with dog Spot. Only here is Dick and Jane run wild. All the words run together and the passage abruptly cuts off the word "happy" at the "h". Obviously the Breedloves are not, nor will they ever be, the Dick and Jane family. No happy ever after tale here, and in this chapter, as in the novel, Morrison shows us not necessarily "why" but "how."

The Breedloves are a poor black family from Lorraine, Ohio, who live in the projects. Not one of them has much of what we refer to in 90s jargon as "self-esteem." Bluntly, Morrison calls them ugly because they accept their less-than state with conviction. While Cholly is weak and violent, Mrs. Breedlove, called so by her children Sammy and Pecola, wears her ugliness as martyrdom. Sammy hurts people out of his self-hatred and Pecola, the main subject of this chapter, hides herself and yearns to disappear, to be different, to be white. Pecola imagines that having blue eyes and blonde hair, like Shirley Temple, will make her free from pain.

When one wants what one cannot have, or tries to be what one cannot, there is chaos, confusion, and in Pecola's case, madness. In this chapter, the Breedloves, driven by despair and futility, fight against each other, each vicious in his or her own right. Cholly, drinking and out of work, has lost self-respect. Pauline, later called Polly by the white family she serves as a maid, is tormented by the loss of her dreams, her desire for affluence, for beauty, and for what she once felt marriage might deliver. The Breedloves beat on each other with words, frying pans, and angry silences for what the world does not provide. Pecola tries to disappear when she hears her parents fighting, in much the same way she will try to disappear later when her father rapes her. She makes herself small, imagining that she is no longer the tormented child. She cannot be the white girl with blue eyes on the Mary Jane candies. She can only long for those blue eyes and all that they, like the white house with the picket fence in Dick-and-Jane-land, promise. Eating Mary Janes, in spite of disdain by the white merchant who hands Pecola the candy and almost spits on her, is the closest she can get to pure joy. The American dream, Toni Morri-

son tells us, is not possible for this black family. And possibly not
for any of us.

The tale makes us asks important questions about responsibility. Is it Cholly's fault that Pecola disappears? Is it the parents'
lack of love for each other, for their children, or for themselves?
Claudia, the narrator of much of the rest of the novel, comes to
understand that Pecola is a victim of her times, of her community,
of her family. But the family is also disowned by our country,
drowned by the illusion of the American dream.

RPW—

The Breedloves are at the bottom of that hierarchical system
that defines beauty and privilege in America. They have black
skin in a world that celebrates whiteness. They have no possessions in a world that celebrates material wealth. And every school
book, every movie, every billboard, every glance replicates this
dominant belief system: they are ugly. How could they possibly
know anything about the breeding of love?

Living in "the anonymous misery of their storefront," the
Breedlove family has shaped itself according to the established
definition of ugliness, a definition they cannot escape. Mrs. Breedlove has adopted the role of the martyr acting in the name of
Christ the Judge (but not Christ the Redeemer). Cholly has become the sinner beyond redemption, the abuser bringing his ritual
of drunkeness to the family ceremony of violence. Sammy, the son,
is the sadist, the intimidator, though anxious to run from his family whenever he has the chance. Pecola, the daughter, unable to
run, can only endure the pain, praying for a miracle, for blue eyes.

The Breedloves do not hate the white people who have defined
them; instead, they have internalized those definitions. They believe those categories are natural ones. As a result, they hate themselves. Like Cholly, who despises not the white men with their
flashlights but the country girl beneath him, the Breedlove family
believes in the hierarchical system created by a white society, a
system that determines their lives as if it were their fate.

Pecola would like to disappear. And who can blame her? But
she is continually haunted by the reality of her dark eyes. She
knows that "if those eyes of hers were different, that is to say,
beautiful, she herself would be different." Her teachers would call
on her in school. Her schoolmates would not insult her. Her family would be transformed by the presence of their pretty-eyes doll.

Pecola craves affection because she is capable of giving it. But, like the dandelions, she has been declared a worthless weed, battered by shame and humiliation.

Mr. Yacobowski, the fifty-two-year-old white immigrant store-keeper, cannot see Pecola because she exists in that invisible world of darkness. Pecola wants Mary Jane candy from him. For Pecola, the Mary Janes could transform her, could give her those blue eyes, the beauty that the white world celebrates. On the wrapper of that candy is Pecola's dream: the smiling white face, blond hair, blue eyes, clean comfort. "To eat the candy is somehow to eat the eyes, eat Mary Jane. Love Mary Jane. Be Mary Jane." For Pecola this is religious ecstasy, a ritual to take her from the violence of the Breedlove storefront. But where could it possibly lead her in such a world?

FRIENDSHIP/LOVE

INTRODUCTION

Love makes the world go round, or so goes the saying. But is that true? Surely we have seen that violence also makes the world go round. Is love the antidote to violence or just another part of the human condition? What really is love? Is it a feeling or a combination of actions? How is it shown and how do we know it is or isn't there?

Love in literature is not a unique theme because so many of us are driven by needs for connection and so many writers create characters with those same needs. But the young passionate love we see in *Romeo and Juliet* is far different from the mature love of the aging couple in *On Golden Pond*. Some of us call dependency "love," and others of us get confused about love and lust. Without some "love interest," television and films could never make it. But as Steve Martin says in *Roxanne*, his delightful movie based on Edmund Rostand's *Cyrano de Bergerac*, the word "love" is overused in the twentieth century. How can we love a car wax or a shampoo, using the same word we use for a lover?

The purpose of this section is to ask questions about the nature of love as it is shown through the characters in these pieces, and to examine the different kinds of love that endear, confuse, anger, delight, drive, destroy, and comfort us.

Platonic love or friendship is certainly one kind of love we find in the pieces included in this section. In John Steinbeck's *Of Mice and Men*, Lenny and George, two men who work together and travel from place to place, are friends. In spite of the fact that George must take care of the lumbering, slow, and slightly retarded Lenny, Lenny is as loyal as can be. Before the selection included here, George and Lenny have dreamed of what their life will be like in the future when they move to their own farm. After a tragedy in which Lenny kills boss Curly's wife, George insists that he will take Lenny to his final resting-place. He does not want to see his friend brutalized by people who are not his friends. What is it, Steinbeck asks us to consider, that makes friendship? The friendship we see in this piece brings up issues of loyalty and betrayal, and asks us to consider what we would do for or against our beloved friends.

The deceit and horrors of perverse friendships and addictive love are shown in Harry Crews' *The Knockout Artist*. This piece exemplifies how easily we use the word "love" today when we more often mean attachment. The low-life world of the boxer shown by Crews is no different than the slick underbellies of New Orleans or L.A., where relationships are all based on using. Love is no more than a shot of heroin, and friendship is the guy who holds your head over the toilet when you've had too much to drink. Can there be friendship or love in the darkest places?

Another relationship that falls on the dark side of friendship is that between two violent men, mildly unhappy in their marriages and somewhat bored in their lives. Jerry and Bill, in Raymond Carver's "Tell the Women We're Going," represent two average Joes who go too far, and they go there together. The influence of friends and how they affect each other is explored in this short story, and as readers, we must again define what makes friendship and what values we want in our friends. Whereas Crews shows us friendship with exploitation, Carver forces us to consider if we can indeed call it friendship when "friends" destroy lives.

Romantic love, that with which we are most familiar, is the kind found between Janie and Tea Cake in Zora Neale Hurston's *Their Eyes Were Watching God*. Janie, having left one man and been widowed by another, is now in a secure financial position. Into her life comes Tea Cake, many years her junior, a gambler and every woman's bad boy. Janie falls head over heels, and Tea Cake too considers Janie the love of his life. They marry, and so begins Janie's adventure of the heart. What is it to marry for love versus security? What is it that makes love last and how is love tested? Can we love someone who hurts us and why or why not? Tough questions about love must be answered in this selection, and Hurston leads us squarely into the heart of the matter.

Love that is pure and love that can save lives is the subject of Gloria Naylor's *The Women of Brewster Place*. In "Lucelia Louise Turner," Mattie is the earth mother who lives out her broken dreams in the New York tenement of Brewster Place. When her neighbor Ciel is destroyed by a man, she comes to Ciel's aid. The scene between these two women makes us think about the power of love to save us from our worst selves and its ability to heal our wounds. What is it that love can and cannot do?

Although the selections here show us that love is not without pain, we can begin to unravel the complicated strands of this emotion. How love hurts and how love heals are not always so far apart as we see in *Their Eyes Were Watching God* and *Of Mice and Men*. Love can be an excuse. It can be an addiction. And certainly, love can be something we strive towards, a way of defining what is best in us, as we see in Mattie in *The Women of Brewster Place*.

from OF MICE AND MEN

John Steinbeck

CHAPTER 5

One end of the great barn was piled high with new hay and over the pile hung the four-taloned Jackson fork suspended from its pulley. The hay came down like a mountain slope to the other end of the barn, and there was a level place as yet unfilled with the new crop. At the sides the feeding racks were visible, and between the slats the heads of horses could be seen.

It was Sunday afternoon. The resting horses nibbled the remaining wisps of hay, and they stamped their feet and they bit the wood of the mangers and rattled the halter chains. The afternoon sun sliced in through the cracks of the barn walls and lay in bright lines on the hay. There was the buzz of flies in the air, the lazy afternoon humming.

From outside came the clang of horseshoes on the playing peg and the shouts of men, playing, encouraging, jeering. But in the barn it was quiet and humming and lazy and warm.

Only Lennie was in the barn, and Lennie sat in the hay beside a packing case under a manger in the end of the barn that had not been filled with hay. Lennie sat in the hay and looked at a little dead puppy that lay in front of him. Lennie looked at it for a long time, and then he put out his huge hand and stroked it, stroked it clear from one end to the other.

And Lennie said softly to the puppy, "Why do you got to get killed? You ain't so little as mice. I didn't bounce you hard." He bent the pup's head up and looked in its face, and he said to it, "Now maybe George ain't gonna let me tend no rabbits, if he fin's out you got killed."

He scooped a little hollow and laid the puppy in it and covered it over with hay, out of sight; but he continued to stare at the mound he had made. He said, "This ain't no bad thing like I got to go hide in the brush. Oh! no. This ain't. I'll tell George I foun' it dead."

He unburied the puppy and inspected it, and he stroked it from ears to tail. He went on sorrowfully, "But he'll know. George always knows. He'll say, 'You done it. Don't try to put nothing over on me.' An' he'll say, 'Now jus' for that you don't get to tend no rabbits!' "

Suddenly his anger arose. "God damn you," he cried. "Why do you got to get killed? You ain't so little as mice." He picked up the pup and hurled it from him. He turned his back on it. He sat bent over his knees and he whispered, "Now I won't get to tend the rabbits. Now he won't let me." He rocked himself back and forth in his sorrow.

From outside came the clang of horseshoes on the iron stake, and then a little chorus of cries. Lennie got up and brought the puppy back and laid it on the hay and sat down. He stroked the pup again. "You wasn't big enough," he said. "They tol' me and tol' me you wasn't. I di'n't know you'd get killed so easy." He worked his fingers on the pup's limp ear. "Maybe George won't care," he said. "This here God damn little son-of-a-bitch wasn't nothing to George."

Curley's wife came around the end of the last stall. She came very quietly, so that Lennie didn't see her. She wore her bright cotton dress and the mules with the red ostrich feathers. Her face was made up and the little sausage curls were all in place. She was quite near to him before Lennie looked up and saw her.

In a panic he shoveled hay over the puppy with his fingers. He looked sullenly up at her.

She said, "What you got there, sonny boy?"

Lennie glared at her. "George says I ain't to have nothing to do with you—talk to you or nothing."

She laughed. "George giving you orders about everything?"

Lennie looked down at the hay. "Says I can't tend no rabbits if I talk to you or anything."

She said quietly, "He's scared Curley'll get mad. Well, Curley got his arm in a sling—an' if Curley gets tough, you can break his other han'. You didn't put nothing over on me about gettin' it caught in no machine."

But Lennie was not to be drawn. "No, sir. I ain't gonna talk to you or nothing."

She knelt in the hay beside him. "Listen," she said. "All the guys got a horseshoe tenement goin' on. It's on'y about four o'clock. None of them guys is goin' to leave that tenement. Why can't I talk to you? I never get to talk to nobody. I get awful lonely."

Lennie said, "Well, I ain't supposed to talk to you or nothing."

"I get lonely," she said. "You can talk to people, but I can't talk to nobody but Curley. Else he gets mad. How'd you like not to talk to anybody?"

Lennie said, "Well, I ain't supposed to. George's scared I'll get in trouble."

She changed the subject. "What you got covered up there?"

Then all of Lennie's woe came back on him. "Jus' my pup," he said sadly. "Jus' my little pup." And he swept the hay from on top of it.

"Why, he's dead," she cried.

"He was so little," said Lennie. "I was jus' playin' with him . . . an' he made like he's gonna bite me . . . an' I made like I was gonna smack him . . . an' . . . an' I done it. An' then he was dead."

She consoled him. "Don't you worry none. He was jus' a mutt. You can get another one easy. The whole country is fulla mutts."

"It ain't that so much," Lennie explained miserably. "George ain't gonna let me tend no rabbits now."

"Why don't he?"

"Well, he said if I done any more bad things he ain't gonna let me tend the rabbits."

She moved closer to him and she spoke soothingly. "Don't you worry about talkin' to me. Listen to the guys yell out there. They got four dollars bet in that tenement. None of them ain't gonna leave till it's over."

"If George sees me talkin' to you he'll give me hell," Lennie said cautiously. "He tol' me so."

Her face grew angry. "Wha's the matter with me?" she cried. "Ain't I got a right to talk to nobody? Whatta they think I am, anyways? You're a nice guy. I don't know why I can't talk to you. I ain't doin' no harm to you."

"Well, George says you'll get us in a mess."

"Aw, nuts!" she said. "What kinda harm am I doin' to you? Seems like they ain't none of them cares how I gotta live. I tell you I ain't used to livin' like this. I coulda made somethin' of myself." She said darkly, "Maybe I will yet." And then her words tumbled out in a passion of communication, as though she hurried before her listener could be taken away. "I lived right in Salinas," she said. "Come there when I was a kid. Well, a show come through, an' I met one of the actors. He says I could go with that show. But my ol' lady wouldn' let me. She says because I was on'y fifteen.

But the guy says I coulda. It I'd went, I wouldn't be livin' like this, you bet."

Lennie stroked the pup back and forth. "We gonna have a little place—an' rabbits," he explained.

She went on with her story quickly, before she should be interrupted. "'Nother time I met a guy, an' he was in pitchers. Went out to the Riverside Dance Palace with him. He says he was gonna put me in the movies. Says I was a natural. Soon's he got back to Hollywood he was gonna write to me about it." She looked closely at Lennie to see whether she was impressing him. "I never got that letter," she said. "I always thought my ol' lady stole it. Well, I wasn't gonna stay no place where I couldn't get nowhere or make something of myself, an' where they stole your letters. I ast her if she stole it, too, an' she says no. So I married Curley. Met him out to the Riverside Dance Palace that same night." She demanded, "You listenin'?"

"Me? Sure."

"Well, I ain't told this to nobody before. Maybe I ought'n to. I don' *like* Curley. He ain't a nice fella." And because she had confided in him, she moved closer to Lennie and sat beside him. "Coulda been in the movies, an' had nice clothes—all them nice clothes like they wear. An' I coulda sat in them big hotels, an' had pitchers took of me. When they had them previews I coulda went to them, an' spoke in the radio, an' it wouldn'ta cost me a cent because I was in the pitcher. An' all them nice clothes like they wear. Because this guy says I was a natural." She looked up at Lennie, and she made a small grand gesture with her arm and hand to show that she could act. The fingers trailed after her leading wrist, and her little finger stuck out grandly from the rest.

Lennie sighed deeply. From outside came the clang of a horseshoe on metal, and then a chorus of cheers. "Somebody made a ringer," said Curley's wife.

Now the light was lifting as the sun went down, and the sun streaks climbed up the wall and fell over the feeding racks and over the heads of the horses.

Lennie said, "Maybe if I took this pup out and throwed him away George wouldn't never know. An' then I could tend the rabbits without no trouble."

Curley's wife said angrily, "Don't you think of nothing but rabbits?"

"We gonna have a little place," Lennie explained patiently. "We gonna have a house an' a garden and a place for alfalfa, an' that alfalfa is for the rabbits, an' I take a sack and get it all fulla alfalfa and then I take it to the rabbits."

She asked, "What makes you so nuts about rabbits?"

Lennie had to think carefully before he could come to a conclusion. He moved cautiously close to her, until he was right against her. "I like to pet nice things. Once at a fair I seen some of them long-hair rabbits. An' they was nice, you bet. Sometimes I've even pet mice, but not when I could get nothing better."

Curley's wife moved away from him a little. "I think you're nuts," she said.

"No I ain't," Lennie explained earnestly. "George says I ain't. I like to pet nice things with my fingers, sof' things."

She was a little bit reassured. "Well, who don't?" she said. "Ever'body likes that. I like to feel silk an' velvet. Do you like to feel velvet?"

Lennie chuckled with pleasure. "You bet, by God," he cried happily. "An' I had some, too. A lady give me some, an' that lady was—my own Aunt Clara. She give it right to me—'bout this big a piece. I wisht I had that velvet right now." A frown came over his face. "I lost it," he said. "I ain't seen it for a long time."

Curley's wife laughed at him. "You're nuts," she said. "But you're a kinda nice fella. Jus' like a big baby. But a person can see kinda what you mean. When I'm doin' my hair sometimes I jus' set an' stroke it 'cause it's so soft." To show how she did it, she ran her fingers over the top of her head. "Some people got kinda coarse hair," she said complacently. "Take Curley. His hair is jus' like wire. But mine is soft and fine. 'Course I brush it a lot. That makes it fine. Here—feel right here." She took Lennie's hand and put it on her head. "Feel right aroun' there an' see how soft it is."

Lennie's big fingers fell to stroking her hair.

"Don't you muss it up," she said.

Lennie said, "Oh! That's nice," and he stroked harder. "Oh, that's nice."

"Look out, now, you'll muss it." And then she cried angrily, "You stop it now, you'll mess it all up." She jerked her head sideways, and Lennie's fingers closed on her hair and hung on. "Let go," she cried. "You let go!"

Lennie was in a panic. His face was contorted. She screamed then, and Lennie's other hand closed over her mouth and nose.

"Please don't," he begged. "Oh! Please don't do that. George'll be mad."

She struggled violently under his hands. Her feet battered on the hay and she writhed to be free; and from under Lennie's hand came a muffled screaming. Lennie began to cry with fright. "Oh! Please don't do none of that," he begged. "George gonna say I done a bad thing. He ain't gonna let me tend no rabbits." He moved his hand a little and her hoarse cry came out. Then Lennie grew angry. "Now don't," he said. "I don't want you to yell. You gonna get me in trouble jus' like George says you will. Now don't you do that." And she continued to struggle, and her eyes were wild with terror. He shook her then, and he was angry with her. "Don't you go yellin'," he said, and he shook her; and her body flopped like a fish. And then she was still, for Lennie had broken her neck.

He looked down at her, and carefully he removed his hand from over her mouth, and she lay still. "I don't want ta hurt you," he said, "but George'll be mad if you yell." When she didn't answer nor move he bent closely over her. He lifted her arm and let it drop. For a moment he seemed bewildered. And then he whispered in fright, "I done a bad thing. I done another bad thing."

He pawed up the hay until it partly covered her.

From outside the barn came a cry of men and the double clang of shoes on metal. For the first time Lennie became conscious of the outside. He crouched down in the hay and listened. "I done a real bad thing," he said. "I shouldn't of did that. George'll be mad. An' . . . he said . . . an' hide in the brush till he come. He's gonna be mad. In the brush till he come. Tha's what he said." Lennie went back and looked at the dead girl. The puppy lay close to her. Lennie picked it up. "I'll throw him away," he said. "It's bad enough like it is." He put the pup under his coat, and he crept to the barn wall and peered out between the cracks, toward the horseshoe game. And then he crept around the end of the last manger and disappeared.

The sun streaks were high on the wall by now, and the light was growing soft in the barn. Curley's wife lay on her back, and she was half covered with hay.

It was very quiet in the barn, and the quiet of the afternoon was on the ranch. Even the clang of the pitched shoes, even the voices of the men in the game seemed to grow more quiet. The air in the barn was dusky in advance of the outside day. A pigeon flew in through the open hay door and circled and flew out again. Around the last stall came a shepherd bitch, lean and long, with heavy, hanging dugs. Halfway to the packing box where the puppies were she caught the dead scent of Curley's wife, and the hair rose along her spine. She whimpered and cringed to the packing box, and jumped in among the puppies.

Curley's wife lay with a half-covering of yellow hay. And the meanness and the plannings and the discontent and the ache for attention were all gone from her face. She was very pretty and simple, and her face was sweet and young. Now her rouged cheeks and her reddened lips made her seem alive and sleeping very lightly. The curls, tiny little sausages, were spread on the hay behind her head, and her lips were parted.

As happens sometimes, a moment settled and hovered and remained for much more than a moment. And sound stopped and movement stopped for much, much more than a moment.

Then gradually time awakened again and moved sluggishly on. The horses stamped on the other side of the feeding racks and the halter chains clinked. Outside, the men's voices became louder and clearer.

From around the end of the last stall old Candy's voice came. "Lennie," he called. "Oh, Lennie! You in here? I been figuring some more. Tell you what we can do, Lennie." Old Candy appeared around the end of the last stall. "Oh, Lennie!" he called again; and then he stopped, and his body stiffened. He rubbed his smooth wrist on his white stubble whiskers. "I di'n't know you was here," he said to Curley's wife.

When she didn't answer, he stepped nearer. "You oughten to sleep out here," he said disapprovingly; and then he was beside her and—"Oh, Jesus Christ!" He looked about helplessly, and he rubbed his beard. And then he jumped up and went quickly out of the barn.

But the barn was alive now. The horses stamped and snorted, and they chewed the straw of their bedding and they clashed the chains of their halters. In a moment Candy came back, and George was with him.

George said, "What was it you wanted to see me about?"

Candy pointed at Curley's wife. George stared. "What's the matter with her?" he asked. He stepped closer, and then he echoed Candy's words. "Oh, Jesus Christ!" He was down on his knees beside her. He put his hand over her heart. And finally, when he stood up, slowly and stiffly, his face was as hard and tight as wood, and his eyes were hard.

Candy said, "What done it?"

George looked coldly at him. "Ain't you got any idear?" he asked. And Candy was silent. "I should of knew," George said hopelessly. "I guess maybe way back in my head I did."

Candy asked, "What we gonna do now, George. What we gonna do now?"

George was a long time in answering. "Guess . . . we gotta tell the . . . guys. I guess we gotta get 'im an' lock 'im up. We can't let 'im get away. Why, the poor bastard'd starve." And he tried to re-assure himself. "Maybe they'll lock 'im up an' be nice to 'im."

But Candy said excitedly, "We oughtta let 'im get away. You don't know that Curley. Curley gon'ta wanta get 'im lynched. Curley'll get 'im killed."

George watched Candy's lips. "Yeah," he said at last, "that's right, Curley will. An' the other guys will." And he looked back at Curley's wife.

Now Candy spoke his greatest fear. "You an' me can get that little place, can't we, George? You an' me can go there an' live nice, can't we, George? Can't we?"

Before George answered, Candy dropped his head and looked down at the hay. He knew.

George said softly, "—I think I knowed from the very first. I think I knowed we'd never do her. He usta like to hear about it so much I got to thinking maybe we would."

"Then—it's all off?" Candy asked sulkily.

George didn't answer his question. George said, "I'll work my month an' I'll take my fifty bucks an' I'll stay all night in some lousy cat house. Or I'll set in some poolroom till ever'body goes home. An' then I'll come back an' work another month an' I'll have fifty bucks more."

Candy said, "He's such a nice fella. I didn' think he'd do nothing like this."

George still stared at Curley's wife. "Lennie never done it in meanness," he said. "All the time he done bad things, but he never done one of 'em mean." He straightened up and looked back at Candy. "Now listen. We gotta tell the guys. They got to bring him in, I guess. They ain't no way out. Maybe they won't hurt 'im." He said sharply, "I ain't gonna let 'em hurt Lennie. Now you listen. The guys might think I was in on it. I'm gonna go in the bunk house. Then in a minute you come out and tell the guys about her, and I'll come along and make like I never seen her. Will you do that? So the guys won't think I was in on it?"

Candy said, "Sure, George. Sure I'll do that."

"O.K. Give me a couple of minutes then, and you come runnin' out an' tell like you jus' found her. I'm going now." George turned and went quickly out of the barn.

Old Candy watched him go. He looked helplessly back at Curley's wife, and gradually his sorrow and his anger grew into words. "You God damn tramp," he said viciously. "You done it, di'n't you? I s'pose you're glad. Ever'body knowed you'd mess things up. You wasn't no good. You ain't no good now, you lousy tart." He sniveled, and his voice shook. "I could of hoed in the garden and washed dishes for them guys." He paused, and then went on in a singsong. And he repeated the old words: "If they was a circus or a baseball game . . . we would of went to her . . . jus' said 'ta hell with work,' an' went to her. Never ast nobody's say so. An' they'd of been a pig and chickens . . . an' in the winter . . . the little fat stove . . . an' the rain comin' . . . an' us jus' settin' there." His eyes blinded with tears and he turned and went weakly out of the barn, and he rubbed his bristly whiskers with his wrist stump.

Outside the noise of the game stopped. There was a rise of voices in question, a drum of running feet and the men burst into the barn. Slim and Carlson and young Whit and Curley, and Crooks keeping back out of attention range. Candy came after them, and last of all came George. George had put on his blue denim coat and buttoned it, and his black hat was pulled down low over his eyes. The men raced around the last stall. Their eyes found Curley's wife in the gloom, they stopped and stood still and looked.

Then Slim went quietly over to her, and he felt her wrist. One lean finger touched her cheek, and then his hand went under her slightly twisted neck and his fingers explored her neck. When he stood up the men crowded near and the spell was broken.

Curley came suddenly to life. "I know who done it," he cried. "That big son-of-a-bitch done it. I know he done it. Why— ever'body else was out there playin' horseshoes." He worked himself into a fury. "I'm gonna get him. I'm going for my shotgun. I'll kill the big son-of-a-bitch myself. I'll shoot 'im in the guts. Come on, you guys." He ran furiously out of the barn. Carlson said, "I'll get my Luger," and he ran out too.

Slim turned quietly to George. "I guess Lennie done it, all right," he said. "Her neck's bust. Lennie coulda did that."

George didn't answer, but he nodded slowly. His hat was so far down on his forehead that his eyes were covered.

Slim went on, "Maybe like that time in Weed you was tellin' about."

Again George nodded.

Slim sighed. "Well, I guess we got to get him. Where you think he might of went?"

It seemed to take George some time to free his words. "He— would of went south," he said. "We come from north so he would of went south."

"I guess we gotta get 'im," Slim repeated.

George stepped close. "Couldn' we maybe bring him in an' they'll lock him up? He's nuts, Slim. He never done this to be mean."

Slim nodded. "We might," he said. "If we could keep Curley in, we might. But Curley's gonna want to shoot 'im. Curley's still mad about his hand. An' s'pose they lock him up an' strap him down and put him in a cage. That ain't no good, George."

"I know," said George. "I know."

Carlson came running in. "The bastard's stole my Luger," he shouted. "It ain't in my bag." Curley followed him, and Curley carried a shotgun in his good hand. Curley was cold now.

"All right, you guys," he said. "The nigger's got a shotgun. You take it, Carlson. When you see 'um, don't give 'im no chance. Shoot for his guts. That'll double 'im over."

Whit said excitedly, "I ain't got a gun."

Curley said, "You go in Soledad an' get a cop. Get Al Wilts, he's deputy sheriff. Le's go now." He turned suspiciously on George. "You're comin' with us, fella."

"Yeah," said George. "I'll come. But listen, Curley. The poor bastard's nuts. Don't shoot 'im. He di'n't know what he was doin'."

"Don't shoot 'im?" Curley cried. "He got Carlson's Luger. 'Course we'll shoot 'im."

George said weakly, "Maybe Carlson lost his gun."

"I seen it this morning," said Carlson. "No, it's been took."

Slim stood looking down at Curley's wife. He said, "Curley— maybe you better stay here with your wife."

Curley's face reddened. "I'm goin'," he said. "I'm gonna shoot the guts outa that big bastard myself, even if I only got one hand. I'm gonna get 'im."

Slim turned to Candy. "You stay here with her then, Candy. The rest of us better get goin'."

They moved away. George stopped a moment beside Candy and they both looked down at the dead girl until Curley called, "You George! You stick with us so we don't think you had nothin' to do with this."

George moved slowly after them, and his feet dragged heavily.

And when they were gone, Candy squatted down in the hay and watched the face of Curley's wife. "Poor bastard," he said softly.

The sound of the men grew fainter. The barn was darkening gradually and, in their stalls, the horses shifted their feet and rattled the halter chains. Old Candy lay down in the hay and covered his eyes with his arm.

CHAPTER 6

The deep green pool of the Salinas River was still in the late afternoon. Already the sun had left the valley to go climbing up the slopes of the Gabilan mountains, and the hilltops were rosy in the sun. But by the pool among the mottled sycamores, a pleasant shade had fallen.

A water snake glided smoothly up the pool, twisting its periscope head from side to side; and it swam the length of the pool and came to the legs of a motionless heron that stood in the shallows. A silent head and beak lanced down and plucked it out by the head, and the beak swallowed the little snake while its tail waved frantically.

A far rush of wind sounded and a gust drove through the tops of the trees like a wave. The sycamore leaves turned up their silver sides, the brown, dry leaves on the ground scudded a few feet. And row on row of tiny wind waves flowed up the pool's green surface.

As quickly as it had come, the wind died, and the clearing was quiet again. The heron stood in the shallows, motionless and waiting. Another little water snake swam up the pool, turning its periscope head from side to side.

Suddenly Lennie appeared out of the brush, and he came as silently as a creeping bear moves. The heron pounded the air with its wings, jacked itself clear of the water and flew off down river. The little snake slid in among the reeds at the pool's side.

Lennie came quietly to the pool's edge. He knelt down and drank, barely touching his lips to the water. When a little bird skittered over the dry leaves behind him, his head jerked up and he strained toward the sound with eyes and ears until he saw the bird, and then he dropped his head and drank again.

When he finished, he sat down on the bank, with his side to the pool, so that he could watch the trail's entrance. He embraced his knees and laid his chin down on his knees.

The light climbed on out of the valley, and as it went, the tops of the mountains seemed to blaze with increasing brightness.

Lennie said softly, "I di'n't forget, you bet, God damn. Hide in the brush an' wait for George." He pulled his hat down low over his eyes. "George gonna give me hell," he said. "George gonna wish he was alone an' not have me botherin' him." He turned his head and looked at the bright mountain tops. "I can go right off there an' find a cave," he said. And he continued sadly, "—an' never have no ketchup—but I won't care. If George don't want me . . . I'll go away. I'll go away."

And then from out of Lennie's head there came a little fat old woman. She wore thick bull's-eye glasses and she wore a huge gingham apron with pockets, and she was starched and clean. She stood in front of Lennie and put her hands on her hips, and she frowned disapprovingly at him.

And when she spoke, it was in Lennie's voice. "I tol' you an tol' you," she said. "I tol' you, 'Min' George because he's such a nice fella an' good to you.' But you don't never take no care. You do bad things."

And Lennie answered her, "I tried, Aunt Clara, ma'am. I tried and tried. I couldn' help it."

"You never give a thought to George," she went on in Lennie's voice. "He been doin' nice things for you alla time. When he got a piece a pie you always got half or more'n half. An' if they was any ketchup, why he'd give it all to you."

"I know," said Lennie miserably. "I tried, Aunt Clara, ma'am. I tried and tried."

She interrupted him. "All the time he coulda had such a good time if it wasn't for you. He woulda took his pay an' raised hell in a whore house, and he coulda set in a pool room an' played snooker. But he got to take care of you."

Lennie moaned with grief. "I know, Aunt Clara, ma'am. I'll go right off in the hills an' I'll fin' a cave an' I'll live there so I won't be no more trouble to George."

"You jus' say that," she said sharply. "You're always sayin' that, an' you know sonofabitching well you ain't never gonna do it. You'll jus' stick around an' stew the b'Jesus outa George all the time."

Lennie said, "I might jus' as well go away. George ain't gonna let me tend no rabbits now."

Aunt Clara was gone, and from out of Lennie's head there came a gigantic rabbit. It sat on its haunches in front of him, and it waggled its ears and crinkled its nose at him. And it spoke in Lennie's voice too.

"Tend rabbits," it said scornfully. "You crazy bastard. You ain't fit to lick the boots of no rabbit. You'd forget 'em and let 'em go hungry. That's what you'd do. An' then what would George think?"

"I would *not* forget," Lennie said loudly.

"The hell you wouldn'," said the rabbit. "You ain't worth a greased jack-pin to ram you into hell. Christ knows George done ever'thing he could to jack you outa the sewer, but it don't do no good. If you think George gonna let you tend rabbits, you're even crazier'n usual. He ain't. He's gonna beat hell outa you with a stick, that's what he's gonna do."

Now Lennie retorted belligerently, "He ain't neither. George won't do nothing like that. I've knew George since—I forget when—and he ain't never raised his han' to me with a stick. He's nice to me. He ain't gonna be mean."

"Well he's sick of you," said the rabbit. "He's gonna beat hell outa you an' then go away an' leave you."

"He won't," Lennie cried frantically. "He won't do nothing like that. I know George. Me an' him travels together."

But the rabbit repeated softly over and over, "He gonna leave you, ya crazy bastard. He gonna leave ya all alone. He gonna leave ya, crazy bastard."

Lennie put his hands over his ears. "He ain't, I tell ya he ain't." And he cried, "Oh! George—George—George!"

George came quietly out of the brush and the rabbit scuttled back into Lennie's brain.

George said quietly, "What the hell you yellin' about?"

Lennie got up on his knees. "You ain't gonna leave me, are ya, George? I know you ain't."

George came stiffly near and sat down beside him. "No."

"I knowed it," Lennie cried. "You ain't that kind."

George was silent.

Lennie said, "George."

"Yeah?"

"I done another bad thing."

"It don't make no difference," George said, and he fell silent again.

Only the topmost ridges were in the sun now. The shadow in the valley was blue and soft. From the distance came the sound of men shouting to one another. George turned his head and listened to the shouts.

Lennie said, "George."

"Yeah?"

"Ain't you gonna give me hell?"

"Give ya hell?"

"Sure, like you always done before. Like, 'If I di'n't have you I'd take my fifty bucks—'"

"Jesus Christ, Lennie! You can't remember nothing that happens, but you remember ever' word I say."

"Well, ain't you gonna say it?"

George shook himself. He said woodenly, "If I was alone I could live so easy." His voice was monotonous, had no emphasis. "I could get a job an' not have no mess." He stopped.

"Go on," said Lennie. "An' when the enda the month come—"

"An' when the end of the month come I could take my fifty bucks an' go to a . . . cat house . . . " He stopped again.

Lennie looked eagerly at him. "Go on, George. Ain't you gonna give me no more hell?"

"No," said George.

"Well, I can go away," said Lennie. "I'll go right off in the hills an' find a cave if you don' want me."

George shook himself again. "No," he said. "I want you to stay with me here."

Lennie said craftily "Tell me like you done before."

"Tell you what?"

"'Bout the other guys an' about us."

George said, "Guys like us got no fambly. They make a little stake an' then they blow it in. They ain't got nobody in the worl' that gives a hoot in hell about 'em—"

"*But not us,*" Lennie cried happily. "Tell about us now."

George was quiet for a moment. "But not us," he said.

"Because—"

"Because I got you an'—"

"An' I got you. We got each other, that's what, that gives a hoot in hell about us," Lennie cried in triumph.

The little evening breeze blew over the clearing and the leaves rustled and the wind waves flowed up the green pool. And the shouts of men sounded again, this time much closer than before.

George took off his hat. He said shakily, "Take off your hat, Lennie. The air feels fine."

Lennie removed his hat dutifully and laid it on the ground in front of him. The shadow in the valley was bluer, and the evening came fast. On the wind the sound of crashing in the brush came to them.

Lennie said, "Tell how it's gonna be."

George had been listening to the distant sounds. For a moment he was business-like. "Look acrost the river, Lennie an' I'll tell you so you can almost see it."

Lennie turned his head and looked off across the pool and up the darkening slopes of the Gabilans. "We gonna get a little place," George began. He reached in his side pocket and brought out Carlson's Luger; he snapped off the safety, and the hand and gun lay on the ground behind Lennie's back. He looked at the back of Lennie's head, at the place where the spine and skull were joined.

A man's voice called from up the river, and another man answered.

"Go on," said Lennie.

George raised the gun and his hand shook, and he dropped his hand to the ground again.

"Go on," said Lennie. "How's it gonna be. We gonna get a little place."

"We'll have a cow," said George. "An' we'll have maybe a pig an' chickens . . . an' down the flat we'll have a . . . little piece alfalfa—"

"For the rabbits," Lennie shouted.

"For the rabbits," George repeated.

"And I get to tend the rabbits."

"An' you get to tend the rabbits."

Lennie giggled with happiness. "An' live on the fatta the lan'."

"Yes."

Lennie turned his head.

"No, Lennie. Look down there acrost the river, like you can almost see the place."

Lennie obeyed him. George looked down at the gun.

There were crashing footsteps in the brush now. George turned and looked toward them.

"Go on, George. When we gonna do it?"

"Gonna do it soon."

"Me an' you."

"You . . . an' me. Ever'body gonna be nice to you. Ain't gonna be no more trouble. Nobody gonna hurt nobody nor steal from 'em."

Lennie said, "I thought you was mad at me, George."

"No," said George. "No, Lennie. I ain't mad. I never been mad, an' I ain't now. That's a thing I want ya to know."

The voices came close now. George raised the gun and listened to the voices.

Lennie begged, "Le's do it now. Le's get that place now."

"Sure, right now. I gotta. We gotta."

And George raised the gun and steadied it, and he brought the muzzle of it close to the back of Lennie's head. The hand shook violently, but his face set and his hand steadied. He pulled the trigger. The crash of the shot rolled up the hills and rolled down again. Lennie jarred, and then settled slowly forward to the sand, and he lay without quivering.

George shivered and looked at the gun, and then he threw it from him, back up on the bank, near the pile of old ashes.

The brush seemed filled with cries and with the sound of running feet. Slim's voice shouted, "George. Where you at, George?"

But George sat stiffly on the bank and looked at his right hand that had thrown the gun away. The group burst into the clearing, and Curley was ahead. He saw Lennie lying on the sand. "Got him, by God." He went over and looked down at Lennie, and then he looked back at George. "Right in the back of the head," he said softly.

Slim came directly to George and sat down beside him, sat very close to him. "Never you mind," said Slim. "A guy got to sometimes."

But Carlson was standing over George. "How'd you do it?" he asked.

"I just done it," George said tiredly.

"Did he have my gun?"

"Yeah. He had your gun."

"An' you got it away from him and you took it an' you killed him?"

"Yeah. Tha's how." George's voice was almost a whisper. He looked steadily at his right hand that had held the gun.

Slim twitched George's elbow. "Come on, George. Me an' you'll go in an' get a drink."

George let himself be helped to his feet. "Yeah, a drink."

Slim said, "You hadda, George. I swear you hadda. Come on with me." He led George into the entrance of the trail and up toward the highway.

Curley and Carlson looked after them. And Carlson said, "Now what the hell ya suppose is eatin' them two guys?"

——For Discussion——

RPW—

George and Lennie have traveled together on the road since Aunt Clara died, finding work as they go, dreaming about the future when they will finally have their own home, their own land, their own rabbits to feed. Lennie needs George to care for him, but George also needs Lennie as a companion, a friend to relieve the loneliness of a rootless existence.

In his feeble innocence, Lennie loves the softness of velvet and silk, the touch of small mice and young puppies, but he has little control of his large physical presence or his massive grip. Before arriving with George at the ranch, he had frightened a woman in the town of Weed by pulling at her dress, and he has crushed Curley's hand here in a fight in the bunk house.

Curley's wife also suffers from loneliness, but the men believe she is a dangerous flirt, a woman who can only bring trouble. When Lennie panics in the barn, he is worried that he will lose his dream, his friendship with George, his opportunity to feed the rabbits. He does not want to hurt Curley's wife, only stop her screams. Ironically, by killing her, he is trying to prevent an inevitable loss.

Candy had hoped to join George and Lennie in their quest for the American dream of land and friendship. When he discov-

ers the body of Curley's wife, however, he knows the dream is dead. The only question left then is how the final scene will play itself out.

Curley wants revenge, not only for the death of his wife, but also for the harm done to his hand. George could run again with Lennie as he had done in Weed, but Lennie has now killed a human being, and Curley is determined to lock him in a cage and perhaps kill him.

George and Lennie are family. They "give a hoot" about each other. George, at times, may think Lennie is a burden, but when he shoots Lennie with Carlson's Luger, I think he is executing a final act of friendship. He cannot do otherwise. As the wise foreman Slim puts it: "You hadda, George. I swear you hadda. Come on with me." That they walk off together leaves the only trace of hope.

JRT—

Lennie is a lump of a man whom others would have shipped off to a mental institution long ago. He would have lived out his days among the "criminally insane," doing hard labor or just being confined if he got belligerent. After all, Lennie is dangerous. He's killed mice and puppies because he loves to touch them; he pets them to death, breaking their bones with his enormous strength. And in this first chapter, he inadvertently kills Curley's wife. This death is not forgivable, as many of his other smaller acts of violence have been.

George, crusty and macho as he is, a regular guy making his way on a farm and doing odd jobs to earn enough money for the future, has been Lennie's caretaker. He is also Lennie's friend, and when he hears that Lennie has killed Curley's wife, he knows that the farmhands and Curley will kill Lennie. Steinbeck makes us question how we can best be our brother's keeper. Should George turn the murder of his retarded companion over to the farm mob, in a sense the society at large? Or is there a moral law operating here? Does George owe it to Lennie to take his life even though it isn't legal? What rights does a man have to take action?

Dreaming for what one cannot have also seems to be at the heart of this text. Lennie dreams for a place where he and George can live happily ever after, a place free from bosses and the ugliness of city life. Candy, the old farm hand, has also joined in George and Lennie's fantasies, planning a place for himself with them. He blames Curley's wife for the loss of his dream after Lennie kills her, calling her a tramp, sure that she has tempted Lennie and caused the murder.

It has always been interesting to me that Curley's wife has no name. She is no more to blame than Lennie. Also a dreamer, she muses about a world she might have had if she hadn't married Curley. She is set up here to be the innocent too, another victim of society's cruelty. Curley, her husband, gives her no space, no regard, and treats her like property. No wonder she wants to talk to someone, have some fun, be appreciated, have a voice.

Curley, the pragmatist and the representation of a man who must make himself important by controlling a woman, has no dreams. He wants to keep up illusions that he has power. After he learns of his wife's death, he sees no way out but killing Lennie. An eye for an eye, a tooth for a tooth. He immediately turns to anger instead of grief. He seems to have no heart, and unlike George, he has no pain in the seeking of Lennie's life.

The illusion of the American dream, a place where we can work for ourselves, own land, and tend our own, is at question here. What love has to do with it is very much at stake. If Curley remains in charge, the Georges of the world will suffer, the women will be brutalized, and the Lennies will be lost.

from THE KNOCKOUT ARTIST

Harry Crews

CHAPTER 10

With the exception of the time it took Mr. Blasingame to take two
calls on his cordless telephone, the three of them talked boxing
without interruption all the way downriver to the Gulf of Mex-
ico, and by the time the yacht broke into open water they had the
terms of their venture settled to everybody's satisfaction. Eugene
was impressed with Pete in a way he had never been impressed
before. Eugene would not have known what to ask for from Mr.
Blasingame. He had never had any kind of signed agreement with
Budd, nothing even verbal that was very specific. But Pete was specific, very specific. About everything.

"This whole thing is going to cost a lot of money," Pete said.

Mr. Blasingame smiled his humorless smile. "Doesn't everything?"

"If the conditions are right, I can find the boy, but even that
won't be cheap."

"Anything worthwhile never is," Mr. Blasingame said.

"You ought to know going in that with the breaks going our
way—and they probably won't—nobody may see a profit for three,
even five years. The only money in any division is for the top two
or three guys. The only real money is having a champion, a popular champion."

"Then for five years, perhaps forever," said Mr. Blasingame, "it
will simply be a tax write-off, won't it?"

"I wouldn't know about that," said Pete.

"My accountants would. And in the meantime, it would give
me pleasure."

"A very expensive pleasure."

"Most of my pleasures are."

This talk of money and accountants and championships had
stunned Eugene more than a little. Besides that, Pete sounded as
though he were trying to talk Mr. Blasingame out of owning a
fighter, talk the two of them out of a job. Eugene glanced at the
waiter hovering just out of earshot and the waiter was instantly at
the table, where Eugene handed him his empty glass. Pete pushed

his own empty glass toward the waiter without ever taking his eyes off Mr. Blasingame or missing a beat in what he was saying. Eugene watched him, amazed. Was this the same guy whose bedroom was hardly bigger than a closet and who had slept in rank, dead air until he paid a hundred dollars to a girl, who did a nasty act with a teddy bear, for a howling mob, to fall in love with him for six hours before she finally fell in love with him forever for nothing?

Mr. Blasingame spread his dead-white bony fingers on the table and said: "So that we may enjoy the afternoon and the other guests, why don't you just put it all in front of me. You too, Eugene. You've been too quiet."

"Pete was a better fighter than me," said Eugene, "and he's doing this better than I could, too."

Mr. Blasingame frowned. "I hate to see a man sell himself short."

Eugene said: "Who's selling who short? I brought the best mouth in New Orleans with me, didn't I? He sound like he knows what he's doing or he sound like he knows what he's doing?"

"A point well taken."

"A really good kid," said Pete, "say a National Golden Gloves champion, will still usually have to hold down a job and train in the evening. But if we can feed him, give him someplace to put his head down, put clothes on his back, a little pocket money on his hip, and cover his gym expenses, we can have the pick of some very good boys. Eugene and I will go straight salary, say four hundred apiece a week, plus expenses. Kick it up a hundred every time the kid wins, lose a hundred every time he loses. You own, Mr. Blasingame, twenty percent of the kid forever. Eugene and me take ten percent apiece. We never make a nickel on our ten until you make back what you pay us and what it costs to keep the boy. The boy knows all this going in. He starts taking sixty percent when his fights make back what we—you—got in him. It's a good deal. A fair deal. We'll get a contract, lawyers, make it right. Nobody gets fu . . . screwed."

"I have no shortage of lawyers," said Mr. Blasingame.

"Fine," said Pete. "Use'm. Eugene and me'll get our own."

Mr. Blasingame said: "If I were not hiring you for this, Pete, I would hire you for something else. You're a good man at the table."

"Then it's a deal?" said Pete.

"No," said Mr. Blasingame.

And so with Pete and Mr. Blasingame bargaining back and forth, Eugene drank steadily as they sailed through the bright air down the Mississippi River. It all got more and more complex and more and more specific. Mr. Blasingame did not want to give up twenty percent of his fighter. Pete settled on fifteen percent—seven and a half percent for himself, the same for Eugene—but in return, Pete got the salary raised to five hundred a week. To go up to five hundred, though, Mr. Blasingame made the bonus in salary for the fighter winning only fifty dollars, while the penalty for losing was still a hundred-dollar reduction in salary. Pete and Eugene had the right to sell their interests in the fighter, but Mr. Blasingame retained first option to buy them out. The right to sell and first refusal option were not, on the other hand, reciprocal. Pete pointed out that neither he nor Eugene had transportation, unless you could call Eugene's motorcycle transportation, and surely Mr. Blasingame did not want his fighter's handlers riding around on a motorcycle. Certainly he did not. He had a lease agreement for automobiles for certain of his employees. Mr. Blasingame offered a Ford Maverick. Pete wanted a Cadillac. Eugene wanted another drink. Through a vodka mist that grew gradually redder, Eugene could see how much Mr. Blasingame was enjoying this bargaining and jockeying for leverage, which did not surprise him at all. After all, the man owned a fucking building in the CBD, and a mansion on St. Charles Avenue, and they were sitting on his yacht. What did surprise him was how much Pete was also enjoying the give-and-take, and how good he was at it. And Pete, to his certain knowledge, did not own a goddam thing, except a competitive instinct and a will to fight that might have won him the world. Eugene, happy and stunned with drink, relaxed and watched the seagulls wheeling and turning over the water. He was so happy and so stunned, in fact, that he did not realize the discussion was over until Mr. Blasingame was already on his feet.

"I look forward to working with you," said Mr. Blasingame. "The finer points are best left until later. I have guests to look after. May I show you about the craft? Introduce you to some of the other guests, perhaps?"

"I think I'd just like to sit here and think about all this for a minute," Eugene said.

Pete said: "We've got a couple of ladies aboard somewhere. We'll run'm down after my man here gets his sea legs."

"They're with Jake," said Eugene.

"Then they're in fine hands," Mr. Blasingame said.

"She's good people," Eugene said. "I didn't always know that, but she's good people." Only when he heard himself say what he said did he realize how over-the-top drunk he was.

"That she is, Eugene," Mr. Blasingame said. "That she is."

"We're going to do it up tight and right," said Pete. "Good doing business with you."

Mr. Blasingame lifted his glass of carrot juice in toast. "Pleasure, gentlemen. Let pleasure rule the day." He turned and strode across the deck.

"Absofuckinglutely amazing," said Pete when he was gone.

"Some better than I thought it might be," Eugene said.

"I'll believe all this when I see the money."

"I don't think it's jive, man. I think it's for real."

"Cut buddy, you ain't said shit that whole time. I'm in up to my ass and don't know half what I'm talking about and all you do is sit here breathing and drinking. Drinking some. Tell me I'm wrong. You are about three-quarters twisted, ain't you?"

"Why should I say anything when I got you," said Eugene. "And yeah, drunk some."

Pete reached over and threw his arm around Eugene's neck. "You sweet son of a bitch, I may shuck Tulip and marry you. This is a bitch of a day, sweetheart. I don't know how you fell in this and I don't want to know, but Jesus, thanks for the leg up for me."

"Why ain't you drunk?" said Eugene.

"Because I was talking. *You* was drinking."

"You think they got any food on this thing? I need a bottom for my stomach."

"What they ain't got on this boat, nobody needs. You want food, we find food. Come on."

Eugene put his hand on Pete's arm. "Hold it a second."

"Yeah?"

"About Mr. Blasingame."

"What about him?"

That was exactly what Eugene had been turning over and over. How much of what he knew of Mr. Blasingame should he tell Pete? Anything? Everything?

"He's . . . he's a shark."

"Eugene, you drunk and you do need a bottom. Bad. Where the hell you think I been all my life? I don't know how the dude got his bucks or what kind of tree he swings from, but two minutes after I started talking to him, I saw that old familiar face, man. That face been gnawing my ass since I left my mama's knees. They ain't two cents' worth of difference in that sucker and the jiveass iceman I been making it on the corner with my whole life. Be easy, sweetheart, Pete know these waters. I been here before."

"You ain't been here before."

"You know how much of my ass I owned when I was seven in the world? I never told you this. You know how much?" Eugene only sat watching him. "Not a fucking ounce. I'd been beat out of ever piece of my skin. Everybody else riding and I was walking. It ain't gone happen again. Count on it. Rest easy. Now let's you and me go find that food." He turned and pointed to a huge glass-enclosed room in which they could see men and women standing about with glasses in their hands. "Wouldn't surprise me if it was food right in there somewhere."

"I magine," said Eugene.

"You need a shoulder?"

"Steady as a rock, man," Eugene said, but he put a hand on Pete's shoulder when they stood up.

The waveless, blue-green Gulf was flat as a pond, and walking over the deck was like walking on the street. Pete opened the door and Eugene immediately felt a little better as the chill air of the room washed over him. The four old black men playing muted blues at the far end of the room on a little platform covered in blue velvet reminded Eugene of the college students' party. He had not known what he was walking into then, and he reminded himself that he did not know what he was walking into now.

"Look yonder, old son," said Pete.

A long line of food was set up at right angles to the corner where the musicians, looking bored and sleepy, played. Two men in starched linen jackets and wearing high chefs' caps stood looking equally bored and sleepy because nobody was paying much attention to the food they were obviously there to serve. The action centered on the round mahogany bar in the middle of the room where two bartenders worked to fill and refill the glasses being shoved at them.

"Well, I thought you'd never," a voice said as a soft, heavy hand touched his elbow.

Eugene turned his slowly spinning head, trying to stop the

spinning but fearing it was going to spin faster. It was Purvis, enormous in a satin jumpsuit which the creases of his fat caught and held under his sloping breasts, on his stomach, at his groin.

"We'd never what, man?" said Pete pleasantly.

"Come in from that savage, savage heat and join the party."

"I don't believe I know you, biggun," Pete said.

Purvis looked at Eugene. "Aren't you going to introduce me to your friend, Eugene?"

"No."

"That's not the right answer," said Purvis, "and not the right attitude." He put out his thick, soft hand. "My name is Purvis, Purvis Reeker. I'm Mr. Blasingame's man."

"Hell, ain't we all," Pete said, shaking hands with Purvis. "And don't mind Eugene here. He sometimes gets out of step with the parade. But he comes back quick, Eugene does. My name's Pete Turner and . . . "

"I know," said Purvis.

"You do?" said Pete.

"I was just giving Eugene a chance to be polite. You're here with Miss Josephine, perfectly delightful creature, and just there"—he pointed across the room to Charity, who was talking with Mr. Blasingame while holding lightly to Jake's arm—"and just there is Miss Charity, the third member of Mr. Biggs' party."

Pete slapped Purvis good-naturedly on the ass and said, "Now ain't you a hip, magic motherfucker."

Purvis blushed and his fat face jerked in a shy smile. "Not magic at all, really. Ernesto—he's the one who met you when you came aboard—is my man."

"Your man?" said Pete.

"In Mr. Blasingame's world it's like medieval times when every man had his man and God had the king."

"Kiss my ass," said Pete, "God had the king, you say."

"And Ernesto reported immediately to me because he knew I needed to know because I'm Mr. Blasingame's man and since you're one of the special ones on board today, I'm here to make sure you have everything you need."

"Say everything I need?"

"Or want," said Purvis. "Alas, they're not always the same." And again a faint blush rushed up his creased neck and chins into his face.

"Hear that, Eugene? I'm special and I get what I want. Or need. Afuckinglas."

"Oh, everyone in your party aboard is special today."

Eugene said: "Will you believe me if I tell you it's raining, Purvis, when I puke on you shoes?"

"Do be happy," pleaded Purvis in a voice that was sad and strangely girlish, his face now darkly frowning, "and don't say terrible things. You'll just spoil the day."

"We need to feed him," said Pete. "He get cranky when he get hungry."

"Well, for God's sake, for God's sake, I can understand that. Why didn't you say so? Let me take care of that for you." He pointed again. "Take that table back there. I'll have a steward bring you something wild and Cajun and delicious. Everybody else is ignoring the food. I'm glad somebody is hungry. I certainly appreciate that."

He danced away toward the buffet table in a step surprisingly light for a man so heavy. They watched him go and Pete said, "Boy's got his full growth, ain't he? He ain't but a biscuit away from four hundred pounds. How come you so mean to him?"

"Because I don't like him."

"Ain't a hell of a lot you do like anymore, seems like."

"Seems like," said Eugene, raising his hand to take Pete's shoulder again. "Let's go sit down."

They took a table covered by a white linen cloth beside a tinted glass wall through which they could see oceangoing freighters steaming for New Orleans and sailboats—everything from two-man catamarans to three-masters as big as the yacht they were on—and heavy, low-riding shrimp boats with nets winched into their rigging. The water through which they moved was a blue mirror reflecting light.

A waiter appeared at the table almost before they had a chance to settle in their chairs. He carried a round tray on which there were glasses of iced water and hot bread wrapped in cloth in wicker baskets and dishes of mounded butter. "Would the gentlemen like wine with lunch?" he asked.

"I'll have vodka straight up," said Pete. He hooked his thumb at Eugene. "Coffee for him."

"Very good, sir."

"No coffee," said Eugene. "A vodka for me, too."

"Of course, sir," said the waiter and was gone.

"I thought you had the dark twirlies, man."

"I said I wanted a bottom, I didn't say I didn't want a drink. We've done our business, I'm ready to go home. But we're in the middle of the fucking ocean. I'm not going to hold up to the rest of this sober. Need a little grease for the machinery, boss man, a little grease."

"You strange, Eugene, you know that? Hold up to what? The man said we got anything we wanted, so what's the problem?"

"No problem."

"Good."

They watched Purvis coming toward them, driving two waiters carrying trays loaded with dishes before him. As they put the food on the table, Purvis said: "Here's a little bit of heaven for you. My own favorite. I do hope you like it. Roasted quail stuffed with crawfish dressing, a touch of corn maque choux, and a steaming bowl of gumbo." He shuffled where he stood, his great body swaying in a little dance of anticipation. "Well, go on! Go on! Try it!"

Pete ripped a drumstick about the size of his thumb off the quail, put it in his mouth and stripped the meat off the bone. He chewed slowly and swallowed, nothing showing on his face. Then he cracked the little bone with his teeth and sucked the marrow.

"Well?" said Purvis.

Pete looked up from the dish and a great, open smile spread over his face. "Purvis, your taste and my taste fit like spoons. If you was a woman, I'd marry you. Man'd have to die and go to heaven to git better meat than that."

Eugene, who had been sucking a piece of bread he'd torn off a hot loaf and soaked in gumbo, said, "You done good, Purvis, you done real good." He sipped from the ice-cold vodka the waiter had brought in a frosted goblet. "Everything is just right."

Pete had ripped open the quail and was spooning the dressing into his mouth. He paused with the spoon in the air, and looked about the room. "Say, Purvis, where's Tulip?"

"Tulip?" said Purvis.

"Josephine," said Eugene.

"Uh, she's below."

"Below what?" Pete said.

"Decks."

"Break it down for me, Purvis, I ain't a sailor."

"Downstairs. She's downstairs in the greenroom."

"And what would that be, the greenroom?"

"That's where people wait."

Now Pete put his spoon down and pushed his plate aside. "Wait for what?"

"For what they want. See, it's called the greenroom because in the theater . . . "

Pete waved him silent. "I don't need to know nothing about that shit. What's my woman *doing* down there?"

"Anything she wants, I suspect," Purvis said in a voice that was at once shy and contemptuous.

Pete stood up, reached for the front of Purvis's jumpsuit, and jerked him close, their noses almost touching. "Talk straight, man. I don't play when I'm talking about my woman."

Purvis leaned to the side and whispered something that Eugene could not hear. He could not imagine why Pete was so hot, but Eugene was more than a little drunk, and he knew it. Maybe Pete knew something he didn't know.

"Show me," said Pete, releasing Purvis. Then to Eugene, "Hold it down here, Eugene. Back in a flash. Got to check on something." And he was gone, following Purvis through a doorway on the other side of the bar.

Eugene would have gone with him but he did not trust himself on his feet. He finished the food and sat sipping from Pete's drink after he had finished his own. Charity was sitting beside him before he saw her. Jake didn't sit down but lounged there before the table. She had changed her clothes and was now in a white cotton shirt and trousers with a light-yellow snap-brim Panama hat pulled low over her eyes. An unlit black cheroot was caught between her pouting lips.

"Mr. Blasingame says you're going to do business," said Charity.

"We'll see," said Eugene.

Jake cocked one of her thin model's hips and said: "Why so pale and wan, fair lover?"

"What?"

"Why the hangdog glum?" she said. Then: "What the fuck ails you?"

"I don't think I like boats," he said. "And these ain't my kind of people."

"Well, I want you to know you've made me very happy," said Charity, "and I'm grateful."

"That's good," said Eugene. He felt better—steadier—now that he'd eaten.

"So," Jake said, "except for not liking the boat and the people on it, what do you think of the day so far? Glad you came?"

"I already thanked you. I already did that."

"Hey, that was a straight question. There's plenty of people to bite without biting your friends."

"Is that what I was doing, biting my friend? I'm glad I came, O.K.?"

Charity reached across the table and touched his chin with one of her long, slender fingers. "You didn't tell me Mr. Blasingame was interested in a fighter, in owning one you could work with. I think that's just wonderful—for him and for you. And for Pete, of course."

"The deal ain't done yet," said Eugene. "So far, it's only talk."

Jake said: "If Mr. B says the deal is done, it's done. You can put his word in the bank."

The four old black men had swung into a slow, waltzy kind of jazz number, and a few couples were swaying together across the floor to the music. Charity caught Eugene's hand in hers. "Dance with me."

"Not hardly," Eugene said.

Jake uncocked her hip, leaned and took Charity's hand in hers. "Come," she said. "I'll dance with you."

Charity hesitated for just a second, and Eugene thought he saw her cheeks darken with blood, before her lips parted, smiling, over her sharp, perfect teeth, and she rose to be embraced by Jake. They moved to the music, out over the floor, moved gracefully and naturally, and Eugene couldn't help thinking, as he watched Jake's narrow-hipped back, what a lovely couple they made. He felt a moment of uneasy fear for Jake. She no doubt thought she was the odd one out, when in fact she held, in the person of Charity, a bundle of snakes. But Eugene felt Jake could take care of herself, and he didn't want to think about it.

He watched the door through which Pete had disappeared and waited for him to return. But he did not. He started to have another drink, but thought better of it. His head had cleared and he remembered the urgency and anger in Pete's voice. The number the musicians were playing ended, and they segued into another. Jake and Charity remained on the dance floor.

A waiter came by the table and Eugene caught his arm. The waiter stopped, turned toward Eugene, balancing the tray he was carrying.

"The greenroom," said Eugene.

"You wish something, sir?" The waiter had an accent that he did not recognize.

"My friend went to the greenroom. Where is it?"

"I'm afraid I don't understand, sir."

Eugene stood up. He still had the sleeve of the man's jacket caught in his fist. "Take me to the greenroom, cocksucker." He had spoken louder than he meant to and realized, for the first time, that a tiny fear had been gnawing at him. Eugene had not brought Pete here to drop him into something he could not handle.

"Please, sir. The cursing . . . Mr. Blasingame."

"Take me now to the greenroom or I'll tear your head off and puke down your lungs."

"Just let me get Mr. Reeker, he'll know . . . "

"Purvis already told me. And he's got my friend down there."

Eugene saw the waiter's eyes lift and focus on something over his left shoulder. When he turned to look, Eugene saw Mr. Blasingame across the room nodding his head to the waiter. He gave Eugene his tight, lipless smile and raised his carrot juice in toast.

"If you would follow me, sir," the waiter said.

"Why the fuck couldn't you save me all that to start with?" said Eugene, as they stepped out of the room into a long corridor.

"You should not curse here because . . . "

Eugene reached out and slapped the waiter hard on the back of his head. The waiter flinched and jerked his head into his shoulders but did not turn. "Shut up," hissed Eugene. "Don't talk to me." He didn't like any of this. Something smacked of kink here, and Blasingame had promised him that kink was not what this trip was about. Well, son, he thought, ain't the first time you been lied to, is it?

The corridor took them to the very back of the yacht, where they descended a narrow iron stairwell. At the bottom of the stairwell was a pale green door. The waiter stepped to the side of the door and averted his eyes.

"The greenroom, sir." The waiter turned and Eugene could hear his feet on the stairs as he rushed away.

Eugene opened the door and stepped inside. The room was not

only painted pale green but it was lit indirectly from some secret source in an even paler shade of green that caused the heavy
chairs, the couches, and the people moving through the dim light
to glow like phosphorus on the sea at night. There were no windows. Eugene stood very still just inside the door, waiting for his
senses to adjust. Then he felt, rather than saw, someone at his elbow. When he turned, Purvis loomed there, enormous, glowing,
with a flaking cream pie in either hand. Some white substance was
smeared on his lips, and his powerful jaws worked and worked before he finally swallowed.

"Hello, Knockout," he said.

"Eugene, goddammit. Eugene Biggs." His throat was so tight
that he did not recognize the voice as his own.

Purvis looked at the ceiling, and raised a pie. "Up there, you're
Eugene. Down here, you're Knockout. And don't get superior with
me just because I'm heavy. Heavy people need love, too."

"Jesus," said Eugene, "this is a bad dream."

"This is everybody's worst dream," Purvis said around a
mouthful of cream pie, chewing, smiling. "Your worst dream come
true. Mr. B is a dreamer, a purveyor of dreams."

He looked at Purvis, and the expression on Eugene's face made
Purvis take a step backward. "You're not going to run amuck are
you?"

"What?" Eugene said.

"Amuck. You are not going to run amuck." It was a statement
now, not a question. "Because Mr. B does not like amuck. He will
not deal with amuck. So don't. It's too far to swim home."

The phosphorescent figures moving through the green light
had become more distinct now, recognizable. Across the room a
tiny man dressed as a jockey was riding a wooden rocking horse.
At regular intervals he savagely lashed the horse with a leather
whip. A group of people stood in one far corner, and as Eugene
watched, they parted briefly, and he saw Russell Muscle, naked, his
body oiled, flexing in front of a huge mirror while the young man
he had seen earlier at the end of the dock, tall and lean and very
blond in his bleached-out and wrinkled denims and tuxedo jacket,
directed a long-snouted camera with one hand and waved wildly
with the other.

"Yes, I know," said Purvis in a sympathetic voice. "Always
something of a shock the first time. But you'll get used to it if you

want to." He took another bite of the last remaining pie. "Or need to. But do try to remember that it is not Mr. B's pleasure to force anybody into anything. Or even to suggest, for that matter. He only provides the opportunity. Opportunity is his pleasure."

"Where is Pete?"

"You don't want to know."

"I came down here, didn't I? Don't hurt yourself, Purvis."

"I'll not, and neither will you. You're in our game now. This is our arena. And, yes, as a matter of fact, you did come down here of your own free will."

"Show me Pete, you fat tub of guts. I'm tired of talking."

Purvis said: "You've already established what you think of my body, Knocker. I do wish you didn't feel compelled to make continual reference to the fact that I'm heavy."

"You've gone way past heavy, Purvis. You've gone all the way to something else."

"There you go again," said Purvis, but he turned as he spoke and Eugene followed him past the tiny man lashing the rocking horse, to a section of the room partitioned off by a bamboo screen. Purvis stopped, licked his fingers, and pointed.

"Through there. And remember, amuck will not be tolerated."

"Eat shit and die," said Eugene.

Eugene parted the bamboo screen and stepped through. It was a small room and dimly lit by a small, shaded green light on a low table beside a narrow bed. Josephine sat on the edge of the bed, her face slack as though she might be asleep, even though her hooded eyes were open. Her left arm was tied off above the elbow by a looped belt, the end of which she held in her teeth.

Pete stood in front of her, holding a hypodermic syringe raised toward the dim light. He turned, glanced at Eugene, then back at the syringe, and thumped it with his finger. Eugene could not speak. He knew what he was seeing but looking dead at it could not believe it. He moved closer.

Pete bent and took Josephine's elbow and inserted the needle into the bulging vein there in the crook of her arm. He drew back the plunger and the syringe filled with blood. Eugene had seen more blood in the ring and in the gym than most men saw in a lifetime, but looking at the blood in the syringe, he felt his gorge rising.

"I'm in, darling," Pete whispered softly.

Josephine opened her mouth, releasing the belt, and as it loosened on her arm, Pete slowly depressed the plunger. Josephine's mouth opened wider and she licked her dry, cracked lips.

In a distant voice, she said, "Oh, God." She watched the syringe. "Boot it," she whispered.

Pete drew back the plunger, filling the syringe again with blood. He slowly depressed the plunger until it was empty.

"Again," she said.

He drew the plunger back and when the syringe filled with blood, he depressed it again.

"Once more," she said, her voice dreamy. "Just once more."

"You've got the hit," Pete said. "You're just playing now."

He withdrew the needle, placed a piece of cotton where the needle had entered the vein, and pushed her hand up against her shoulder to hold the cotton in place.

In a barely audible voice she said: "Thank you. Oh, thank you, God."

Pete placed one of his hands on the back of her head and eased her down on the bed, where she lay smiling, her eyes half closed.

"Ahhh, Pete," Eugene said.

Pete said: "She'll be all right by the time we get back to the marina."

"She ain't going to be all right for a long time, man . . . if she ever is."

"Well, at least now you know."

"I don't know shit," said Eugene.

"None of us do," Pete said.

——*For Discussion*——

RPW—

Eugene Talmadge Biggs from southern Georgia had a sublime dream of becoming a world boxing champion until the day it became clear that he had a glass jaw. His manager Budd abandoned him, and filled with humiliation and shame, Eugene descended to the perverse underworld of New Orleans, becoming "the knockout artist" with the bizarre talent of knocking himself unconscious. In this underworld, Eugene's friend Pete, once a potential contender for the championship, now works as a projectionist at the Flesh and Flash porno and snuff movie house; Josephine (a.k.a. Tulip), Pete's new girlfriend, stages a sex show with a teddy bear doll each night in the French Quarter; Jake, a bisexual prostitute, sells sex for survival; and Charity, a snake-like seductress and opportunist, has made Eugene a subject to be studied as part of her lustful field research.

In this selection from the story, Eugene believes that Mr. Blasingame, whom he also knows from a previous encounter as Oyster Boy (the kinky underside of the business tycoon), can deliver him from the hopeless round of despair and shame. But, as we see, Blasingame cannot be part of Eugene's solution, because he is part of the problem. Blasingame is not what he appears to be.

Blasingame wants to invest in a boxer, buy him, and have Eugene and Pete manage and train him. Blasingame can afford it just as he can afford the building he owns in the Central Business District, the mansion on St. Charles Avenue, the yacht where the party and negotiations are taking place, and the rigid hierarchy of servants from the obese Purvis on down. By contrast, Eugene and Pete have never owned anything; in fact, they seem to know much more about being owned than about ownership. On this yacht, however, they supposedly can get whatever they want.

"The man said we got anything we wanted, so what's the problem?"

"No problem."

But in this fake paradise, there is a problem. What people driven by humiliation and shame want is what they crave, but not what they need. In this world, Mr. Blasingame provides the opportunities and the dreams. His pleasure is derived from controlling the show. Unfortunately, his pleasure is not the pleasure of a god, but of the devil in disguise.

Below deck, Eugene glimpses the horror of hell, the addictions fueled by false desire and by the illusion of always craving "something else." In the end, Eugene will only have one option if he is to survive: break forever from Blasingame, from Charity, from Pete and Tulip, and from his sublime dreams.

JRT—

It's difficult not to feel sorry for Eugene, who seems swept up in a world of illicit drugs, lousy deals, seamy morals, and machismo. He just wants to fight, I say to myself. After all, why shouldn't he rely on the Petes of the world and get to go around in cruise ships? Isn't that all part of the glamour that comes with success in sports?

The problem is that soon into the chapter, I begin to wonder if that is really all that boxing is about. Fresh from the 1997 bout where Mike Tyson bites Evander Holyfield's ear, we know that boxing is not exempt from the slimy side of life. Money governs reruns of that HBO special and in some parts of the country, you can now buy chocolate ears, dedicated to the fighters. But here, in Crews' tough view of reality, where Eugene sees Pete's woman, Josephine, shoot up in the "greenroom," a sort of den of iniquity on the open seas, fighting seems less sport than a way of life.

Crews is a fierce writer and his portraits of cons are powerful. First there's the sleazebag, Purvis, a four-hundred-pounder who shines with sweat and sleaze; his "man," the dealmaker, Mr. Blasingame, whom we can just imagine in an expensive suit, with cheap cigars, diamond rings and ear studs; Jake, a lesbian man-looking woman who's "good people" and who dances with Charity, Eugene's lover; and finally, Josephine, or Tulip, Pete's junkie girlfriend whom we watch shoot up. I am both drawn to the scene in the ship for its grotesqueness and to the scene in the greenroom for its horror—complete with weird naked muscle-men and whips—and repelled by the brutality they evoke.

It is a sad commentary on our world to see through Crews' eyes, but perhaps the fault is not Crews'. The world he sees is too real and too hopeless. Eugene must exit from this den of iniquity to redeem his spirit.

Tell the Women We're Going

Raymond Carver

Bill Jamison had always been best friends with Jerry Roberts. The two grew up in the south area, near the old fairgrounds, went through grade school and junior high together, and then on to Eisenhower, where they took as many of the same teachers as they could manage, wore each other's shirts and sweaters and pegged pants, and dated and banged the same girls—whichever came up as a matter of course.

Summers they took jobs together—swamping peaches, picking cherries, stringing hops, anything they could do that paid a little and where there was no boss to get on your ass. And then they bought a car together. The summer before their senior year, they chipped in and bought a red '54 Plymouth for $325.

They shared it. It worked out fine.

But Jerry got married before the end of the first semester and dropped out of school to work steady at Robby's Mart.

As for Bill, he'd dated the girl too. Carol was her name, and she went just fine with Jerry, and Bill went over there every chance he got. It made him feel older, having married friends. He'd go over there for lunch or for supper, and they'd listen to Elvis or to Bill Haley and the Comets.

But sometimes Carol and Jerry would start making out right with Bill still there, and he'd have to get up and excuse himself and take a walk to Dezorn's Service Station to get some Coke because there was only the one bed in the apartment, a hide-away that came down in the living room. Or sometimes Jerry and Carol would head off to the bathroom, and Bill would have to move to the kitchen and pretend to be interested in the cupboards and the refrigerator and not trying to listen.

So he stopped going over so much; and then June he graduated, took a job at the Darigold plant, and joined the National Guard. In a year he had a milk route of his own and was going steady with Linda. So Bill and Linda would go over to Jerry and Carol's, drink beer, and listen to records.

Carol and Linda got along fine, and Bill was flattered when Carol said that, confidentially, Linda was "a real person."

Jerry liked Linda too. "She's great," Jerry said.

When Bill and Linda got married, Jerry was best man. The reception, of course, was at the Donnelly Hotel, Jerry and Bill cutting up together and linking arms and tossing off glasses of spiked punch. But once, in the middle of all this happiness, Bill looked at Jerry and thought how much older Jerry looked, a lot older than twenty-two. By then Jerry was the happy father of two kids and had moved up to assistant manager at Robby's, and Carol had one in the oven again.

They saw each other every Saturday and Sunday, sometimes oftener if it was a holiday. If the weather was good, they'd be over at Jerry's to barbecue hot dogs and turn the kids loose in the wading pool Jerry had got for next to nothing, like a lot of other things he got from the Mart.

Jerry had a nice house. It was up on a hill overlooking the Naches. There were other houses around, but not too close. Jerry was doing all right. When Bill and Linda and Jerry and Carol got together, it was always at Jerry's place because Jerry had the barbecue and the records and too many kids to drag around.

It was a Sunday at Jerry's place the time it happened.

The women were in the kitchen straightening up. Jerry's girls were out in the yard throwing a plastic ball into the wading pool, yelling, and splashing after it.

Jerry and Bill were sitting in the reclining chairs on the patio, drinking beer and just relaxing.

Bill was doing most of the talking—things about people they knew, about Darigold, about the four-door Pontiac Catalina he was thinking of buying.

Jerry was staring at the clothesline, or at the '68 Chevy hardtop that stood in the garage. Bill was thinking how Jerry was getting to be deep, the way he stared all the time and hardly did any talking at all.

Bill moved in his chair and lighted a cigarette.

He said, "Anything wrong, man? I mean, you know."

Jerry finished his beer and then mashed the can. He shrugged.

"You know," he said.

Bill nodded.

Then Jerry said, "How about a little run?"

"Sounds good to me," Bill said. "I'll tell the women we're going."

They took the Naches River highway out to Gleed, Jerry driving. The day was sunny and warm, and air blew through the car.

"Where we headed?" Bill said.

"Let's shoot a few balls."

"Fine with me," Bill said. He felt a whole lot better just seeing Jerry brighten up.

"Guy's got to get out," Jerry said. He looked at Bill. "You know what I mean?"

Bill understood. He liked to get out with the guys from the plant for the Friday-night bowling league. He liked to stop off twice a week after work to have a few beers with Jack Broderick. He knew a guy's got to get out.

"Still standing," Jerry said, as they pulled up onto the gravel in front of the Rec Center.

They went inside, Bill holding the door for Jerry, Jerry punching Bill lightly in the stomach as he went on by.

"Hey there!"

It was Riley.

"Hey, how you boys keeping?"

It was Riley coming around from behind the counter, grinning. He was a heavy man. He had on a short-sleeved Hawaiian shirt that hung outside his jeans. Riley said, "So how you boys been keeping?"

"Ah, dry up and give us a couple of Olys," Jerry said, winking at Bill. "So how you been, Riley?" Jerry said.

Riley said, "So how you boys doing? Where you been keeping yourselves? You boys getting any on the side? Jerry, the last time I seen you, your old lady was six months gone."

Jerry stood a minute and blinked his eyes.

"So how about the Olys?" Bill said.

They took stools near the window. Jerry said, "What kind of place is this, Riley, that it don't have any girls on a Sunday afternoon?"

Riley laughed. He said, "I guess they're all in church praying for it."

They each had five cans of beer and took two hours to play three racks of rotation and two racks of snooker, Riley sitting on a stool and talking and watching them play, Bill always looking at his watch and then looking at Jerry.

Bill said, "So what do you think, Jerry? I mean, what do you think?" Bill said.

Jerry drained his can, mashed it, then stood for a time turning the can in his hand.

Back on the highway, Jerry opened it up—little jumps of eighty-five and ninety. They'd just passed an old pickup loaded with furniture when they saw the two girls.

"Look at that!" Jerry said, slowing. "I could use some of that."

Jerry drove another mile or so and then pulled off the road. "Let's go back," Jerry said. "Let's try it."

"Jesus," Bill said. "I don't know."

"I could use some," Jerry said.

Bill said, "Yeah, but I don't know."

"For Christ's sake," Jerry said.

Bill glanced at his watch and then looked all around. He said, "You do the talking. I'm rusty."

Jerry hooted as he whipped the car around.

He slowed when he came nearly even with the girls. He pulled the Chevy onto the shoulder across from them. The girls kept on going on their bicycles, but they looked at each other and laughed. The one on the inside was dark-haired, tall, and willowy. The other was light-haired and smaller. They both wore shorts and halters.

"Bitches," Jerry said. He waited for the cars to pass so he could pull a Y.

"I'll take the brunette," he said. He said, "The little one's yours."

Bill moved his back against the front seat and touched the bridge of his sunglasses. "They're not going to do anything," Bill said.

"They're going to be on your side," Jerry said.

He pulled across the road and drove back. "Get ready," Jerry said.

"Hi," Bill said as the girls bicycled up. "My name's Bill," Bill said.

"That's nice," the brunette said.

"Where are you going?" Bill said.

The girls didn't answer. The little one laughed. They kept bicycling and Jerry kept driving.

"Oh, come on now. Where you going?" Bill said.

"No place," the little one said.

"Where's no place?" Bill said.

"Wouldn't you like to know," the little one said.

"I told you my name," Bill said. "What's yours? My friend's Jerry," Bill said.

The girls looked at each other and laughed.

A car came up from behind. The driver hit his horn.

"Cram it!" Jerry shouted.

He pulled off a little and let the car go around. Then he pulled back up alongside the girls.

Bill said, "We'll give you a lift. We'll take you where you want. That's a promise. You must be tired riding those bicycles. You look tired. Too much exercise isn't good for a person. Especially for girls."

The girls laughed.

"You see?" Bill said. "Now tell us your names."

"I'm Barbara, she's Sharon," the little one said.

"All right!" Jerry said. "Now find out where they're going."

"Where you girls going?" Bill said. "Barb?"

She laughed. "No place," she said. "Just down the road."

"Where down the road?"

"Do you want me to tell them?" she said to the other girl.

"I don't care," the other girl said. "It doesn't make any difference," she said. "I'm not going to go anyplace with anybody anyway," the one named Sharon said.

"Where you going?" Bill said. "Are you going to Picture Rock?"

The girls laughed.

"That's where they're going," Jerry said.

He fed the Chevy gas and pulled up off onto the shoulder so that the girls had to come by on his side.

"Don't be that way," Jerry said. He said, "Come on." He said, "We're all introduced."

The girls just rode on by.

"I won't bite you!" Jerry shouted.

The brunette glanced back. It seemed to Jerry she was looking at him in the right kind of way. But with a girl you could never be sure.

Jerry gunned it back onto the highway, dirt and pebbles flying from under the tires.

"We'll be seeing you!" Bill called as they went speeding by.

"It's in the bag," Jerry said. "You see the look that cunt gave me?"

"I don't know," Bill said. "Maybe we should cut for home."

"We got it made!" Jerry said.

He pulled off the road under some trees. The highway forked here at Picture Rock, one road going on to Yakima, the other heading for Naches, Enumclaw, the Chinook Pass, Seattle.

A hundred yards off the road was a high, sloping, black mound of rock, part of a low range of hills, honeycombed with footpaths and small caves, Indian sign-painting here and there on the cave walls. The cliff side of the rock faced the highway and all over it there were things like this: NACHES 67—GLEED WILDCATS—JESUS SAVES—BEAT YAKIMA—REPENT NOW.

They sat in the car, smoking cigarettes. Mosquitoes came in and tried to get at their hands.

"Wish we had a beer now," Jerry said. "I sure could go for a beer," he said.

Bill said, "Me too," and looked at his watch.

When the girls came into view, Jerry and Bill got out of the car. They leaned against the fender in front.

"Remember," Jerry said, starting away from the car, "the dark one's mine. You got the other one."

The girls dropped their bicycles and started up one of the paths. They disappeared around a bend and then reappeared again, a little higher up. They were standing there and looking down.

"What're you guys following us for?" the brunette called down.

Jerry just started up the path.

The girls turned away and went off again at a trot.

Jerry and Bill kept climbing at a walking pace. Bill was smoking a cigarette, stopping every so often to get a good drag. When the path turned, he looked back and caught a glimpse of the car.

"Move it!" Jerry said.

"I'm coming," Bill said.

They kept climbing. But then Bill had to catch his breath. He couldn't see the car now. He couldn't see the highway, either. To his left and all the way down, he could see a strip of the Naches like a strip of aluminum foil.

Jerry said, "You go right and I'll go straight. We'll cut the cock-teasers off."

Bill nodded. He was too winded to speak.

He went higher for a while, and then the path began to drop, turning toward the valley. He looked and saw the girls. He saw them crouched behind an outcrop. Maybe they were smiling.

Bill took out a cigarette. But he could not get it lit. Then Jerry showed up. It did not matter after that.

Bill had just wanted to fuck. Or even to see them naked. On the other hand, it was okay with him if it didn't work out.

He never knew what Jerry wanted. But it started and ended with a rock. Jerry used the same rock on both girls, first on the girl called Sharon and then on the one that was supposed to be Bill's.

——*For Discussion*——

RPW—

Jerry Roberts and Bill Jamison have always been best buddies, sharing the same clothes, the same car, the same classes, and the same girls. Their male friendship came first, long before marriage and the trappings of adult responsibility. They are bonded for life.

Something is bothering Jerry. He is "getting to be deep, the way he star[es] all the time and hardly [does] any talking at all." What can it be? Is it his wife Carol? His two daughters? Another baby "in the oven again"? He's looking "a lot older than twenty-two" these days. Too bad he got married the beginning of his senior year and dropped out of high school. Carol must have been pregnant then too. Jerry must be feeling hemmed in. He needs some open space. Time to hit the road. "Tell the women we're going."

Where to? Male territory, that's where: the local bar to shoot some pool, drink some beer, talk some guy talk, maybe find some girls. In the end, girls are always the problem and the solution for folks like Jerry and Bill.

Five beers later, they're on the road again, headed home (that's OK with Bill), but ready for the hunt (Jerry needs it). Then they spot their prey, two "bitches" wearing shorts and halters—Sharon for Jerry, Barbara for Bill. It's all arranged. If Bill is hesitant and uncertain, Jerry has no doubt. He exudes male confidence and aggression.

"It's in the bag," Jerry said. "You see the look that cunt gave me. . . . We got it made."

The last scene up on Picture Rock shouldn't surprise us, but it does. Jerry uses the same rock on both girls, once for him and once for his buddy. They share everything. No doubt Jerry and Bill are blood brothers.

JRT—

Here we have a picture of two rapists. Although this story is well written in terms of some of the truths of the two men—as rapists and ultimately as murderers—it is not a story I would use with women in Changing Lives. So then, why is it included in our text?

It is a story that provokes us to think. It is not offensive to women because it is graphic (it isn't) or because the characters are caricatures (they aren't), but the story seems to say that a boring American life can lead to rape and murder. It is almost as though the backgrounds of the two men, Bill and Jerry, aren't important to their becoming violent criminals. There is no voice of conscience in the story; there are no second thoughts. There is only the beer and another boring day in the life of two mediocre men who marry, Carver suggests, out of predictability. The men stay together (is this friendship?) even though they grow apart from their wives after children and houses and after lack of deep communication. And lo and behold, they end up at a bar, looking for whatever comes their way. The men's cryptic "You know" seems to be the big answer for why they end up there.

It seems to me that this story could be useful for men to consider what's really going on in the lives of the two men in the story, lives that Carver does not show. And it might even be something that a woman could use to say, "See, here's how it was in my life." However, I tend to choose stories for women that have some hope and offer a possibility of redemption for the characters. Carver's story denigrates the average guy, and I do not buy the assumption that these rapists/murderers could be any two men. Whatever makes a man commit violent acts, or a woman for that matter, comes in large part from his particular background and not just from the American society or from the expectations we have of men and women.

The Carver story does not present young men like those in Boyle's "Greasy Lake," young men who have the potential, Boyle *says, to change their ways. If it is the institution of marriage and the lack of communication, the assumptions of friendship and good pals drinking together, that are supposed to "lead" Jerry and Bill onto the darkest path, I heartily protest such notions. Jerry and Bill are responsible for their behavior. And most women know this already, too well.*

from THEIR EYES WERE WATCHING GOD

Zora Neale Hurston

CHAPTER 10

One day Hezekiah asked off from work to go off with the ball team. Janie told him not to hurry back. She could close up the store herself this once. He cautioned her about the catches on the windows and doors and swaggered off to Winter Park.

Business was dull all day, because numbers of people had gone to the game. She decided to close early, because it was hardly worth the trouble of keeping open on an afternoon like this. She had set six o'clock as her limit.

At five-thirty a tall man came into the place. Janie was leaning on the counter making aimless pencil marks on a piece of wrapping paper. She knew she didn't know his name, but he looked familiar.

"Good evenin', Mis' Starks," he said with a sly grin as if they had a good joke together. She was in favor of the story that was making him laugh before she even heard it.

"Good evenin'," she answered pleasantly. "You got all de advantage 'cause Ah don't know yo' name."

"People wouldn't know me lak dey would *you*."

"Ah guess standin' in uh store do make uh person git tuh be known in de vicinity. Look lak Ah seen you somewhere."

"Oh, Ah don't live no further than Orlandah. Ah'm easy tuh see on Church Street most any day or night. You got any smokin' tobacco?"

She opened the glass case. "What kind?"

"Camels."

She handed over the cigarettes and took the money. He broke the pack and thrust one between his full, purple lips.

"You got a lil piece uh fire over dere, lady?"

They both laughed and she handed him two kitchen matches out of a box for that purpose. It was time for him to go but he didn't. He leaned on the counter with one elbow and cold-cocked her a look.

"Why ain't *you* at de ball game, too? Everybody else is dere."

"Well, Ah see somebody else besides me ain't dere. Ah just sold some cigarettes." They laughed again.

"Dat's 'cause Ah'm dumb. Ah got de thing all mixed up. Ah thought de game was gointuh be out at Hungerford. So Ah got uh ride tuh where dis road turns off from de Dixie Highway and walked over here and then Ah find out de game is in Winter Park."

That was funny to both of them too.

"So what you gointuh do now? All de cars in Eatonville is gone."

"How about playin' *you* some checkers? You looks hard tuh beat."

"Ah is, 'cause Ah can't play uh lick."

"You don't cherish de game, then?"

"Yes, Ah do, and then agin Ah don't know whether Ah do or not, 'cause nobody ain't never showed me how."

"Dis is de last day for *dat* excuse. You got uh board round heah?"

"Yes indeed. De men folks treasures de game round heah. Ah just ain't never learnt how."

He set it up and began to show her and she found herself glowing inside. Somebody wanted her to play. Somebody thought it natural for her to play. That was even nice. She looked him over and got little thrills from every one of his good points. Those full, lazy eyes with the lashes curling sharply away like drawn scimitars. The lean, over-padded shoulders and narrow waist. Even nice!

He was jumping her king! She screamed in protest against losing the king she had had such a hard time acquiring. Before she knew it she had grabbed his hand to stop him. He struggled gallantly to free himself. That is he struggled, but not hard enough to wrench a lady's fingers.

"Ah got uh right tuh take it. You left it right in mah way."

"Yeah, but Ah wuz lookin' off when you went and stuck yo' men right up next tuh mine. No fair!"

"You ain't supposed tuh look off, Mis' Starks. It's de biggest part uh de game tuh watch out! Leave go mah hand."

"No suh! Not mah king. You kin take another one, but not dat one."

They scrambled and upset the board and laughed at that.

"Anyhow it's time for uh Coca-Cola," he said. "Ah'll come teach yuh some mo' another time."

"It's all right tuh come teach me, but don't come tuh cheat me."

"Yuh can't beat uh woman. Dey jes won't stand fuh it. But Ah'll come teach yuh agin. You gointuh be uh good player too, after while."

"You reckon so? Jody useter tell me Ah never would learn. It wuz too heavy fuh mah brains."

"Folks is playin' it wid sense and folks is playin' it without. But you got good meat on yo' head. You'll learn. Have uh cool drink on me."

"Oh all right, thank yuh. Got plenty cold ones tuhday. Nobody ain't been heah tuh buy none. All gone off tuh de game."

"You oughta be at de next game. 'Tain't no use in *you* stayin' heah if everybody else is gone. You don't buy from yo'self, do yuh?"

"You crazy thing! 'Course Ah don't. But Ah'm worried 'bout you uh little."

"How come? 'Fraid Ah ain't gointuh pay fuh dese drinks?"

"Aw naw! How you gointuh git back home?"

"Wait round heah fuh a car. If none don't come, Ah got good shoe leather. 'Tain't but seben miles no how. Ah could walk dat in no time. Easy."

"If it wuz me, Ah'd wait on uh train. Seben miles is uh kinda long walk."

"It would be for you, 'cause you ain't used to it. But Ah'm seen women walk further'n dat. You could too, if yuh had it tuh do."

"Maybe so, but Ah'll ride de train long as Ah got railroad fare."

"Ah don't need no pocket-full uh money to ride de train lak uh woman. When Ah takes uh notion Ah rides anyhow—money or no money."

"Now ain't you somethin'! Mr. er—er—You never did tell me whut yo' name wuz."

"Ah sho didn't. Wuzn't expectin' fuh it to be needed. De name mah mama gimme is Vergible Woods. Dey calls me Tea Cake for short."

"Tea Cake! So you sweet as all dat?" She laughed and he gave her a little cut-eye look to get her meaning.

"Ah may be guilty. You better try me and see."

She did something halfway between a laugh and a frown and he set his hat on straight.

"B'lieve Ah done cut uh hawg, so Ah guess Ah better ketch air." He made an elaborate act of tipping to the door stealthily. Then looked back at her with an irresistible grin on his face. Janie burst out laughing in spite of herself. "You crazy thing!"

He turned and threw his hat at her feet. "If she don't throw it at me, Ah'll take a chance on comin' back," he announced, making gestures to indicate he was hidden behind a post. She picked up the hat and threw it after him with a laugh. "Even if she had uh brick she couldn't hurt yuh wid it," he said to an invisible companion. "De lady can't throw." He gestured to his companion, stepped out from behind the imaginary lamp post, set his coat and hat and strolled back to where Janie was as if he had just come in the store.

"Evenin', Mis' Starks. Could yuh lemme have uh pound uh knuckle puddin'* till Saturday? Ah'm sho tuh pay yuh then."

"You needs ten pounds, Mr. Tea Cake. Ah'll let yuh have all Ah got and you needn't bother 'bout payin' it back."

They joked and went on till the people began to come in. Then he took a seat and made talk and laughter with the rest until closing time. When everyone else had left he said, "Ah reckon Ah done over-layed mah leavin' time, but Ah figgured you needed somebody tuh help yuh shut up de place. Since nobody else ain't round heah, maybe Ah kin git de job."

"Thankyuh, Mr. Tea Cake. It is kinda strainin' fuh me."

"Who ever heard of uh teacake bein' called Mister! If you wanta be real hightoned and call me Mr. Woods, dat's de way you feel about it. If yuh wants tuh be uh lil friendly and call me Tea Cake, dat would be real nice." He was closing and bolting windows all the time he talked.

"All right, then. Thank yuh, Tea Cake. How's dat?"

"Jes lak uh lil girl wid her Easter dress on. Even nice!" He locked the door and shook it to be sure and handed her the key. "Come on now, Ah'll see yuh inside yo' door and git on down de Dixie."

Janie was halfway down the palm-lined walk before she had a thought for her safety. Maybe this strange man was up to something! But it was no place to show her fear there in the darkness between the house and the store. He had hold of her arm too. Then in a moment it was gone. Tea Cake wasn't strange. Seemed as if she had known him all her life. Look how she had been able to talk with him right off! He tipped his hat at the door and was off with the briefest good night.

So she sat on the porch and watched the moon rise. Soon its

*A beating with the fist.

amber fluid was drenching the earth, and quenching the thirst of
the day.

CHAPTER 11

Janie wanted to ask Hezekiah about Tea Cake, but she was
afraid he might misunderstand her and think she was interested.
In the first place he looked too young for her. Must be around
twenty-five and here *she* was around forty. Then again he didn't
look like he had too much. Maybe he was hanging around to get
in with her and strip her of all that she had. Just as well if she never
saw him again. He was probably the kind of man who lived with
various women but never married. Fact is, she decided to treat him
so cold if he ever did foot the place that he'd be sure not to come
hanging around there again.

He waited a week exactly to come back for Janie's snub. It was
early in the afternoon and she and Hezekiah were alone. She heard
somebody humming like they were feeling for pitch and looked towards the door. Tea Cake stood there mimicking the tuning of a
guitar. He frowned and struggled with the pegs of his imaginary
instrument watching her out of the corner of his eye with that secret joke playing over his face. Finally she smiled and he sung middle C, put his guitar under his arm and walked on back to where
she was.

"Evenin', folks. Thought y'all might lak uh lil music this
evenin' so Ah brought long mah box."

"Crazy thing!" Janie commented, beaming out with light.

He acknowledged the compliment with a smile and sat down
on a box. "Anybody have uh Coca-Cola wid me?"

"Ah just had one," Janie temporized with her conscience.

"It'll hafter be done all over agin, Mis' Starks."

"How come?"

"'Cause it wasn't done right dat time. 'Kiah bring us two bottles from de bottom uh de box."

"How you been makin' out since Ah seen yuh last, Tea Cake?"

"Can't kick. Could be worse. Made four days dis week and got
de pay in mah pocket."

"We got a rich man round here, then. Buyin' passenger trains
uh battleships this week?"

"Which one do *you* want? It all depends on you."

"Oh, if you'se treatin' me tuh it, Ah b'lieve Ah'll take de passenger train. If it blow up Ah'll still be on land."

"Choose de battleship if dat's whut you really want. Ah know where one is right now. Seen one round Key West de other day."

"How you gointuh git it?"

"Ah shucks, dem Admirals is always ole folks. Can't no ole man stop me from gittin' no ship for yuh if dat's whut you want. Ah'd git dat ship out from under him so slick till he'd be walkin' de water lak ole Peter befo' he knowed it."

They played away the evening again. Everybody was surprised at Janie playing checkers but they liked it. Three or four stood behind her and coached her moves and generally made merry with her in a restrained way. Finally everybody went home but Tea Cake.

"You kin close up, 'Kiah," Janie said. "Think Ah'll g'wan home."

Tea Cake fell in beside her and mounted the porch this time. So she offered him a seat and they made a lot of laughter out of nothing. Near eleven o'clock she remembered a piece of pound cake she had put away. Tea Cake went out to the lemon tree at the corner of the kitchen and picked some lemons and squeezed them for her. So they had lemonade too.

"Moon's too pretty fuh anybody tuh be sleepin' it away," Tea Cake said after they had washed up the plates and glasses. "Less us go fishin'."

"Fishin'? Dis time uh night?"

"Unhhunh, fishin'. Ah know where de bream is beddin'. Seen 'em when Ah come round de lake dis evenin'. Where's yo' fishin' poles? Less go set on de lake."

It was so crazy digging worms by lamp light and setting out for Lake Sabelia after midnight that she felt like a child breaking rules. That's what made Janie like it. They caught two or three and got home just before day. Then she had to smuggle Tea Cake out by the back gate and that made it seem like some great secret she was keeping from the town.

"Mis' Janie," Hezekiah began sullenly next day, "you oughtn't 'low dat Tea Cake tuh be walkin' tuh de house wid yuh. Ah'll go wid yuh mahself after dis, if you'se skeered."

"What's de matter wid Tea Cake, 'Kiah? Is he uh thief uh somethin'?"

"Ah ain't never heard nobody say he stole nothin'."

"Is he bad 'bout totin' pistols and knives tuh hurt people wid?"

"Dey don't say he ever cut nobody or shot nobody neither."

"Well, is he   he is he got uh wife or something lak dat? Not dat it's any uh mah business." She held her breath for the answer.

"No'm. And nobody wouldn't marry Tea Cake tuh starve tuh death lessen it's somebody jes lak him—ain't used to nothin'. 'Course he always keep hisself in changin' clothes. Dat long-legged Tea Cake ain't got doodly squat. He ain't got no business makin' hissef familiar wid nobody lak you. Ah said Ah wuz goin' to tell yuh so yuh could know."

"Oh dat's all right, Hezekiah. Thank yuh mighty much."

The next night when she mounted her steps Tea Cake was there before her, sitting on the porch in the dark. He had a string of fresh-caught trout for a present.

"Ah'll clean 'em, you fry 'em and let's eat," he said with the assurance of not being refused. They went out into the kitchen and fixed up the hot fish and corn muffins and ate. Then Tea Cake went to the piano without so much as asking and began playing blues and singing, and throwing grins over his shoulder. The sounds lulled Janie to soft slumber and she woke up with Tea Cake combing her hair and scratching the dandruff from her scalp. It made her more comfortable and drowsy.

"Tea Cake, where you git uh comb from tuh be combin' mah hair wid?"

"Ah brought it wid me. Come prepared tuh lay mah hands on it tuhnight."

"Why, Tea Cake? Whut good do combin' mah hair do *you?* It's *mah* comfortable, not yourn."

"It's mine too. Ah ain't been sleepin' so good for more'n uh week cause Ah been wishin' so bad tuh git mah hands in yo' hair. It's so pretty. It feels jus' lak underneath uh dove's wing next to mah face."

"Umph! You'se mighty easy satisfied. Ah been had dis same hair next tuh mah face ever since Ah cried de fust time, and 'tain't never gimme me no thrill."

"Ah tell you lak you told me—you'se mighty hard tuh satisfy. Ah betcha dem lips don't satisfy yuh neither."

"Dat's right, Tea Cake. They's dere and Ah make use of 'em whenever it's necessary, but nothin' special tuh me."

"Umph! umph! umph! Ah betcha you don't never go tuh de lookin' glass and enjoy yo' eyes yo'self. You lets other folks git all de enjoyment out of 'em 'thout takin' in any of it yo'self."

"Naw, Ah never gazes at 'em in de lookin' glass. If anybody else gits any pleasure out of 'em Ah ain't been told about it."

"See dat? You'se got de world in uh jug and make out you don't know it. But Ah'm glad tuh be de one tuh tell yuh."

"Ah guess you done told plenty women all about it."

"Ah'm de Apostle Paul tuh de Gentiles. Ah tells 'em and then agin Ah shows 'em."

"Ah thought so." She yawned and made to get up from the sofa. "You done got me so sleepy wid yo' head-scratchin' Ah kin hardly make it tuh de bed." She stood up at once, collecting her hair. He sat still.

"Naw, you ain't sleepy, Mis' Janie. You jus' want me tuh go. You figger Ah'm uh rounder and uh pimp and you done wasted too much time talkin' wid me."

"Why, Tea Cake! Whut ever put dat notion in yo' head?"

"De way you looked at me when Ah said whut Ah did. Yo' face skeered me so bad till mah whiskers drawed up."

"Ah ain't got no business bein' mad at nothin' you do and say. You got it all wrong. Ah ain't mad atall."

"Ah know it and dat's what puts de shamery on me. You'se jus' disgusted wid me. Yo' face jus' left here and went off somewhere else. Naw, you ain't mad wid me. Ah be glad if you was, 'cause then Ah might do somethin' tuh please yuh. But lak it is—"

"Mah likes and dislikes ought not tuh make no difference wid you, Tea Cake. Dat's fuh yo' lady friend. Ah'm jus' uh sometime friend uh yourn."

Janie walked towards the stairway slowly, and Tea Cake sat where he was, as if he had frozen to his seat, in fear that once he got up, he'd never get back in it again. He swallowed hard and looked at her walk away.

"Ah didn't aim tuh let on tuh yuh 'bout it, leastways not right away, but Ah ruther be shot wid tacks than fuh you tuh act wid me lak you is right now. You got me in de go-long."

At the newel post Janie whirled around and for the space of a thought she was lit up like a transfiguration. Her next thought brought her crashing down. He's just saying anything for the time being, feeling he's got me so I'll b'lieve him. The next thought buried her under tons of cold futility. He's trading on being younger than me. Getting ready to laugh at me for an old fool. But oh, what wouldn't I give to be twelve years younger so I could b'lieve him!

"Aw, Tea Cake, you just say dat tuhnight because de fish and corn bread tasted sort of good. Tomorrow yo' mind would change."

"Naw, it wouldn't neither. Ah know better."

"Anyhow from what you told me when we wuz back dere in de kitchen Ah'm nearly twelve years older than you."

"Ah done thought all about dat and tried tuh struggle aginst it, but it don't do me no good. De thought uh mah youngness don't satisfy me lak yo' presence do."

"It makes uh whole heap uh difference wid most folks, Tea Cake."

"Things lak dat got uh whole lot tuh do wid convenience, but it ain't got nothin' tuh do wid love."

"Well, Ah love tuh find out whut you think after sun-up to-morrow. Dis is jus' yo' night thought."

"You got yo' ideas and Ah got mine. Ah got uh dollar dat says you'se wrong. But Ah reckon you don't bet money, neither."

"Ah never have done it so fur. But as de old folks always say, Ah'm born but Ah ain't dead. No tellin' whut Ah'm liable tuh do yet."

He got up suddenly and took his hat. "Good night, Mis' Janie. Look lak we done run our conversation from grass roots tuh pine trees. G'bye." He almost ran out of the door.

Janie hung over the newel post thinking so long that she all but went to sleep there. However, before she went to bed she took a good look at her mouth, eyes and hair.

All next day in the house and store she thought resisting thoughts about Tea Cake. She even ridiculed him in her mind and was a little ashamed of the association. But every hour or two the battle had to be fought all over again. She couldn't make him look just like any other man to her. He looked like the love thoughts of women. He could be a bee to a blossom—a pear tree blossom in the spring. He seemed to be crushing scent out of the world with his footsteps. Crushing aromatic herbs with every step he took. Spices hung about him. He was a glance from God.

So he didn't come that night and she laid in bed and pretended to think scornfully of him. "Bet he's hangin' round some jook or 'nother. Glad Ah treated him cold. Whut do Ah want wid some trashy nigger out de streets? Bet he's livin' wid some woman or 'nother and takin' me for uh fool. Glad Ah caught mahself in time." She tried to console herself that way.

The next morning she awoke hearing a knocking on the front door and found Tea Cake there.

"Hello, Mis' Janie, Ah hope Ah woke you up."

"You sho did, Tea Cake. Come in and rest yo' hat. Whut you doin' out so soon dis mornin'?"

"Thought Ah'd try tuh git heah soon enough tuh tell yuh mah daytime thoughts. Ah see yuh needs tuh know mah daytime feelings. Ah can't sense yuh intuh it at night."

"You crazy thing! Is dat whut you come here for at daybreak?"

"Sho is. You needs tellin' and showin', and dat's whut Ah'm doin'. Ah picked some strawberries too, Ah figgered you might like."

"Tea Cake, Ah 'clare Ah don't know whut tuh make outa you. You'se so crazy. You better lemme fix you some breakfast."

"Ain't got time. Ah got uh job uh work. Gottuh be back in Orlandah at eight o'clock. See yuh later, tell you straighter."

He bolted down the walk and was gone. But that night when she left the store, he was stretched out in the hammock on the porch with his hat over his face pretending to sleep. She called him. He pretended not to hear. He snored louder. She went to the hammock to shake him and he seized and pulled her in with him. After a little, she let him adjust her in his arms and laid there for a while.

"Tea Cake, Ah don't know 'bout you, but Ah'm hongry, come on let's eat some supper."

They went inside and their laughter rang out first from the kitchen and all over the house.

Janie awoke next morning by feeling Tea Cake almost kissing her breath away. Holding her and caressing her as if he feared she might escape his grasp and fly away. Then he must dress hurriedly and get to his job on time. He wouldn't let her get him any breakfast at all. He wanted her to get her rest. He made her stay where she was. In her heart she wanted to get his breakfast for him. But she stayed in bed long after he was gone.

So much had been breathed out by the pores that Tea Cake still was there. She could feel him and almost see him bucking around the room in the upper air. After a long time of passive happiness, she got up and opened the window and let Tea Cake leap forth and mount to the sky on a wind. That was the beginning of things.

In the cool of the afternoon the fiend from hell specially sent to lovers arrived at Janie's ear. Doubt. All the fears that circumstance could provide and the heart feel, attacked her on every side. This was a new sensation for her, but no less excruciating. If only Tea Cake would make her certain! He did not return that night nor the next and so she plunged into the abyss and descended to the ninth darkness where light has never been.

But the fourth day after he came in the afternoon driving a battered car. Jumped out like a deer and made the gesture of tying it to a post on the store porch. Ready with his grin! She adored him and hated him at the same time. How could he make her suffer so and then come grinning like that with that darling way he had? He pinched her arm as he walked inside the door.

"Brought me somethin' tuh haul you off in," he told her with that secret chuckle. "Git yo' hat if you gointuh wear one. We got tuh go buy groceries."

"Ah sells groceries right here in dis store, Tea Cake, if you don't happen tuh know." She tried to look cold but she was smiling in spite of herself.

"Not de kind we want fuh de occasion. You sells groceries for ordinary people. We'se gointuh buy for *you*. De big Sunday School picnic is tomorrow—bet you done forget it—and we got tuh be dere wid uh swell basket and ourselves."

"Ah don't know 'bout dat, Tea Cake. Tell yuh whut you do. G'wan down tuh de house and wait for me. Be dere in uh minute."

As soon as she thought it looked right she slipped out of the back and joined Tea Cake. No need of fooling herself. Maybe he was just being polite.

"Tea Cake, you sure you want me tuh go tuh dis picnic wid yuh?"

"Me scramble 'round tuh git de money tuh take yuh—been workin' lak uh dawg for two whole weeks—and she come astin' me if Ah want her tuh go! Puttin' mahself tuh uh whole heap uh trouble tuh git dis car so you kin go over tuh Winter Park or Orlandah tuh buy de things you might need and dis woman set dere and ast me if Ah want her tuh go!"

"Don't git mad, Tea Cake, Ah just didn't want you doin' nothin' outa politeness. If dere's somebody else you'd ruther take, it's all right wid me."

"Naw, it ain't all right wid you. If it was you wouldn't be sayin' dat. Have de nerve tuh say whut you mean."

"Well, all right, Tea Cake, Ah wants tuh go wid you real bad, but,—oh, Tea Cake, don't make no false pretense wid me!"

"Janie, Ah hope God may kill me, if Ah'm lyin'. Nobody else on earth kin hold uh candle tuh you, baby. You got de keys to de kingdom."

——For Discussion——

RPW—

The attractive mulatto Janie, around forty years old, has been married twice, once to the landowner Logan Killicks and more recently to the town builder Jody Starks, the first mayor of the all-colored town of Eatonville. Janie's grandmother had wanted her to be protected through marriage and economic well-being, but neither man has given Janie a chance to find her voice and define herself. Logan Killicks and Jody Starks were capitalists who measured success by the standards set in the mirror of white men. They believed Janie was part of their value, part of their possessions. By contrast, Janie had never lost the dream of "the love embrace," the dream of having "a dust-bearing bee sink into the sanctum of (her) bloom." Now widowed and wealthy by Eatonville standards, Janie takes care of the store with her helper, Hezekiah.

In contrast to Killicks and Starks, Tea Cake is not interested in business propositions, property, or formal titles, but in "the love game." He plays checkers with Janie, goes fishing with her, combs out her long hair. He is the bee to her blossom, and for him, she has "de keys to de kingdom." Tea Cake helps Janie rediscover herself by reawakening her desire and by giving her the desire of which she dreams. As Tea Cake tells Janie: "See dat? You'se got de world in uh jug and make out you don't know it. But Ah'm glad tuh be de one tuh tell yuh."

Tea Cake lives with the passion and intensity of the moment. He is a guitar man filled with joy and laughter. But he is twelve years younger than Janie, and he "ain't got doodly squat." Janie

*does not need money, but she fears the uncertainty of the relation-
ship. She knows her neighbors disapprove, but she also knows that
her neighbors reflect the values of her previous husbands. In the
presence of Tea Cake, she is transfigured, shining inside and out.
For her, Tea Cake is "a glance from God."*

JRT—
   *Janie is nearly forty and a widow of two marriages: the first
to a hardworking farmer arranged by her grandmother to bring her
security; and the other to the politician who wants Janie to be his
showpiece more than his equal partner. As a strong black woman
in the 1930s whose parents have died and who is far away from
where she grew up, Janie is not, however, living in loss. She has
kept her head on her shoulders, owns a store, and is self-sufficient.
It is when Tea Cake walks into her life that we see how she is still
struggling to find herself in the eyes of her beloved, to allow herself
to be an independent woman, and to trust and love a man who
sees her as an equal.*
   *The problem, at first, with Tea Cake is that he is twelve years
younger than Janie, a gambler, and a heartthrob with a reputation
for wildness. Here is a man who surprises, offering to teach her
how to play checkers, taking her fishing at midnight. "She felt like
a child breaking rules. That's what made Janie like it." Tea Cake,
or as one woman I know calls him, "Tea Bag," is a man who
seems to have no strings attached. Yet, when he doesn't show up
for a couple of days after the first night they spend together, Janie
is terrified, thrown into the fear that she'll lose him, that he's the
no-good guy her employed store assistant, Hezekiah, warned her
about.*
   *I am of two minds about Tea Cake, and it seems to me that
most of the women I have encountered in our reading groups feel
the same way, to a greater or lesser extent. On the one hand, we
have a real romantic hero, someone who adores Janie, can't sleep
because he longs to comb her hair, and works extra hours just to
earn enough to take her to a picnic. Who wouldn't want a man
like that? And he has the best lines in the chapter: "Nobody else
can hold a candle tuh you, baby. You got de keys to de kingdom."
But later in the book, Tea Cake steals from Janie, hits her, and
almost sleeps with another woman. He is the perfect "dangerous
man" that women fantasize about. The fact that he is unpredict-
able shows us that Tea Cake is lovable but not necessarily some-*

one who can last in a woman's life. Imagining Tea Cake with kids in diapers or a Tea Cake bringing home a paycheck is impossible. He's "the stuff that dreams are made of," and yet he is flawed. Like Romeo and Juliet, Janie and Tea Cake could never be "forever."

Janie does learn to be her own person, and Tea Cake helps her along that path. "He was a glance from God." By the end of the novel, Janie has lost him, first to the madness of rabies and later to death. She has to shoot him to keep him, in his madness, from killing her. Then she must defend herself in a trial to the town. It is a lot for anyone to go through, but Hurston shows us a Janie who is credible, has dignity, and ultimately comes to look at life as an adventure to be fully lived.

from THE WOMEN OF BREWSTER PLACE

Gloria Naylor

LUCIELIA LOUISE TURNER

The sunlight was still watery as Ben trudged into Brewster Place, and the street had just begun to yawn and stretch itself. He eased himself onto his garbage can, which was pushed against the sagging brick wall that turned Brewster into a dead-end street. The metallic cold of the can's lid seeped into the bottom of his thin trousers. Sucking on a piece of breakfast sausage caught in his back teeth, he began to muse. Mighty cold, these spring mornings. The old days you could build a good trash fire in one of them barrels to keep warm. Well, don't want no summons now, and can't freeze to death. Yup, can't freeze to death.

His daily soliloquy completed, he reached into his coat pocket and pulled out a crumpled brown bag that contained his morning sun. The cheap red liquid moved slowly down his throat, providing immediate justification as the blood began to warm in his body. In the hazy light a lean dark figure began to make its way slowly up the block. It hesitated in front of the stoop at 316, but looking around and seeing Ben, it hurried over.

"Yo, Ben."

"Hey, Eugene, I thought that was you. Ain't seen ya round for a coupla days."

"Yeah." The young man put his hands in his pockets, frowned into the ground, and kicked the edge of Ben's can. "The funeral's today, ya know."

"Yeah."

"You going?" He looked up into Ben's face.

"Naw, I ain't got no clothes for them things. Can't abide 'em no way—too sad—it being a baby and all."

"Yeah. I was going myself, people expect it, ya know?"

"Yeah."

"But, man, the way Ciel's friends look at me and all—like I was filth or something. Hey, I even tried to go see Ciel in the hospital, heard she was freaked out and all."

"Yeah, she took it real bad."

"Yeah, well, damn, I took it bad. It was my kid, too, ya know. But Mattie, that fat, black bitch, just standin' in the hospital hall sayin' to me—to me, now, 'Whatcha want?' Like I was a fuckin' germ or something. Man, I just turned and left. You gotta be treated with respect, ya know?"

"Yeah."

"I mean, I should be there today with my woman in the limo and all, sittin' up there, doin' it right. But how you gonna be a man with them ball-busters tellin' everybody it was my fault and I should be the one dead? Damn!"

"Yeah, a man's gotta be a man." Ben felt the need to wet his reply with another sip. "Have some?"

"Naw, I'm gonna be heading on—Ciel don't need me today. I bet that frig, Mattie, rides in the head limo, wearing the pants. Shit—let 'em." He looked up again. "Ya know?"

"Yup."

"Take it easy, Ben." He turned to go.

"You too, Eugene."

"Hey, you going?"

"Naw."

"Me neither. Later."

"Later, Eugene."

Funny, Ben thought, Eugene ain't stopped to chat like that for a long time—near on a year, yup, a good year. He took another swallow to help him bring back the year-old conversation, but it didn't work; the second and third one didn't either. But he did remember that it had been an early spring morning like this one, and Eugene had been wearing those same tight jeans. He had hesitated outside of 316 then, too. But that time he went in . . .

Lucielia had just run water into the tea kettle and was putting it on the burner when she heard the cylinder turn. He didn't have to knock on the door; his key still fit the lock. Her thin knuckles gripped the handle of the kettle, but she didn't turn around. She knew. The last eleven months of her life hung compressed in the air between the click of the lock and his "Yo, baby."

The vibrations from those words rode like parasites on the air waves and came rushing into her kitchen, smashing the compression into indistinguishable days and hours that swirled dizzily before her. It was all there: the frustration of being left alone, sick,

with a month-old baby; her humiliation reflected in the case-
worker's blue eyes for the unanswerable "you can find him to have
it, but can't find him to take care of it" smile; the raw urges that
crept, uninvited, between her thighs on countless nights; the eternal whys all meshed with the explainable hate and unexplainable
love. They kept circling in such a confusing pattern before her that
she couldn't seem to grab even one to answer him with. So there
was nothing in Lucielia's face when she turned it toward Eugene,
standing in her kitchen door holding a ridiculously pink Easter
bunny, nothing but sheer relief. . . .

"So he's back." Mattie sat at Lucielia's kitchen table, playing
with Serena. It was rare that Mattie ever spoke more than two sentences to anybody about anything. She didn't have to. She chose
her words with the grinding precision of a diamond cutter's drill.

"You think I'm a fool, don't you?"

"I ain't said that."

"You didn't have to," Ciel snapped.

"Why you mad at me, Ciel? It's your life, honey."

"Oh, Mattie, you don't understand. He's really straightened up
this time. He's got a new job on the docks that pays real good, and
he was just so depressed before with the new baby and no work.
You'll see. He's even gone out now to buy paint and stuff to fix up
the apartment. And, and Serena needs a daddy."

"You ain't gotta convince me, Ciel."

No, she wasn't talking to Mattie, she was talking to herself.
She was convincing herself it was the new job and the paint and
Serena that let him back into her life. Yet, the real truth went beyond her scope of understanding. When she laid her head in the
hollow of his neck there was a deep musky scent to his body that
brought back the ghosts of the Tennessee soil of her childhood. It
reached up and lined the inside of her nostrils so that she inhaled
his presence almost every minute of her life. The feel of his sooty
flesh penetrated the skin of her fingers and coursed through her
blood and became one, somewhere, wherever it was, with her actual being. But how do you tell yourself, let alone this practical
old woman who loves you, that he was back because of that. So
you don't.

You get up and fix you both another cup of coffee, calm the
fretting baby on your lap with her pacifier, and you pray silently—
very silently—behind veiled eyes that the man will stay.

Ciel was trying to remember exactly when it had started to go wrong again. Her mind sought for the slender threads of a clue that she could trace back to—perhaps—something she had said or done. Her brow was set tightly in concentration as she folded towels and smoothed the wrinkles over and over, as if the answer lay concealed in the stubborn creases of the terry cloth.

The months since Eugene's return began to tick off slowly before her, and she examined each one to pinpoint when the nagging whispers of trouble had begun in her brain. The friction on the towels increased when she came to the month that she had gotten pregnant again, but it couldn't be that. Things were different now. She wasn't sick as she had been with Serena, he was still working—no it wasn't the baby. It's not the baby, it's not the baby—the rhythm of those words sped up the motion of her hands, and she had almost yanked and folded and pressed them into a reality when, bewildered, she realized that she had run out of towels.

Ciel jumped when the front door slammed shut. She waited tensely for the metallic bang of his keys on the coffee table and the blast of the stereo. Lately that was how Eugene announced his presence home. Ciel walked into the living room with the motion of a swimmer entering a cold lake.

"Eugene, you're home early, huh?"

"You see anybody else sittin' here?" He spoke without looking at her and rose to turn up the stereo.

He wants to pick a fight, she thought, confused and hurt. He knows Serena's taking her nap, and now I'm supposed to say, Eugene, the baby's asleep, please cut the music down. Then he's going to say, you mean a man can't even relax in his own home without being picked on? I'm not picking on you, but you're going to wake up the baby. Which is always supposed to lead to: You don't give a damn about me. Everybody's more important than me—that kid, your friends, everybody. I'm just chickenshit around here, huh?

All this went through Ciel's head as she watched him leave the stereo and drop defiantly back down on the couch. Without saying a word, she turned and went into the bedroom. She looked down on the peaceful face of her daughter and softly caressed her small cheek. Her heart became full as she realized, this is the only thing I have ever loved without pain. She pulled the sheet gently over the tiny shoulders and firmly closed the door, protecting her from the music. She then went into the kitchen and began washing the rice for their dinner.

Eugene, seeing that he had been left alone, turned off the stereo and came and stood in the kitchen door.

"I lost my job today," he shot at her, as if she had been the cause.

The water was turning cloudy in the rice pot, and the force of the stream from the faucet caused scummy bubbles to rise to the surface. These broke and sprayed tiny starchy particles onto the dirty surface. Each bubble that broke seemed to increase the volume of the dogged whispers she had been ignoring for the last few months. She poured the dirty water off the rice to destroy and silence them, then watched with a malicious joy as they disappeared down the drain.

"So now, how in the hell I'm gonna make it with no money, huh? And another brat comin' here, huh?"

The second change of the water was slightly clearer, but the starch-speckled bubbles were still there, and this time there was no way to pretend deafness to their message. She had stood at that sink countless times before, washing rice, and she knew the water was never going to be totally clear. She couldn't stand there forever—her fingers were getting cold, and the rest of the dinner had to be fixed, and Serena would be waking up soon and wanting attention. Feverishly she poured the water off and tried again.

"I'm fuckin' sick of never getting ahead. Babies and bills, that's all you good for."

The bubbles were almost transparent now, but when they broke they left light trails of starch on top of the water that curled around her fingers. She knew it would be useless to try again. Defeated, Ciel placed the wet pot on the burner, and the flames leaped up bright red and orange, turning the water droplets clinging on the outside into steam.

Turning to him, she silently acquiesced. "All right, Eugene, what do you want me to do?"

He wasn't going to let her off so easily. "Hey, baby, look, I don't care what you do. I just can't have all these hassles on me right now, ya know?"

"I'll get a job. I don't mind, but I've got no one to keep Serena, and you don't want Mattie watching her."

"Mattie—no way. That fat bitch'll turn the kid against me. She hates my ass, and you know it."

"No, she doesn't, Eugene." Ciel remembered throwing that at Mattie once. "You hate him, don't you?" "Naw, honey," and she had cupped both hands on Ciel's face. "Maybe I just loves you too much."

"I don't give a damn what you say—she ain't minding my kid."

"Well, look, after the baby comes, they can tie my tubes—I don't care." She swallowed hard to keep down the lie.

"And what the hell we gonna feed it when it gets here, huh— air? With two kids and you on my back, I ain't never gonna have nothin'." He came and grabbed her by the shoulders and was shouting into her face. "Nothin', do you hear me, nothin'!"

"Nothing to it, Mrs. Turner." The face over hers was as calm and antiseptic as the room she lay in. "Please, relax. I'm going to give you a local anesthetic and then perform a simple D&C, or what you'd call a scraping to clean out the uterus. Then you'll rest here for about an hour and be on your way. There won't even be much bleeding." The voice droned on in its practiced monologue, peppered with sterile kindness.

Ciel was not listening. It was important that she keep herself completely isolated from these surroundings. All the activities of the past week of her life were balled up and jammed on the right side of her brain, as if belonging to some other woman. And when she had endured this one last thing for her, she would push it up there, too, and then one day give it all to her—Ciel wanted no part of it.

The next few days Ciel found it difficult to connect herself up again with her own world. Everything seemed to have taken on new textures and colors. When she washed the dishes, the plates felt peculiar in her hands, and she was more conscious of their smoothness and the heat of the water. There was a disturbing split second between someone talking to her and the words penetrating sufficiently to elicit a response. Her neighbors left her presence with slight frowns of puzzlement, and Eugene could be heard mumbling, "Moody bitch."

She became terribly possessive of Serena. She refused to leave her alone, even with Eugene. The little girl went everywhere with Ciel, toddling along on plump uncertain legs. When someone asked to hold or play with her, Ciel sat nearby, watching every move. She found herself walking into the bedroom several times when the child napped to see if she was still breathing. Each time she chided herself for this unreasonable foolishness, but within the next few minutes some strange force still drove her back.

Spring was slowly beginning to announce itself at Brewster Place. The arthritic cold was seeping out of the worn gray bricks, and the tenants with apartment windows facing the street were awakened by six o'clock sunlight. The music no longer blasted inside of 3C, and Ciel grew strong with the peacefulness of her household. The playful laughter of her daughter, heard more often now, brought a sort of redemption with it.

"Isn't she marvelous, Mattie? You know she's even trying to make whole sentences. Come on, baby, talk for Auntie Mattie."

Serena, totally uninterested in living up to her mother's proud claims, was trying to tear a gold-toned button off the bosom of Mattie's dress.

"It's so cute. She even knows her father's name. She says, my da da is Gene."

"Better teach her your name," Mattie said, while playing with the baby's hand. "She'll be using it more."

Ciel's mouth flew open to ask her what she meant by that, but she checked herself. It was useless to argue with Mattie. You could take her words however you wanted. The burden of their truth lay with you, not her.

Eugene came through the front door and stopped short when he saw Mattie. He avoided being around her as much as possible. She was always polite to him, but he sensed a silent condemnation behind even her most innocent words. He constantly felt the need to prove himself in front of her. These frustrations often took the form of unwarranted rudeness on his part.

Serena struggled out of Mattie's lap and went toward her father and tugged on his legs to be picked up. Ignoring the child and cutting short the greetings of the two women, he said coldly, "Ciel, I wanna talk to you."

Sensing trouble, Mattie rose to go. "Ciel, why don't you let me take Serena downstairs for a while. I got some ice cream for her."

"She can stay right here," Eugene broke in. "If she needs ice cream, I can buy it for her."

Hastening to soften his abruptness, Ciel said, "That's okay,

Mattie, it's almost time for her nap. I'll bring her later—after dinner."

"All right. Now you all keep good." Her voice was warm. "You too, Eugene," she called back from the front door.

The click of the lock restored his balance to him. "Why in the hell is she always up here?"

"You just had your chance—why didn't you ask her yourself? If you don't want her here, tell her to stay out," Ciel snapped back confidently, knowing he never would.

"Look, I ain't got time to argue with you about that old hag. I got big doings in the making, and I need you to help me pack." Without waiting for a response, he hurried into the bedroom and pulled his old leather suitcase from under the bed.

A tight, icy knot formed in the center of Ciel's stomach and began to melt rapidly, watering the blood in her legs so that they almost refused to support her weight. She pulled Serena back from following Eugene and sat her in the middle of the living room floor.

"Here, honey, play with the blocks for Mommy—she has to talk to Daddy." She piled a few plastic alphabet blocks in front of the child, and on her way out of the room, she glanced around quickly and removed the glass ashtrays off the coffee table and put them on a shelf over the stereo.

Then, taking a deep breath to calm her racing heart, she started toward the bedroom.

Serena loved the light colorful cubes and would sometimes sit for an entire half-hour, repeatedly stacking them up and kicking them over with her feet. The hollow sound of their falling fascinated her, and she would often bang two of them together to re-create the magical noise. She was sitting, contentedly engaged in this particular activity, when a slow dark movement along the baseboard caught her eye.

A round black roach was making its way from behind the couch toward the kitchen. Serena threw one of her blocks at the insect, and, feeling the vibrations of the wall above it, the roach sped around the door into the kitchen. Finding a totally new game to amuse herself, Serena took off behind the insect with a block in each hand. Seeing her moving toy trying to bury itself under the linoleum by the garbage pail she threw another block, and the frantic roach now raced along the wall and found security in the electric wall socket under the kitchen table.

Angry at losing her plaything, she banged the block against the socket, attempting to get it to come back out. When that failed, she unsuccessfully tried to poke her chubby finger into the thin horizontal slit. Frustrated, tiring of the game, she sat under the table and realized she had found an entirely new place in the house to play. The shiny chrome of the table and chair legs drew her attention, and she experimented with the sound of the block against their smooth surfaces.

This would have entertained her until Ciel came, but the roach, thinking itself safe, ventured outside of the socket. Serena gave a cry of delight and attempted to catch her lost playmate, but it was too quick and darted back into the wall. She tried once again to poke her finger into the slit. Then a bright slender object, lying dropped and forgotten, came into her view. Picking up the fork, Serena finally managed to fit the thin flattened prongs into the electric socket.

Eugene was avoiding Ciel's eyes as he packed. "You know, baby, this is really a good deal after me bein' out of work for so long." He moved around her still figure to open the drawer that held his T-shirts and shorts. "And hell, Maine ain't far. Once I get settled on the docks up there, I'll be able to come home all the time."

"Why can't you take us with you?" She followed each of his movements with her eyes and saw herself being buried in the case under the growing pile of clothes.

"'Cause I gotta check out what's happening before I drag you and the kid up there."

"I don't mind. We'll make do. I've learned to live on very little."

"No, it just won't work right now. I gotta see my way clear first."

"Eugene, please." She listened with growing horror to herself quietly begging.

"No, and that's it!" He flung his shoes into the suitcase.

"Well, how far is it? Where did you say you were going?" She moved toward the suitcase.

"I told ya—the docks in Newport."

"That's not in Maine. You said you were going to Maine."

"Well, I made a mistake."

"How could you know about a place so far up? Who got you the job?"

"A friend."

"Who?"

"None of your damned business!" His eyes were flashing with the anger of a caged animal. He slammed down the top of the suitcase and yanked it off the bed.

"You're lying, aren't you? You don't have a job, do you? Do you?"

"Look, Ciel, believe whatever the fuck you want to. I gotta go." He tried to push past her.

She grabbed the handle of the case. "No, you can't go."

"Why?"

Her eyes widened slowly. She realized that to answer that would require that she uncurl that week of her life, pushed safely up into her head, when she had done all those terrible things for that other woman who had wanted an abortion. She and she alone would have to take responsibility for them now. He must understand what those actions had meant to her, but somehow, he had meant even more. She sought desperately for the right words, but it all came out as—

"Because I love you."

"Well, that ain't good enough."

Ciel had let the suitcase go before he jerked it away. She looked at Eugene, and the poison of reality began to spread through her body like gangrene. It drew his scent out of her nostrils and scraped the veil from her eyes, and he stood before her just as he really was—a tall, skinny black man with arrogance and selfishness twisting his mouth into a strange shape. And, she thought, I don't feel anything now. But soon, very soon, I will start to hate you. I promise—I will hate you. And I'll never forgive myself for not having done it sooner—soon enough to have saved my baby. Oh, dear God, my baby.

Eugene thought the tears that began to crowd into her eyes were for him. But she was allowing herself this one last luxury of brief mourning for the loss of something denied to her. It troubled her that she wasn't sure exactly what that something was, or which one of them was to blame for taking it away. Ciel began to feel the overpowering need to be near someone who loved her. I'll get Serena and we'll go visit Mattie now, she thought in a daze.

Then they heard the scream from the kitchen.

The church was small and dark. The air hung about them like a stale blanket. Ciel looked straight ahead, oblivious to the seats filling up behind her. She didn't feel the damp pressure of Mattie's heavy arm or the doubt that invaded the air over Eugene's absence. The plaintive Merciful Jesuses, lightly sprinkled with sobs, were lost on her ears. Her dry eyes were locked on the tiny pearl-gray casket, flanked with oversized arrangements of red-carnationed bleeding hearts and white-lilied eternal circles. The sagging chords that came loping out of the huge organ and mixed with the droning voice of the black-robed old man behind the coffin were also unable to penetrate her.

Ciel's whole universe existed in the seven feet of space between herself and her child's narrow coffin. There was not even room for this comforting God whose melodious virtues floated around her sphere, attempting to get in. Obviously, He had deserted or damned her, it didn't matter which. All Ciel knew was that her prayers had gone unheeded—that afternoon she had lifted her daughter's body off the kitchen floor, those blank days in the hospital, and now. So she was left to do what God had chosen not to.

People had mistaken it for shock when she refused to cry. They thought it some special sort of grief when she stopped eating and even drinking water unless forced to; her hair went uncombed and her body unbathed. But Ciel was not grieving for Serena. She was simply tired of hurting. And she was forced to slowly give up the life that God had refused to take from her.

After the funeral the well-meaning came to console and offer their dog-eared faith in the form of coconut cakes, potato pies, fried chicken, and tears. Ciel sat in the bed with her back resting against the headboard; her long thin fingers, still as midnight frost on a frozen pond, lay on the covers. She acknowledged their kindnesses with nods of her head and slight lip movements, but no sound. It was as if her voice was too tired to make the journey from the diaphragm through the larynx to the mouth.

Her visitors' impotent words flew against the steel edge of her pain, bled slowly, and returned to die in the senders' throats. No one came too near. They stood around the door and the dressing table, or sat on the edges of the two worn chairs that needed upholstering, but they unconsciously pushed themselves back against the wall as if her hurt was contagious.

A neighbor woman entered in studied certainty and stood in the middle of the room. "Child, I know how you feel, but don't do this to yourself. I lost one, too. The Lord will ... " And she choked, because the words were jammed down into her throat by the naked force of Ciel's eyes. Ciel had opened them fully now to look at the woman, but raw fires had eaten them worse than lifeless—worse than death. The woman saw in that mute appeal for silence the ragings of a personal hell flowing through Ciel's eyes. And just as she went to reach for the girl's hand, she stopped as if a muscle spasm had overtaken her body and, cowardly, shrank back. Reminiscences of old, dried-over pains were no consolation in the face of this. They had the effect of cold beads of water on a hot iron—they danced and fizzled up while the room stank from their steam.

Mattie stood in the doorway, and an involuntary shudder went through her when she saw Ciel's eyes. Dear God, she thought, she's dying, and right in front of our faces.

"Merciful Father, no!" she bellowed. There was no prayer, no bended knee or sackcloth supplication in those words, but a blasphemous fireball that shot forth and went smashing against the gates of heaven, raging and kicking, demanding to be heard.

"No! No! No!" Like a black Brahman cow, desperate to protect her young, she surged into the room, pushing the neighbor woman and the others out of her way. She approached the bed with her lips clamped shut in such force that the muscles in her jaw and the back of her neck began to ache.

She sat on the edge of the bed and enfolded the tissue-thin body in her huge ebony arms. And she rocked. Ciel's body was so hot it burned Mattie when she first touched her, but she held on and rocked. Back and forth, back and forth—she had Ciel so tightly she could feel her young breasts flatten against the buttons of her dress. The black mammoth gripped so firmly that the slightest increase of pressure would have cracked the girl's spine. But she rocked.

And somewhere from the bowels of her being came a moan from Ciel, so high at first it couldn't be heard by anyone there, but the yard dogs began an unholy howling. And Mattie rocked. And then, agonizingly slow, it broke its way through the parched lips in a spaghetti-thin column of air that could be faintly heard in the frozen room.

Ciel moaned. Mattie rocked. Propelled by the sound, Mattie rocked her out of that bed, out of that room, into a blue vastness just underneath the sun and above time. She rocked her over Aegean seas so clean they shone like crystal, so clear the fresh blood of sacrificed babies torn from their mother's arms and given to Neptune could be seen like pink froth on the water. She rocked her on and on, past Dachau, where soul-gutted Jewish mothers swept their children's entrails off laboratory floors. They flew past the spilled brains of Senegalese infants whose mothers had dashed them on the wooden sides of slave ships. And she rocked on.

She rocked her into her childhood and let her see murdered dreams. And she rocked her back, back into the womb, to the nadir of her hurt, and they found it—a slight silver splinter, embedded just below the surface of the skin. And Mattie rocked and pulled—and the splinter gave way, but its roots were deep, gigantic, ragged, and they tore up flesh with bits of fat and muscle tissue clinging to them. They left a huge hole, which was already starting to pus over, but Mattie was satisfied. It would heal.

The bile that had formed a tight knot in Ciel's stomach began to rise and gagged her just as it passed her throat. Mattie put her hand over the girl's mouth and rushed her out the now-empty room to the toilet. Ciel retched yellowish-green phlegm, and she brought up white lumps of slime that hit the seat of the toilet and rolled off, splattering onto the tiles. After a while she heaved only air, but the body did not seem to want to stop. It was exorcising the evilness of pain.

Mattie cupped her hands under the faucet and motioned for Ciel to drink and clean her mouth. When the water left Ciel's mouth, it tasted as if she had been rinsing with a mild acid. Mattie drew a tub of hot water and undressed Ciel. She let the nightgown fall off the narrow shoulders, over the pitifully thin breasts and jutting hipbones. She slowly helped her into the water, and it was like a dried brown autumn leaf hitting the surface of a puddle.

And slowly she bathed her. She took the soap, and, using only her hands, she washed Ciel's hair and the back of her neck. She raised her arms and cleaned the armpits, soaping well the downy brown hair there. She let the soap slip between the girl's breasts, and she washed each one separately, cupping it in her hands. She took each leg and even cleaned under the toenails. Making Ciel rise and kneel in the tub, she cleaned the crack in her behind, soaped her pubic hair, and gently washed the creases in her vagina—slowly, reverently, as if handling a newborn.

She took her from the tub and toweled her in the same manner she had been bathed—as if too much friction would break the skin tissue. All of this had been done without either woman saying a word. Ciel stood there, naked, and felt the cool air play against the clean surface of her skin. She had the sensation of fresh mint coursing through her pores. She closed her eyes and the fire was gone. Her tears no longer fried within her, killing her internal organs with their steam. So Ciel began to cry—there, naked, in the center of the bathroom floor.

Mattie emptied the tub and rinsed it. She led the still-naked Ciel to a chair in the bedroom. The tears were flowing so freely now Ciel couldn't see, and she allowed herself to be led as if blind. She sat on the chair and cried—head erect. Since she made no effort to wipe them away, the tears dripped down her chin and landed on her chest and rolled down to her stomach and onto her dark pubic hair. Ignoring Ciel, Mattie took away the crumpled linen and made the bed, stretching the sheets tight and fresh. She beat the pillows into a virgin plumpness and dressed them in white cases.

And Ciel sat. And cried. The unmolested tears had rolled down her parted thighs and were beginning to wet the chair. But they were cold and good. She put out her tongue and began to drink in their saltiness, feeding on them. The first tears were gone. Her thin shoulders began to quiver, and spasms circled her body as new tears came—this time, hot and stinging. And she sobbed, the first sound she'd made since the moaning.

Mattie took the edges of the dirty sheet she'd pulled off the bed and wiped the mucus that had been running out of Ciel's nose. She then led her freshly wet, glistening body, baptized now, to the bed. She covered her with one sheet and laid a towel across the pillow—it would help for a while.

And Ciel lay down and cried. But Mattie knew the tears would end. And she would sleep. And morning would come.

——For Discussion——

JRT—
Gloria Naylor writes her heart out in this chapter, and within Ciel's tragedy, we also see the gift of friendship and the beauty of new beginnings. We get a glimpse here of how to bear the unbearable. Naylor seems to be saying that friendship and commitment, particularly of one woman to another, are crucial to survival.

Ciel is not atypical. She is a woman who has made a man more important than her own safety, her health, her children, and in a sense, her sanity. Women relate to her. We too give up dreams. Ciel has an abortion in spite of the fact that she wants to keep the baby, because her man, Eugene, wants to be free. Eugene loses his job and blames Ciel for all his losses. In spite of the fact that he leaves her whenever he wants—deserts her, some might say—she has the abortion. After all, she still is mother to Serena. "He must understand what those actions had meant to her, but somehow, he had meant even more." Why, we ask, does she let Eugene mean more to her than her own dreams and desires?

Just when we think we can't handle any more, we discover that Serena has electrocuted herself, and we are left, like Ciel, without hope. Mattie arrives at the house of mourning and literally saves Ciel in a scene that is so beautiful that it becomes like a baptism itself, taking us through the fire with Ciel. We have to get back hope too. As Mattie holds, rocks, and bathes her friend, we feel the exorcism of pain. And when the tears finally come, we cry too. The first time I read this chapter, I wept, both because it is so touching to see Mattie be a friend to Ciel, and also because Naylor writes with religious fervor about Ciel's grief.

It would be easy to discount Eugene, and yet, Naylor doesn't. She lets him have a dialogue with Ben, the janitor, and we see that he isn't welcome at the funeral of his daughter, Serena. He is immersed in his own pain, but he handles it without grace. When women tell me they got into crime "because of the wrong man," I think of Eugene. He must be pretty captivating in his charms.

I am always left gladdened by reading this chapter because Ciel does end with hope. She has lost her man, both her children, and her dreams. But she has someone who loves her standing by her side, saying silently that her life is worth valuing.

RPW—

Brewster Place was first integrated several years ago with the hiring of Ben as janitor and handyman for the buildings. It is now an African-American neighborhood especially fond of its colored daughters like Lucielia Louise Turner. Ciel's story, like all the stories of the women of Brewster Place, is that of an ebony phoenix, a rebirth from the ashes of degradation and despair.

Ciel's lover, Eugene, cannot hold a job, cannot support his family, and cannot find the respect demanded by his manhood. For Eugene, a man has got to be a man, but he finds himself in the position of a caged animal overwhelmed by bills and babies. He does not deserve the respect that his manhood demands, and no matter

what he does, it seems all but impossible for him to earn that respect.

Ciel does not want to lose the touch of Eugene's body if she
can help it, but it is a painful love she has with Eugene. For Ciel,
only her baby, Serena, offers love without pain. Ciel seems willing
to sacrifice her own best self to keep Eugene close, and at one level
that seems a tragedy. But I can understand her desire to keep her
lover close. It is never easy to figure out where the line should be
drawn. When do you stop sacrificing for the person you desire?

When Ciel becomes pregnant for a second time, she is willing to endure an abortion because she knows another baby would
drive Eugene away. Ciel can try to remove the memory of the abortion from her consciousness, but she can never totally forget. It is
an everlasting part of her body.

Not surprisingly, the abortion doesn't save her relationship
with Eugene. A man filled with rage and shame, Eugene is destined to run just as he is destined to feel contempt and jealousy
for the bond between the old wise woman Mattie and Ciel, spiri-
tual kin.

While Eugene in the bedroom tells Ciel that he is leaving,
Serena, left alone to play in the living room, electrocutes herself. Ciel too seems to die. "She was simply tired of hurting. And
she was forced to slowly give up the life that God refused to take
from her."

Only Mattie, with the rage of "a blasphemous fireball" and the
desperate desire "to protect her young," can save Ciel. Rocking
Ciel back and forth as if through the deepest pain of the collective
unconscious, Mattie alone exorcises the evil of the pain embedded
in Ciel's body. And then she bathes her, "reverently, as if handling
a newborn," allowing Ciel's tears to flow and her body to be
cleansed and baptized through the ritual of bodily affection and
compassion.

In the end, Ciel is purified, reborn out of the ashes of her burning pain, and Mattie knows that the morning will come. The rebirth of this ebony phoenix hints to me of the power and compassion of female friendship and love—just what Eugene could not
tolerate or understand.

FAMILY

INTRODUCTION

The primary focus of this section is to help you begin thinking about the complex relationships and unique construct we call "family." Although for many years, the "ideal" American family was represented as a mother and father with 2.5 children, a dog, a cat, and a white picket fence, "family" today is not so clearly defined. Families include single parents with children, divorced parents remarried, each with children of their own, married partners without offspring, same sex couples who've adopted, and a variety of other combinations. Families may even be of our own making, a group choosing to live together in community. No longer are we slaves to traditional paradigms with mother at home and father out working; "dysfunctional" seems to be the word of the times as we seek to understand more fully who we are in relationship to where we come from. One of our basic assumptions is that family plays a role in our lives; that is why it is such a prevalent subject in great pieces of literature.

We have tried to pick works that tackle a variety of tough contemporary issues about family. Although many other themes are wound together in these pieces, we encourage you to discuss your preconceived notions about family as you approach these pieces and use them as a stepping-off point to discuss other aspects of the relationships on the page. The stories and chapters will challenge you to define what you think makes family such a compelling issue for writers.

Alice Walker's "Everyday Use" takes us to a poor Southern family strapped by the death of a father. The narrator, the mother, awaits the arrival of one of her two daughters, who has gone off to "make it" at college, trying to escape the poverty of her background. The mother, who lives in a shack with her other daughter, is faced in this story with issues dealing with her offspring. We, the readers, are faced with issues of whom we identify with, and how we feel about these siblings. What is loyalty in a family? What is it to know your roots? As you read this short story, you might consider the values of getting out of a family versus staying in the neighborhood. You might consider how a parent teaches values to a child and how that child puts those values to "everyday use."

In "Sonny's Blues," James Baldwin asks us to consider what it is to be our brother's keeper. Although Baldwin might want us to think about this in metaphorical terms, he takes us to two brothers, each leading very different lives in Harlem. In spite of the well-to-do life of one and the almost desperate life of the other, the two are linked together in ways we must uncover through the story. The brothers find ways to reach each other and sustain themselves, perhaps even heal their lives through their connection to each other. What is it that connects us to our family members? How do we keep or break that bond?

Dorothy Allison takes us to the deep South, a far cry from the streets of New York, to show us a brutal side of family life in *Bastard Out of Carolina*. A young girl, Bone, born out of wedlock, cannot find protection and safety within her nuclear family. Her stepdaddy abuses her emotionally, physically, and sexually, and her mother cannot choose Bone's safety over her own crippled love for Daddy Glen. The aunt turns out to provide the only safe haven for Bone, causing us to ask, what makes us feel safe in a family? What makes us feel violated? How does trust play a part here in helping us to find our way? If we must survive without safety, what are the consequences?

Creating a family of our own is one of the upshots of life in Ken Kesey's idiosyncratic mental hospital in *One Flew Over the Cuckoo's Nest*. As we watch the newest patient, McMurphy, make a place for himself on the ward and create friendships with the other men, we see how a group bonds. Here are men who focus around a common enemy, the hospital, as represented by Big Nurse. In spite of their illnesses, they, like us, become stronger when they work together, weaker when they are not functioning as a unit. The power of the recreated family is explored in this passage. We ask you to think about the untraditional in terms of family and to consider how each family member finds his place.

While we recognize that each of us defines family in our own way, this section seeks to explore how family issues play into our actions. If Bone had not been raped by Daddy Glen, she might not have been abandoned by her mother, but she also might not have developed such a close connection to her aunt. Without a brother, Sonny might not have survived, yet sibling rivalry in "Everyday Use" might have caused an irreparable split in the family. As you plunge into the discussion of the following pieces, take note that our comments may prod you to argue, agree, or go off on other strands, but always, with these selections, an option is to return to the question of what makes a family.

Everyday Use

Alice Walker

FOR YOUR GRANDMAMA

I will wait for her in the yard that Maggie and I made so clean and wavy yesterday afternoon. A yard like this is more comfortable than most people know. It is not just a yard. It is like an extended living room. When the hard clay is swept clean as a floor and the fine sand around the edges lined with tiny, irregular grooves, anyone can come and sit and look up into the elm tree and wait for the breezes that never come inside the house.

Maggie will be nervous until after her sister goes: she will stand hopelessly in corners, homely and ashamed of the burn scars down her arms and legs, eying her sister with a mixture of envy and awe. She thinks her sister has held life always in the palm of one hand, that "no" is a word the world never learned to say to her.

You've no doubt seen those TV shows where the child who has "made it" is confronted, as a surprise, by her own mother and father, tottering in weakly from backstage. (A pleasant surprise, of course: What would they do if parent and child came on the show only to curse out and insult each other?) On TV mother and child embrace and smile into each other's faces. Sometimes the mother and father weep, the child wraps them in her arms and leans across the table to tell how she would not have made it without their help. I have seen these programs.

Sometimes I dream a dream in which Dee and I are suddenly brought together on a TV program of this sort. Out of a dark and soft-seated limousine I am ushered into a bright room filled with many people. There I meet a smiling, gray, sporty man like Johnny Carson who shakes my hand and tells me what a fine girl I have. Then we are on the stage and Dee is embracing me with tears in her eyes. She pins on my dress a large orchid, even though she has told me once that she thinks orchids are tacky flowers.

In real life I am a large, big-boned woman with rough, man-working hands. In the winter I wear flannel nightgowns to bed and overalls during the day. I can kill and clean a hog as mercilessly as a man. My fat keeps me hot in zero weather. I can work outside all day, breaking ice to get water for washing, I can eat pork liver cooked over the open fire minutes after it comes steaming from the hog. One winter I knocked a bull calf straight in the brain between the eyes with a sledge hammer and had the meat hung up to chill before nightfall. But of course all this does not show on television. I am the way my daughter would want me to be: a hundred pounds lighter, my skin like an uncooked barley pancake. My hair glistens in the hot bright lights. Johnny Carson has much to do to keep up with my quick and witty tongue.

But that is a mistake. I know even before I wake up. Who ever knew a Johnson with a quick tongue? Who can even imagine me looking a strange white man in the eye? It seems to me I have talked to them always with one foot raised in flight, with my head turned in whichever way is farthest from them. Dee, though. She would always look anyone in the eye. Hesitation was no part of her nature.

"How do I look, Mama?" Maggie says, showing just enough of her thin body enveloped in pink skirt and red blouse for me to know she's there, almost hidden by the door.

"Come out into the yard," I say.

Have you ever seen a lame animal, perhaps a dog run over by some careless person rich enough to own a car, sidle up to someone who is ignorant enough to be kind to him? That is the way my Maggie walks. She has been like this, chin on chest, eyes on ground, feet in shuffle, ever since the fire that burned the other house to the ground.

Dee is lighter than Maggie, with nicer hair and a fuller figure. She's a woman now, though sometimes I forget. How long ago was it that the other house burned? Ten, twelve years? Sometimes I can still hear the flames and feel Maggie's arms sticking to me, her hair smoking and her dress falling off her in little black papery flakes. Her eyes seemed stretched open, blazed open by the flames reflected in them. And Dee. I see her standing off under the sweet gum tree she used to dig gum out of; a look of concentration on her face as she watched the last dingy gray board of the house fall in toward the red-hot brick chimney. Why don't you do a dance around the ashes? I'd wanted to ask her. She had hated the house that much.

I used to think she hated Maggie, too. But that was before we raised the money, the church and me, to send her to Augusta to school. She used to read to us without pity; forcing words, lies, other folks' habits, whole lives upon us two, sitting trapped and ignorant underneath her voice. She washed us in a river of make believe, burned us with a lot of knowledge we didn't necessarily need to know. Pressed us to her with the serious way she read, to shove us away at just the moment, like dimwits, we seemed about to understand.

Dee wanted nice things. A yellow organdy dress to wear to her graduation from high school; black pumps to match a green suit she'd made from an old suit somebody gave me. She was determined to stare down any disaster in her efforts. Her eyelids would not flicker for minutes at a time. Often I fought off the temptation to shake her. At sixteen she had a style of her own: and knew what style was.

I never had an education myself. After second grade the school was closed down. Don't ask me why: in 1927 colored asked fewer questions than they do now. Sometimes Maggie reads to me. She stumbles along good-naturedly but can't see well. She knows she is not bright. Like good looks and money, quickness passed her by. She will marry John Thomas (who has mossy teeth in an earnest face) and then I'll be free to sit here and I guess just sing church songs to myself. Although I never was a good singer. Never could carry a tune. I was always better at a man's job. I used to love to milk till I was hooked in the side in '49. Cows are soothing and slow and don't bother you, unless you try to milk them the wrong way.

I have deliberately turned my back on the house. It is three rooms, just like the one that burned, except the roof is tin; they don't make shingle roofs any more. There are no real windows, just some holes cut in the sides, like the portholes in a ship, but not round and not square, with rawhide holding the shutters up on the outside. This house is in a pasture, too, like the other one. No doubt when Dee sees it she will want to tear it down. She wrote me once that no matter where we "choose" to live, she will manage to come see us. But she will never bring her friends. Maggie and I thought about this and Maggie asked me, "Mama, when did Dee ever *have* any friends?"

She had a few. Furtive boys in pink shirts hanging about on washday after school. Nervous girls who never laughed. Impressed with her they worshiped the well-turned phrase, the cute shape, the scalding humor that erupted like bubbles in lye. She read to them.

When she was courting Jimmy T she didn't have much time to pay to us, but turned all her faultfinding power on him. He *flew* to marry a cheap city girl from a family of ignorant flashy people. She hardly had time to recompose herself.

When she comes I will meet—but there they are!

Maggie attempts to make a dash for the house, in her shuffling way, but I stay her with my hand. "Come back here," I say. And she stops and tries to dig a well in the sand with her toe.

It is hard to see them clearly through the strong sun. But even the first glimpse of leg out of the car tells me it is Dee. Her feet were always neat-looking, as if God himself had shaped them with a certain style. From the other side of the car comes a short, stocky man. Hair is all over his head a foot long and hanging from his chin like a kinky mule tail. I hear Maggie suck in her breath. "Uhnnnh," is what it sounds like. Like when you see the wriggling end of a snake just in front of your foot on the road. "Uhnnnh."

Dee next. A dress down to the ground, in this hot weather. A dress so loud it hurts my eyes. There are yellows and oranges enough to throw back the light of the sun. I feel my whole face warming from the heat waves it throws out. Earrings gold, too, and hanging down to her shoulders. Bracelets dangling and making noises when she moves her arm up to shake the folds of the dress out of her armpits. The dress is loose and flows, and as she walks closer, I like it. I hear Maggie go "Uhnnnh" again. It is her sister's hair. It stands straight up like the wool on a sheep. It is black as night and around the edges are two long pigtails that rope about like small lizards disappearing behind her ears.

"Wa-su-zo-Tean-o!"[1] she says, coming on in that gliding way the dress makes her move. The short stocky fellow with the hair to his navel is all grinning and he follows up with "Asalamalakim,[2] my mother and sister!" He moves to hug Maggie but she falls back, right up against the back of my chair. I feel her trembling there and when I look up I see the perspiration falling off her chin.

"Don't get up," says Dee. Since I am stout it takes something

[1]Swahili greeting.
[2]Arabic greeting.

of a push. You can see me trying to move a second or two before I make it. She turns, showing white heels through her sandals, and goes back to the car. Out she peeks next with a Polaroid. She stoops down quickly and lines up picture after picture of me sitting there in front of the house with Maggie cowering behind me. She never takes a shot without making sure the house is included. When a cow comes nibbling around the edge of the yard she snaps it and me and Maggie *and* the house. Then she puts the Polaroid in the back seat of the car, and comes up and kisses me on the forehead.

Meanwhile Asalamalakim is going through motions with Maggie's hand. Maggie's hand is as limp as a fish, and probably as cold, despite the sweat, and she keeps trying to pull it back. It looks like Asalamalakim wants to shake hands but wants to do it fancy. Or maybe he don't know how people shake hands. Anyhow, he soon gives up on Maggie.

"Well," I say. "Dee."

"No, Mama," she says. "Not 'Dee,' Wangero Leewanika Kemanjo!"

"What happened to 'Dee'?" I wanted to know.

"She's dead," Wangero said. "I couldn't bear it any longer, being named after the people who oppress me."

"You know as well as me you was named after your aunt Dicie," I said. Dicie is my sister. She named Dee. We called her "Big Dee" after Dee was born.

"But who was *she* named after?" asked Wangero.

"I guess after Grandma Dee," I said.

"And who was she named after?" asked Wangero.

"Her mother," I said, and saw Wangero was getting tired. "That's about as far back as I can trace it," I said. Though, in fact, I probably could have carried it back beyond the Civil War through the branches.

"Well," said Asalamalakim, "there you are."

"Uhnnnh," I heard Maggie say.

"There I was not," I said, "before 'Dicie' cropped up in our family, so why should I try to trace it that far back?"

He just stood there grinning, looking down on me like somebody inspecting a Model A car. Every once in a while he and Wangero sent eye signals over my head.

"How do you pronounce this name?" I asked.

"You don't have to call me by it if you don't want to," said Wangero.

"Why shouldn't I?" I asked. "If that's what you want us to call you, we'll call you."

"I know it might sound awkward at first," said Wangero.

"I'll get used to it," I said. "Ream it out again."

Well, soon we got the name out of the way. Asalamalakim had a name twice as long and three times as hard. After I tripped over it two or three times he told me to just call him Hakim-a-barber. I wanted to ask him was he a barber, but I didn't really think he was, so I didn't ask.

"You must belong to those beef-cattle peoples down the road," I said. They said "Asalamalakim" when they met you, too, but they didn't shake hands. Always too busy: feeding the cattle, fixing the fences, putting up salt-lick shelters, throwing down hay. When the white folks poisoned some of the herd the men stayed up all night with rifles in their hands. I walked a mile and a half just to see the sight.

Hakim-a-barber said, "I accept some of their doctrines, but farming and raising cattle is not my style." (They didn't tell me, and I didn't ask, whether Wangero (Dee) had really gone and married him.)

We sat down to eat and right away he said he didn't eat collards and pork was unclean. Wangero, though, went on through the chitlins and corn bread, the greens and everything else. She talked a blue streak over the sweet potatoes. Everything delighted her. Even the fact that we still used the benches her daddy made for the table when we couldn't afford to buy chairs.

"Oh, Mama!" she cried. Then turned to Hakim-a-barber. "I never knew how lovely these benches are. You can feel the rump prints," she said, running her hands underneath her and along the bench. Then she gave a sigh and her hand closed over Grandma Dee's butter dish. "That's it!" she said. "I knew there was something I wanted to ask you if I could have." She jumped up from the table and went over in the corner where the churn stood, the milk in it clabber by now. She looked at the churn and looked at it.

"This churn top is what I need," she said. "Didn't Uncle Buddy whittle it out of a tree you all used to have?"

"Yes," I said.

"Uh huh," she said happily. "And I want the dasher, too."

"Uncle Buddy whittle that, too?" asked the barber.

Dee (Wangero) looked up at me.

"Aunt Dee's first husband whittled the dash," said Maggie so low you almost couldn't hear her. "His name was Henry, but they called him Stash."

"Maggie's brain is like an elephant's," Wangero said, laughing. "I can use the churn top as a centerpiece for the alcove table," she said, sliding a plate over the churn, "and I'll think of something artistic to do with the dasher."

When she finished wrapping the dasher the handle stuck out. I took it for a moment in my hands. You didn't even have to look close to see where hands pushing the dasher up and down to make butter had left a kind of sink in the wood. In fact, there were a lot of small sinks; you could see where thumbs and fingers had sunk into the wood. It was beautiful light yellow wood, from a tree that grew in the yard where Big Dee and Stash had lived.

After dinner Dee (Wangero) went to the trunk at the foot of my bed and started rifling through it. Maggie hung back in the kitchen over the dishpan. Out came Wangero with two quilts. They had been pieced by Grandma Dee and then Big Dee and me had hung them on the quilt frames on the front porch and quilted them. One was in the Lone Star pattern. The other was Walk Around the Mountain. In both of them were scraps of dresses Grandma Dee had worn fifty and more years ago. Bits and pieces of Grandpa Jarrell's Paisley shirts. And one teeny faded blue piece, about the size of a penny matchbox, that was from Great Grandpa Ezra's uniform that he wore in the Civil War.

"Mama," Wangero said sweet as a bird. "Can I have these old quilts?"

I heard something fall in the kitchen, and a minute later the kitchen door slammed.

"Why don't you take one or two of the others?" I asked. "These old things was just done by me and Big Dee from some tops your grandma pieced before she died."

"No," said Wangero. "I don't want those. They are stitched around the borders by machine."

"That'll make them last better," I said.

"That's not the point," said Wangero. "These are all pieces of dresses Grandma used to wear. She did all this stitching by hand. Imagine!" She held the quilts securely in her arms, stroking them.

"Some of the pieces, like those lavender ones, come from old clothes her mother handed down to her," I said, moving up to touch the quilts. Dee (Wangero) moved back just enough so that I couldn't reach the quilts. They already belonged to her.

"Imagine!" she breathed again, clutching them closely to her bosom.

"The truth is," I said, "I promised to give them quilts to Maggie, for when she marries John Thomas."

She gasped like a bee had stung her.

"Maggie can't appreciate these quilts!" she said. "She'd probably be backward enough to put them to everyday use."

"I reckon she would," I said. "God knows I been saving 'em for long enough with nobody using 'em. I hope she will!" I didn't want to bring up how I had offered Dee (Wangero) a quilt when she went away to college. Then she had told me they were old-fashioned, out of style.

"But they're *priceless!*" she was saying now, furiously; for she has a temper. "Maggie would put them on the bed and in five years they'd be in rags. Less than that!"

"She call always make some more," I said. "Maggie knows how to quilt."

Dee (Wangero) looked at me with hatred. "You just will not understand. The point is these quilts, *these* quilts!"

"Well," I said, stumped. "What would *you* do with them?"

"Hang them," she said. As if that was the only thing you *could* do with quilts.

Maggie by now was standing in the door. I could almost hear the sound her feet made as they scraped over each other.

"She can have them, Mama," she said, like somebody used to never winning anything, or having anything reserved for her. "I can 'member Grandma Dee without the quilts."

I looked at her hard. She had filled her bottom lip with check-erberry snuff and it gave her face a kind of dopey, hangdog look. It was Grandma Dee and Big Dee who taught her how to quilt herself. She stood there with her scarred hands hidden in the folds of her skirt. She looked at her sister with something like fear but she wasn't mad at her. This was Maggie's portion. This was the way she knew God to work.

When I looked at her like that something hit me in the top of my head and ran down to the soles of my feet. Just like when I'm in church and the spirit of God touches me and I get happy and shout. I did something I never had done before: hugged Maggie to me, then dragged her on into the room, snatched the quilts out of Miss Wangero's hands and dumped them into Maggie's lap. Maggie just sat there on my bed with her mouth open.

"Take one or two of the others," I said to Dee.

But she turned without a word and went out to Hakim-a-barber.

"You just don't understand," she said, as Maggie and I came out to the car.

"What don't I understand?" I wanted to know.

"Your heritage," she said. And then she turned to Maggie, kissed her, and said, "You ought to try to make something of yourself, too, Maggie. It's really a new day for us. But from the way you and Mama still live you'd never know it."

She put on some sunglasses that hid everything above the tip of her nose and her chin.

Maggie smiled; maybe at the sunglasses. But a real smile, not scared. After we watched the car dust settle I asked Maggie to bring me a dip of snuff. And then the two of us sat there just enjoying, until it was time to go in the house and go to bed.

——*For Discussion*——

RPW—

Mama Johnson, with her slow tongue and big-boned man-working hands, wears flannel nightgowns and overalls, stays fat eating "pork liver cooked over the open fire," and has killed a bull calf with a sledgehammer. She is a black woman in the rural South, endless miles from the sophisticated world of style and celebrity, of quick wit and popular culture. She is not the television dream, and she knows it.

Her daughter Maggie, with burn scars, has walked like "a lame animal" since a fire destroyed their house ten or twelve years ago, a fire that her other daughter Dee watched while "standing off" under the gum tree. Now they are waiting for the stylish and confident Dee to pay the family a visit.

When Dee arrives with her boyfriend, she is wearing African dress, has changed her name to Wangero, and snaps picture after picture with her Polaroid camera. She wants to escape her slave identity and return to her roots, but she has apparently forgotten that she was named after her Aunt Dee and Grandma Dee and that cultural artifacts ripped from their context do not create a sustained sense of family heritage. Dee is sophisticated and well-educated, a modern woman, but she cannot appreciate the material culture born from toil and everyday use.

Mama Johnson will not allow Dee to take the quilts woven from the scraps and pieces of the family past, the quilts promised to Maggie as a dowry for her marriage to John Thomas. To Dee, the quilts would make artistic wall hangings; for Maggie, they are part of ordinary life. In the end, Dee (a.k.a. Wangero) can only find fault with a mother and sister who, according to her, refuse to make something of themselves in this new modern age. Standing off behind her sunglasses, Dee leaves with the same confidence and arrogance that she had when she arrived. Mama and Maggie remain together, sharing a dip of snuff, sitting and enjoying their inherited portion in life. Dee might have a point about making a new self in the modern world, but in this story, I'll take Maggie and Mama every time.

JRT—

It is easy to embrace Alice Walker's main character in "Everyday Use." Mama is a big woman with "rough man-working hands" who values family and tradition, raised two girls by herself, and takes life as it comes to her. Maggie too, the shy daughter bound to marry a man with "mossy teeth," creeps in corners and asks for little; she engages our pity and later our respect as the one who has learned to quilt, carrying on her family's heritage. Only Dee, the daughter who craves nice things, leaves her home for the city, changes her name, and seeks to make a new life for herself; she lingers outside our sympathies.

Dee is most interesting to me because she represents the one who goes after higher education. She is also the most selfish and possibly the one who is most wounded. It seems that Maggie and her mother are close and might have always been special to each other. As one of my students pointed out, Maggie might have had a different father from Dee. Walker also hints that Dee, in her loneliness, might have started the fire that burned down their first shack. Who knows what desperation she felt, poor, fatherless, a stranger in some ways to her world, outside her mother's innermost circle?

Dee is the quick one, but as Walker reminds us, education is not everything. It must be coupled with good values. Maggie has spent time learning how to run the farm and to take care of the necessities for survival that common sense insists on. She is her mother's right hand. Unattractive, crouching around strangers, and slow, she nevertheless loves faithfully and dutifully. She will be the one to use quilts and not hang them like her sister. She will be the one to take care of her family's most precious treasures. Her education is of the spirit and not just of the mind.

We love to reject Dee because of her selfishness, to embrace Maggie because of her sense of goodness, and to enjoy the earthiness of the mother who stands up to Dee's demands. It seems important to look at each of the characters here for what they lack as well as for what they stand for. Maggie is not a young woman in many ways that we honestly want to be. She is overprotected and shy to a painful point. And in some ways, she is the one who will never strive for much. Dee has sought to find her way in the world and is determined to get ahead. She has ignored some of the lessons of her past. But she has guts too. It seems to me we need some of Dee and Maggie in order to fully appreciate our heritage and make use of ourselves.

Sonny's Blues

James Baldwin

I read about it in the paper, in the subway, on my way to work. I read it, and I couldn't believe it, and I read it again. Then perhaps I just stared at it, at the newsprint spelling out his name, spelling out the story. I stared at it in the swinging lights of the subway car, and in the faces and bodies of the people, and in my own face, trapped in the darkness which roared outside.

It was not to be believed and I kept telling myself that, as I walked from the subway station to the high school. And at the same time I couldn't doubt it. I was scared, scared for Sonny. He became real to me again. A great block of ice got settled in my belly and kept melting there slowly all day long, while I taught my classes algebra. It was a special kind of ice. It kept melting, sending trickles of ice water all up and down my veins, but it never got less. Sometimes it hardened and seemed to expand until I felt my guts were going to come spilling out or that I was going to choke or scream. This would always be at a moment when I was remembering some specific thing Sonny had once said or done.

When he was about as old as the boys in my classes his face had been bright and open, there was a lot of copper in it; and he'd had wonderfully direct brown eyes, and great gentleness and privacy. I wondered what he looked like now. He had been picked up the evening before, in a raid on an apartment downtown, for peddling and using heroin.

I couldn't believe it: but what I mean by that is that I couldn't find any room for it anywhere inside me. I had kept it outside me for a long time. I hadn't wanted to know. I had had suspicions, but I didn't name them, I kept putting them away. I told myself that Sonny was wild, but he wasn't crazy. And he'd always been a good boy, he hadn't ever turned hard or evil or disrespectful, the way kids can, so quick, especially in Harlem. I didn't want to believe that I'd ever see my brother going down, coming to nothing, all that light in his face gone out, in the condition I'd already seen so many others. Yet it had happened and here I was, talking about algebra to a lot of boys who might, every one of them for all I knew, be popping off needles every time they went to the head. Maybe it did more for them than algebra could.

I was sure that the first time Sonny had ever had horse,[1] he couldn't have been much older than these boys were now. These boys, now, were living as we'd been living then, they were growing up with a rush and their heads bumped abruptly against the low ceiling of their actual possibilities. They were filled with rage. All they really knew were two darknesses, the darkness of their lives, which was now closing in on them, and the darkness of the movies, which had blinded them to that other darkness, and in which they now, vindictively, dreamed, at once more together than they were at any other time, and more alone.

When the last bell rang, the last class ended, I let out my breath. It seemed I'd been holding it for all that time. My clothes were wet—I may have looked as though I'd been sitting in a steam bath, all dressed up all afternoon. I sat alone in the classroom a long time. I listened to the boys outside, downstairs, shouting and cursing and laughing. Their laughter struck me for perhaps the first time. It was not the joyous laughter which—God knows why—one associates with children. It was mocking and insular, its intent was to denigrate. It was disenchanted, and in this, also, lay the authority of their curses. Perhaps I was listening to them because I was thinking about my brother and in them I heard my brother. And myself.

One boy was whistling a tune, at once very complicated and very simple, it seemed to be pouring out of him as though he were a bird, and it sounded very cool and moving through all that harsh, bright air, only just holding its own through all those other sounds.

I stood up and walked over to the window and looked down into the courtyard. It was the beginning of the spring and the sap was rising in the boys. A teacher passed through them every now and again, quickly, as though he or she couldn't wait to get out of that courtyard, to get those boys out of their sight and off their minds. I started collecting my stuff. I thought I'd better get home and talk to Isabel.

The courtyard was almost deserted by the time I got downstairs. I saw this boy standing in the shadow of a doorway, look-

[1]Heroin.

ing just like Sonny. I almost called his name. Then I saw that it wasn't Sonny, but somebody we used to know, a boy from around our block. He'd been Sonny's friend. He'd never been mine, having been too young for me, and, anyway, I'd never liked him. And now, even though he was a grown-up man, he still hung around that block, still spent hours on the street corners, was always high and raggy. I used to run into him from time to time and he'd often work around to asking me for a quarter or fifty cents. He always had some real good excuse too, and I always gave it to him, I don't know why.

But now, abruptly I hated him. I couldn't stand the way he looked at me, partly like a dog, partly like a cunning child. I wanted to ask him what the hell he was doing in the school courtyard.

He sort of shuffled over to me, and he said, "I see you got the papers. So you already know about it."

"You mean about Sonny? Yes, I already know about it. How come they didn't get you?"

He grinned. It made him repulsive and it also brought to mind what he'd looked like as a kid. "I wasn't there. I stay away from them people."

"Good for you." I offered him a cigarette and I watched him through the smoke. "You come all the way down here just to tell me about Sonny?"

"That's right." He was sort of shaking his head and his eyes looked strange, as though they were about to cross. The bright sun deadened his damp dark brown skin and it made his eyes look yellow and showed up the dirt in his kinked hair. He smelled funky. I moved a little way away from him and I said, "Well, thanks. But I already know about it and I got to get home."

"I'll walk you a little ways," he said. We started walking. There were a couple of kids still loitering in the courtyard and one of them said goodnight to me and looked strangely at the boy beside me.

"What're you going to do?" he asked me. "I mean, about Sonny?"

"Look. I haven't seen Sonny for over a year. I'm not sure I'm going to do anything. Anyway, what the hell can I do?"

"That's right," he said quickly, "ain't nothing you can do. Can't much help old Sonny no more, I guess."

It was what I was thinking and so it seemed to me he had no right to say it.

"I'm surprised at Sonny, though," he went on—he had a funny way of talking, he looked straight ahead as though he were talking to himself—"I thought Sonny was a smart boy, I thought he was too smart to get hung."

"I guess he thought so too," I said sharply, "and that's how he got hung. And how about you? You're pretty goddamn smart, I bet."

Then he looked directly at me, just for a minute. "I ain't smart," he said. "If I was smart, I'd have reached for a pistol a long time ago."

"Look. Don't tell *me* your sad story, if it was up to me, I'd give you one." Then I felt guilty—guilty, probably, for never having supposed that the poor bastard *had* a story of his own, much less a sad one, and I asked, quickly, "What's going to happen to him now?"

He didn't answer this. He was off by himself some place. "Funny thing," he said, and from his tone we might have been discussing the quickest way to get to Brooklyn, "when I saw the papers this morning, the first thing I asked myself was if I had anything to do with it. I felt sort of responsible."

I began to listen more carefully. The subway station was on the corner, just before us, and I stopped. He stopped, too. We were in front of a bar and he ducked slightly, peering in, but whoever he was looking for didn't seem to be there. The juke box was blasting away with something black and bouncy and I half watched the barmaid as she danced her way from the juke box to her place behind the bar. And I watched her face as she laughingly responded to something someone said to her, still keeping time to the music. When she smiled one saw the little girl, one sensed the doomed, still struggling woman beneath the battered face of the semi-whore.

"I never *give* Sonny nothing," the boy said finally, "but a long time ago I come to school high and Sonny asked me how it felt." He paused, I couldn't bear to watch him, I watched the barmaid, and I listened to the music which seemed to be causing the pavement to shake. "I told him it felt great." The music stopped, the barmaid paused and watched the juke box until the music began again. "It did."

All this was carrying me some place I didn't want to go. I certainly didn't want to know how it felt. It filled everything, the people, the houses, the music, the dark, quicksilver barmaid, with menace, and this menace was their reality.

"What's going to happen to him now?" I asked again.

"They'll send him away some place and they'll try to cure him." He shook his head. "Maybe he'll even think he's kicked the habit. Then they'll let him loose"—he gestured, throwing his cigarette into the gutter. "That's all."

"What do you mean that's *all?*"

But I knew what he meant.

"I *mean,* that's *all.*" He turned his head and looked at me, pulling down the corners of his mouth. "Don't you know what I mean?" he asked, softly.

"How the hell *would* I know what you mean?" I almost whispered it, I don't know why.

"That's right," he said to the air, "how would *he* know what I mean?" He turned toward me again, patient and calm, and yet I somehow felt him shaking, shaking as though he were going to fall apart. I felt that ice in my guts again, the dread I'd felt all afternoon; and again I watched the barmaid, moving about the bar, washing glasses, and singing. "Listen. They'll let him out and then it'll just start all over again. That's what I mean."

"You mean—they'll let him out. And then he'll just start working his way back in again. You mean he'll never kick the habit. Is that what you mean?"

"That's right," he said cheerfully. "*You* see what I mean."

"Tell me," I said at last, "why does he want to die? He must want to die, he's killing himself, why does he want to die?"

He looked at me in surprise. He licked his lips. "He don't want to die. He wants to live. Don't nobody want to die, ever."

Then I wanted to ask him—too many things. He could not have answered, or if he had, I could not have borne the answers. I started walking. "Well, I guess it's none of my business."

"It's going to be rough on old Sonny," he said. We reached the subway station. "This is your station?" he asked. I nodded. I took one step down. "Damn!" he said suddenly. I looked up at him. He grinned again. "Damn it if I didn't leave all my money home. You ain't got a dollar on you, have you? Just for a couple of days, is all."

All at once something inside gave and threatened to come pouring out of me. I didn't hate him any more. I felt that in another moment I'd start crying like a child.

"Sure," I said. "Don't sweat." I looked in my wallet and didn't have a dollar, I only had five. "Here." I said. "That hold you?"

He didn't look at it—he didn't want to look at it. A terrible closed look came over his face, as though he were keeping the number on the bill a secret from him and me. "Thanks," he said, and now he was dying to see me go. "Don't worry about Sonny. Maybe I'll write him or something."

"Sure," I said. "You do that. So long."

"Be seeing you," he said. I went on down the steps.

And I didn't write Sonny or send him anything for a long time. When I finally did, it was just after my little girl died, he wrote me back a letter which made me feel like a bastard.

Here's what he said:

Dear brother,

You don't know how much I needed to hear from you. I wanted to write you many a time but I dug how much I must have hurt you and so I didn't write. But now I feel like a man who's been trying to climb up out of some deep, real deep and funky hole and just saw the sun up there, outside. I got to get outside.

I can't tell you much about how I got here. I mean I don't know how to tell you. I guess I was afraid of something or I was trying to escape from something and you know I have never been very strong in the head (smile). I'm glad Mama and Daddy are dead and can't see what's happened to their son and I swear if I'd known what I was doing I would never have hurt you so, you and a lot of other fine people who were nice to me and who believed in me.

I don't want you to think it had anything to do with me being a musician. It's more than that. Or maybe less than that. I can't get anything straight in my head down here and I try not to think about what's going to happen to me when I get outside again. Sometime I think I'm going to flip and *never* get outside and sometime I think I'll come straight back. I tell you one thing, though, I'd rather blow my brains out than go through this again. But that's what they all say, so they tell me. If I tell you when I'm coming to New York and if you could meet me, I sure would appreciate it. Give my love to Isabel and the kids and I was sure sorry to hear about little Gracie. I wish I could be like Mama and say the Lord's will be done, but I don't know it seems to me that trouble is the one thing that never does get stopped and I don't know what good it does to blame it on the Lord. But maybe it does some good if you believe it.

Your brother,
Sonny

Then I kept in constant touch with him and I sent him whatever I could and I went to meet him when he came back to New York. When I saw him many things I thought I had forgotten came flooding back to me. This was because I had begun, finally, to wonder about Sonny, about the life that Sonny lived inside. This life, whatever it was, had made him older and thinner and it had deepened the distant stillness in which he had always moved. He looked very unlike my baby brother. Yet, when he smiled, when we shook hands, the baby brother I'd never known looked out from the depths of his private life, like an animal waiting to be coaxed into the light.

"How you been keeping?" he asked me.

"All right. And you?"

"Just fine." He was smiling all over his face. "It's good to see you again."

"It's good to see you."

The seven years' difference in our ages lay between us like a chasm: I wondered if these years would ever operate between us as a bridge. I was remembering, and it made it hard to catch my breath, that I had been there when he was born; and I had heard the first words he had ever spoken. When he started to walk, he walked from our mother straight to me. I caught him just before he fell when he took the first steps he ever took in this world.

"How's Isabel?"

"Just fine. She's dying to see you."

"And the boys?"

"They're fine, too. They're anxious to see their uncle."

"Oh, come on. You know they don't remember me."

"Are you kidding? Of course they remember you."

He grinned again. We got into a taxi. We had a lot to say to each other, far too much to know how to begin.

As the taxi began to move, I asked, "You still want to go to India?"

He laughed. "You still remember that. Hell, no. This place is Indian enough for me."

"It used to belong to them," I said.

And he laughed again. "They damn sure knew what they were doing when they got rid of it."

Years ago, when he was around fourteen, he'd been all hipped on the idea of going to India. He read books about people sitting on rocks, naked, in all kinds of weather, but mostly bad, naturally, and walking barefoot through hot coals and arriving at wisdom. I used to say that it sounded to me as though they were getting away from wisdom as fast as they could. I think he sort of looked down on me for that.

"Do you mind," he asked, "if we have the driver drive alongside the park? On the west side—I haven't seen the city in so long."

"Of course not," I said. I was afraid that I might sound as though I were humoring him, but I hoped he wouldn't take it that way.

So we drove along, between the green of the park and the stony, lifeless elegance of hotels and apartment buildings, toward the vivid, killing streets of our childhood. These streets hadn't changed, though housing projects jutted up out of them now like rocks in the middle of a boiling sea. Most of the houses in which we had grown up had vanished, as had the stores from which we had stolen, the basements in which we had first tried sex, the roof-tops from which we had hurled tin cans and bricks. But houses exactly like the houses of our past yet dominated the landscape, boys exactly like the boys we once had been found themselves smothering in these houses, came down into the streets for light and air and found themselves encircled by disaster. Some escaped the trap, most didn't. Those who got out always left something of themselves behind, as some animals amputate a leg and leave it in the trap. It might be said, perhaps, that I had escaped, after all, I was a school teacher; or that Sonny had, he hadn't lived in Harlem for years. Yet, as the cab moved uptown through streets which seemed, with a rush, to darken with dark people, and as I covertly studied Sonny's face, it came to me that what we both were seeking through our separate cab windows was that part of ourselves which had been left behind. It's always at the hour of trouble and confrontation that the missing member aches.

We hit 110th Street and started rolling up Lenox Avenue. And I'd known this avenue all my life, but it seemed to me again, as it had seemed on the day I'd first heard about Sonny's trouble, filled with a hidden menace which was its very breath of life.

"We almost there," said Sonny.

"Almost." We were both too nervous to say anything more.

We live in a housing project. It hasn't been up long. A few days after it was up it seemed uninhabitably new, now, of course, it's already rundown. It looks like a parody of the good, clean, faceless life — God knows the people who live in it do their best to make it a parody. The beat-looking grass lying around isn't enough to make their lives green, the hedges will never hold out the streets, and they know it. The big windows fool no one, they aren't big enough to make space out of no space. They don't bother with the windows, they watch the TV screen instead. The playground is most popular with the children who don't play at jacks, or skip rope, or roller skate, or swing, and they can be found in it after dark. We moved in partly because it's not too far from where I teach, and partly for the kids; but it's really just like the houses in which Sonny and I grew up. The same things happen, they'll have the same things to remember. The moment Sonny and I started into the house I had the feeling that I was simply bringing him back into the danger he had almost died trying to escape.

Sonny has never been talkative. So I don't know why I was sure he'd be dying to talk to me when supper was over the first night. Everything went fine, the oldest boy remembered him, and the youngest boy liked him, and Sonny had remembered to bring something for each of them; and Isabel, who is really much nicer than I am, more open and giving, had gone to a lot of trouble about dinner and was genuinely glad to see him. And she's always been able to tease Sonny in a way that I haven't. It was nice to see her face so vivid again and to hear her laugh and watch her make Sonny laugh. She wasn't, or, anyway, she didn't seem to be, at all uneasy or embarrassed. She chatted as though there were no subject which had to be avoided and she got Sonny past his first, faint stiffness. And thank God she was there, for I was filled with that icy dread again. Everything I did seemed awkward to me, and everything I said sounded freighted with hidden meaning. I was trying to remember everything I'd heard about dope addiction and I couldn't help watching Sonny for signs. I wasn't doing it out of malice. I was trying to find out something about my brother. I was dying to hear him tell me he was safe.

"Safe!" my father grunted, whenever Mamma suggested trying

to move to a neighborhood which might be safer for children. "Safe, hell! Ain't no place safe for kids, nor nobody."

He always went on like this, but he wasn't, ever, really as bad as he sounded, not even on weekends, when he got drunk. As a matter of fact, he was always on the lookout for "something a little better," but he died before he found it. He died suddenly, during a drunken weekend in the middle of the war, when Sonny was fifteen. He and Sonny hadn't ever got on too well. And this was partly because Sonny was the apple of his father's eye. It was because he loved Sonny so much and was frightened for him, that he was always fighting with him. It doesn't do any good to fight with Sonny. Sonny just moves back, inside himself, where he can't be reached. But the principal reason that they never hit it off is that they were so much alike. Daddy was big and rough and loud-talking, just the opposite of Sonny, but they both had—that same privacy.

Mama tried to tell me something about this, just after Daddy died. I was home on leave from the army.

This was the last time I ever saw my mother alive. Just the same, this picture gets all mixed up in my mind with pictures I had of her when she was younger. The way I always see her is the way she used to be on a Sunday afternoon, say, when the old folks were talking after the big Sunday dinner. I always see her wearing pale blue. She'd be sitting on the sofa. And my father would be sitting in the easy chair, not far from her. And the living room would be full of church folks and relatives. There they sit, in chairs all around the living room, and the night is creeping up outside, but nobody knows it yet. You can see the darkness growing against the window-panes and you hear the street noises every now and again, or maybe the jangling beat of a tambourine from one of the churches close by, but it's real quiet in the room. For a moment nobody's talking, but every face looks darkening, like the sky outside. And my mother rocks a little from the waist, and my father's eyes are closed. Everyone is looking at something a child can't see. For a minute they've forgotten the children. Maybe a kid is lying on the rug, half asleep. Maybe somebody's got a kid in his lap and is absent-mindedly stroking the kid's head. Maybe there's a kid, quiet and big-eyed, curled up in a big chair in the corner. The silence, the darkness coming, and the darkness in the faces frightens the child obscurely. He hopes that the hand which strokes his forehead will never stop—will never die. He hopes that there will never come a time when the old folks won't be sitting around the living room, talking about where they've come from, and what they've seen, and what's happened to them and their kinfolk.

But something deep and watchful in the child knows that this is bound to end, is already ending. In a moment someone will get up and turn on the light. Then the old folks will remember the children and they won't talk any more that day. And when light fills the room, the child is filled with darkness. He knows that every time this happens he's moved just a little closer to that darkness outside. The darkness outside is what the old folks have been talking about. It's what they've come from. It's what they endure. The child knows that they won't talk any more because if he knows too much about what's happening to *them*, he'll know too much too soon, about what's going to happen to *him*.

The last time I talked to my mother, I remember I was restless. I wanted to get out and see Isabel. We weren't married then and we had a lot to straighten out between us.

There Mama sat, in black, by the window. She was humming an old church song, *Lord you brought me from a long ways off.* Sonny was out somewhere. Mama kept watching the streets.

"I don't know," she said, "if I'll ever see you again, after you go off from here. But I hope you'll remember the things I tried to teach you."

"Don't talk like that," I said, and smiled. "You'll be here a long time yet."

She smiled, too, but she said nothing. She was quiet for a long time. And I said, "Mama, don't you worry about nothing. I'll be writing all the time, and you be getting the checks. . . . "

"I want to talk to you about your brother," she said, suddenly. "If anything happens to me he ain't going to have nobody to look out for him."

"Mama," I said, "ain't nothing going to happen to you *or* Sonny. Sonny's all right. He's a good boy and he's got good sense."

"It ain't a question of his being a good boy," Mama said, "nor of his having good sense. It ain't only the bad ones, nor yet the dumb ones that gets sucked under." She stopped, looking at me. "Your Daddy once had a brother," she said, and she smiled in a way that made me feel she was in pain. "You didn't never know that, did you?"

"No," I said, "I never knew that," and I watched her face.

"Oh, yes," she said, "your Daddy had a brother." She looked

out of the window again. "I know you never saw your Daddy cry. But *I* did—many a time, through all these years."

I asked her, "What happened to his brother? How come nobody's ever talked about him?"

This was the first time I ever saw my mother look old.

"His brother got killed," she said, "when he was just a little younger than you are now. I knew him. He was a fine boy. He was maybe a little full of the devil, but he didn't mean nobody no harm."

Then she stopped and the room was silent, exactly as it had sometimes been on those Sunday afternoons. Mama kept looking out into the streets.

"He used to have a job in the mill," she said, "and, like all young folks, he just liked to perform on Saturday nights. Saturday nights, him and your father would drift around to different places, go to dances and things like that, or just sit around with people they knew, and your father's brother would sing, he had a fine voice, and play along with himself on his guitar. Well, this particular Saturday night, him and your father was coming home from some place, and they were both a little drunk and there was a moon that night, it was bright like day. Your father's brother was feeling kind of good, and he was whistling to himself, and he had his guitar slung over his shoulder. They was coming down a hill and beneath them was a road that turned off from the highway. Well, your father's brother, being always kind of frisky, decided to run down this hill, and he did, with that guitar banging and clanging behind him, and he ran across the road, and he was making water behind a tree. And your father was sort of amused at him and he was still coming down the hill, kind of slow. Then he heard a car motor and that same minute his brother stepped from behind the tree, into the road, in the moonlight. And he started to cross the road. And your father started to run down the hill, he says he don't know why. This car was full of white men. They was all drunk, and when they seen your father's brother they let out a great whoop and holler and they aimed the car straight at him. They was having fun, they just wanted to scare him, the way they do sometimes, you know. But they was drunk. And I guess the boy, being drunk, too, and scared, kind of lost his head. By the time he jumped it was too late. Your father says he heard his brother scream when the car rolled over him, and he heard the wood of that guitar when it give, and he heard them strings go flying, and he heard them white men shouting, and the car kept on a-going and it ain't stopped till this day. And, time your father got down the hill, his brother weren't nothing but blood and pulp."

Tears were gleaming on my mother's face. There wasn't anything I could say.

"He never mentioned it," she said, "because I never let him mention it before you children. Your Daddy was like a crazy man that night and for many a night thereafter. He says he never in his life seen anything as dark as that road after the lights of that car had gone away. Weren't nothing, weren't nobody on that road, just your Daddy and his brother and that busted guitar. Oh, yes. Your Daddy never did really get right again. Till the day he died he weren't sure but that every white man he saw was the man that killed his brother."

She stopped and took out her handkerchief and dried her eyes and looked at me.

"I ain't telling you all this," she said, "to make you scared or bitter or to make you hate nobody. I'm telling you this because you got a brother. And the world ain't changed."

I guess I didn't want to believe this. I guess she saw this in my face. She turned away from me, toward the window again, searching those streets.

"But I praise my Redeemer," she said at last, "that He called your Daddy home before me. I ain't saying it to throw no flowers at myself, but, I declare, it keeps me from feeling too cast down to know I helped your father get safely through this world. Your father always acted like he was the roughest, strongest man on earth. And everybody took him to be like that. But if he hadn't had *me* there— to see his tears!"

She was crying again. Still I couldn't move. I said, "Lord, Lord, Mama, I didn't know it was like that."

"Oh, honey," she said, "there's a lot that you don't know. But you are going to find it out." She stood up from the window and came over to me. "You got to hold on to your brother," she said, "and don't let him fall, no matter what it looks like is happening to him and no matter how evil you gets with him. You going to be evil with him many a time. But don't you forget what I told you, you hear?"

"I won't forget," I said. "Don't you worry, I won't forget. I won't let nothing happen to Sonny."

My mother smiled as though she were amused at something

she saw in my face. Then, "You may not be able to stop nothing from happening. But you got to let him know you's *there.*"

Two days later I was married, and then I was gone. And I had a lot of things on my mind and I pretty well forgot my promise to Mama until I got shipped home on a special furlough for her funeral.

And, after the funeral, with just Sonny and me alone in the empty kitchen, I tried to find out something about him.

"What do you want to do?" I asked him.

"I'm going to be a musician," he said.

For he had graduated, in the time I had been away, from dancing to the juke box to finding out who was playing what, and what they were doing with it, and he had bought himself a set of drums.

"You mean, you want to be a drummer?" I somehow had the feeling that being a drummer might be all right for other people but not for my brother Sonny.

"I don't think," he said, looking at me very gravely, "that I'll ever be a good drummer. But I think I can play a piano."

I frowned. I'd never played the role of the older brother quite so seriously before, had scarcely ever, in fact, *asked* Sonny a damn thing. I sensed myself in the presence of something I didn't really know how to handle, didn't understand. So I made my frown a litle deeper as I asked: "What kind of musician do you want to be?"

He grinned. "How many kinds do you think there are?"

"Be *serious,*" I said.

He laughed, throwing his head back, and then looked at me. "I *am* serious."

"Well, then, for Christ's sake, stop kidding around and answer a serious question. I mean, do you want to be a concert pianist, or want to play classical music and all that, or—or what?" Long before I finished he was laughing again. "For Christ's *sake,* Sonny!"

He sobered, but with difficulty. "I'm sorry. But you sound so— *scared!*" and he was off again.

"Well, you may think it's funny now, baby, but it's not going to be so funny when you have to make your living at it, let me tell you *that.*" I was furious because I knew he was laughing at me and I didn't know why.

"No," he said, very sober now, and afraid, perhaps, that he'd hurt me, "I don't want to be a classical pianist. That isn't what interests me. I mean"—he paused, looking hard at me, as though his eyes would help me to understand, and then gestured helplessly, as though perhaps his hand would help—"I mean, I'll have a lot of studying to do, and I'll have to study *everything*, but, I mean, I want to play *with*—jazz musicians." He stopped. "I want to play jazz," he said.

Well, the word had never before sounded as heavy, as real, as it sounded that afternoon in Sonny's mouth. I just looked at him and I was probably frowning a real frown by this time. I simply couldn't see why on earth he'd want to spend his time hanging around nightclubs, clowning around on bandstands, while people pushed each other around a dance floor. It seemed—beneath him, somehow. I had never thought about it before, had never been forced to, but I suppose I had always put jazz musicians in a class with what Daddy called "good-time people."

"Are you *serious?*"

"Hell, *yes*, I'm serious."

He looked more helpless than ever, and annoyed, and deeply hurt.

I suggested helpfully: "You mean—like Louis Armstrong?"

His face closed as though I'd struck him. "No. I'm not talking about none of that old-time, down home crap."

"Well, look Sonny, I'm sorry, don't get mad. I just don't altogether get it, that's all. Name somebody—you know, a jazz musician you admire."

"Bird."

"Who?"

"Bird! Charlie Parker! Don't they teach you nothing in the goddamn army?"

I lit a cigarette. I was surprised and then a little amused to discover that I was trembling. "I've been out of touch," I said. "You'll have to be patient with me. Now. Who's this Parker character?"

"He's just one of the greatest jazz musicians alive," said Sonny, sullenly, his hands in his pockets, his back to me. "Maybe *the* greatest," he added, bitterly, "that's probably why *you* never heard of him."

"All right," I said, "I'm ignorant. I'm sorry. I'll go out and buy all the cat's records right away, all right?"

"It don't," said Sonny, with dignity, "make any difference to me. I don't care what you listen to. Don't do me no favors."

I was beginning to realize that I'd never seen him so upset before. With another part of my mind I was thinking that this would probably turn out to be one of those things kids go through and that I shouldn't make it seem important by pushing it too hard. Still, I didn't think it would do any harm to ask: "Doesn't all this take a lot of time? Can you make a living at it?"

He turned back to me and half leaned, half sat, on the kitchen table. "Everything takes time," he said, "and—well, yes, sure, I can make a living at it. But what I don't seem to be able to make you understand is that it's the only thing I want to do."

"Well, Sonny," I said gently, "you know people can't always do exactly what they *want* to do—"

"*No,* I don't know that," said Sonny, surprising me. "I think people *ought* to do what they want to do, what else are they alive for?"

"You are getting to be a big boy," I said desperately, "it's time you started thinking about your future."

"I'm thinking about my future," said Sonny, grimly. "I think about it all the time."

I gave up. I decided, if he didn't change his mind, that we could always talk about it later. "In the meantime," I said, "you got to finish school." We had already decided that he'd have to move in with Isabel and her folks. I knew this wasn't the ideal arrangement because Isabel's folks are inclined to be dicty[2] and they hadn't especially wanted Isabel to marry me. But I didn't know what else to do. "And we have to get you fixed up at Isabel's."

There was a long silence. He moved from the kitchen table to the window. "That's a terrible idea. You know it yourself."

"Do you have a *better* idea?"

He just walked up and down the kitchen for a minute. He was as tall as I was. He had started to shave. I suddenly had the feeling that I didn't know him at all.

He stopped at the kitchen table and picked up my cigarettes. Looking at me with a kind of mocking, amused defiance, he put one between his lips. "You mind?"

"You smoking already?"

He lit the cigarette and nodded, watching me through the smoke. "I just wanted to see if I'd have the courage to smoke in front of you." He grinned and blew a great cloud of smoke to the

[2]Snobbish.

ceiling. "It was easy." He looked at my face. "Come on, now. I bet you was smoking at my age, tell the truth."

I didn't say anything but the truth was on my face, and he laughed. But now there was something very strained in his laugh. "Sure. And I bet that ain't all you was doing."

He was frightening me a little. "Cut the crap," I said. "We already decided that you was going to go and live at Isabel's. Now what's got into you all of a sudden?"

"*You* decided it," he pointed out. "*I* didn't decide nothing." He stopped in front of me, leaning against the stove, arms loosely folded. "Look, brother. I don't want to stay in Harlem no more, I really don't." He was very earnest. He looked at me, then over toward the kitchen window. There was something in his eyes I'd never seen before, some thoughtfulness, some worry all his own. He rubbed the muscle of one arm. "It's time I was getting out of here."

"Where do you want to *go*, Sonny?"

"I want to join the army. Or the navy, I don't care. If I say I'm old enough, they'll believe me."

Then I got mad. It was because I was so scared. "You must be crazy. You goddamn fool, what the hell do you want to go and join the *army* for?"

"I just told you. To get out of Harlem."

"Sonny, you haven't even finished *school*. And if you really want to be a musician, how do you expect to study if you're in the *army*?"

He looked at me, trapped, and in anguish. "There's ways. I might be able to work out some kind of deal. Anyway, I'll have the G.I. Bill when I come out."

"*If* you come out." We stared at each other. "Sonny, please. Be reasonable. I know the setup is far from perfect. But we got to do the best we can."

"I ain't learning nothing in school," he said. "Even when I go." He turned away from me and opened the window and threw his cigarette out into the narrow alley. I watched his back. "At least, I ain't learning nothing you'd want me to learn." He slammed the window so hard I thought the glass would fly out, and turned back to me. "And I'm sick of the stink of these garbage cans!"

"Sonny," I said, "I know how you feel, but if you don't finish school now, you're going to be sorry later that you didn't." I grabbed him by the shoulders. "And you only got another year. It ain't so bad. And I'll come back and I swear I'll help you do *whatever* you want to do. Just try to put up with it till I come back. Will you please do that? For me?"

He didn't answer and he wouldn't look at me.

"Sonny. You hear me?"

He pulled away. "I hear you. But you never hear anything *I* say."

I didn't know what to say to that. He looked out of the window and then back at me. "OK," he said, and sighed. "I'll try."

Then I said, trying to cheer him up a little, "They got a piano at Isabel's. You can practice on it."

And as a matter of fact, it did cheer him up for a minute. "That's right," he said to himself. "I forgot that." His face relaxed a little. But the worry, the thoughtfulness, played on it still, the way shadows play on a face which is staring into the fire.

But I thought I'd never hear the end of that piano. At first, Isabel would write me, saying how nice it was that Sonny was so serious about his music and how, as soon as he came in from school, or wherever he had been when he was supposed to be at school, he went straight to that piano and stayed there until suppertime. And, after supper, he went back to that piano and stayed there until everybody went to bed. He was at the piano all day Saturday and all day Sunday. Then he bought a record player and started playing records. He'd play one record over and over again, all day long sometimes, and he'd improvise along with it on the piano. Or he'd play one section of the record, one chord, one change, one progression, then he'd do it on the piano. Then back to the record. Then back to the piano.

Well, I really don't know how they stood it. Isabel finally confessed that it wasn't like living with a person at all, it was like living with sound. And the sound didn't make any sense to her, didn't make any sense to any of them—naturally. They began, in a way, to be afflicted by this presence that was living in their home. It was as though Sonny were some sort of god, or monster. He moved in an atmosphere which wasn't like theirs at all. They fed him and he ate, he washed himself, he walked in and out of their door; he certainly wasn't nasty or unpleasant or rude, Sonny isn't any of those things; but it was as though he were all wrapped up in some cloud, some fire, some vision all his own; and there wasn't any way to reach him.

At the same time, he wasn't really a man yet, he was still a child, and they had to watch out for him in all kinds of ways. They certainly couldn't throw him out. Neither did they dare to make a great scene about that piano because even they dimly sensed, as I sensed, from so many thousands of miles away, that Sonny was at that piano playing for his life.

But he hadn't been going to school. One day a letter came from the school board and Isabel's mother got it—there had, apparently, been other letters but Sonny had torn them up. This day, when Sonny came in, Isabel's mother showed him the letter and asked where he'd been spending his time. And she finally got it out of him that he'd been down in Greenwich Village, with musicians and other characters, in a white girl's apartment. And this scared her and she started to scream at him and what came up, once she began—though she denies it to this day—was what sacrifices they were making to give Sonny a decent home and how little he appreciated it.

Sonny didn't play the piano that day. By evening, Isabel's mother had calmed down but then there was the old man to deal with, and Isabel herself. Isabel says she did her best to be calm but she broke down and started crying. She says she just watched Sonny's face. She could tell, by watching him, what was happening with him. And what was happening was that they penetrated his cloud, they had reached him. Even if their fingers had been a thousand times more gentle than human fingers ever are, he could hardly help feeling that they had stripped him naked and were spitting on that nakedness. For he also had to see that his presence, that music, which was life or death to him, had been torture for them and that they had endured it, not at all for his sake, but only for mine. And Sonny couldn't take that. He can take it a little better today than he could then but he's still not very good at it and, frankly, I don't know anybody who is.

The silence of the next few days must have been louder than the sound of all the music ever played since time began. One morning, before she went to work, Isabel was in his room for something and she suddenly realized that all of his records were gone. And she knew for certain that he was gone. And he was. He went as far as the navy would carry him. He finally sent me a postcard from some place in Greece and that was the first I knew that Sonny was still alive. I didn't see him any more until we were both back in New York and the war had long been over.

He was a man by then, of course, but I wasn't willing to see it.

He came by the house from time to time, but we fought almost
every time we met. I didn't like the way he carried himself, loose
and dreamlike all the time, and I didn't like his friends, and his
music seemed to be merely an excuse for the life he led. It sounded
just that weird and disordered.

Then we had a fight, a pretty awful fight, and I didn't see him
for months. By and by I looked him up, where he was living, in a
furnished room in the Village, and I tried to make it up. But there
were lots of other people in the room and Sonny just lay on his bed,
and he wouldn't come downstairs with me, and he treated these
other people as though they were his family and I weren't. So I got
mad and then he got mad, and then I told him that he might just
as well be dead as live the way he was living. Then he stood up
and he told me not to worry about him any more in life, that he
was dead as far as I was concerned. Then he pushed me to the door
and the other people looked on as though nothing were happening,
and he slammed the door behind me. I stood in the hallway, staring
at the door. I heard somebody laugh in the room and then the tears
came to my eyes. I started down the steps, whistling to keep from
crying, I kept whistling to myself, *You going to need me, baby, one
of these cold, rainy days.*

I read about Sonny's trouble in the spring. Little Grace died in
the fall. She was a beautiful little girl. But she only lived a little
over two years. She died of polio and she suffered. She had a slight
fever for a couple of days, but it didn't seem like anything and we
just kept her in bed. And we would certainly have called the doctor, but the fever dropped, she seemed to be all right. So we thought
it had just been a cold. Then, one day, she was up, playing, Isabel
was in the kitchen fixing lunch for the two boys when they'd come
in from school, and she heard Grace fall down in the living room.
When you have a lot of children you don't always start running
when one of them falls, unless they start screaming or something.
And, this time, Grace was quiet. Yet, Isabel says that when she
heard that *thump* and then that silence, something happened in
her to make her afraid. And she ran to the living room and there
was little Grace on the floor, all twisted up, and the reason she
hadn't screamed was that she couldn't get her breath. And when
she did scream, it was the worst sound, Isabel says, that she'd ever
heard in all her life, and she still hears it sometimes in her dreams.
Isabel will sometimes wake me up with a low, moaning, strangled

sound and I have to be quick to awaken her and hold her to me and where Isabel is weeping against me seems a mortal wound.

I think I may have written Sonny the very day that little Grace was buried. I was sitting in the living room in the dark, by myself, and I suddenly thought of Sonny. My trouble made his real.

One Saturday afternoon, when Sonny had been living with us, or, anyway, been in our house, for nearly two weeks, I found myself wandering aimlessly about the living room, drinking from a can of beer, and trying to work up the courage to search Sonny's room. He was out, he was usually out whenever I was home, and Isabel had taken the children to see their grandparents. Suddenly I was standing still in front of the living room window, watching Seventh Avenue. The idea of searching Sonny's room made me still. I scarcely dared to admit to myself what I'd be searching for. I didn't know what I'd do if I found it. Or if I didn't.

On the sidewalk across from me, near the entrance to a barbecue joint, some people were holding an old-fashioned revival meeting. The barbecue cook, wearing a dirty white apron, his conked hair reddish and metallic in the pale sun, and a cigarette between his lips, stood in the doorway, watching them. Kids and older people paused in their errands and stood there, along with some older men and a couple of very tough-looking women who watched everything that happened on the avenue, as though they owned it, or were maybe owned by it. Well, they were watching this, too. The revival was being carried on by three sisters in black, and a brother. All they had were their voices and their Bibles and a tambourine. The brother was testifying and while he testified two of the sisters stood together, seeming to say, amen, and the third sister walked around with the tambourine outstretched and a couple of people dropped coins into it. Then the brother's testimony ended and the sister who had been taking up the collection dumped the coins into her palm and transferred them to the pocket of her long black robe. Then she raised both hands, striking the tambourine against the air, and then against one hand, and she started to sing. And the two other sisters and the brother joined in.

It was strange, suddenly, to watch, though I had been seeing these street meetings all my life. So, of course, had everybody else down there. Yet, they paused and watched and listened and I stood still at the window. *"Tis the old ship of Zion,"* they sang, and the sister with the tambourine kept a steady, jangling beat, *"it has rescued many a thousand!"* Not a soul under the sound of their voices was hearing this song for the first time, not one of them had been rescued. Nor had they seen much in the way of rescue work being done around them. Neither did they especially believe in the holiness of the three sisters and the brother, they knew too much about them, knew where they lived, and how. The woman with the tambourine, whose voice dominated the air, whose face was bright with joy, was divided by very little from the woman who stood watching her, a cigarette between her heavy, chapped lips, her hair a cuckoo's nest, her face scarred and swollen from many beatings, and her black eyes glittering like coal. Perhaps they both knew this, which was why, when, as rarely, they addressed each other, they addressed each other as Sister. As the singing filled the air the watching, listening faces underwent a change, the eyes focusing on something within; the music seemed to soothe a poison out of them; and time seemed, nearly, to fall away from the sullen, belligerent, battered faces, as though they were fleeing back to their first condition, while dreaming of their last. The barbecue cook half shook his head and smiled, and dropped his cigarette and disappeared into his joint. A man fumbled in his pockets for change and stood holding it in his hand impatiently, as though he had just remembered a pressing appointment further up the avenue. He looked furious. Then I saw Sonny, standing on the edge of the crowd. He was carrying a wide, flat notebook with a green cover, and it made him look, from where I was standing, almost like a schoolboy. The coppery sun brought out the copper in his skin, he was very faintly smiling, standing very still. Then the singing stopped, the tambourine turned into a collection plate again. The furious man dropped in his coins and vanished, so did a couple of the women, and Sonny dropped some change in the plate, looking directly at the woman with a little smile. He started across the avenue, toward the house. He has a slow, loping walk, something like the way Harlem hipsters walk, only he's imposed on this his own half-beat. I had never really noticed it before.

I stayed at the window, both relieved and apprehensive. As Sonny disappeared from my sight, they began singing again. And they were still singing when his key turned in the lock.

"Hey," he said.

"Hey, yourself. You want some beer?"

"No. Well, maybe." But he came up to the window and stood beside me, looking out. "What a warm voice," he said.

They were singing *If I could only hear my mother pray again!*

"Yes," I said, "and she can sure beat that tambourine."

"But what a terrible song," he said, and laughed. He dropped his notebook on the sofa and disappeared into the kitchen. "Where's Isabel and the kids?"

"I think they went to see their grandparents. You hungry?"

"No." He came back into the living room with his can of beer. "You want to come some place with me tonight?"

I sensed, I don't know how, that I couldn't possibly say no. "Sure. Where?"

He sat down on the sofa and picked up his notebook and started leafing through it. "I'm going to sit in with some fellows in a joint in the Village."

"You mean, you're going to play, tonight?"

"That's right." He took a swallow of his beer and moved back, to the window. He gave me a sidelong look. "If you can stand it."

"I'll try," I said.

He smiled to himself and we both watched as the meeting across the way broke up. The three sisters and the brother, heads bowed, were singing *God be with you till we meet again*. The faces around them were very quiet. Then the song ended. The small crowd dispersed. We watched the three women and the lone man walk slowly up the avenue.

"When she was singing before," said Sonny, abruptly, "her voice reminded me for a minute of what heroin feels like some-times—when it's in your veins. It makes you feel sort of warm and cool at the same time. And distant. And—and sure." He sipped his beer, very deliberately not looking at me. I watched his face. "It makes you feel—in control. Sometimes you've got to have that feeling."

"Do you?" I sat down slowly in the easy chair.

"Sometimes." He went to the sofa and picked up his notebook again. "Some people do."

"In order," I asked, "to play?" And my voice was very ugly, full of contempt and anger.

"Well"—he looked at me with great, troubled eyes, as though, in fact, he hoped his eyes would tell me things he could never otherwise say—"they *think* so. And *if* they think so—!"

"And what do *you* think?" I asked.

He sat on the sofa and put his can of beer on the floor. "I don't know," he said, and I couldn't be sure if he were answering my question or pursuing his thoughts. His face didn't tell me. "It's not so much to *play*. It's to *stand* it, to be able to make it at all. On any level." He frowned and smiled: "In order to keep from shaking to pieces."

"But these friends of yours," I said, "they seem to shake themselves to pieces pretty goddamn fast."

"Maybe." He played with the notebook. And something told me that I should curb my tongue, that Sonny was doing his best to talk, that I should listen. "But of course you only know the ones that've gone to pieces. Some don't—or at least they haven't *yet* and that's just about all *any* of us can say." He paused. "And then there are some who just live, really, in hell, and they know it and they see what's happening, and they go right on. I don't know." He sighed, dropped the notebook, folded his arms. "Some guys, you can tell from the way they play, they on something *all* the time. And you can see that, well, it makes something real for them. But of course," he picked up his beer from the floor and sipped it and put the can down again, "they *want* to, too, you've got to see that. Even some of them that say they don't—*some*, not all."

"And what about you?" I asked—I couldn't help it. "What about you? Do *you* want to?"

He stood up and walked to the window and remained silent for a long time. Then he sighed. "Me," he said. Then: "While I was downstairs before, on my way here, listening to that woman sing, it struck me all of a sudden how much suffering she must have had to go through—to sing like that. It's *repulsive* to think you have to suffer that much."

I said: "But there's no way not to suffer—is there, Sonny?"

"I believe not," he said and smiled, "but that's never stopped anyone from trying." He looked at me. "Has it?" I realized, with this mocking look, that there stood between us, forever, beyond the power of time or forgiveness, the fact that I had held silence—so long!—when he had needed human speech to help him. He turned back to the window. "No, there's no way not to suffer. But you try all kinds of ways to keep from drowning in it, to keep on top of it, and to make it seem—well, like *you*. Like you did something, all right, and now you're suffering for it. You know?" I said nothing. "Well you know," he said, impatiently, "why *do* people suffer? Maybe it's better to do something to give it a reason, *any* reason."

"But we just agreed," I said, "that there's no way not to suffer. Isn't it better, then, just to—take it?"

"But nobody just takes it," Sonny cried, "that's what I'm telling you! *Everybody* tries not to. You're just hung up on the *way* some people try—it's not *your* way!"

The hair on my face began to itch, my face felt wet. "That's not true," I said, "that's not true. I don't give a damn what other people do, I don't even care how they suffer. I just care how *you* suffer." And he looked at me. "Please believe me," I said. "I don't want to see you—die—trying not to suffer."

"I won't," he said, flatly, "die trying not to suffer. At least, not any faster than anybody else."

"But there's no need," I said, trying to laugh, "is there? in killing yourself."

I wanted to say more, but I couldn't. I wanted to talk about will power and how life could be—well, beautiful. I wanted to say that it was all within; but was it? or, rather, wasn't that exactly the trouble? And I wanted to promise that I would never fail him again. But it would all have sounded—empty words and lies.

So I made the promise to myself and prayed that I would keep it.

"It's terrible sometimes, inside," he said, "that's what's the trouble. You walk these streets, black and funky and cold, and there's not really a living ass to talk to, and there's nothing shaking, and there's no way of getting it out—that storm inside. You can't talk it and you can't make love with it, and when you finally try to get with it and play it, you realize *nobody's* listening. So *you've* got to listen. You got to find a way to listen."

And then he walked away from the window and sat on the sofa again, as though all the wind had suddenly been knocked out of him. "Sometimes you'll do *anything* to play, even cut your mother's throat." He laughed and looked at me. "Or your brother's." Then he sobered. "Or your own." Then: "Don't worry. I'm all right now and I think I'll *be* all right. But I can't forget—where I've been. I don't mean just the physical place I've been, I mean where I've *been*. And *what* I've been."

"What have you been, Sonny?" I asked.

He smiled—but sat sideways on the sofa, his elbow resting on the back, his fingers playing with his mouth and chin, not looking at me. "I've been something I didn't recognize, didn't know I could be. Didn't know anybody could be." He stopped, looking inward, looking helplessly young, looking old. "I'm not talking about it now because I feel *guilty* or anything like that—maybe it would be better if I did, I don't know. Anyway, I can't really talk about it. Not to you, not to anybody," and now he turned and faced me. "Sometimes, you know and it was actually when I was most *out* of the world. I felt that I was in it, that I was *with* it, really, and I could play or I didn't really have to *play*, it just came out of me, it was there. And I don't know how I played, thinking about it now, but I know I did awful things, those times, sometimes, to people. Or it wasn't that I *did* anything to them—it was that they weren't real." He picked up the beer can; it was empty; he rolled it between his palms: "And other times—well, I needed a fix, I needed to find a place to lean, I needed to clear a space to *listen*—and I couldn't find it, and I—went crazy, I did terrible things to *me*, I was terrible *for* me." He began pressing the beer can between his hands, I watched the metal begin to give. It glittered, as he played with it, like a knife, and I was afraid he would cut himself, but I said nothing. "Oh well. I can never tell you. I was all by myself at the bottom of something, stinking and sweating and crying and shaking, and I smelled it, you know? *my* stink, and I thought I'd die if I couldn't get away from it and yet, all the same, I knew that everything I was doing was just locking me in with it. And I didn't know," he paused, still flattening the beer can, "I didn't know, I still *don't* know, something kept telling me that maybe it was good to smell your own stink, but I didn't think that *that* was what I'd been trying to do—and—who can stand it?" and he abruptly dropped the ruined beer can, looking at me with a small, still smile, and then rose, walking to the window as though it were the lodestone rock. I watched his face, he watched the avenue. "I couldn't tell you when Mama died—but the reason I wanted to leave Harlem so bad was to get away from drugs. And then, when I ran away, that's what I was running from—really. When I came back, nothing had changed, *I* hadn't changed, I was just—older." And he stopped drumming with his fingers on the windowpane. The sun had vanished, soon darkness would fall. I watched his face. "It can come again," he said, almost as though speaking to himself. Then he turned to me. "It can come again," he repeated. "I just want you to know that."

"All right," I said, at last. "So it can come again, All right."

He smiled, but the smile was sorrowful. "I had to try to tell you," he said.

"Yes," I said. "I understand that."

"You're my brother," he said, looking straight at me, and not smiling at all.

"Yes," I repeated, "yes. I understand that."

He turned back to the window, looking out. "All that hatred down there," he said, "all that hatred and misery and love. It's a wonder it doesn't blow the avenue apart."

We went to the only nightclub on a short, dark street, downtown. We squeezed through the narrow, chattering, jam-packed bar to the entrance of the big room, where the bandstand was. And we stood there for a moment, for the lights were very dim in this room and we couldn't see. Then, "Hello, boy," said a voice and an enormous black man, much older than Sonny or myself, erupted out of all that atmospheric lighting and put an arm around Sonny's shoulder. "I been sitting right here," he said, "waiting for you."

He had a big voice, too, and heads in the darkness turned toward us.

Sonny grinned and pulled a little away, and said, "Creole, this is my brother. I told you about him."

Creole shook my hand. "I'm glad to meet you, son," he said, and it was clear that he was glad to meet me *there*, for Sonny's sake. And he smiled, "You got a real musician in *your* family," and he took his arm from Sonny's shoulder and slapped him, lightly, affectionately, with the back of his hand.

"Well. Now I've heard it all," said a voice behind us. This was another musician, and a friend of Sonny's, a coal-black, cheerful-looking man, built close to the ground. He immediately began confiding to me, at the top of his lungs, the most terrible things about Sonny, his teeth gleaming like a lighthouse and his laugh coming up out of him like the beginning of an earthquake. And it turned out that everyone at the bar knew Sonny, or almost everyone; some were musicians, working there, or nearby, or not working, some were simply hangers-on, and some were there to hear Sonny play. I was introduced to all of them and they were all very polite to me. Yet, it was clear that, for them, I was only Sonny's brother. Here, I was in Sonny's world. Or, rather: his kingdom. Here, it was not even a question that his veins bore royal blood.

They were going to play soon and Creole installed me, by myself, at a table in a dark corner. Then I watched them, Creole, and the little black man, and Sonny, and the others, while they horsed around, standing just below the bandstand. The light from the bandstand spilled just a little short of them and, watching them laughing and gesturing and moving about, I had the feeling that they, nevertheless, were being most careful not to step into that circle of light too suddenly: that if they moved into the light too suddenly, without thinking, they would perish in flame. Then, while I watched, one of them, the small, black man, moved into the light and crossed the bandstand and started fooling around with his drums. Then—being funny and being, also, extremely ceremonious—Creole took Sonny by the arm and led him to the piano. A woman's voice called Sonny's name and a few hands started clapping. And Sonny, also being funny and being ceremonious, and so touched, I think, that he could have cried, but neither hiding it nor showing it, riding it like a man, grinned, and put both hands to his heart and bowed from the waist.

Creole then went to the bass fiddle and a lean, very bright-skinned brown man jumped up on the bandstand and picked up his horn. So there they were, and the atmosphere on the bandstand and in the room began to change and tighten. Someone stepped up to the microphone and announced them. Then there were all kinds of murmurs. Some people at the bar shushed others. The waitress ran around, frantically getting in the last orders, guys and chicks got closer to each other, and the lights on the bandstand, on the quartet, turned to a kind of indigo. Then they all looked different there. Creole looked about him for the last time, as though he were making certain that all his chickens were in the coop, and then he—jumped and struck the fiddle. And there they were.

All I know about music is that not many people ever really hear it. And even then, on the rare occasions when something opens within, and the music enters, what we mainly hear, or hear corroborated, are personal, private, vanishing evocations. But the man who creates the music is hearing something else, is dealing with the roar rising from the void and imposing order on it as it hits the air. What is evoked in him, then, is of another order, more terrible because it has no words, and triumphant, too, for that same reason. And his triumph, when he triumphs, is ours. I just watched Sonny's face. His face was troubled, he was working hard, but he wasn't with it. And I had the feeling that, in a way, everyone on the bandstand was waiting for him, both waiting for him and pushing him along. But as I began to watch Creole, I realized that it was Creole who held them all back. He had them on a short rein.

Up there, keeping the beat with his whole body, wailing on the fiddle, with his eyes half closed, he was listening to everything, but he was listening to Sonny. He was having a dialogue with Sonny. He wanted Sonny to leave the shoreline and strike out for the deep water. He was Sonny's witness that deep water and drowning were not the same thing—he had been there, and he knew. And he wanted Sonny to know. He was waiting for Sonny to do the things on the keys which would let Creole know that Sonny was in the water.

And, while Creole listened, Sonny moved, deep within, exactly like someone in torment. I had never before thought of how awful the relationship must be between the musician and his instrument. He has to fill it, this instrument, with the breath of life, his own. He has to make it do what he wants it to do. And a piano is just a piano. It's made out of so much wood and wires and little hammers and big ones, and ivory. While there's only so much you can do with it, the only way to find this out is to try; to try and make it do everything.

And Sonny hadn't been near a piano for over a year. And he wasn't on much better terms with his life, not the life that stretched before him now. He and the piano stammered, started one way, got scared, stopped; started another way, panicked, marked time, started again; then seemed to have found a direction, panicked again, got stuck. And the face I saw on Sonny I'd never seen before. Everything had been burned out of it, and, at the same time, things usually hidden were being burned in, by the fire and fury of the battle which was occurring in him up there.

Yet, watching Creole's face as they neared the end of the first set, I had the feeling that something had happened, something I hadn't heard. Then they finished, there was scattered applause, and then, without an instant's warning, Creole started into something else, it was almost sardonic, it was *Am I Blue.* And, as though he commanded, Sonny began to play. Something began to happen. And Creole let out the reins. The dry, low, black man said something awful on the drums, Creole answered, and the drums talked back. Then the horn insisted, sweet and high, slightly detached perhaps, and Creole listened, commenting now and then, dry, and driving, beautiful and calm and old. Then they all came together again, and Sonny was part of the family again. I could tell this from his face. He seemed to have found, right there beneath his fingers, a damn brand-new piano. It seemed that he couldn't get over it. Then, for awhile, just being happy with Sonny, they seemed to be agreeing with him that brand-new pianos certainly were a gas.

Then Creole stepped forward to remind them that what they were playing was the blues. He hit something in all of them, he hit something in me, myself, and the music tightened and deepened, apprehension began to beat the air. Creole began to tell us what the blues were all about. They were not about anything very new. He and his boys up there were keeping it new, at the risk of ruin, destruction, madness, and death, in order to find new ways to make us listen. For, while the tale of how we suffer, and how we are delighted, and how we may triumph is never new, it always must be heard. There isn't any other tale to tell, it's the only light we've got in all this darkness.

And this tale, according to that face, that body, those strong hands on those strings, has another aspect in every country, and a new depth in every generation. Listen, Creole seemed to be saying, listen. Now these are Sonny's blues. He made the little black man on the drums know it, and the bright, brown man on the horn. Creole wasn't trying any longer to get Sonny in the water. He was wishing him Godspeed. Then he stepped back, very slowly, filling the air with the immense suggestion that Sonny speak for himself.

Then they all gathered around Sonny and Sonny played. Every now and again one of them seemed to say, amen. Sonny's fingers filled the air with life, his life. But that life contained so many others. And Sonny went all the way back, he really began with the spare, flat statement of the opening phrase of the song. Then he began to make it his. It was very beautiful because it wasn't hurried and it was no longer a lament. I seemed to hear with what burning he had made it his, with what burning we had yet to make it ours, how we could cease lamenting. Freedom lurked around us and I understood, at last, that he could help us to be free if we would listen, that he would never be free until we did. Yet, there was no battle in his face now. I heard what he had gone through, and would continue to go through until he came to rest in earth. He had made it his: that long line, of which we knew only Mama and Daddy. And he was giving it back, as everything must be given back, so that, passing through death, it can live forever. I saw my mother's face again, and felt, for the first time, how the stones of the road she had walked on must have bruised her feet. I saw the moonlit road where my father's brother died. And it brought something else back to me, and carried me past it, I saw my little girl again and felt Isabel's tears again, and I felt my own tears begin to rise. And I was yet aware that this was only a moment, that the world waited outside, as hungry as a tiger, and that trouble stretched above us, longer than the sky.

Then it was over. Creole and Sonny let out their breath, both soaking wet, and grinning. There was a lot of applause and some of it was real. In the dark, the girl came by and I asked her to take drinks to the bandstand. There was a long pause, while they talked up there in the indigo light and after awhile I saw the girl put a Scotch and milk on top of the piano for Sonny. He didn't seem to notice it, but just before they started playing again he sipped from it and looked toward me, and nodded. Then he put it back on top of the piano. For me, then, as they began to play again, it glowed and shook above my brother's head like the very cup of trembling.

——*For Discussion*——

RPW—

This is a story about the inevitability of suffering, the importance of listening to that pain, and the significance of music, art, and stories. The narrator, Sonny's older brother by seven years, wants to keep the pain and suffering outside of himself, at a convenient distance. When Sonny is arrested for peddling and using heroin, his brother cannot find "any room for it" inside himself. He is reluctant to listen to Sonny's friend who has a story to tell, and for several months, he avoids writing to Sonny in jail. Yet despite his resistance and denial, the news of Sonny's arrest opens something in the narrator. It forces him to listen to the disenchanted laughter of his high school students and reminds him of Sonny and himself. Only when his little girl Gracie dies, however, will he communicate with Sonny in a moment of compassion born from a sense of shared suffering. His troubles make his brother's real.

Both the narrator and Sonny have attempted to escape the darkness that roars through the streets of Harlem: the narrator by becoming a schoolteacher, Sonny by using drugs. But they cannot escape the menace anymore than they can leave Harlem behind. They still feel the ache of the streets just as an amputee suffers the pain of a missing limb. There is no safe place in this world, as their father would say, thinking perhaps about the violent death of his own brother on a dark road: "Safe, hell. Ain't no place safe for kids, nor nobody."

After their mother dies, the narrator tries to talk to Sonny, tries to protect him. But as Sonny says to his brother: "But you never hear anything I say." Sonny stays for awhile playing his music in Isabel's family's house, then heads down to the Village, attempting to define his suffering through jazz and drugs. He is arrested, and when he gets out of jail, he continues to surround himself with music. Like the singing that fills the air at the revival meetings on the street, such moments seem "to soothe a poison" oozing from the mortal wound that all brothers and sisters share.

Sonny tries to explain to his brother: We need to get out "that storm inside"; we need to express that suffering; we need to listen to it. Through jazz and the blues, through art and story, we enter into a dialogue with pain, expressing it, listening to it, building a community of human compassion.

In the end, Sonny's brother goes to hear him play at a nightclub downtown. Guided by the bandleader, Creole, Sonny becomes "part of the family again," playing "Am I Blue" and making the music of eternal suffering new. As Sonny moves deeply into the music, deeply into the past, he makes the music his own. His brother becomes part of the expression and, at least for a moment, understands. As Creole says: "There isn't any other tale to tell, it's the only light we've got in all this darkness." And by listening to "Sonny's Blues," the narrator hears what Sonny has gone through and what he will continue to go through, "that long line" of suffering that stretches endlessly through time.

JRT—

What moves me most about "Sonny's Blues" is Baldwin's ability to take us to the most fragile places, past hurts and losses to loneliness that comes at us like a wail, a long low horn, or the piano riff that Sonny plays. Amidst the world of fragility that Baldwin creates where a child dies, parents pass on, and heroin offers temporary relief from pain, two brothers have the opportunity to connect. Likewise, we all have the opportunity to help each other bear the terrors of the night.

It is not often that a piece of writing leaves me just wanting to hear more, but Baldwin's lines go deep. Sonny is a young man who turns to music as a way "to climb up out of some deep, real deep and funky hole," and it provides connectedness, home, love, and passion. It also is a reflection of the terrors that he has felt, the addiction, the fragile edge of life. Baldwin doesn't trivialize this darkness but doesn't dwell on why either. He makes it clear that it is part of the human condition and so is our ability to connect with our brothers, literally and metaphorically. That is our redemption.

"It's always at the hour of trouble and confrontation that the missing member aches," says Sonny's brother, the narrator. And so, after losing his daughter, the narrator keeps the promise he made to his mother to look after Sonny. After all, some brothers cannot keep their brethren safe, Mama reminds us, telling the story of how her husband's brother was run over by a carload of drunk white men. We must be vigilant: "You got to hold on to your brother. . . . You may not be able to stop nothing from happening. But you got to let him know you's there."

The epiphany for the narrator seems to be his realization that Sonny needs him, needs his attention, his language, his inquiry into Sonny's well-being. Sonny opens up and they talk about human suffering; how some try to avoid it with heroin and drink, as Sonny has done; how suffering cannot be avoided; how human it is to want to escape. Sonny has seen that his brother can hold pain, can find words, can break the silence. He too shares his world when they go to a nightclub and Sonny plays his blues. "There isn't any other tale to tell, it's the only light we've got in all this darkness."

Language and music share this ability for Baldwin. The brothers, he tells us, are of every generation, of every place, and we can conclude, of every race. The bottle will always be there, Baldwin reminds us, showing us a Scotch waiting for Sonny atop the piano. He may drink again and he may lose his way as he seeks to bridge the darkness. It is not easy to be our brother's keeper, a job filled with "the very cup of trembling."

from BASTARD OUT OF CAROLINA

Dorothy Allison

CHAPTER 21

Aunt Alma has a scrapbook full of newspaper clippings, with a few wedding invitations, funeral announcements, and baby pictures pasted down beside page after page of headlines. "Oh, we're always turning up in the news," she used to joke when she'd show people that book. Her favorite is the four-page spread the *Greenville News* did when Uncle Earle's convertible smashed into the barbershop across the street from the county courthouse a few months before it burned down. There are pictures of the front end of the car propped up on a barber stool just a few feet short of splintered silvered mirrors, another of Earle sitting on the curb leaning forward with his head in his hands, and a series of the barber picking through the remains of his shop with the help of a highway patrolman and Granny Boatwright. The barber looks funny, holding up his shaving brush and cup in fingers that blur a little so that you can see he must have still been shaking.

HE DIDN'T COME IN FOR A SHAVE, the headline reads under the picture of the car on the stool.

BOATWRIGHT captions the close-up of Earle's numb face.

In those pictures, Uncle Earle looks scary, like a thief or a murderer, the kind of gaunt, poorly shaven face sketched on a post office wall. In that washed-out gray print, he looks like a figure from a horror show, an animated corpse. Granny, my mama, uncles, aunts, cousins—all of us look dead on the black-and-white page.

"We look worse than other people ever seem to look," I once complained to Aunt Alma.

"Oh, piss," she said. "Watery ink and gray paper makes everybody look a little crazy." I think she was annoyed that I didn't take more pride in her scrapbook, but it seemed to me nobody looked quite like my family. Worse than crazy; we looked moon-eyed, rigid, openmouthed, and stupid. Even our wedding announcement pictures were bad. Aunt Alma insisted it had nothing to do with us, that Boatwrights weren't bad-looking seen head on.

"We just make bad pictures," she said. "The difference is money. It takes a lot of money to make someone look alive on newsprint," she told me, "to keep some piece of the soul behind the eyes."

I'm in Aunt Alma's book now.

As soon as I saw the picture of me on the front page of the *News*, I knew it would wind up in her scrapbook, and I hated it. In it, I was leaning against Raylene's shoulder, my face all pale and long, my chin sticking out too far, my eyes sunk into shadows. I was a Boatwright there for sure, as ugly as anything. I was a freshly gutted fish, my mouth gaping open above my bandaged shoulder and arm, my neck still streaked dark with blood. Like a Boatwright all right—it wasn't all my blood.

Coming back to myself at Greenville General, I kept my teeth clamped together, not even screaming when the doctor rotated my arm in the bruised shoulder socket, put a cast on my wrist, washed out the cuts, and then wrapped the whole tight to my midriff. Mama had been there, had carried me in from the car and made the doctor look at me right away. The nurse took me out of her arms, and Mama stepped back, her bloody knuckles still outstretched, touching my cheek lightly. I looked into the nurse's face and then looked back for Mama, but she was gone. Before she could give her name or mine, she had disappeared.

"Come on, honey." The soft-voiced nurse ran her fingers through my hair, then stroked lightly all over my head. I looked for her nametag but saw none. "Don't jump, now. You'll hurt yourself." Her fingers smelled of alcohol and talcum powder. She seemed kind. I wondered if she had children.

"Feeling for bumps or cuts," she told me while the doctor was still busy with my wrist. There was just the scrape on my temple and the cut along my ear, but those had bled all down my neck and shoulder. It was hard to believe all that blood had come from so few cuts. The nurse was gentle and slow. I let her touch me as she pleased, turning my head to follow her smile like an infant watching the nipple. I watched, but didn't speak. I didn't tell her how much I hurt. I figured she could see the bruises on my throat and my torn lips. She could certainly see the look in my eyes. The one glance I'd got at my face in the mirror-black pane of the examining-room door scared me. I was a stranger with eyes sunk in shadowy caves above sharp cheekbones and a mouth so tight the lips had disappeared.

"That shoulder's gonna ache for a while." The doctor didn't look at me when he spoke, just made notes on a clipboard. "And that wrist is badly sprung. It'll be a couple of months healing completely." The nurse was washing dried blood from my cheek with an alcohol swab. I watched her instead of him.

"We're going to have to wait a while before we give you anything." The doctor's eyes wandered up from the clipboard and down my body, pausing at the bruises on my thighs and sliding down to the swollen knees, one of which was scraped raw. He put his palm on my hip and squeezed slightly. "You tell me now if anything else hurts you."

It might have been a question. It might not. I looked up at him with no expression. I kept wondering where Mama had gone. What had happened to Daddy Glen? I didn't remember the ride in from Alma's place, didn't remember Mama saying anything to me. Had she told them what had happened? Did anyone know? Where was Mama, and why wasn't she with me?

The deputy leaned against the door until the nurse brought him a folding metal chair he could prop back against the wall. He was a red-faced boy with sandy hair cut so short you could see his pink scalp under the fuzz. He reminded me of the twins when they came back from the county farm, stiff-backed, crew-cut, and proud of themselves. This one was proud of himself too; kept smoothing down his uniform shirt and pulling at the material so the sweaty wrinkles under his arms wouldn't show. His mouth was soft and his chin small, but when he looked at me, he would poke his lips out and try to make his face stern. Watched too much television, probably thought of himself as some public defender type. I tried to feel dangerous, but my eyelids were damp and swollen, my neck itchy, and my mouth too painful for me to frown. He kept fiddling with his shirt and looking over at me. After a while I began to feel more and more like a child, a girl, hurt and alone.

By the time Sheriff Cole came in, walking stiffly as if his big wide belt weighted him down and hurt his back, I felt so small I didn't know if I could talk.

"Ruth Anne." He greeted me by name.

He pulled a stool over beside the hip-high table I was propped up on, grunted as he shifted his butt onto the stool, then rolled his head so that his neck made a loud cracking noise. At the sound he grinned and put both hands flat on his thighs.

"You want to talk to me? Tell me what happened?"

I swallowed. Olive complexion, big nose, bigger ears, strong chin, and thin gray hair combed straight back off his face—Sheriff Cole didn't look like anybody else I knew. People said he came from Maryland and that he would never have made sheriff if he hadn't been such a churchgoing Baptist, a deacon, and well-off even before he married a Greenville girl. He looked more like a frycook than a sheriff, big-bellied, greasy, and soft.

I looked up into his wide, dark eyes. His voice was soft, almost lazy, his tone both polite and respectful. He made me wish I could talk, tell him what had happened, what I thought had happened. But it all seemed so complicated in my head, so long and difficult. How could I begin? Where would I begin? With Aunt Alma going crazy? With the moment Daddy Glen grabbed me and tore my shirt? I thought of that moment in the parking lot so long ago, waiting to find out about Mama and his son.

"You're not hurt too bad," he told me. "Doctor says you'll be fine."

I lifted my head, knowing fear showed in my face.

"No concussion, the doctor says." He took the little notebook out of his pocket, opened it. "You're a little shocky, need to be careful for a while. Some of your people are out there. I got the doctor talking to them."

"Mama?" My voice was a hoarse croak.

"I an't talked to your mama yet. Your aunts are here, though. We'll let you see them soon." He flipped pages, took out a pen, and looked at me. "Now, we need to know what happened, Ruth Anne. I know you're not feeling too good, but I want you to try to talk to me." His mouth softened, as if he were trying to look comforting. "You tell me what happened and we can work on getting you home soon." He put the point of the pen to the paper.

I closed my eyes. Mama hadn't talked to him. I felt suddenly so tired I could barely draw breath.

"They call you Bone, don't they?"

I said nothing.

"Bone, I want you to know that no one is gonna hurt you. No one is gonna be allowed to hurt you. We can see that you've been through enough. Just tell me who beat you, girl. Tell me." His voice was calm, careful, friendly. He was Daddy Glen in a uniform. The world was full of Daddy Glens, and I didn't want to be in the world anymore.

"Honey," the sheriff said again. I hated him for calling me that. He didn't know me. "We're gonna have to know everything that happened."

No. My tongue swelled in my mouth. I didn't want anyone to know anything. Mama, I almost whispered, but clamped my teeth together. I couldn't tell this man anything. He didn't care about me. No one cared about me. I didn't even care about myself anymore.

"Ruth Anne." He leaned forward, his face close to mine, his whispery voice too big in my ear. "I want to help you. I want you to tell me what happened, girl. I'll take care of everything. I promise you. You'll be all right."

No. He thought he knew everything. Son of a bitch in his smug uniform could talk like Santa Claus, promise anything, but I was alone.

"I want to go home," I said. "I want my mama."

Sheriff Cole put his hand on mine and sighed. "All right. All right, girl."

I looked at him, remembering what Raylene had said that night on the landing when I told her how much I hated people who looked at us like trash. What must it be like to be Sheriff Cole? What made him who he was? I'd think about that sometime, but not now. I didn't want to think at all right now.

The double door swung open. I turned eagerly, but the struggling angry figure there wasn't Mama. Raylene was wrestling with a nurse, pushing the woman away and almost losing her black pea coat in the process. "Let me go," she said in a voice bigger than the room. "You let me go." She shoved the woman away and came forward like a tree falling, massive, inevitable, and reassuringly familiar.

"Bone. Baby." Her words echoed hollowly against the stark white walls.

"Oh, my girl, what'd they do to you?" Raylene leaned over me, and the smell of her wrapped me around. I opened my mouth like a baby bird, cried out, and reached up to her with my good arm. I said her name twice and lay against her breasts. Her arms were so strong, so safe. Don't let me go, I thought. Just please, don't let me go.

"What are you doing to this child?" I felt her turn slightly, her voice loud and insistent above me. "You tell me what right you got to be in here with her alone, and keeping me outside?"

Sheriff Cole's voice was patient. "We need to know what happened," he said.

"You can see what happened," Raylene snapped. "Look at her. She's hurt and scared and don't need nobody hurting her any more. Were you gonna keep me away from her till you had her ready to jump out the window or say anything you wanted her to?"

"Miss Boatwright, I'm sorry, but there's been an assault. There has to be an investigation."

"She's just twelve years old, you fool. Right now she needs to feel safe and loved, not alone and terrified. You're right, there has to be justice. There has to be a judgment day too, when God will judge us all. What you gonna tell him you did to this child when that day comes?"

"There's no need—" he began, but she interrupted him.

"There's need," she said. "God knows there's need." Her voice was awesome, biblical. "God knows."

The notebook snapped closed. I looked sideways out of Raylene's embrace and saw Sheriff Cole glare at her and stuff his notebook back in his pocket. "You call me," he said. "You call me when she's ready to tell us what happened."

Aunt Raylene grunted contemptuously, and held me close as he stomped away. "My girl," she whispered in that strong voice, and stroked my hair back off my face. "Oh, my poor little girl, you just lay still. We'll get you home. Don't you worry. Don't you worry about nothing. I'll get you home and safe."

CHAPTER 22

There was no stopping Aunt Raylene. When the doctor insisted I stay overnight, she planted herself in a chair by my bed and refused to move. She held my hand all night while I lay unsleeping and restless. My arm throbbed, and my mouth was so bruised I could only whimper.

"I can't give her anything," the nurse told Raylene each time she checked on us.

"I know," Raylene nodded. "Just give me a straw, why don't you?" She fed me sips of Coke and hummed quietly while I stared up at the ceiling.

In the morning, the doctor felt all over the back of my head while Raylene glared at him from her chair. I was numb with exhaustion and pain, couldn't even smile when he grumbled and signed the release forms. The nurse took me to the entry in a wheelchair. I could see the photographer waiting outside, but Raylene just harrumphed and picked me up like a baby doll, not looking left or right as she carried me out to her truck.

Raylene settled me close to her right hip before she started the engine, but I slid away, over to where I could hang on to the door and look out through the window. I could not look at her, could not listen to the words she kept trying to speak softly in my direction. Murmurs of comfort, meaningless phrases that did not register. The one thing I wanted her to say went unspoken. Where was Mama? What had happened to her?

When we pulled up in Raylene's yard, the sun was beating down on the muddy spring grass. The river ran flat and fast, and there was no breeze at all. I wiped sweat off my neck and watched a big unfamiliar yellow dog creep out from under the porch and stand by the steps with his head canted to one side. Raylene sighed and cut the engine.

"I need to say something to you." Raylene sounded uncertain. "The thing you need to understand, that's the one thing I'm afraid you're too young to hear." She didn't look at me. Her words came out in a rush. "But it's simple enough, and one day maybe you will understand it." She turned to look at me then.

"One time you talked to me about how I live, with no husband or children or even a good friend. Well, I had me a friend when I was with the carnival, somebody I loved better than myself, a lover I would have spent my life with and should have. But I was crazy with love, too crazy to judge what I was doing. I did a terrible thing, Bone." Her skin looked tighter over her cheekbones, as if her whole frame were swelling with shame. She shook her head but didn't look away from my eyes.

"Bone, no woman can stand to choose between her baby and her lover, between her child and her husband. I made the woman I loved choose. She stayed with her baby, and I came back here alone. It should never have come to that. It never should. It just about killed her. It just about killed me."

Aunt Raylene covered her eyes for a moment, then pushed her hair back with both hands. "God!" She dropped her hands and turned back to me. "We do terrible things to the ones we love sometimes," she said. "We can't explain it. We can't excuse it. It eats us up, but we do them just the same. You want to know about your mama, I know. But I can't tell you anything. None of us can. No one knows where she's gone. I can't explain that to you, Bone. I just can't, but I know your mama loves you. Don't doubt that. She loves you more than her life, and she an't never gonna forgive herself for what she's done to you, what she allowed to happen."

Aunt Raylene gripped the steering wheel fiercely and stared at me. "I shouldn't talk so much. I've said enough." She wiped her mouth. "We need some time. You need some time. You know what you look like, girl?"

I turned away. I knew what I looked like. At the hospital when they had left me alone in the bathroom for a minute, I had looked at myself in the mirror and known I was a different person. Older, meaner, rawboned, crazy, and hateful. I was full of hate. I had spit on the glass, spit on my life, not caring anymore who I was or would be. I had wanted to laugh at everyone, Raylene and the nurses, all of them watching me like some fragile piece of glass ready to shatter around boiling water. I was boiling inside. I was cooking away. I was who I was going to be, and she was a terrible person.

"Ruth Anne," Aunt Raylene whispered. "Girl, look at me. Stop thinking about what happened. Don't think about it. Don't try to think about nothing. You can't understand it yet. You don't have to. It don't make sense, and I can't explain it to you. You can't explain it to yourself. Your mama . . . " She stopped, and I looked back at her. "Your mama loves you. Just hang on, girl. Just hang on. It'll be better in time, I promise you."

I promise you, she said. My mouth twisted. I stared at her hatefully.

Raylene looked at me as if my rage hurt her, but she said nothing, just climbed heavily out of the truck. She moved slowly, hugging her old purse to her bosom and stopping only to give the panting dog a quick pat on the head before she went up and laid the purse on the steps. She came back and took me up again as easily as if I weighed no more than that purse. She carried me inside the house, the dog following, and put me in her bed. The dog settled himself on the rug, comfortably. I lay still, ignoring Aunt Raylene's movements but thinking even so about the woman she had loved, the woman who had loved her child more. It was too much for me. I'd have to think about it some other time.

The dog turned to me with hopeful brown eyes, his tongue hanging down as if he wanted me to invite him up on the bed. Big dumb sad eyes waited on me. I wanted to beat my fists until bones splintered, kick my heels into raw meat, scream until my tongue pulled loose and split at the root, but everything was slow, words and feelings just moved across my brain. I was slow, numb, and stupid. The pain in my arm was comforting, the throbbing at my temple was a music I needed in order to keep breathing.

Everything hurt me: my arm in its cotton sling; the memory of the nurse's careful fingers; the light that glinted into my eyes from the flawed glass of Raylene's window; my hip where it pressed against the mattress. Most of all my heart hurt me, a huge swollen obstruction in my chest. Every time I closed my eyes there was a flash of Glen's face as he had looked above me. I kept turning my head as if Mama's prayers still echoed in my ears, and even the slow drag of that dog's eyes raked over my skin like a pitchfork cutting furrows in dust. I had seen my whole life in Sheriff Cole's eyes, contemptible, small, meaningless. My mama had abandoned me, and that was the only thing that mattered. When Raylene brought me some soup later, I refused to eat. "I hate her," I whispered through torn lips. "I hate her."

"You'll forgive her," Raylene said.

I pulled the sheet up over my mouth.

How do you forgive somebody when you cannot even speak her name, when you cannot stand to close your eyes and see her face? I did not understand. If I thought of Mama, I thought of her with her head thrown back and her mouth open, Glen's bloody face pressed to her belly. I could not stand to remember that, could not watch it again. I turned away, closed my eyes, and prayed for the darkness to come back. I wanted to die. I refused to eat, refused to speak, covered my face, and would not let Aunt Raylene coax me out of bed. She left me alone, and I woke up with my eyes wet and my mouth open, but with no memory of dreaming. The only sound was the yellow dog's tail thumping the rug. My heart, the pulse that pounded in my head, beat to that rhythm. Everything in me said no, repeated it, drummed it, hummed and sang it. I had no more spirit of meanness than a bug had. I was just a whisper in the dark saying no and hoping to die.

Raylene came in the morning and fed me grits with a spoon. She let me be quiet that day, but the next, she picked me up and carried me out to the porch to sit on her rocker in the sun. I wouldn't look at her, wouldn't speak, but she didn't seem to care. She watered her plants, fed her dogs and chickens, and stood smoking on the steps until the cool air came up from the river. Then she carried me back to bed. The next day, grudgingly, I dragged myself up, ate a little on my own, and went out to the rocker on the porch. But it was not a surrender. I was willing to eat and sit up, but not to speak.

I stayed on the porch and would not talk to anyone, not to Raylene and not to Earle when he brought me his battered record player and tried to make me laugh. He played some of the same records I had listened to with Aunt Ruth, but I sat unmoving, dry-eyed and distant. Eventually he left me alone. Raylene didn't try to talk to me. She brought me beans to pick over, which I did with no interest. She also asked me to rip out the hem on some old curtains, but that I refused to do. Not that I argued with her. I just left them lying untouched on the dusty boards by the rocker. I would have slept in the rocker, but Raylene threatened to drag me out of it kicking and screaming.

"I an't gonna have you sleeping on the porch," she fumed. So I pulled myself up painfully and crept off to bed like an old lady, bent over and cramped. I did what I had to do so they would leave me alone. I heard Raylene talking to Earle about Mama. They were worried. No one knew where she had gone. No one knew where Glen was either, though the uncles were talking about paying a bounty to anyone who found him. Earle was adamant, Beau had bought a new shotgun, but it was Nevil who scared Raylene.

Nevil came out to Raylene's one evening and stood silently in front of me. He touched my bruised chin with one outstretched finger, traced my hairline, and leaned forward to kiss my left cheekbone with dry chapped lips. I wanted to speak to him but instead held my breath, looking into his dark hooded eyes.

"I promise," he said, and I saw Raylene cover her mouth with one hand. I knew what he meant, and I smiled. He turned and went down the steps abruptly, stomping with his bootheels. Raylene called his name, but he didn't pause. Fay told Raylene that Nevil had stopped sleeping at home. He was living in his truck, driving the county roads at night, searching.

"He'll get himself killed," Raylene told me, but I refused to say anything.

I didn't care anymore who got killed.

The night Mama came, Raylene was at the record player, listening to every record Earle had brought over. That music seemed to echo off the porch ceiling, the silvery river surface, and the night sky. The guitar plunked and became clearly Patsy Cline's voice singing "Walking After Midnight." The driving notes and the dark undertone of the drum paced her voice. I listened closely, heard the pause as the song ended, and then Patsy's voice started again, taking up from the beginning, the scratches and popping of the worn record overwhelming that heartbreaking voice, making me wish I could still cry the way I had with Aunt Ruth.

The silence extended, the soft rustle of the river barely audible. A breeze swelled and died down. The music came back, the chords different. Not Patsy Cline. Kitty Wells. "Talk Back Trembling Lips." Her twangy voice shook and scolded, louder still than Patsy's drawl. Mama always said Kitty had a smoky voice, not as pure as Patsy's, but familiar. That raw accent, like Beau's or Alma's, flattened vowels and stretched-out syllables to fit the chorus. I rocked back and listened to the record play through. The next one was another of Mama's favorites, Patsy Cline telling the world that it wasn't God who made honky-tonk angels. Grief filled me.

I stared up into the pattern of rusty dried paint and spider-fine traceries on the porch ceiling. I opened my mouth to cry, but no cry came. Tears kept running down my face into my collar, but I didn't make a sound. Children cried. I was not a child. Maybe, I told myself, I should go stay with Aunt Carr up in Baltimore or go out to Eustis and visit Aunt Maybelle and Aunt Marvella. I closed my eyes and licked my lips.

The screen door swung closed with a thud. I turned my head.

Mama stood motionless in one of her old short-sleeved dresses, her arms crossed under her breasts and her head up. She was looking at me from slitted eyes. My heart raced at the sight of her.

Aunt Ruth had told her after Lyle Parsons's funeral that she would look the same till she died. "Now you look like a Boatwright. Now you got the look," she'd said. In all the years since, that prophecy had held true. Age and exhaustion had worn lines under Mama's mouth and eyes, narrowed her chin, and deepened the indentations beside her nose, but you could still see the beautiful girl she had been. Now that face was made new. Bones seemed to have moved, flesh fallen away, and lines deepened into gullies, while shadows darkened to streaks of midnight.

I breathed hard, feeling like I was underwater looking at her. She came across the porch, her face stern, her mouth set in a rigid line. The muscles in her neck stood out in high relief. I pushed myself up. She came straight to the rocker. My face felt plaster-stiff. The music was still playing. It wasn't God who made us like this, I thought. We'd gotten ourselves messed up on our own.

"Baby." Mama's voice was a raspy whisper.

I did not move, did not speak.

"Bone." She touched my shoulder. "Oh, girl."

I could not pull away, but still I did not speak. I wondered if she could see herself in my pupils.

She drew back a little and dropped down to half-kneel beside me. "I know," she said. "I know you must feel like I don't love you, like I didn't love you enough."

She took hold of her own shoulders, hugging herself and shivering as if she were cold. "Bone, I never wanted you to be hurt. I wanted you to be safe. I wanted us all to be happy. I never thought it would go the way it did. I never thought Glen would hurt you like that."

Mama shut her eyes and turned her head as if she could no longer stand to look into my face. Her mouth opened and closed several times. I saw tears at the corners of her eyes.

"And I just loved him. You know that. I just loved him so I couldn't see him that way. I couldn't believe. I couldn't imagine . . . " She swallowed several times, then opened her eyes and looked at me directly.

I looked back, saw her face pale and drawn, her eyes red-rimmed, her lips trembling. I wanted to tell her lies, tell her that I had never doubted her, that nothing could make any difference to my love for her, but I couldn't. I had lost my mama. She was a stranger, and I was so old my insides had turned to dust and stone. Every time I closed my eyes, I could see again the blood on Glen's hairline, his face pressed to her belly, feel that black despair whose only relief would be death. I had prayed for death. Maybe it wasn't her fault. It wasn't mine. Maybe it wasn't a matter of anybody's fault. Maybe it was like Raylene said, the way the world goes, the way hearts get broken all the time.

"You don't know how much I love you," she said, her face as

stark as a cracked white plate. "How much I have always loved you."

My heart broke all over again. I wanted my life back, my mama, but I knew I would never have that. The child I had been was gone with the child she had been. We were new people, and we didn't know each other anymore. I shook my head desperately.

"Mama," I said, not wanting to speak but not able to stop the rush of that cry. I shuddered, and the word came out like a bird's call, high and piercing. The sobs that followed were hoarse and ugly. I grabbed the front of Mama's dress with my good arm, ignoring the pain in my shoulder as I pushed forward into her embrace. She caught me, pressing my face against her throat and whispering into my ear.

"It's all right, baby. You just cry. You just go on and cry." Her hands touched me gently, lifted, and came back down as if she were afraid she might hurt me but couldn't keep from reaching for me again. "You're my own baby girl. I'm not gonna let you go."

Over Mama's shoulder, I saw Raylene in the doorway, her face as red as a new apple. Mama's hands stroked my hair back off my face, cupped my head, held me safe. I pressed my face into her neck, and let it all go. The grief. The anger. The guilt and the shame. It would come back later. It would come back forever. We had all wanted the simplest thing, to love and be loved and be safe together, but we had lost it and I didn't know how to get it back.

The music stopped, and the sound of the river water filled the night. My crying eased and then stopped. Mama rocked back on her heels. A jaybird dropped off the porch lintel and streaked up into the darkening sky. The dog loped out to nose its track in the dusty grass. Raylene called Mama's name softly, then mine, her voice as scratchy and penetrating as the chords of a steel guitar, as familiar as Kitty Wells or a gospel chorus. Mama looked back at her and shook her head. She straightened and gave my hand on the rocker's arm a little pat. Her smell, that familiar salt-and-butter smell, almost made me cry again, but I felt empty. I just watched her.

Raylene had been right. I didn't understand anything. But I didn't want to understand. Seeing Mama hurt me almost as bad as not seeing her had.

There was an envelope on my lap. Mama had put it there. She leaned forward and kissed my cheek just below where Nevil had kissed me. The memory of his burning eyes startled me. He would not forgive. He was out there hunting. I almost cried out. Mama's finger touched my lips. Her eyes burned into me.

"I love you, Bone," she said. "Never forget that. You're my baby girl, and I love you." Her ravaged cheeks shone in the light from the house, her eyes glittered. She bent, kissed my fingers, and stood up. Aunt Raylene came through the door, but Mama backed away quickly, shaking her head again. We watched her cross the yard, heard her start the Pontiac in the darkness past the curve of the road.

"Damn," Raylene cursed. Her fist drummed on the doorjamb. "Damn," she said again, and dropped her hand as if she could think of nothing else to say, to do. I held the envelope and watched her shoulders. They were shaking, but she made no sound.

"Do you know where she's going?" I asked.

"No." The word was a whisper. Raylene lifted her hands slightly, dropped them again. She did not turn to me, and I knew she did not want me to see her face.

"California," I said. "Or Florida, maybe. He always talked about taking us off there sometime, someplace where they grew oranges and a man could find decent work." My voice sounded so rough and mean I barely recognized it. I felt old and chilled, though I knew the night was warm. I looked down my bandaged arm to the envelope. It was oversized, yellow, official-looking, and unsealed. I opened it.

Folded into thirds was a certificate. RUTH ANNE BOATWRIGHT. Mother: ANNEY BOATWRIGHT. Father: UNKNOWN. I almost laughed, reading down the page. Greenville General Hospital and the embossed seal of the county, the family legend on imitation parchment. I had never seen it before, but had heard all about it. I unfolded the bottom third.

It was blank, unmarked, unstamped.

I looked out into the dark night, past Raylene's hip and the porch railing. What had she done? I shook my head and swallowed. I knew nothing, understood nothing. Maybe I never would. Who had Mama been, what had she wanted to be or do before I was born? Once I was born, her hopes had turned, and I had climbed up her life like a flower reaching for the sun. Fourteen and terrified, fifteen and a mother, just past twenty-one when she married Glen. Her life had folded into mine. What would I be like when I was fifteen, twenty, thirty? Would I be as strong as she had been, as hungry for love, as desperate, determined, and ashamed?

My eyes were dry, the night a blanket that covered me. I wasn't old. I would be thirteen in a few weeks. I was already who I was going to be. I tucked the envelope inside my pocket. When Raylene came to me, I let her touch my shoulder, let my head tilt to lean against her, trusting her arm and her love. I was who I was going to be, someone like her, like Mama, a Boatwright woman. I wrapped my fingers in Raylene's and watched the night close in around us.

——*For Discussion*——

JRT—

What is it to be born into a Southern family where you are known as "bastard," "white trash," and one of those with the "Boatwright" look? Who can you turn to when your mama can't give up your stepfather even though he beats and rapes you, and when your uncles believe in blind justice and stalk anyone who hurts the family? How can there be hope in a book filled with the bleakness of a twelve-year-old's abuse and abandonment?

Bone, the determined and soulful spirit of the book, finds some solace in her family and in the comfort of her Aunt Raylene, one of her mother's sisters. After a gruesome scene at the county hospital where Bone has been examined for rape and brutal beatings by her stepfather, Daddy Glen, it is Aunt Raylene, not her mother, who stands by her side. Allison shows us both the heartbreak and heroism in this act. Although Bone suffers because her mother deserts her, leaving for Florida or California or some such dream of a new life, she is better off in the care of one who has learned how to love.

Raylene says that she is alone now because she made the woman she loved better than herself choose between Raylene and the woman's child. "We do terrible things to the ones we love sometimes," she tells Bone, speaking the truth that so many never say. "We can't explain it. It eats us up, but we do it just the same." Raylene, who owns her own home, makes her own way in the world, and has heart, is a role model for Bone. She sees that Bone's mother has not yet learned how to love herself and sees the pain that she causes Bone. In spite of the fact that Bone does not yet recognize the gift she has in her relationship with Raylene, we do. Raylene offers strength and wisdom to the young girl as well as her love and a place to live, a real home. With Raylene, Allison gives us a woman who is dependable and solid, like a tree in a world filled with broken branches. With Raylene, Allison also allows us the chance to explore our own family conflicts and see how painful love can be. Bone has someone to care for her but not a father or a mother by her side.

RPW—

In these last two chapters of the novel, Ruth Anne, usually called Bone, makes it into the news and into her Aunt Alma's scrapbook of Boatwrights at the age of twelve. Her original birth certificate marked her as a bastard from South Carolina, but now it is clear that she is a member of the Boatwright family, white trash, perceived as ugly and stupid, cut off from the world.

Daddy Glen, her stepfather, has brutally raped her, and her mother, Anney, has left her at the hospital to return to Glen, the man she desperately needs and loves. For Bone the world is full of Daddy Glens, and she doesn't want to be in that world anymore. In the hospital, only Aunt Raylene seems to understand: right now Bone "needs to feel safe and loved, not alone and terrified." I think she needs compassion to fill the hole in her heart, not the justice of a sheriff or the revenge of an uncle, but the love of a mother's embrace.

But even the temporary embrace of a mother cannot heal Bone's heart. Aunt Raylene knows that people pay for what they allow themselves to become. They pay for it "by the lives they lead." Bone's mother loves Bone more than she loves herself, and she will never forgive herself for what she has done to Bone. But she cannot bring Bone back to her innocent childhood. I wish she could penetrate beyond Bone's numbness and hatred, but I am afraid that Bone has lost too much.

While Bone listens silently in her grief to the heartbreaking music of Patsy Cline and Kitty Wells, her mother appears at the screen door, and Bone seems to believe that it isn't God who shapes their destiny. "We'd gotten ourselves messed up on our own," she reflects, indicating perhaps that her destiny is all too human.

Blinded by her love for Glen, Bone's mother couldn't see him any other way, and now she seems destined to travel with him just as Bone seems destined to be a Boatwright woman as strong as her mother, "as hungry for love, as desperate, determined, and ashamed." Bone's new unmarked, unstamped birth certificate is a gift from her mother, a legacy that she cannot yet fully understand, but one that inevitably makes her part of the family legend.

from ONE FLEW OVER THE CUCKOO'S NEST

Ken Kesey

Come morning, McMurphy is up before I am, the first time anybody been up before me since Uncle Jules the Wallwalker was here. Jules was a shrewd old white-haired Negro with a theory the world was being tipped over on its side during the night by the black boys; he used to slip out in the early mornings, aiming to catch them tipping it. Like Jules, I'm up early in the mornings to watch what machinery they're sneaking onto the ward or installing in the shaving room, and usually it's just me and the black boys in the hall for fifteen minutes before the next patient is out of bed. But this morning I hear McMurphy out there in the latrine as I come out of the covers. Hear him singing! Singing so you'd think he didn't have a worry in the world. His voice is clear and strong slapping up against the cement and steel.

" 'Your horses are hungry, that's what she did say.' " He's enjoying the way the sound rings in the latrine. " 'Come sit down beside me, an' feed them some hay.' " He gets a breath, and his voice jumps a key, gaining pitch and power till it's joggling the wiring in all the walls. " 'My horses ain't hungry, they won't eat your hay-ay-aeee.' " He holds the note and plays with it, then swoops down with the rest of the verse to finish it off. " 'So fare-thee-well, darlin', I'm gone on my way.' "

Singing! Everybody's thunderstruck. They haven't heard such a thing in years, not on this ward. Most of the Acutes in the dorm are up on their elbows, blinking and listening. They look at one another and raise their eyebrows. How come the black boys haven't hushed him up out there? They never let anybody raise that much racket before, did they? How come they treat this new guy different? He's a man made outa skin and bone that's due to get weak and pale and die, just like the rest of us. He lives under the same laws, gotta eat, bumps up against the same troubles; these things make him just as vulnerable to the Combine as anybody else, don't they?

But the new guy *is* different, and the Acutes can see it, different from anybody been coming on this ward for the past ten years, different from anybody they ever met outside. He's just as vulnerable, maybe, but the Combine didn't get him.

" 'My wagons are loaded,' " he sings, " 'my whip's in my hand. . . . ' "

How'd he manage to slip the collar? Maybe, like old Pete, the Combine missed getting to him soon enough with controls. Maybe he growed up so wild all over the country, batting around from one place to another, never around one town longer'n a few months when he was a kid so a school never got much a hold on him, logging, gambling, running carnival wheels, traveling lightfooted and fast, keeping on the move so much that the Combine never had a chance to get anything installed. Maybe that's it, he never gave the Combine a chance, just like he never gave the black boy a chance to get to him with the thermometer yesterday morning, because a moving target is hard to hit.

No wife wanting new linoleum. No relatives pulling at him with watery old eyes. No one to *care* about, which is what makes him free enough to be a good con man. And maybe the reason the black boys don't rush into that latrine and put a stop to his singing is because they *know* he's out of control, and they remember that time with old Peter and what a man out of control can do. And they can see that McMurphy's a lot bigger than old Pete; if it comes down to getting the best of him, it's going to take all three of them and the Big Nurse waiting on the sidelines with a needle. The Acutes nod at one another; that's the reason, they figure, that the black boys haven't stopped his singing where they would stop any of the rest of us.

I come out of the dorm into the hall just as McMurphy comes out of the latrine. He's got his cap on and not much else, just a towel grabbed around his hips. He's holding a toothbrush in his other hand. He stands in the hall, looking up and down, rocking up on his toes to keep off the cold tile as much as he can. Picks him out a black boy, the least one, and walks up to him and whaps him on the shoulder just like they'd been friends all their lives.

"Hey there, old buddy, what's my chance of gettin' some toothpaste for brushin' my grinders?"

The black boy's dwarf head swivels and comes nose to knuckle with that hand. He frowns at it, then takes a quick check where's

the other two black boys just in case, and tells McMurphy they
don't open the cabinet till six-forty-five. "It's a policy," he says.

"Is that right? I mean, is that where they keep the toothpaste?
In the cabinet?"

"Tha's right, locked in the cabinet."

The black boy tries to go back to polishing the baseboards, but
that hand is still lopped over his shoulder like a big red clamp.

"Locked in the cabinet, is it? Well well well, now why do you
reckon they keep the toothpaste locked up? I mean, it ain't like
it's dangerous, is it? You can't poison a man with it, can you? You
couldn't brain some guy with the tube, could you? What reason
you suppose they have for puttin' something as harmless as a little
tube of toothpaste under lock and key?"

"It's ward policy, Mr. McMurphy, tha's the reason," And when
he sees that this last reason don't affect McMurphy like it should,
he frowns at that hand on his shoulder and adds, "What you s'pose
it'd be like if *evahbody* was to brush their teeth whenever they
took a notion to brush?"

McMurphy turns loose the shoulder, tugs at the tuft of red wool
at his neck, and thinks this over. "Uh-huh, uh-huh, I think I can
see what you're drivin' at: ward policy is for those that can't brush
after every meal."

"My *gaw*, don't you *see?*"

"Yes, now, I do. You're saying people'd be brushin' their teeth
whenever the spirit moved them."

"Tha's right, tha's why we—"

"And, lordy, can you imagine? Teeth bein' brushed at six-
thirty, six-twenty—who can tell? maybe even six o'clock. Yeah, I
can see your point."

He winks past the black boy at me standing against the wall.

"I gotta get this baseboard cleaned, McMurphy."

"Oh. I didn't mean to keep you from your job." He starts to
back away as the black boy bends to his work again. Then he comes
forward and leans over to look in the can at the black boy's side.
"Well, look here; what do we have here?"

The black boy peers down. "Look where?"

"Look here in this old can, Sam. What is the stuff in this old
can?"

"Tha's . . . soap powder."

"Well, I generally use paste, but"—McMurphy runs his tooth-

brush down in the powder and swishes it around and pulls it out
and taps it on the side of the can—"but this will do fine for me. I
thank you. We'll look into that ward policy business later."

And he heads back to the latrine, where I can hear his singing
garbled by the piston beat of his toothbrushing.

That black boy's standing there looking after him with his
scrub rag hanging limp in his gray hand. After a minute he blinks
and looks around and sees I been watching and comes over and
drags me down the hall by the drawstring on my pajamas and
pushes me to a place on the floor I just did yesterday.

"There! Damn you, right there! That's where I want you
workin', not gawkin' around like some big useless cow! There!
There!"

And I lean over and go to mopping with my back to him so he
won't see me grin. I feel good, seeing McMurphy get that black
boy's goat like not many men could. Papa used to be able to do
it—spraddle-legged, dead-panned, squinting up at the sky that first
time the government men showed up to negotiate about buying off
the treaty. "Canada honkers up there," Papa says, squinting up.
Government men look, rattling papers. "What are you—? In July?
There's no—uh—geese this time of year. Uh, no geese."

They had been talking like tourists from the East who figure
you've got to talk to Indians so they'll understand. Papa didn't
seem to take any notice of the way they talked. He kept looking at
the sky. "Geese up there, white man. You know it. Geese this year.
And last year. And the year before and the year before."

The men looked at one another and cleared their throats. "Yes.
Maybe true, Chief Bromden. Now. Forget geese. Pay attention to
contract. What we offer could greatly benefit you—your people—
change the lives of the red man."

Papa said, " . . . and the year before and the year before and the
year before . . . "

By the time it dawned on the government men that they were
being poked fun at, all the council who'd been sitting on the porch
of our shack, putting pipes in the pockets of their red and black
plaid wool shirts and taking them back out again, grinning at one
another and at Papa—they had all busted up laughing fit to kill.
Uncle R & J Wolf was rolling on the ground, gasping with laughter
and saying, "You know it, white man."

It sure did get their goat; they turned without saying a word

and walked off toward the highway, red-necked, us laughing behind
them. I forget sometimes what laughter can do.

The Big Nurse's key hits the lock, and the black boy is up to her
soon as she's in the door, shifting from foot to foot like a kid asking to pee. I'm close enough I hear McMurphy's name come into
his conversation a couple of times, so I know he's telling her about
McMurphy brushing his teeth, completely forgetting to tell her
about the old Vegetable who died during the night. Waving his arms
and trying to tell her what that fool redhead's been up to already,
so early in the morning—disrupting things, goin' contrary to ward
policy, can't she *do* something?

She glares at the black boy till he stops fidgeting, then looks
up the hall to where McMurphy's singing is booming out of the
latrine door louder than ever. " 'Oh, your parents don't like me,
they say I'm too po-o-or; they say I'm not worthy to enter your
door.' "

Her face is puzzled at first; like the rest of us, it's been so long
since she's heard singing it takes her a second to recognize what
it is.

" 'Hard livin's my pleasure, my money's my o-o-own, an' them
that don't like me, they can leave me alone.' "

She listens a minute more to make sure she isn't hearing
things; then she goes to puffing up. Her nostrils flare open, and
every breath she draws she gets bigger, as big and tough-looking's
I seen her get over a patient since Taber was here. She works the
hinges in her elbows and fingers. I hear a small squeak. She starts
moving, and I get back against the wall, and when she rumbles past
she's already big as a truck, trailing that wicker bag behind in her
exhaust like a semi behind a Jimmy Diesel. Her lips are parted,
and her smile's going out before her like a radiator grill. I can smell
the hot oil and magneto spark when she goes past, and every step
hits the floor she blows up a size bigger, blowing and puffing, roll
down anything in her path! I'm scared to think *what* she'll do.

Then, just as she's rolling along at her biggest and meanest,
McMurphy steps out of the latrine door right in front of her, holding that towel around his hips—stops her *dead!* She shrinks to
about head-high to where that towel covers him, and he's grinning
down on her. Her own grin is giving way, sagging at the edges.

"Good morning, Miss Rat-shed! How's things on the outside?"

"You can't run around here—in a *towel!*"

"No?" He looks down at the part of the towel she's eye to eye with, and it's wet and skin tight. "Towels against ward policy too? Well, I guess there's nothin' to do exce—"

"*Stop!* don't you dare. You get back in that dorm and get your clothes on this *instant!*"

She sounds like a teacher bawling out a student, so McMurphy hangs his head like a student and says in a voice sounds like he's about to cry, "I can't do that, ma'am. I'm afraid some thief in the night boosted my clothes whilst I slept. I sleep awful sound on the mattresses you have here."

"Somebody boosted . . . ?"

"Pinched. Jobbed. Swiped. Stole," he says happily. "You know, man, like somebody boosted my threads." Saying this tickles him so he goes into a little barefooted dance before her.

"Stole your clothes?"

"That looks like the whole of it."

"But—prison clothes? Why?"

He stops jigging around and hangs his head again. "All I know is that they were there when I went to bed and gone when I got up. Gone slick as a whistle. Oh, I do *know* they were nothing but prison clothes, coarse and faded and uncouth, ma'am, well I know it—and prison clothes may not seem like much to those as has *more.* But to a nude man—"

"That outfit," she says, realizing, "was *supposed* to be picked up. You were issued a uniform of green convalescents this morning."

He shakes his head and sighs, but still don't look up. "No. No, I'm afraid I wasn't. Not a thing this morning but the cap that's on my head and—"

"Williams," she hollers down to the black boy who's still at the ward door like he might make a run for it. "Williams, can you come here a moment?"

He crawls to her like a dog to a whipping.

"Williams, why doesn't this patient have an issue of convalescents?"

The black boy is relieved. He straightens up and grins, raises that gray hand and points down the other end of the hall to one of the big ones. "Mistuh Washington over there is 'signed to the laundry duty this mornin'. Not me. No."

"Mr. *Washington!*" She nails him with his mop poised over the bucket, freezes him there. "Will you come here a moment!"

The mop slides without a sound back in the bucket, and with slow, careful movements he leans the handle against the wall. He turns around and looks down at McMurphy and the least black boy and the nurse. He looks then to his left and to his right, like she might be yelling at somebody else.

"Come down here!"

He puts his hands in his pockets and starts shuffling down the hall to her. He never walks very fast, and I can see how if he don't get a move on she might freeze him and shatter him all to hell by just looking; all the hate and fury and frustration she was planning to use on McMurphy is beaming out down the hall at the black boy, and he can feel it blast against him like a blizzard wind, slowing him more than ever. He has to lean into it, pulling his arms around him. Frost forms in his hair and eyebrows. He leans farther forward, but his steps are getting slower; he'll never make it.

Then McMurphy takes to whistling "Sweet Georgia Brown," and the nurse looks away from the black boy just in time. Now she's madder and more frustrated than ever, madder'n I ever saw her get. Her doll smile is gone, stretched tight and thin as a red-hot wire. If some of the patients could be out to see her now, McMurphy could start collecting his bets.

The black boy finally gets to her, and it took him two hours. She draws a long breath. "Washington, why wasn't this man issued a change of greens this morning? Couldn't you see he had nothing on but a towel?"

"And my cap," McMurphy whispers, tapping the brim with his finger.

"Mr. Washington?"

The big black boy looks at the little one who pointed him out, and the little black boy commences to fidget again. The big boy looks at him a long time with those radio-tube eyes, plans to square things with *him* later; then the head turns and he looks McMurphy up and down, taking in the hard, heavy shoulders, the lopsided grin, the scar on the nose, the hand clamping the towel in place, and then he looks at the nurse.

"I guess—" he starts out.

"You *guess!* You'll do more than *guess!* You'll get him a uniform this instant, Mr. Washington, or spend the next two weeks

working on Geriatrics Ward! Yes. You may need a month of bed-
pans and slab baths to refresh your appreciation of just how little work you aides have to do on this ward. If this was one of the
other wards, who do you think would be scouring the hall all
day? Mr. Bromden here? No, you know who it would be. We excuse
you aides from most of your housekeeping duties to enable you to
see to the patients. And that means seeing that they don't parade
around exposed. What do you think would have happened if one
of the young nurses had come in early and found a patient running
round the halls without a uniform? What do you think!"

The big black boy isn't too sure what, but he gets her drift and
ambles off to the linen room to get McMurphy a set of greens—
probably ten sizes too small—and ambles back and holds it out to
him with a look of the clearest hate I ever saw. McMurphy just
looks confused, like he don't know how to take the outfit the black
boy's handing to him, what with one hand holding the toothbrush
and the other hand holding up the towel. He finally winks at the
nurse and shrugs and unwraps the towel, drapes it over her shoulder like she was a wooden rack.

I see he had his shorts on under the towel all along.

I think for a fact that she'd rather he'd of been stark naked under that towel than had on those shorts. She's glaring at those big
white whales leaping round on his shorts in pure wordless outrage.
That's more'n she can take. It's a full minute before she can pull
herself together enough to turn on the least black boy; her voice is
shaking out of control, she's so mad.

"Williams . . . I believe . . . you were supposed to have the windows of the Nurses' Station polished by the time I arrived this
morning." He scuttles off like a black and white bug. "And
you, Washington—and you . . . " Washington shuffles back to his
bucket in almost a trot. She looks around again, wondering who
else she can light into. She spots me, but by this time some of the
other patients are out of the dorm and wondering about the little
clutch of us here in the hall. She closes her eyes and concentrates.
She can't have them see her face like this, white and warped with
fury. She uses all the power of control that's in her. Gradually the
lips gather together again under the little white nose, run together,
like the red-hot wire had got hot enough to melt, shimmer a second, then click solid as the molten metal sets, growing cold and
strangely dull. Her lips part, and her tongue comes between them,

a chunk of slag. Her eyes open again, and they have that strange dull and cold and flat look the lips have, but she goes into her good-morning routine like there was nothing different about her, figuring the patients'll be too sleepy to notice.

"Good morning, Mr. Sefelt, are your teeth any better? Good morning, Mr. Fredrickson, did you and Mr. Sefelt have a good night last night? You bed right next to each other, don't you? Incidentally, it's been brought to my attention that you two have made some arrangement with your medication—you are letting Bruce have your medication, aren't you, Mr. Sefelt? We'll discuss that later. Good morning, Billy; I saw your mother on the way in, and she told me to be sure to tell you she thought of you all the time and *knew* you wouldn't disappoint her. Good morning, Mr. Harding   why, look, your fingertips are red and raw. Have you been chewing your fingernails again?"

Before they could answer, even if there was some answer to make, she turns to McMurphy still standing there in his shorts. Harding looks at the shorts and whistles.

"And you, Mr. McMurphy," she says, smiling, sweet as sugar, "if you are finished showing off your manly physique and your gaudy underpants. I think you had better go back in the dorm and put on your greens."

He tips his cap to her and to the patients ogling and poking fun at his white-whale shorts, and goes to the dorm without a word. She turns and starts off in the other direction, her flat red smile going out before her; before she's got the door closed on her glass station, his singing is rolling from the dorm door into the hall again.

"'She took me to her parlor, and coo-oo-ooled me with her fan'"—I can hear the whack as he slaps his bare belly—"'whispered low in her mamma's ear, I luh-uhvvv that gamblin' man.'"

Sweeping the dorm soon's it's empty, I'm after dust mice under his bed when I get a smell of something that makes me realize for the first time since I been in the hospital that this big dorm full of beds, sleeps forty grown men, has always been sticky with a thousand other smells—smells of germicide, zinc ointment, and foot powder, smell of piss and sour old-man manure, of Pablum and eyewash, of musty shorts and socks musty even when they're fresh back from the laundry, the stiff odor of starch in the linen, the acid stench of morning mouths, the banana smell of machine oil, and sometimes the smell of singed hair—but never before now, before he came in, the man smell of dust and dirt from the open fields, and sweat, and work.

All through breakfast McMurphy's talking and laughing a mile a minute. After this morning he thinks the Big Nurse is going to be a snap. He don't know he just caught her off guard and, if anything, made her strengthen herself.

He's being the clown, working at getting some of the guys to laugh. It bothers him that the best they can do is grin weakly and snigger sometimes. He prods at Billy Bibbit, sitting across the table from him, says in a secret voice, "Hey, Billy boy, you remember that time in Seattle you and me picked up those two twitches? One of the best rolls I ever had."

Billy's eyes bob up from his plate. He opens his mouth but can't say a thing. McMurphy turns to Harding.

"We'd never have brought it off, neither, picking them up on the spur of the moment that way, except that they'd heard tell of Billy Bibbit. Billy 'Club' Bibbit, he was known as in them days. Those girls were about to take off when one looked at him and says 'Are you *the* renowned Billy Club Bibbit? Of the famous fourteen inches?' And Billy ducked his head and blushed—like he's doin' now—and we were a shoo-in. And I remember, when we got them up to the hotel, there was this woman's voice from over near Billy's bed, says, 'Mister Bibbit, I'm disappointed in you; I heard that you had four—four—for goodness *sakes!*' "

And whoops and slaps his leg and gooses Billy with his thumb till I think Billy will fall in a dead faint from blushing and grinning.

McMurphy says that as a matter of fact a couple of sweet twitches like those two is the *only* thing this hospital does lack. The bed they give a man here, finest he's ever slept in, and what a fine table they do spread. He can't figure why everybody's so glum about being locked up here.

"Look at me now," he tells the guys and lifts a glass to the light, "getting my first glass of orange juice in six months. Hooee, that's good. I ask you, what did I get for breakfast at that work farm? What was I served? Well, I can describe what it *looked* like, but I sure couldn't hang a name on it; morning noon and night it was burnt black and had potatoes in it and looked like roofing glue. I know one thing; it wasn't orange juice. Look at me now: bacon, toast, butter, eggs—coffee the little honey in the kitchen even asks me if I like it black or white thank you—and a great! big! cold glass of orange juice. Why, you couldn't *pay* me to leave this place!"

He gets seconds on everything and makes a date with the girl who pours coffee in the kitchen for when he gets discharged, and he compliments the Negro cook on sunnysiding the best eggs he ever ate. There's bananas for the corn flakes, and he gets a handful, tells the black boy that he'll filch him one 'cause he looks so starved, and the black boy shifts his eyes to look down the hall to where the Nurse is sitting in her glass case, and says it ain't allowed for the help to eat with the patients.

"Against ward policy?"

"Tha's right."

"Tough luck"—and peels three bananas right under the black boy's nose and eats one after the other, tells the boy that any time you want one snuck outa the mess hall for you, Sam, you just give the word.

When McMurphy finishes his last banana he slaps his belly and gets up and heads for the door, and the big black boy blocks the door and tells him the rule that patients sit in the mess hall till they all leave at seven-thirty. McMurphy stares at him like he can't believe he's hearing right, then turns and looks at Harding. Harding nods his head, so McMurphy shrugs and goes back to his chair. "I sure don't want to go against that goddamned policy."

The clock at the end of the mess hall shows it's a quarter after seven, lies about how we been sitting here fifteen minutes when you can tell it's been at least an hour. Everybody is finished eating and leaned back, watching the big hand to move to seven-thirty. The black boys take away the Vegetables' splattered trays and wheel the two old men down to get hosed off. In the mess hall about half the guys lay their heads on their arms, figuring to get a little sleep before the black boys get back. There's nothing else to do, with no cards or magazines or picture puzzles. Just sleep or watch the clock.

But McMurphy can't keep still for that; he's got to be up to something. After about two minutes of pushing food scraps around his plate with his spoon, he's ready for more excitement. He hooks his thumbs in his pockets and tips back and one-eyes that clock up on the wall. Then he rubs his nose.

"You know—that old clock up there puts me in mind of the *targets* at the target range at Fort Riley. That's where I got my first medal, a sharpshooter medal. Dead-Eye McMurphy. Who wants to lay me a pore little dollar that I can't put this dab of butter square in the center of the face of that clock up there, or at least *on* the face?"

He gets three bets and takes up his butter pat and puts it on his knife, gives it a flip. It sticks a good six inches or so to the left of the clock, and everybody kids him about it until he pays his bets. They're still riding him about did he mean Dead-Eye or Dead-Eyes when the least black boy gets back from hosing Vegetables and everybody looks into his plate and keeps quiet. The black boy senses something is in the air, but he can't see what. And he probably never would of known except old Colonel Matterson is gazing around, and *he* sees the butter stuck up on the wall and this causes him to point up at it and go into one of his lessons, explaining to us all in his patient, rumbling voice, just like what he said made sense.

"The but-ter . . . is the Re-pub-li-can party. . . . "

The black boy looks where the colonel is pointing, and there that butter is, easing down the wall like a yellow snail. He blinks at it but he doesn't say a word, doesn't even bother looking around to make certain who flipped it up there.

McMurphy is whispering and nudging the Acutes sitting around him, and in a minute they all nod, and he lays three dollars on the table and leans back. Everybody turns in his chair and watches that butter sneak on down the wall, starting, hanging still, shooting ahead and leaving a shiny trail behind it on the paint. Nobody says a word. They look at the butter, then at the clock, then back at the butter. The clock's moving now.

The butter makes it down to the floor about a half minute before seven-thirty, and McMurphy gets back all the money he lost.

The black boy wakes up and turns away from the greasy stripe on the wall and says we can go, and McMurphy walks out of the mess hall, folding his money in his pocket. He puts his arms around the black boy's shoulders and half walks, half carries him, down the hall toward the day room. "The day's half gone, Sam, ol' buddy, an' I'm just barely breaking even. I'll have to hustle to catch up. How about breaking out that deck of cards you got locked securely in that cabinet, and I'll see if I can make myself heard over that loudspeaker."

Spends most of that morning hustling to catch up by dealing more blackjack, playing for IOUs now instead of cigarettes. He moves the blackjack table two or three times to try to get out from under the speaker. You can tell it's getting on his nerves. Finally he goes to the Nurses' Station and raps on a pane of glass till the Big Nurse swivels in her chair and opens the door, and he asks her how about turning that infernal noise off for a while. She's calmer than ever now, back in her seat behind her pane of glass; there's no heathen running around half-naked to unbalance her. Her smile is settled and solid. She closes her eyes and shakes her head and tells McMurphy very pleasantly, No.

"Can't you even ease down the volume? It ain't like the whole state of Oregon needed to hear Lawrence Welk play 'Tea for Two' three times every hour, all day long! If it was soft enough to hear a man shout his bets across the table I might get a game of poker going—"

"You've been told, Mr. McMurphy, that it's against the policy to gamble for money on the ward."

"Okay, then down soft enough to gamble for matches, for fly buttons—just turn the damn thing down!"

"Mr. McMurphy"—she waits and lets her calm schoolteacher tone sink in before she goes on; she knows every Acute on the ward is listening to them—"do you want to know what I think? I think you are being very selfish. Haven't you noticed there are others in this hospital besides yourself? There are old men here who couldn't hear the radio at all if it were lower, old fellows who simply aren't capable of reading, or working puzzles—or playing cards to win other men's cigarettes. Old fellows like Matterson and Kittling, that music coming from the loudspeaker is all they have. And you want to take that away from them. We like to hear suggestions and requests whenever we can, but I should think you might at least give some thought to others before you make your requests."

He turns and looks over at the Chronic side and sees there's something to what she says. He takes off his cap and runs his hand in his hair, finally turns back to her. He knows as well as she does that all the Acutes are listening to everything they say.

"Okay—I never thought about that."

"I thought you hadn't."

He tugs at that little tuft of red showing out of the neck of his greens, then says. "Well, hey; what do you say to us taking the card game someplace else? Some other room? Like, say, that room you people put the tables in during that meeting. There's nothing in there all the rest of the day. You could unlock that room and let the card-players go in there, and leave the old men out here with their radio—a good deal all around."

She smiles and closes her eyes again and shakes her head gently. "Of course, you take the suggestion up with the rest of the staff at some time, but I'm afraid everyone's feelings will correspond with mine: we do not have adequate coverage for two day rooms. There isn't enough personnel. And I wish you wouldn't lean against the glass there, please; your hands are oily and staining the window. That means extra work for some of the other men."

He jerks his hand away, and I see he starts to say something and then stops, realizing she didn't leave him anything else to say, unless he wants to start cussing at her. His face and neck are red. He draws a long breath and concentrates on his will power, the way she did this morning, and tells her that he is very sorry to have bothered her, and goes back to the card table.

Everybody on the ward can feel that it's started.

At eleven o'clock the doctor comes to the day-room door and calls over to McMurphy that he'd like to have him come down to his office for an interview. "I interview all new admissions on the second day."

McMurphy lays down his cards and stands up and walks over to the doctor. The doctor asks him how his night was, but McMurphy just mumbles an answer.

"You look deep in thought today, Mr. McMurphy."

"Oh, I'm a thinker all right," McMurphy says, and they walk off together down the hall. When they come back what seems like days later, they're both grinning and talking and happy about something. The doctor is wiping tears off his glasses and looks like he's actually been laughing, and McMurphy is back as loud and full of brass and swagger as ever. He's that way all through lunch, and at one o'clock he's the first one in his seat for the meeting, his eyes blue and ornery from his place in the corner.

The Big Nurse comes into the day room with her covey of student nurses and her basket of notes. She picks the log book up from the table and frowns into it a minute (nobody's informed on anybody all day long), then goes to her seat beside the door. She picks up some folders from the basket on her lap and riffles through them till she finds the one on Harding.

"As I recall, we were making quite a bit of headway yesterday with Mr. Harding's problem—"

"Ah—before we go into that," the doctor says, "I'd like to interrupt a moment, if I might. Concerning a talk Mr. McMurphy and I had in my office this morning. Reminiscing, actually. Talking over old times. You see Mr. McMurphy and I find we have something in common—we went to the same high school."

The nurses look at one another and wonder what's got into this man. The patients glance at McMurphy grinning from his corner and wait for the doctor to go on. He nods his head.

"Yes, the same high school. And in the course of our reminiscing we happened to bring up the carnivals the school used to sponsor—marvelous, noisy, gala occasions. Decorations, crepe streamers, booths, games—it was always one of the prime events of the year. I—as I mentioned to McMurphy—was the chairman of the high-school carnival both my junior and senior years—wonderful carefree years . . . "

It's got real quiet in the day room. The doctor raises his head, peers around to see if he's making a fool of himself. The Big Nurse is giving him a look that shouldn't leave any doubts about it, but he doesn't have on his glasses and the look misses him.

"Anyway—to put an end to this maudlin display of nostalgia—in the course of our conversation McMurphy and I wondered what would be the attitude of some of the men toward a carnival here on the ward?"

He puts on his glasses and peers around again. Nobody's jumping up and down at the idea. Some of us can remember Taber trying to engineer a carnival a few years back, and what happened to it. As the doctor waits, a silence rears up from out of the nurse and looms over everybody, daring anybody to challenge it. I know McMurphy can't because he was in on the planning of the carnival, and just as I'm thinking that nobody will be fool enough to break that silence, Cheswick, who sits right next to McMurphy, gives a grunt and is on his feet, rubbing his ribs, before he knows what happened.

"Uh—I personally believe, see"—he looks down at McMurphy's fist on the chair arm beside him, with that big stiff thumb sticking straight up out of it like a cow prod—"that a carnival is a real good idea. Something to break the monotony."

"That's right, Charley," the doctor says, appreciating Cheswick's support, "and not altogether without therapeutic value."

"Certainly not," Cheswick says, looking happier now. "No. Lots of therapeutics in a carnival. You bet."

"It would b-b-be fun," Billy Bibbit says.

"Yeah, that too," Cheswick says. "We could do it, Doctor Spivey, sure we could. Scanlon can do his human bomb act, and I can make a ring toss in Occupational Therapy."

"I'll tell fortunes," Martini says and squints at a spot above his head.

"I'm rather good at diagnosing pathologies from palm reading, myself," Harding says.

"Good, good," Cheswick says and claps his hands. He's never had anybody support anything he said before.

"Myself," McMurphy drawls, "I'd be honored to work a skillo wheel. Had a little experience . . . "

"Oh, there are numerous possibilities," the doctor says, sitting up straight in his chair and really warming to it. "Why, I've got a million ideas. . . . "

He talks fall steam ahead for another five minutes. You can tell a lot of the ideas are ideas he's already talked over with McMurphy. He describes games, booths, talks of selling tickets, then stops as suddenly as though the Nurse's look had hit him right between the eyes. He blinks at her and asks, "What do you think of the idea, Miss Ratched? Of a carnival? Here, on the ward?"

"I agree that it may have a number of therapeutic possibilities," she says, and waits. She lets that silence rear up from her again. When she's sure nobody's going to challenge it, she goes on. "But I also believe that an idea like this should be discussed in staff meeting before a decision is reached. Wasn't that your idea, Doctor?"

"Of course. I merely thought, understand, I would feel out some of the men first. But certainly, a staff meeting first. Then we'll continue our plans."

Everybody knows that's all there is to the carnival.

The Big Nurse starts to bring things back into hand by rattling the folio she's holding. "Fine. Then if there is no other new business—and if Mr. Cheswick will be seated—I think we might go right on into the discussion. We have"—she takes her watch from the basket and looks at it—"forty-eight minutes left. So, as I—"

"Oh. Hey, wait. I remember there is some other new business."

McMurphy has his hand up, fingers snapping. She looks at the hand for a long time before she says anything.

"Yes, Mr. McMurphy?"

"Not me, Doctor Spivey has. Doc, tell 'em what you come up with about the hard-of-hearing guys and the radio."

The nurse's head gives one little jerk, barely enough to see, but my heart is suddenly roaring. She puts the folio back in the basket, turns to the doctor.

"Yes," says the doctor. "I very nearly forgot." He leans back and crosses his legs and puts his fingertips together; I can see he's still in good spirits about his carnival. "You see, McMurphy and I were talking about that age-old problem we have on this ward: the mixed population, the young and the old together. It's not the most ideal surroundings for our Therapeutic Community, but Administration says there's no helping it with the Geriatric Building overloaded the way it is. I'll be the first to admit it's not an absolutely pleasant situation for anyone concerned. In our talk, however, McMurphy and I did happen to come up with an idea which might make things more pleasant for both age groups. McMurphy mentioned that he had noticed some of the old fellows seemed to have difficulty hearing the radio. He suggested the speaker be turned up louder so the Chronics with auditory weaknesses could hear it. A very humane suggestion, I think."

McMurphy gives a modest wave of his hand, and the doctor nods at him and goes on.

"But I told him I had received previous complaints from some of the younger men that the radio is already so loud it hinders conversation and reading. McMurphy said he hadn't thought of this, but mentioned that it did seem a shame that those who wished to read couldn't get off by themselves where it was quiet and leave the radio for those who wished to listen. I agreed with him that it did seem a shame and was ready to drop the matter when I happened to think of the old tub room where we store the tables during the ward meeting. We don't use the room at all otherwise; there's no longer a need for the hydrotherapy it was designed for, now that we have the new drugs. So how would the group like to have that room as a sort of second day room, a *game* room, shall we say?"

The group isn't saying. They know whose play it is next. She folds Harding's folio back up and puts it on her lap and crosses her hands over it, looking around the room just like somebody might dare have something to say. When it's clear nobody's going to talk till she does, her head turns again to the doctor. "It sounds like a fine plan, Doctor Spivey, and I appreciate Mr. McMurphy's interest in the other patients, but I'm terribly afraid we don't have the personnel to cover a second day room."

  ⸰ And is so certain that this should be the end of it she starts to open the folio again. But the doctor has thought this through more than she figured.

"I thought of that, too, Miss Ratched. But since it will be largely the Chronic patients who remain here in the day room with the speaker—most of whom are restricted to lounges or wheel chairs— one aide and one nurse in here should easily be able to put down any riots or uprisings that might occur, don't you think?"

She doesn't answer, and she doesn't care much for his joking about riots and uprisings either, but her face doesn't change. The smile stays.

"So the other two aides and nurses can cover the men in the tub room, perhaps even better than here in a larger area. What do you think, men? Is it a workable idea? I'm rather enthused about it myself, and I say we give it a try, see what it's like for a few days. If it doesn't work, well, we've still got the key to lock it back up, haven't we?"

"Right!" Cheswick says, socks his fist into his palm. He's still standing, like he's afraid to get near that thumb of McMurphy's again. "Right, Doctor Spivey, if it don't work, we've still got the key to lock it back up. You bet."

The doctor looks around the room and sees all the other Acutes nodding and smiling and looking so pleased with what he takes to be him and his idea that he blushes like Billy Bibbit and has to polish his glasses a time or two before he can go on. It tickles me to see the little man so happy with himself. He looks at all the guys nodding, and nods himself and says, "Fine, fine," and settles his hands on his knees. "Very good. Now. If that's decided—I seem to have forgotten what we were planning to talk about this morning?"

The nurse's head gives that one little jerk again, and she bends over her basket, picks up a folio. She fumbles with the papers, and it looks like her hands are shaking. She draws out a paper, but once more, before she can start reading out of it, McMurphy is standing and holding up his hand and shifting from foot to foot, giving a long, thoughtful, "Saaaay," and her fumbling stops, freezes as though the sound of his voice froze her just like her voice froze that black boy this morning. I get that giddy feeling inside me again when she freezes. I watch her close while McMurphy talks.

"Saaaaay, Doctor, what I been dyin' to know is what did this dream I dreamt the other night mean? You see, it was like I was *me*, in the dream, and then again kind of like I *wasn't* me—like I was somebody else that looked like me—like—like my *daddy!* Yeah, that's who it was. It was my daddy because sometimes when I saw me—him—I saw there was this iron bolt through the jawbone like daddy used to have—"

"Your father has an iron *bolt* through his jawbone?"

"Well, not any more, but he did once when I was a kid. He went around for about ten months with this big metal bolt going in *here* and coming out *here!* God, he was a regular Frankenstein. He'd been clipped on the jaw with a pole ax when he got into some kinda hassle with this pond man at the logging mill—Hey! Let me tell you how *that* incident came about. . . . "

Her face is still calm, as though she had a cast made and painted to just the look she wants. Confident, patient, and unruffled. No more little jerk, just that terrible cold face, a calm smile stamped out of red plastic; a clean, smooth forehead, not a line in it to show weakness or worry; flat, wide, painted-on green eyes, painted on with an expression that says I can wait, I might lose a yard now and then but I can wait, and be patient and calm and confident, because I know there's no real losing for me.

I thought for a minute there I saw her whipped. Maybe I did. But I see now that it don't make any difference. One by one the patients are sneaking looks at her to see how she's taking the way McMurphy is dominating the meeting, and they see the same thing. She's too big to be beaten. She covers one whole side of the room like a Jap statue. There's no moving her and no help against her. She's lost a little battle here today, but it's a minor battle in a big war that she's been winning and that she'll go on winning. We mustn't let McMurphy get our hopes up any different, lure us into making some kind of dumb play. She'll go on winning, just like the Combine, because she has all the power of the Combine behind her. She don't lose on her losses, but she wins on ours. To beat her you don't have to whip her two out of three or three out of five, but every time you meet. As soon as you let down your guard, as soon as you lose *once*, she's won for good. And eventually we all got to lose. Nobody can help that.

Right now, she's got the fog machine switched on, and it's rolling in so fast I can't see a thing but her face, rolling in thicker and thicker, and I feel as hopeless and dead as I felt happy a minute ago, when she gave that little jerk—even more hopeless than ever before, on account of I know now there is no real help against her or her Combine. McMurphy can't help any more than I could. Nobody can help. And the more I think about how nothing can be helped, the faster the fog rolls in.

And I'm glad when it gets thick enough you're lost in it and can let go, and be safe again.

There's a Monopoly game going on in the day room. They've been at it for three days, houses and hotels everywhere, two tables pushed together to take care of all the deeds and stacks of play money. McMurphy talked them into making the game interesting by paying a penny for every dollar the bank issues them; the monopoly box is loaded with change.

"It's your roll, Cheswick."

"Hold it a minute before he rolls. What's a man need to buy thum hotels?"

"You need four houses on every lot of the same color, Martini. Now let's *go*, for Christsakes."

"Hold it a minute."

There's a flurry of money from that side of the table, red and green and yellow bills blowing in every direction.

"You buying a hotel or you playing happy new year, for Christsakes?"

"It's your dirty roll, Cheswick."

"Snake eyes? Hooooee, Cheswicker, where does that put you? That don't put you on my Marvin Gardens by any chance? That don't mean you have to pay me, let's see, three hundred and fifty dollars?"

"Boogered."

"What's thum other things? Hold it a minute. What's thum other things *all* over the board?"

"Martini, you been seeing them other things all over the board for two days. No wonder I'm losing my ass. McMurphy, I don't see how you can concentrate with Martini sitting there hallucinating a mile a minute."

"Cheswick, you never mind about Martini. He's doing real good. You just come on with that three fifty, and Martini will take care of himself; don't we get rent from him every time one of his 'things' lands on our property?"

"Hold it a minute. There's so many of thum."

"That's okay, Mart. You just keep us posted whose property they land on. You're still the man with the dice, Cheswick. You rolled a double, so you roll again. Atta boy. *Faw!* a big six."

"Takes me to . . . Chance: 'You Have Been Elected Chairman of the Board; Pay Every Player—' Boogered and double boogered!"

"Whose hotel is this here for Christsakes on the Reading Railroad?"

"My friend, that, as anyone can see, is not a hotel; it's a depot."

"Now *hold* it a minute—"

McMurphy surrounds his end of the table, moving cards, rearranging money, evening up his hotels. There's a hundred-dollar bill sticking out of the brim of his cap like a press card; mad money, he calls it.

"Scanlon? I believe it's your turn, buddy."

"Gimme those dice. I'll blow this board to pieces. Here we go. Lebenty Leben, count me over eleven, Martini."

"Why, all right."

"Not that one, you crazy bastard; that's not my piece, that's my *house.*"

"It's the same color."

"What's this little house doing on the Electric Company?"

"That's a power station."

"Martini, those ain't the dice you're shaking—"

"Let him be; what's the difference?"

"Those are a couple of houses!"

"*Faw.* And Martini rolls a big, let me see, a big nineteen. Good goin', Mart; that puts you—Where's your piece, buddy?"

"Eh? Why here it is."

"He had it in his mouth, McMurphy. Excellent. That's two moves over the second and third bicuspid, four moves to the board, which takes you on to—to Baltic Avenue, Martini. Your own and only property. How fortunate can a man get, friends? Martini has been playing three days and lit on his property practically every time."

"Shut up and roll, Harding. It's your turn."

Harding gathers the dice up with his long fingers, feeling the smooth surfaces with his thumb as if he was blind. The fingers are the same color as the dice and look like they were carved by his other hand. The dice rattle in his hand as he shakes it. They tumble to a stop in front of McMurphy.

"*Faw.* Five, six, seven. Tough luck, buddy. That's another o' my vast holdin's. You owe me—oh, two hundred dollars should about cover it."

"Pity."

The game goes round and round, to the rattle of dice and the shuffle of play money.

There's long spells—three days, years—when you can't see a thing, know where you are only by the speaker sounding overhead like a bell buoy clanging in the fog. When I can see, the guys are usually moving around as unconcerned as though they didn't notice so much as a mist in the air. I believe the fog affects their memory some way it doesn't affect mine.

Even McMurphy doesn't seem to know he's been fogged in. If he does, he makes sure not to let on that he's bothered by it. He's making sure none of the staff sees him bothered by anything; he knows that there's no better way in the world to aggravate somebody who's trying to make it hard for you than by acting like you're not bothered.

He keeps up his high-class manners around the nurses and the black boys in spite of anything they might say to him, in spite of every trick they pull to get him to lose his temper. A couple of times some stupid rule gets him mad, but he just makes himself act more polite and mannerly than ever till he begins to see how funny the whole thing is—the rules, the disapproving looks they use to enforce the rules, the ways of talking to you like you're nothing but a three-year-old—and when he sees how funny it is he goes to laughing, and this aggravates them no end. He's safe as long as he can laugh, he thinks, and it works pretty fair. Just once he loses control and shows he's mad, and then it's not because of the black boys or the Big Nurse and something they did, but it's because of the patients, and something they *didn't* do.

It happened at one of the group meetings. He got mad at the guys for acting too cagey—too chicken-shit, he called it. He'd been taking bets from all of them on the World Series coming up Friday. He'd had it in mind that they would get to watch the games on TV, even though they didn't come on during regulation TV time. During the meeting a few days before he asks if it wouldn't be okay if they did the cleaning work at night, during TV time, and watched the games during the afternoon. The nurse tells him no, which is about what he expected. She tells him how the schedule has been set up for a delicately balanced reason that would be thrown into turmoil by the switch of routines.

This doesn't surprise him, coming from the nurse; what does surprise him is how the Acutes act when he asks them what they think of the idea. Nobody says a thing. They're all sunk back out of sight in little pockets of fog. I can barely see them.

"Now look here," he tells them, but they don't look. He's been waiting for somebody to say something, answer his question. Nobody acts like they've heard it. "Look here, damn it," he says when nobody moves, "there's at least twelve of you guys I know of myself got a leetle personal *interest* who wins these games. Don't you guys care to watch them?"

"I don't know, Mack," Scanlon finally says, "I'm pretty used to seeing that six-o'clock news. And if switching times would really mess up the schedule as bad as Miss Ratched says—"

"The hell with the schedule. You can get back to the bloody schedule next week, when the Series is over. What do you say, buddies? Let's take a vote on watching the TV during the afternoon instead of at night. All those in favor?"

"Ay," Cheswick calls out and gets to his feet.

"I mean all those in favor raise their hands. Okay, all those in favor?"

Cheswick's hand comes up. Some of the other guys look around to see if there's any other fools. McMurphy can't believe it.

"Come on now, what is this crap? I thought you guys could vote on policy and that sort of thing. Isn't that the way it is, Doc?"

The doctor nods without looking up.

"Okay then; now who wants to watch those games?"

Cheswick shoves his hand higher and glares around. Scanlon shakes his head and then raises his hand, keeping his elbow on the arm of the chair. And nobody else. McMurphy can't say a word.

"If that's settled, then," the nurse says, "perhaps we should get on with the meeting."

"Yeah," he says, slides down in his chair till the brim of his cap nearly touches his chest. "Yeah, perhaps we should get on with the sonofabitchin' meeting at that."

"Yeah," Cheswick says, giving all the guys a hard look and sitting down, "yeah, get on with the godblessed meeting." He nods stiffly, then settles his chin down on his chest, scowling. He's pleased to be sitting next to McMurphy, feeling brave like this. It's the first time Cheswick ever had somebody along with him on his lost causes.

After the meeting McMurphy won't say a word to any of them, he's so mad and disgusted. It's Billy Bibbit who goes up to him.

"Some of us have b-been here for fi-fi-five years, Randle," Billy says. He's got a magazine rolled up and is twisting at it with his hands; you can see the cigarette burns on the backs of his hands. "And some of us will b-be here maybe th-that muh-muh-much longer, long after you're g-g-gone, long after this Wo-world Series is over. And . . . don't you see . . . " He throws down the magazine and walks away. "Oh, what's the use of it anyway."

McMurphy stares after him, that puzzled frown knotting his bleached eyebrows together again.

He argues for the rest of the day with some of the other guys about why they didn't vote, but they don't want to talk about it, so he seems to give up, doesn't say anything about it again till the day before the Series starts. "Here it is Thursday," he says, sadly shaking his head.

He's sitting on one of the tables in the tub room with his feet on a chair, trying to spin his cap around one finger. Other Acutes mope around the room and try not to pay any attention to him. Nobody'll play poker or blackjack with him for money any more—after the patients wouldn't vote he got mad and skinned them so bad at cards that they're all so in debt they're scared to go any deeper—and they can't play for cigarettes because the nurse has started making the men keep their cartons on the desk in the Nurses Station, where she doles them out one pack a day, says its for their health, but everybody knows it's to keep McMurphy from winning them all at cards. With no poker or blackjack, it's quiet in the tub room, just the sound of the speaker drifting in from the day room. It's so quiet you can hear that guy upstairs in Disturbed climbing the wall, giving out an occasional signal, loo loo *looo*, a bored, uninterested sound, like a baby yells to yell itself to sleep.

"Thursday," McMurphy says again.

"*Looooo*," yells that guy upstairs.

"That's Rawler," Scanlon says, looking up at the ceiling. He don't want to pay any attention to McMurphy. "Rawler the Squawler. He came through this ward a few years back. Wouldn't keep still to suit Miss Ratched, you remember, Billy? Loo loo loo all the time till I thought I'd go nuts. What they should do with that whole bunch of dingbats up there is toss a couple of grenades in the dorm. They're no use to anybody—"

"And tomorrow is Friday," McMurphy says. He won't let Scanlon change the subject.

"Yeah," Cheswick says, scowling around the room, "tomorrow is Friday."

Harding turns a page of his magazine. "And that will make nearly a week our friend McMurphy has been with us without succeeding in throwing over the government, is that what you're saying, Cheswickle? Lord, to think of the chasm of apathy in which we have fallen—a shame, a pitiful shame."

"The hell with that," McMurphy says. "What Cheswick means is that the first Series game is gonna be played on TV tomorrow, and what are we gonna be doin'? Mopping up this damned nursery again."

"Yeah," Cheswick says. "Ol' Mother Ratched's Therapeutic Nursery."

Against the wall of the tub room I get a feeling like a spy; the mop handle in my hands is made of metal instead of wood (metal's a better conductor) and it's hollow; there's plenty of room inside it to hide a miniature microphone. If the Big Nurse is hearing this, she'll really get Cheswick. I take a hard ball of gum from my pocket and pick some fuzz off it and hold it in my mouth till it softens.

"Let me see again," McMurphy says. "How many of you birds will vote with me if I bring up that time switch again?"

About half the Acutes nod yes, a lot more than would really vote. He puts his hat back on his head and leans his chin in his hands.

"I tell ya, I can't figure it out. Harding, what's wrong with *you*, for crying out loud? You afraid if you raise your hand that old buzzard'll cut it off."

Harding lifts one thin eyebrow. "Perhaps I am; perhaps I *am* afraid she'll cut if off if I raise it."

"What about you, Billy? Is that what you're scared of?"

"No. I don't think she'd d-d-*do* anything, but"—he shrugs and sighs and climbs up on the big panel that controls the nozzles on the shower, perches up there like a monkey—"but I just don't think a vote wu-wu-would do any good. Not in the l-long run. It's just no use, M-Mack."

"Do any *good?* Hooee! It'd do you birds some good just to get the exercise lifting that arm."

"It's still a risk, my friend. She always has the capacity to make things worse for us. A baseball game isn't worth the risk," Harding says.

"Who the hell says so? Jesus, I haven't missed a World Series in years. Even when I was in the cooler one September they let us bring in a TV and watch the *Series;* they'd of had a riot on their hands if they hadn't. I just may have to kick that damned door down and walk to some bar downtown to see the game, just me and my buddy Cheswick."

"Now there's a suggestion with a lot of merit," Harding says, tossing down his magazine. "Why not bring that up for vote in group meeting tomorrow? 'Miss Ratched, I'd like to move that the ward be transported *en masse* to the Idle Hour for beer and television.'"

"I'd second the motion," Cheswick says. "Damn right."

"The hell with that in mass business," McMurphy says. "I'm tired of looking at you bunch of old ladies; when me and Cheswick bust outta here I think by God I'm gonna nail the door shut behind me. You guys better stay behind; your mamma probably wouldn't let you cross the street."

"Yeah? Is that it?" Fredrickson has come up behind McMurphy. "You're just going to raise one of those big he-man boots of yours and *kick* down the door? A real tough guy."

McMurphy don't hardly look at Fredrickson; he's learned that Fredrickson might act hard-boiled now and then, but it's an act that folds under the slightest scare.

"What about it, he-man," Fredrickson keeps on, "are you going to kick down that door and show us how tough you are?"

"No, Fred, I guess not. I wouldn't want to scuff up my boot."

"Yeah? Okay, you been talking so big, just how *would* you go about busting out of here?"

McMurphy takes a look around him. "Well, I guess I could knock the mesh outa one of these windows with a chair when and if I took a notion. . . . "

"Yeah? You could, could you? Knock it right out? Okay, let's see you try. Come on, he-man, I'll bet you ten dollars you can't do it."

"Don't bother trying, Mack," Cheswick says. "Fredrickson knows you'll just break a chair and end up on Disturbed. The first day we arrived over here we were given a demonstration about these screens. They're specially made. A technician picked up a chair just like that one you've got your feet on and beat the screen till the chair was no more than kindling wood. Didn't hardly dent the screen."

"Okay then," McMurphy says, taking a look around him. I can see he's getting more interested. I hope the Big Nurse isn't hearing this; he'll be up on Disturbed in an hour. "We need something heavier. How about a table?"

"Same as the chair. Same wood, same weight."

"All right, by God, let's just figure out what I'd have to toss through that screen to bust out. And if you birds don't think I'd do it if I ever got the urge, then you got another think coming. Okay— something bigger'n a table or a chair . . . Well, if it was night I might throw that fat coon through it; he's heavy enough."

"Much too soft," Harding says. "He'd hit the screen and it would dice him like an eggplant."

"How about one of the beds?"

"A bed is too big even if you could lift it. It wouldn't go through the window."

"I could lift it all right. Well, hell, right over there you are: that thing Billy's sittin' on. That big control panel with all the handles and cranks. That's hard enough, ain't it? And it damn well should be heavy enough."

"Sure," Fredrickson says. "That's the same as you kicking your foot through the steel door at the front."

"What would be wrong with using the panel? It don't look nailed down."

"No, its not bolted—there's probably nothing holding it but a few wires—but *look* at it, for Christsakes."

Everybody looks. The panel is steel and cement, half the size of one of the tables, probably weighs four hundred pounds.

"Okay, I'm looking at it. It don't look any bigger than hay bales I've bucked up onto truck beds."

"I'm afraid, my friend, that this contrivance will weigh a bit more than your bales of hay."

"About a quarter-ton more, I'd bet," Fredrickson says.

"He's right, Mack," Cheswick says. "It'd be awful heavy."

"Hell, are you birds telling me I can't *lift* that dinky little gizmo?"

"My friend, I don't recall anything about psychopaths being

able to move mountains in addition to their other noteworthy as-
sets."

"Okay, you say I can't lift it. Well *by* God . . . "

McMurphy hops off the table and goes to peeling off his green
jacket; the tattoos sticking half out of his T-shirt jump around the
muscles on his arms.

"Then who's willing to lay five bucks? Nobody's gonna convince me I can't do something till I try it. Five bucks . . . "

"McMurphy, this is as foolhardy as your bet about the nurse."

"Who's got five bucks they want to lose? You hit or you sit. . . . "

The guys all go to signing liens at once; he's beat them so many
times at poker and blackjack they can't wait to get back at him,
and this is a certain sure thing. I don't know what he's driving at;
broad and big as he is, it'd take three of him to move that panel,
and he knows it. He can just look at it and see he probably couldn't
even tip it, let alone lift it. It'd take a giant to lift it off the ground.
But when the Acutes all get their IOUs signed, he steps up to the
panel and lifts Billy Bibbit down off it and spits in his big callused
palms and slaps them together, rolls his shoulders.

"Okay, stand outa the way. Sometimes when I go to exertin'
myself I use up all the air nearby and grown men faint from suf-
focation. Stand back. There's liable to be crackin' cement and
flying steel. Get the women and kids someplace safe. Stand
back. . . . "

"By golly, he might do it," Cheswick mutters.

"Sure, maybe he'll talk it off the floor," Fredrickson says.

"More likely he'll acquire a beautiful hernia," Harding says.
"Come now, McMurphy, quit acting like a fool; there's no man can
lift that thing."

"Stand back, sissies, you're using my oxygen."

McMurphy shifts his feet a few times to get a good stance, and
wipes his hands on his thighs again, then leans down and gets hold
of the levers on each side of the panel. When he goes to strain-
ing, the guys go to hooting and kidding him. He turns loose and
straightens up and shifts his feet around again.

"Giving up?" Fredrickson grins.

"Just *limbering* up. Here goes the real effort"—and grabs those
levers again.

And suddenly nobody's hooting at him any more. His arms
commence to swell, and the veins squeeze up to the surface. He
clinches his eyes, and his lips draw away from his teeth. His head

leans back, and tendons stand out like coiled ropes running from his heaving neck down both arms to his hands. His whole body shakes with the strain as he tries to lift something he *knows* he can't lift, something *everybody* knows he can't lift.

But, for just a second, when we hear the cement grind at our feet, we think, by golly, he might do it.

Then his breath exploded out of him, and he falls back limp against the wall. There's blood on the levers where he tore his hands. He pants for a minute against the wall with his eyes shut. There's no sound but his scraping breath; nobody's saying a thing.

He opens his eyes and looks around at us. One by one he looks at the guys—even at me—then he fishes in his pockets for all the IOUs he won the last few days at poker. He bends over the table and tries to sort them, but his hands are froze into red claws, and he can't work the fingers.

Finally he throws the whole bundle on the floor—probably forty or fifty dollars' worth from each man—and turns to walk out of the tub room. He stops at the door and looks back at everybody standing around.

"But I tried, though," he says. "Goddammit, I sure as hell did that much, now, didn't I?"

And walks out and leaves those stained pieces of paper on the floor for whoever wants to sort through them.

——*For Discussion*——

JRT—

McMurphy, the new guy on the psychiatric ward at a mental hospital, is a romantic hero. He swaggers into the bleak hospital, where Big Nurse rules the roost, and immediately bucks the status quo. His triumphs seem like small ones—brushing his teeth with soap rather than waiting for toothpaste to be unlocked, gaming for small change with the motley crew of Acutes on the ward, and getting a room set aside without loud music for those who want to play cards—but in the hospital, these are huge triumphs. In fact, what makes McMurphy romantic is not just his offhand charm, but his ability to influence others to stand up in the face of both fear and conformity. He is what we want to be. In spite of his obvious con background, McMurphy is a voice for the underdog.

It's hard to imagine anyone else but Jack Nicholson as McMurphy, and as we read about the various struggles in these chapters,
I couldn't help hearing his voice, his sarcasm, and his humor from
the famous movie made of this novel. But even without Jack's por-
trayal, the character is appealing. McMurphy takes the other guys
seriously in spite of their strange quirks, known in some circles
as "disorders," but considered by McMurphy as what makes the
guys who they are. Unlike Big Nurse, whose every action pushes
her patients into conformity and fear, McMurphy's ability to have
fun begins to be freeing to them. He takes their money in Monopoly but ironically, this forces them to focus on the game. He challenges their beliefs about what is and is not possible on this ward
when he gets the psychiatrist to suggest a carnival. Even though
he fails to move the control panel, he tries, proving to them that
much of life's winnings may be in the effort to succeed, not just
in the act of success.

It bothers me a bit that once again we have the bad guy per-
sonified by a woman who tries to control men. Big Nurse represents the woman that all men fear, the one who will take away
their individuality and render them "patients." Although she is
known for her big breasts and she certainly notices McMurphy
in his towel, she is minimally sexual, mostly a male view of a
tyrannical mother. Her sense of control, calm and frightening in
its intensity, exerts a pall over the ward, extending even to her rac-
ist attitude towards the black workers on the floor and to her disdain of the patients. Who can like someone standing for order and
loss of individuality in the face of a McMurphy?

Kesey seems most interested in the match between these two
characters, and these few chapters begin to set us up for the rest
of the book, where they will fight to the death. If the struggle is
seen as a gender issue, it seems more problematic to me than if it
is seen as a human battle, one we wage inside ourselves all the
time. In some ways, we are both McMurphy and Big Nurse. We
all want our freedom and to be awakened to ourselves, and we
all struggle to keep ourselves in check. Where Big Nurse says no,
McMurphy says yes.

RPW—

The battle between McMurphy (a counterculture figure leading a revolutionary transformation) and Big Nurse (an establish-
ment figure working to maintain the status quo of the Combine)

is just beginning in these early scenes from the novel. McMurphy is clearly upbeat and optimistic, the playful con-artist able to seduce Dr. Spivey by evoking joyful images of high school carnivals, the gambler who wants to teach everyone that risk is necessary for human growth, the Monopoly player and World Series supporter who knows that energy and movement are better than passivity and paralysis. By contrast, Nurse Ratched (a wretched ratchet, no doubt) works as if she were a tool for the established order, trying to adjust "the nuts" so they will conform to the machinery of her bureaucratic schedule and dehumanized policies.

The narrator, Chief Bromden, believes that Big Nurse controls the clock in the Day Room, making it move faster or slower according to her own agenda, and that she has a fog machine that makes it difficult to see clearly at times. For the Chief, the fog is a place to hide and be safe, although it also keeps him from discovering his freedom and individuality. In a sense, McMurphy has arrived in the ward to draw the Chief, and more generally all these men (Acutes and Chronics alike), out of this fog, out of the fear that keeps them fixed and paralyzed, incapable of even raising their hands to vote.

The men on the ward know how difficult it is to struggle against Big Nurse. Even if they win one round, they seem inevitably to lose the fight. As the Chief puts it: "To beat her you don't have to whip her two out of three or three out of five, but every time you meet. As soon as you let down your guard, as soon as you lose once, she's won for good. And eventually we all got to lose. Nobody can help that."

The men refuse to take chances. They will not risk new movement. So McMurphy gets mad. He wants to watch the World Series on TV even if he has to break out of the asylum to do it. Finally he bets with the men that he can lift the four-hundred-pound control panel in the tub room and throw it through the screen that separates him from freedom. It seems an impossible challenge, but McMurphy doesn't back away. As he says: "Nobody's gonna convince me I can't do something till I try it."

McMurphy knows he can't do it, but he does try. And that seems to be his lesson here. He loses the bet, but he gives it a shot. At the end of the story, the Chief will take that same control panel and hurl it out the window, thanks to McMurphy, I bet.

ACKNOWLEDGMENT OF SOURCES

The authors and the publisher are grateful for permission to publish the selections under copyright in this anthology.

1. "Greasy Lake," from *Greasy Lake and Other Stories* by T. Coraghessan Boyle. Copyright (c) 1979, 1981, 1983, 1984, 1985 by T. Coraghessan Boyle. Used by permission of Viking Penguin, a division of Penguin Books USA Inc.

2. "Where Are You Going, Where Have You Been?" from *Where Are You Going, Where Have You Been? Selected Early Stories* by Joyce Carol Oates. By permission of the author. Copyright (c) Ontario Review, Inc., 1993.

3. Excerpt (pp. 161–175, 286–298) from *Affliction* by Russell Banks. Copyright (c) 1989 by Russell Banks. Reprinted by permission of HarperCollins Publishers, Inc.

4. "Solitude of Blood," by Marta Brunet, in *Landscapes of a New Land*, edited by Marjorie Agosín, translated by Elaine Dorough Johnson. Copyright 1989, 1992. Translation copyright by Elaine Dorough Johnson 1989, 1992. Reprinted with permission of White Pine Press, 10 Village Square, Fredonia, NY 14063.

5. Excerpt (pp. 93–114) from *Deliverance*. Copyright (c) 1970 by James Dickey. Reprinted by permission of Houghton Mifflin Co. All rights reserved.

6. Excerpt from *The Sea-Wolf* by Jack London, published by Bantam Doubleday Dell Publishing Group, Inc. (in the public domain).

7. "The Man Who Killed a Shadow," from *Eight Men* by Richard Wright. Copyright 1940 (c) 1961 by Richard Wright. Copyright renewed 1989 by Ellen Wright. Reprinted by permission of HarperCollins Publishers, Inc.

8. "I Stand Here Ironing," copyright (c) 1956, 1957, 1960, 1961 by Tillie Olsen. From *Tell Me a Riddle* by Tillie Olsen. Introduction by John Leonard. Used by permission of Delacorte Press/

Seymour Lawrence, a division of Bantam Doubleday Dell Publishing Group, Inc.

9. "The Wife's Story," by Ursula K. Le Guin. Copyright (c) 1982 by Ursula K. Le Guin. First appeared in *The Compass Rose: Short Stories* by Ursula K. Le Guin. Reprinted by permission of the author and the author's agent, Virginia Kidd.

10. Excerpt from *The Bluest Eye* by Toni Morrison. Reprinted by permission of International Creative Management, Inc. Copyright (c) 1972, Henry Holt & Co.

11. Excerpt (pp. 92–118) from *Of Mice and Men* by John Steinbeck. Copyright (c) 1937, renewed (c) 1965 by John Steinbeck. Used by permission of Viking Penguin, a division of Penguin Books USA Inc.

12. Excerpt (pp. 154–193) from *The Knockout Artist* by Harry Crews. Copyright (c) 1988 by Harry Crews. Reprinted by permission of John Hawkins & Associates, Inc.

13. "Tell the Women We're Going," by Raymond Carver. From *Short Cuts* by Raymond Carver. Copyright (c) 1993 by Tess Gallagher. Reprinted by permission of Vintage Books, a division of Random House Inc.

14. Excerpt (pp. 146–180) from *Their Eyes Were Watching God* by Zora Neale Hurston. Copyright 1937 by Harper & Row, Publishers, Inc. Renewed 1965 by John C. Hurston and Joel Hurston. Reprinted by permission of HarperCollins Publishers, Inc.

15. "Lucielia Louise Turner," from *The Women of Brewster Place* by Gloria Naylor. Copyright (c) 1980, 1982 by Gloria Naylor. Used by permission of Viking Penguin, a division of Penguin Books USA Inc.

16. "Everyday Use," from *In Love & Trouble: Stories of Black Women*, copyright (c) 1973 by Alice Walker. Reprinted by permission of Harcourt Brace & Company.

17. "Sonny's Blues," by James Baldwin. "Sonny's Blues" was originally published in *Partisan Review*. Collected in *Going to Meet the Man*, copyright 1965 by James Baldwin. Copyright renewed. Published by Vintage Books. Reprinted by arrangement with the James Baldwin Estate.

18. Excerpt (pp. 292–309) from *Bastard Out of Carolina* by Dorothy Allison. Copyright (c) 1992 by Dorothy Allison. Used by permission of Dutton Signet, a division of Penguin Books USA Inc.

19. Excerpt (pp. 83–111) from *One Flew Over the Cuckoo's Nest* by Ken Kesey. Copyright (c) 1962, 1990 by Ken Kesey. Used by permission of Viking Penguin, a division of Penguin Books USA Inc.